MONTY AND THE CANADIAN ARMY

John A. English

T0369798

General Bernard Law Montgomery, affectionately known as "Monty," exerted an influence on the Canadian Army more lasting than that of any other Second World War commander. In 1942 he assumed responsibility for the exercise and training of Canadian formations in England, and by the end of the war Canada's field army was second to none in the practical exercise of combined arms.

In *Monty and the Canadian Army*, John A. English analyses the way Montgomery's operational influence continued to permeate the Canadian Army. For years, the Canadian Army remained a highly professional force largely because it was commanded at almost every lower level by "Monty men" steeped in the Montgomery method. The era of the Canadian Army headed by such men ceased with the integration and unification of Canada's armed forces in 1964.

The embrace of Montgomery by Canadian soldiers stands in marked contrast to largely negative perceptions held by Americans. *Monty and the Canadian Army* aims to correct such perceptions, which are mostly superficial and more often than not wrong, and addresses the anomaly of how this gifted general, one of the greatest field commanders of the Second World War, managed to win over other North American troops.

LT. COL.-DR. JOHN A. ENGLISH is a Canadian Army veteran and past professor of strategy at the U.S. Naval War College.

MONTY
AND THE
CANADIAN
ARMY

JOHN A. ENGLISH

UNIVERSITY OF TORONTO PRESS
Toronto Buffalo London

Reprinted in paperback 2023

ISBN 978-1-4875-0699-5 (cloth)   ISBN 978-1-4875-3537-7 (EPUB)
ISBN 978-1-4875-4581-9 (paper)   ISBN 978-1-4875-3536-0 (PDF)

Publication cataloguing information is available from Library and Archives
Canada.

Cover image: General Bernard Law Montgomery most likely in Fossacesia,
Italy, in 1944. (LAC 3623203).

We wish to acknowledge the land on which the University of Toronto
Press operates. This land is the traditional territory of the Wendat, the
Anishnaabeg, the Haudenosaunee, the Métis, and the Mississaugas of the
Credit First Nation.

University of Toronto Press acknowledges the financial assistance to its
publishing program of the Canada Council for the Arts and the Ontario Arts
Council, an agency of the Government of Ontario.

Printed and bound by CPI Group (UK) Ltd, Croydon, CR0 4YY

Canada Council   Conseil des Arts
for the Arts   du Canada

ONTARIO ARTS COUNCIL
CONSEIL DES ARTS DE L'ONTARIO
an Ontario government agency
un organisme du gouvernement de l'Ontario

Funded by the   Financé par le
Government   gouvernement
of Canada   du Canada

For Valerie, love of my life, and our daughters, Shannon and Laura, with love forever

Contents

Maps and Figures

Maps

Figures

Preface

I have studied Canadian and Allied ground force operations in the Battle of Normandy and beyond for several decades as both a Queen's University PhD candidate and member of the Directing Staff of the Canadian Land Forces Command and Staff College. I also served as a war plans officer in NATO's Central Army Group Headquarters during the Cold War, Chief of Tactics at the Canadian Combat Training Centre, and Professor of Strategy at the US Naval War College.

In the course of my studies, which resulted in three books, I was struck by the marked influence of Field Marshal B.L. Montgomery on Canadian Army training and operations during the Second World War and well on into the post-war period. Here much of his influence flowed vicariously through the actions of his Canadian disciples, most notably Lieutenant General Guy Simonds. Eventually, as the sheer depth and breadth of Montgomery's professionalism and military influence became more and more apparent, I decided to undertake a closer examination of the relationship between him and the Canadian Army.

This proved a vast challenge as Montgomery's mastery of military operations ran the gamut from minor tactics to large-scale formation deployments. The emphasis he placed on basic fighting skills and realistic training for war through properly conducted test exercises and rehearsals set him apart from other generals of the time. His main problem was how to ensure that his fighting methods trickled down to the lowest levels of command,

As a first step I explored the roots of Montgomery's growth and development as a skilled field commander, which are set forth in chapter 1. His first contact with Canadian soldiers occurred in 1917 during the Great War in which the Canadian Corps earned a foremost fighting reputation before passing quietly onto the domestic scene. In the doldrums of peace, described in chapter 2, Canada's army, for lack of serious leadership focus on training for operations, completely lost the military professionalism that characterized this legendary corps.

Montgomery in contrast became the quintessential professional officer and from the crucible of Dunkirk rose to command two British Army corps, as recounted in chapter 3. Canada by this time had entered the war, but with a far different military command structure than either Britain or, later, the United States. As argued in chapter 4, this would eventually produce tensions in the national command of the First Canadian Army, which grew out of the initial deployment of Canada's overseas army, traced in chapter 5.

Montgomery's second and most consequential contact with Canadian soldiers occurred in 1942, when he inspected all units of the Canadian Corps, and is detailed in chapter 6. As the Canadian Corps came under command of his South-Eastern Army, Montgomery also assumed responsibility for the exercise and training of Canadian formations in all phases of war. Here, as explained in chapter 7, he inculcated the Canadian rank and file with the theory and doctrine of war fighting that his Eighth Army would use to defeat the Germans at Alamein. The disastrous Canadian raid on Dieppe that occurred shortly after Montgomery's departure for Egypt is discussed in chapter 8 with a view to establishing his responsibility for that operation.

Chapter 9 examines the underpinnings of Montgomery's victory at Alamein, which catapulted him into international prominence and reinforced the confidence of Canadian soldiers in his command and leadership. This chapter also covers the entry of Simonds's 1st Canadian Infantry Division into the battle for Sicily, where Montgomery personally intervened in Canadian higher-command matters for better and for worse. The later deployment of Lieutenant General H.D.G. Crerar's 1 Canadian Corps to Italy spawned a further high-command altercation that had to be adjudicated by Montgomery, who, by this time, held Simonds in the highest esteem.

During planning for the Normandy invasion Montgomery began to harbour doubts about Crerar's field qualifications to command the First Canadian Army, now comprising the British 1 Corps and 2 Canadian Corps. When the First Canadian Army finally did deploy under Crerar, as explained in chapter 10, he almost immediately got into a quarrel with his 1 Corps commander, which dispute additionally fell on Montgomery to resolve.

The first major attack launched by the First Canadian Army, Operation "Totalize," is analyzed in some detail in chapter 11 because it has been the subject of much debate that continues to this day. Criticisms levelled against Montgomery for his failure to reinforce the First Canadian Army and cut the Germans off at Falaise are also addressed in this chapter.

The First Canadian Army advance eastwards from Normandy is covered in chapter 12 along with Crerar's celebrated spat with Montgomery and Simonds's inspired generalship in the Battle of the Scheldt. Montgomery's alleged lack of focus on opening the port of Antwerp is coincidentally considered from both tactical and strategic perspectives.

Chapter 13 describes the largest action ever fought by Canada's army, the Battle of the Rhineland, as a military triumph that reflected the Montgomery method. Finally, in chapter 14, the continued military influence of Montgomery on Canadian Army training and doctrine in the two decades following the war is traced.

In amassing documentation for this book over the years I received support from many quarters. At the Imperial War Museum, the late Roderick W.A. Suddaby, the Keeper of the Department of Documents, went out of his way to accommodate my visits there. I remain further beholden to the trustees of the Imperial War Museum for allowing me access to the Montgomery Collections and to the late Right Honorable The Viscount Montgomery of Alamein, CMG, CBE, for permission to use quotations from the materials I acquired. Similarly, Patricia J. Methven, Kate O'Brien, and the staff of King's College London provided me with much valuable material, and I am grateful to Katrina DiMuro and the Liddell Hart and Alanbrooke Trustees for permission to use quotations from the Alanbrooke, Liddell Hart, and Pyman papers. Dave Reisch, my guiding editor at Stackpole Books, also kindly granted permission to use excerpts from my published works under the Stackpole imprint.

I would also like to thank the archivists and staff at the Public Records Office in Kew, London, the National Archives and Records Administration II in College Park, Maryland, the Dwight D. Eisenhower Library in Abilene, Kansas, the George C. Marshall Foundation Library and Archives in Lexington, Virginia, the U.S. Army Military History Institute, Carlisle Barracks, Pennsylvania, the U.S. Military Academy Library at West Point, the National Archives of Canada (now Library and Archives Canada), the Royal Military College's Massey Library, and the Queen's University Archives in Kingston, Ontario.

I owe a special debt to David Willis, Richard Palimaka, and the staff at the Fort Frontenac Library of the Canadian Land Forces Command and Staff College, surely the best military library in Canada. David McCarey of the Military Communications & Electronics Museum also allowed me access to the Lieutenant General S.F. Clark papers. Sincere thanks are further due to Mitch Kryzanowski, MA War Studies, and Terry Poulos, an accomplished author of military history who has degrees from the Universities of Toronto and Chicago, where he studied respectively under C.P. Stacey, Michael Geyer, and William H. McNeill. Both offered invaluable criticism and sound counsel that reflected their unsurpassed knowledge and understanding of Canadian and military history. I remain similarly appreciative to John A. Macdonald, MA War Studies, and John Selkirk of Reserves 2000 for reviewing drafts and making suggestions.

Additional thanks are owing to Jack Granatstein, Canada's foremost military historian, and Colonel Phil Meilinger, prolific military history author and former professor of strategy at the Naval War College, for their support. Finally, I would like to express my appreciation to Len Husband for stickhandling this book through to production, to Robin Studniberg for her managing editor skills, and to James Leahy for his superlative copy editing.

MONTY AND THE CANADIAN ARMY

Introduction

Of all commanders associated with the Canadian Army in the Second World War, none exerted a more lasting military influence than Field Marshal Bernard Law Montgomery. Historians may argue over who fathered the First Canadian Army, whether General A.G.L. "Andy" McNaughton its first commander or General H.D.G. "Harry" Crerar who convinced the Canadian government to field it, but the godfather of that army was most certainly Montgomery, who grabbed it by the scruff of the neck and taught it how to fight effectively as an all-arms team.[1] By the end of the war it was the best little army in the world, second to none in the practical exercise of combined arms, and for decades thereafter remained a highly professional force largely because it was commanded by "Monty men" steeped in the Montgomery method. Under his foremost Canadian disciple, Lieutenant General Guy Simonds, Chief of the General Staff (CGS) during the Korean and Cold wars, Montgomery's operational influence continued vicariously to permeate the Canadian Army. Simonds was followed as CGS, in succession, by Howard Graham, whose career had been saved by Montgomery in Sicily, Findlay Clark, Simonds's corps chief signals officer, and Geoffrey Walsh, Simonds's corps chief engineer. Other "Monty men" could also be found at almost every lower level of army command. The era of the Canadian Army headed by such men ceased with the integration and unification of Canada's armed forces from 1964.

The embrace of Montgomery by Canadian soldiers stands in marked contrast to the negative perceptions of him by Americans, only a few of whom have viewed him in a favourable light. He was certainly a far greater commander than most Americans were willing to admit, wrote US historian Carlo D'Este, and there was much to admire in Montgomery, not least of all his determination to abide by his principles. A most misunderstood general, he was above all an intensely dedicated and honourable professional soldier. Noting the general unkindness of historians toward Montgomery, D'Este makes the case that their judgments are mostly superficial and more often than not wrong. In his book on the battle for Sicily, he also devotes an annex to Montgomery and the Canadians, addressing the anomaly of how he managed to win over these North American troops. A more recent work by American authors Williamson Murray and Allan R. Millett further recognizes Montgomery as a gifted commander and one of the great field commanders of the Second World War. Arguably, American dislike of Montgomery stems largely from the Battle of the Bulge where General Dwight D. Eisenhower, the Supreme Allied Commander, saved the day by transferring command of the First US Army from a resentful General Omar Bradley to Montgomery. In dealing with Courtney Hodges, the shattered commander of the First US Army, Montgomery displayed great tact and understanding in giving the necessary leadership and orders to US troops. He also clearly impressed the frontline American commanders whom he met, and his regrouping and redeployment of US forces effectively stabilized a deteriorating situation. Unfortunately, Montgomery turned his possibly finest hour of generalship into a disaster by holding a press conference in which he gave the impression that the British had rescued the humiliated Americans.[2]

Montgomery's capacity for irritating both friend and foe was of course legendary. He was, by his own admission, anything but a nice chap in the mould of the classic English gentleman. Although wedded to the British Army, he never appeared to be the usual careerist, but focused almost entirely upon field operations and battle tactics. Yet, despite his singular pursuit of military excellence, his skills in this area would never have been realized without a war. Even then, he was never a first choice for higher command. When he was eventually chosen, however, he rose self-assuredly to the challenge as he had prepared himself well for the exercise of generalship. His sheer military competence, in turn, generated a supreme confidence that often gave the impression of arrogance. One of Montgomery's greatest strengths was his ability to grasp the essentials of complex issues and express with great clarity exactly what was on his mind. Historians have mocked his childlike handwriting, but what he wrote was always incredibly clear and concise in getting a point across. Never hesitant to voice his views in an honest and straightforward manner, he was often outspoken to the point of rudeness and oblivious to the feelings of others. His strongest supporter, General Sir Alan Brooke, noted this weakness and in a congratulatory letter to Montgomery on his assumption of corps command offered a friendly warning "against doing wild things," stating that "You have got a name for annoying people at times with your ways, and I have found difficulties in backing you at times against this reputation." Brooke assured Montgomery of his continued backing, but implored him "not to let me down by doing anything silly."[3]

This book will consider Montgomery's relationship with the Canadian Army not in the context of his complex character and eccentric personality, but primarily in terms of his military competence and influence. Montgomery first encountered Canadian soldiers in 1917 at the end of the battle of Passchendaele when he was visiting his brother Donald. A graduate of Cambridge University in law, Donald had emigrated to Vancouver, British Columbia, in 1908 and articled with a Canadian legal firm, eventually becoming a Queen's Counsel. During the Great War he served in the Canadian Corps with the 29th Infantry Battalion, receiving the Military Cross for bravery. The Canadian Corps earned a reputation for being one of the finest fighting formations on the Western Front, but Montgomery's first impression of Canadians was that they were magnificent and gallant fighters not fully aware that the art of war called for taking objectives with as few casualties as possible. Having been badly wounded and almost killed in an earlier action, for which he received the Distinguished Service Order, Montgomery subsequently served as an operations staff officer at brigade, division, and corps levels where he developed an abiding aversion to taking unnecessary casualties for lack of planning. He finished the war as a temporary lieutenant colonel, briefly commanding a battalion in the British Army of the Rhine in 1919.[4]

During the interwar years, characterized by war weariness and disillusionment that spawned anti-military sentiment, both the British and Canadian armies retrenched under financial constraints. In the rush to return to normality, they also forgot the hard-earned lessons of the war to end all wars. Montgomery did not forget. He instead absorbed what had been learned, including the need for meticulous planning, training rehearsals, the vital requirement to retain reserves, the benefit of concentrating artillery fire, and the maintenance of morale. Reverted in rank to major, he attended the Staff College at Camberley in 1920, by now convinced that the profession of arms called for lifelong study. By way of comparison, McNaughton attended Camberley the next year and two years later became Deputy CGS in the rank of brigadier. Montgomery in the meantime conducted operations against the Irish Republican Army from 1921 to 1922, which year also saw Canadian troops called out in aid of the civil power to deal with domestic disturbances brought on by rising labour strife. In 1925 Montgomery served as a company commander, finally becoming a substantive major the following year and returning to Camberley as a member of the Directing Staff (DS) in the rank of brevet lieutenant colonel from January 1927. In January 1929, the same month in which McNaughton became CGS in the rank of major general, Montgomery left Camberley to write the Infantry Training Manual on tactics.

On 27 July 1927 Montgomery married Mrs. E.A. "Betty" Carver, ushering in the happiest years of his life. His career chances also rose with his appointment to command his regiment, the Royal Warwickshire Regiment, as a substantive lieutenant colonel in January 1931. In this capacity he took the battalion to Palestine and Egypt in 1932, and Poona, India, in 1933. All the while he continued to emphasize training for war through exercises and study, earning a reputation as an outstanding commanding officer (CO) and one of the finest trainer of troops in the British Army. In June 1934, on promotion to colonel, he assumed the position of Chief Instructor of the junior division at the Indian Army Staff College, Quetta. Here, during his second tour in a primary centre of military professionalism, he refined and dispensed his tactical concepts and teaching techniques applicable to the conduct of battle in war. In May 1937, the year in which Canada commenced limited rearmament, Montgomery departed Quetta to take command of the 9th Infantry Brigade at Portsmouth, England, in the temporary rank of brigadier. Shortly after he issued his first training directive, however, his wife contracted an unexpected illness that resulted in leg amputation and death. This was a devastating blow to Montgomery, who thereafter immersed himself with missionary zeal in the profession of arms.[5]

As commander of the 9th Brigade Montgomery stressed the importance of "the stage management of battle," which meant deploying forces in positions from which they could most effectively achieve the aim of a battle plan. With all arms properly synchronized and supplied, each could then "play to the broad plan" and avoid blundering aimlessly into action and losing the initiative. Montgomery's field performance earned him promotion to command the 8th Division in Palestine, but after the German seizure of Czechoslovakia in March 1939 he was called back to take command of the 3rd Infantry Division. At this point he took seriously ill and had to be evacuated to England and hospitalized, which led him to vow never to smoke or drink again. Declared fit in August, he assumed command of the 3rd Division and trooped to France with the British Expeditionary Force (BEF). Over the next six months during the period of the Phoney War he exercised his division incessantly in movement by night. This paid off immensely during the fighting withdrawal to Dunkirk, where the 3rd Division performed superbly. Unlike some other commanders who went to pieces, Montgomery thrived in the fear and danger of the moment. Dunkirk also convinced him of the importance of being able to persevere when things were not going well. Promoted after returning to England, Montgomery took command of 5 Corps on 12 July 1940 and completed a ruthless housecleaning of this formation to make it fit to defend the south coast of England against German invasion. In May 1941 he side-stepped to command 12 Corps responsible for the defence of the Kentish coast within the South-Eastern Command. Here again he weeded out personnel and instituted a rigorous operational training regime.

On 17 November 1941 Montgomery took charge of the entire South-Eastern Command, which also included the Canadian Corps. The Canadian Corps had been formed on Christmas Day 1940 under the command of McNaughton. This occurred despite the reservations of Prime Minister W.L. Mackenzie King, who would have preferred to send air forces rather than ground troops because of the perception that bombing would produce fewer casualties and negate any need for conscription, which Quebec had strongly opposed in the Great War. Unfolding events, however, forced the government's hand and troops were committed in accordance with the mobilization plan of the Canadian general staff. King nonetheless continued to favour a limited Canadian war effort and for this reason refused to take an active part in the higher direction of the war. This ensured the exclusion of Canada from Allied war policy deliberations and left it without a strategic voice. Canada's own war direction also suffered as King, ever suspicious of military men, never allowed the Canadian Chiefs of Staff (CCOS) to attend his Cabinet War Committee on a regular basis before June 1942. His personal selection of McNaughton for overseas field command further diminished the status of the CGS, not even filled between 26 December 1943 and 3 May 1944, as the former possessed senior rank. This also left McNaughton burdened with non-operational matters to the detriment of field command. Such an arrangement differed from British and American practice in which the Chief of the Imperial General Staff (CIGS) and the Chief of Staff (COS) of the US Army ensured that field commanders concentrated solely on operations. The Canadian anomaly eventually produced some friction with Montgomery, who considered field command a full time job.

By the time Montgomery took over South-Eastern Command the Canadian Army had been in Britain for almost two years. Training, however, remained stuck in the past. Initially, the 1st Canadian Infantry Division under McNaughton had trained for trench warfare, but after Blitzkrieg led to Dunkirk attention focused on defence against German invasion. To meet this threat McNaughton formed nine battalion mobile columns whose constant practice of rapid motor movement by day and night elicited the witty appellation "McNaughton's Flying Circus." As early as 8

June 1940 McNaughton reported to Mackenzie King that he now considered his force to be battle worthy. By this time McNaughton had been built up into a major national figure by a publicity campaign organized at the beginning of the war. Acclaimed by the press as a soldier-scientist and the best soldier in the British Empire, he enjoyed a greater popularity than most other generals. In the darkness of defeat, he also appeared to be a natural choice to lead the Allied invasion of the Continent, and he personally envisioned the Canadian army eventually spearheading the assault on Germany. In September 1941 he proclaimed the Canadian Corps to be "a dagger pointed at the heart of Berlin."

In Montgomery's view, however, the dagger needed sharpening, a task made easier by McNaughton's November departure to Canada on extended medical leave owing to stress and strain. On 23 December Crerar took command of the Canadian Corps and shortly thereafter invited Montgomery to visit each of his formations and offer his personal views. Crerar doubtless got more than he bargained for, but Montgomery convincingly refuted McNaughton's glowing assessments of Canadian Corps readiness for war. During February and March 1942 he inspected all nine Canadian infantry brigades and twenty-seven infantry battalions, employing a highly effective methodology largely based on listening, a rarity for many senior commanders. Following his brigade visits, he offered a number of constructive and critical comments that were in most cases on the mark. Given the seriousness of the military situation, there was no time for niceties, but a compelling need for expedient direction and decisive leadership, in which circumstances Montgomery did not mince words in making his assessments. Most of all he evinced an abiding concern for the welfare of the common soldier who would face the firestorm. In his view, there were no bad soldiers, only bad officers, and he was not prepared to take chances with the latter, even though some might be borderline. To err in favour of the troops was always better than to give the benefit of the doubt to questionable officers. As Montgomery saw it, the Canadian Corps suffered from a fundamental weakness at the top that called for a thorough housecleaning. In administering his solutions, however, he was no more ruthless than he had been in 5 or 12 Corps.

Montgomery's impact on Canadian Army training and preparation for war was far-reaching and profoundly affected all levels from top to bottom. He considered the volunteer soldiers of the Canadian Corps as probably the best material in any army of the empire, but likely to be killed in large numbers unless commanders learned how to launch them properly into battle. The problem was that the Canadian high command did not know how to train troops for such action and, but for Montgomery's intervention, would have left them utterly unprepared for modern war and vulnerable to unnecessary casualties. Crerar took Montgomery's schooling seriously and for the rest of the war attempted to imitate his military approach, echoing his emphasis on stage managing the battle, seizing the initiative, fighting for information, retaining control, and forcing the enemy to dance to your tune. The army was not a mutual congratulation society and bad work had to be stamped upon. In Exercise "Tiger" held 19–30 May 1942 Crerar earned Montgomery's praise for the performance of the Canadian Corps. After two and a half years, Montgomery told his Canadian aide-de-camp (ADC), the Canadian Corps was coming to be known as a good corps.[6] He also noted that Simonds, Crerar's principal operations officer, contributed greatly to corps operational effectiveness.

One of the most important lessons stressed by Montgomery was that tanks alone were never the answer and the punches they were capable of delivering had to be supported by the maximum effort of artillery, infantry, and all other arms. Montgomery placed particular emphasis upon the war-winning capability of artillery. Although he did not devise the British system of artillery fire control, he had a hand in ensuring the integration of gunner commanders in the tactical planning process so that concentrated indirect artillery fire could be generated swiftly in overwhelming force as required. The Germans had nothing like it and neither did the Americans. The superiority of the British system of artillery fire control has not always been recognized, but it was later confirmed on a lesser scale by the Commonwealth Division in Korea. Here the US commander of the Eighth Army, Lieutenant General James A. Van Fleet, who had commanded a corps with distinction in fighting the Germans on the Western Front, recounted:

> The British Commonwealth Division was one of my best divisions. It was a big division, a strong division that knew how to fight ... They had the best artillery, what we called "TOT" (Time on Target) far superior to the American method as taught at Fort Sill. This was the subject of my report back to Washington which said our artillery is too slow getting on target; when you concentrate it on the front, the British can out-do us. I took some of our visiting artillery officers to the British front to an artillery operation and I said, "Now you pick out any point in that far distant terrain that you want, and we will point it out to their division artillery officer and ask them to concentrate all their artillery including some of the US corps artillery that had been assigned to them on that target. Bang! It would come down in a matter of seconds." I said, "We cannot do that with the American units."[7]

Montgomery also emphasized that soldiers had to be mentally fit and physically hard with powers of endurance lasting weeks under rough conditions. On Exercise "Tiger" most units marched over 150 miles and fought simulated actions in the severest test of endurance experienced by Canadian arms. While Montgomery's tough approach and insistence upon standards was not always appreciated, Canadian troops hailed his victory at Alamein with some pride of association. After Operation "Torch," which saw American troops in action before Canadians, with the exception of Dieppe blamed by some on Montgomery, public pressure forced the dispatch of an infantry division and army tank brigade to the Eighth Army for the invasion of Sicily. This brought Canadian troops into close association with Montgomery once more, with the commander of the 1st Division, Simonds, earning his abiding respect. Simonds himself became a protégé of Montgomery. In this, he was not alone for Lieutenant Colonel B.M. Hoffmeister, future commander of the 5th Canadian Armoured Division, professed enormous pride in being a disciple of Montgomery, marvelling at how he could inspire soldiers and get the best out of them. He recalled Monty addressing him by his first name in a visit to his Seaforth battalion. After exchanging pleasantries, Monty asked for the troops dispersed among the trees to gather round, at which point Hoffmeister related

> the whole blinking battalion just surged out and around the jeep in a great solid mass. Monty then looked them all over, smiling in a benign way, and asked, "Well who have we here?" and a great roar answered "Seaforths!" He replied, "Well of course my Seaforths," just as cordial as all get up, but the troops loved it. It was hot as ... hell by the time we started back to our area, but the troops were whistling and singing and happy as all get out marching at ease. They thought it had just been a great experience.[8]

In Sicily Montgomery refereed a dispute between Simonds and Graham. He also caused a furore by not allowing McNaughton to visit Simonds's division in action. Later in Italy, after the politically arranged transfer of 1 Canadian Corps and the 5th Armoured Division to the Eighth Army, Montgomery adjudicated a stormy confrontation between Simonds and Crerar. As a result of this affair and the reaction of Canadian troops in theatre to Crerar's rejection of relaxed Eighth Army dress codes, Montgomery began to harbour doubts about his heretofore reasonably favourable impression of the 1 Corps commander. These reservations carried on into Normandy, where a Crerar favourite, the commander of the assault landing 3rd Canadian Infantry Division Group, came under scrutiny for poor performance. Crerar had meanwhile worked behind the scenes to remove and replace McNaughton as commander of the First Canadian Army, which the departure of 1 Canadian Corps to Italy and its replacement by 1 British Corps had left an Anglo-Canadian formation. The subsequent deployment of 2 Canadian Corps under the Second British Army on 11 July 1944 also effectively placed all Canadian formations in Normandy under Simonds's command. Bridgehead congestion further enabled Montgomery to delay the activation of First Canadian Army headquarters until 23 July, and then only with the British 1 Corps under command as 2 Canadian Corps remained with the Second British Army until 31 July. Almost immediately Crerar got into a squabble with his one and only British corps commander that once more required mediation by Montgomery.

In the ferocious fighting for Caen, which was pivotal to German defence of Normandy, Canadian and British forces faced seven panzer divisions compared with two facing the Americans farther west. Of these seven panzer divisions, four were also Waffen SS, each fielding two more infantry battalions than normal panzer divisions. Limited numbers of British Firefly tanks partly offset German qualitative superiority in Panther and Tiger tanks, but the real solution to dealing with them was using infantry, armour, and artillery in combination as preached by Montgomery. The Germans could not match the swiftly concentrated artillery fire of the Anglo-Canadians, nor the overwhelming air power that the Allies brought to bear. The British 6-pounder anti-tank gun could also tear the turret off a Panther at close range as could the larger 17-pounder at a range close to that of the German 88 mm flak. Simonds's first-time use of improvised armoured personnel carriers (APCs) to transport infantry in support of tanks in a surprise night attack further enabled the First Canadian Army to crack open the German defence in Operation "Totalize." Failure to exploit the opportunity to seal off the Germans by taking Falaise did not constitute a huge setback, however, as Montgomery, who originally aimed to cut the Germans off on the River Seine, merely moved the shorter Falaise envelopment farther to the east. By 25 August Montgomery's four field armies were on the Seine, ten days earlier than anticipated, having inflicted a crushing defeat on the German army in the west. Throughout this period, as in Italy, Montgomery continued to inspire Canadian soldiers, who knew that casualties were inevitable but that he would do everything in his power to keep them to the minimum.

In the breakout from Normandy the Second British Army raced 250 miles to the east, demonstrating as had the Third US Army, that rapid advances could be made against weak opposition. As shown by operations in the Western Desert, the best tank country was not always open terrain but where there were the fewest anti-tank guns. The First Canadian Army charged with the task of taking the Channel ports, including

Le Havre, Dieppe, Boulogne, and Calais, Dunkirk, and Antwerp, followed in train. That it lagged some 100 miles behind the Second British Army caused Montgomery some concern, but his harsh rebuke of Crerar for missing an army commanders' conference to attend a Dieppe parade commemorating Canadian dead sparked greater fireworks of a constitutional nature. Although he did not even bother to send his COS to stand in for him, an enraged Crerar threatened to take the matter up with the Canadian government. When Montgomery's Canadian personal assistant, Lieutenant Colonel Trumbull Warren, told him that the incident would likely turn into a terrible row, Montgomery shrugged it off, saying there was nothing he could do as he was trying to fight a war. At this point Warren bravely suggested that he write an apology, which prompted Montgomery to cut him short. Early the next morning, however, Montgomery called Warren back and with shaving cream on his face and brush in hand waved him to a desk where a drafted apology letter lay. "That suit you?" he asked. When Warren replied yes, Montgomery sent him off to speed the letter to Crerar. Montgomery followed this with a second letter of apology.[9]

At this time, with German armies reeling all along the front, Montgomery sought to thrust into Germany and capture the industrial Ruhr. To accomplish this he planned one of the most imaginative operations of the war, a three-division airborne assault to attain a bridgehead across the Rhine with a ground force link-up by the British 30 Corps to consolidate the gain. This operation, called "Market Garden," received the approval of Eisenhower and would on success have facilitated the capture of the great port of Rotterdam. Clearance of the Scheldt estuary and opening of the port of Antwerp was thus left to First Canadian Army, which was slow in reducing the remaining Channel ports after the impressive two-day capture of Le Havre by two divisions of the British 1 Corps. Here Crerar's faltering health may have impaired his generalship, which stood in contrast to Simonds's imaginative suggestion of masking the Channel ports and getting on with the opening of Antwerp. In any event, Crerar was medically evacuated on 27 September, leaving Simonds in command of the First Canadian Army. Simonds's arrival was described as electrifying and a breath of fresh air. He went on to fight the battle of the Scheldt as an army battle, integrating naval and air operations, including the innovative employment of bombers to breach the dykes on Walcheren Island, which drowned German defences and left them vulnerable to amphibious operations. In his singular insistence on the use of bombers to inundate Walcheren, his first use of amphibians in Europe, and his coordination of land, air, and sea elements, Simonds proved himself to be an outstanding field army commander. The battle of the Scheldt, fought under the most arduous conditions, also constituted First Canadian Army's greatest contribution to the Allied advance as it ensured the sustainment of supply-starved American armies in central Europe.

The failure of "Market Garden" forced Montgomery to concentrate on the opening of Antwerp, the difficulties of which, he later admitted, he had failed to appreciate initially. He nonetheless took a keen interest once focused on the operation, visiting Simonds some six times. Eisenhower, in contrast, never visited First Canadian Army during the fighting, even though American forces more than Anglo-Canadian armies required Antwerp for supplies.[10] The performance of Simonds in the Scheldt battle doubtless reinforced Montgomery's hope that he would remain in command of the First Canadian Army. Crerar not only returned, however, but received a promotion to full general on 16 November. Resigned to accept the inevitable, Montgomery gave a leading role to Crerar in his plans to clear the west bank of the Rhine, which called for a pincer attack by the First Canadian Army descending from the north in Operation "Veritable" and the Ninth US Army advancing from the south in Operation "Grenade." To carry out "Veritable" Montgomery massively reinforced Crerar with 21st Army Group resources. All told, Crerar commanded nearly half a million troops and eleven divisions in the Battle of the Rhineland. This was the largest force ever commanded by a Canadian. In these terms alone, the battle constituted the finest hour of Crerar and his First Canadian Army headquarters.

The liberation of Holland by the First Canadian Army followed, but it never again fought on the scale of the Battle of the Rhineland. After brief occupation duties, the Canadian Army overseas drifted home. A rapid demobilization followed until the period of the Korean conflict and the Cold War. Throughout this period Montgomery's influence continued indirectly and vicariously through Simonds and other Canadian Monty men. In 1946 Montgomery became CIGS, making his first trip to Canada that year, and on relinquishing that appointment two years later, assumed the post of Chairman of the Western Union Committee of Commanders-in-Chief with combined headquarters in Fontainebleau, France. The Western Union of Britain, France, and the Benelux countries had been formed in reaction to the aggressive behaviour of the Soviet Union and provided the kernel for the formation of the North Atlantic Treaty Organization (NATO). In April 1951 Supreme Headquarters Allied Powers Europe (SHAPE), the direct descendant of Fontainebleau, opened in Paris with Eisenhower as Supreme Allied Commander (SACEUR) and Montgomery joining him as Deputy SACEUR. In this capacity Montgomery performed a critical role that influenced the development of strategical and tactical concepts aimed at addressing the military problems confronting NATO. These, in turn, also affected Canadian Army organization and doctrine of the Cold War era.

Chapter One

The Germination of Generalship

Born in London on 17 November 1887, Montgomery was a child of the British Empire and grew up in the colony of Tasmania, where his father ministered as an Anglican bishop. Not quite two years of age when he went to Tasmania in September 1889, Montgomery lived there until he turned fourteen, by which time the colony had become a state of Australia. On return to England in 1902 he attended St. Paul's School London and later the Royal Military Academy Sandhurst in 1907. Commissioned into the Royal Warwickshire Regiment, he joined the 1st Battalion in Peshawar on the North-West Frontier of India in 1908. Two years later his battalion trooped to Bombay, where it remained until returning to England in January 1913. By the fall of 1914 Montgomery was in action with his regiment in France, barely escaping capture in the Battle of Le Cateau during the retreat from Mons. On 13 October while leading his platoon, sword in hand, in a bayonet charge to clear the Germans from the village of Meteren during the first Battle of Ypres, a German sniper shot him through the right lung, leaving him lying bleeding in the pouring rain. Fortunately for Montgomery, a soldier of his platoon who ran to dress his wound was killed and fell across him, saving his life by absorbing numerous more shots intended for Montgomery. Left to lie for hours until medically treated under cover of darkness, he was shot again in the left knee. For his bravery in this action Montgomery received the Distinguished Service Order, a gallantry medal not usually awarded to lieutenants, and field promotion to captain.

After a remarkable recovery despite the permanent loss of half a lung, Montgomery in February 1915 assumed the appointment of brigade major (BM), principal operations staff officer, of the 112th Infantry Brigade and helped train men of the new volunteer citizen army. In January 1916 he returned to France with his brigade, now redesignated the 104th in the 35th (Bantam) Division, where on 26 July he received a third flesh wound from shrapnel during the Battle of the Somme. In January 1917 Montgomery left the 104th Brigade to take up the appointment of General Staff Officer Grade 2 (GSO2) in the 33rd Division just in time for the bloody Battle of Arras. In July, though still a captain, he became senior GSO2 on the staff of 9 Corps in the Second Army commanded by General Sir Herbert Plumer. In August Plumer rejuvenated the flagging Third Battle of Ypres offensive by ordering a three-week pause to allow proper planning, training, and rehearsal that produced highly successful limited attacks at Menin Road Ridge, Polygon Wood, and Broodseinde. Models of preparation and execution, all three attacks secured their objectives with a minimum of casualties and brought the Germans to the verge of serious defeat. The Plumer approach, embraced by Montgomery, showed that properly trained troops supported by creeping barrages could breach even the most heavily manned defences. Finally brevetted major in June 1918, Montgomery received a further promotion to temporary lieutenant colonel on appointment as GSO1 of the 47th (London) Division in July 1918. In emulation of German army practice, however, his divisional commander, Major General G.F. Gorringe, appointed him Chief of Staff (COS) with power to control often more senior ranking administrative and quartermaster staff officers as well as the general staff responsible for operations and intelligence. Montgomery readily embraced this COS system and later promoted it whenever he could.[1]

Montgomery finished the war having gained a wealth of experience in orchestrating operations at formation as opposed to unit level. In the appointment of BM he learned the importance of the brigade commander relationship with his artillery and engineer commanders. On the Somme he became familiar with large formation operations and, as Plumer practised, the value of setting limited, realistic, and identifiable objectives. He also recognized the benefit of massed artillery fire, creeping barrages, leapfrogging fresh units forward, preparations to resist counter-attacks, communications with spotter planes equipped with wireless, the use of aerial photos for intelligence, the establishment of supply and ammunition dumps, specialized training for taking out strongpoints, and full dress rehearsals. He further saw meticulous planning and training exercises as key to preventing unnecessary loss of life and the maintenance of morale. Having noted that higher staffs were out of touch with regimental officers and troops, Montgomery advocated treating soldiers as individuals rather than masses, with the staff acting as sympathetic servants of the troops. The commander who refused to recognize that all men are different and persisted in treating them as all the same, he concluded, would not succeed. Soldiers had to be trained to act collectively in sections, platoons, and companies, but they always remained separate beings in thought and feeling. Acknowledging this reality explained why front-line officers in close contact with their men often developed almost mystical bonds with their troops. Good training coupled with tailoring objectives to suit troop capabilities, while keeping all soldiers in the picture by thorough briefings down to private level, constituted the ingredients of success. Sending untrained troops into battle in poorly planned and badly executed operations merely threw soldiers' lives away.[2]

From the 1918 Armistice when most of the world had had their fill of war, Montgomery could not stop talking about it.[3] He ended the war convinced that the profession of arms was a lifetime study and, considering his mind still untrained, he decided to focus his attention almost entirely upon mastering his vocation. In 1920, on reversion in rank to brevet major, he attended Camberley Staff College, the institutional brain of the British army and the nursery of professionalism. Here students learned how to support field commanders in the conduct of large-scale operations. The staff college used a tutorial system of discussions within a ten-man syndicate, each with students from various arms and services directed by a DS. To allow greater exposure to the knowledge of others, groupings changed every six to eight weeks. Initially, students read relevant précis and manuals, listened to explanatory lectures, and discussed subjects in syndicate. Subsequently, they observed indoor demonstrations on cloth or sand models and outdoor demonstrations of equipment and troops. In the process, students learned how to devise and coordinate battle plans, run headquarters efficiently, draft field correspondence, and give orders under stress. Emphasis throughout highlighted thoroughness and attention to detail, since battlefield success came to depend increasingly upon the calculated deployment, movement, and administration of large formations. As training progressed, students assumed command as well as staff roles in signals exercises, telephone battles, and tactical exercises without troops (TEWTs) on the ground. Although the DS reputedly placed Montgomery in the "bloody menace" category of students who offered opinionated but often uninformed criticism, he thought he got a good staff college report despite later alleging that nobody ever told him whether he did well or not.[4]

After passing out of the staff college in December 1920 Montgomery served as BM of the 17th Infantry Brigade in Cork, where he coordinated the operations of some 9,000 men in nine battalions in a politically vacillating struggle against the Irish Republican Army. In May 1922 he returned to England, posted first as BM of the 8th Infantry Brigade in Plymouth and, within a year, as GSO2 of the 49th (West Riding) Division, Territorial Army (TA), based at York. While so employed Montgomery noted the futility of efforts to conduct collective training without having first carried out the individual instruction of leaders. Adhering to the dictum of teaching the teachers what to teach before they taught the Tommies, he strove to inculcate a high standard of tactical training through the issuance of practical notes and showing officers how to teach classes using the sand table. His efforts lifted training out of dull and boring, repetitious routine and made it varied, challenging, and exciting. In 1923 he set up a school to prepare candidates for the staff college entrance examination and two years later published a remarkable series of five articles on the growth of modern infantry tactics since the seventeenth century. Appearing in the Warwickshire regimental magazine *The Antelope*, these emphasized the ancient master law of tactics – being superior at the point selected to deliver the decisive blow – on which basis he began to develop his theory of modern mechanized battle incorporating new techniques and equipment. During this period he also struck up an intellectual association with renowned military theorist B.H. Liddell Hart, and, perhaps far more importantly, developed an abiding respect for part-time TA troops and a good understanding of how to deal with a citizen soldiery that would be needed to win in war.[5]

In March 1925 Montgomery rejoined the 1st Battalion, The Royal Warwicks, as a company commander armed with a detailed five-month training plan already in hand. Perhaps reflecting his experience with the part-time TA, whose drill he judged hopeless and a waste of time to rectify, he gave priority to tactical training, which at least offered the chance of achieving reasonably high standards. His aim was to ensure that by the end of training every officer, non-commissioned officer (NCO), and man would have a clear idea of the action of his unit in each of the various phases of war. As the Commanding Officer (CO) had spent all of the war in New Zealand and knew little about tactics, he let Montgomery carry on with training the whole battalion. Montgomery's ambitious training plan not surprisingly drew opposition within the peacetime county regiment, the more so as he aggressively pressed his ideas on everyone at every opportunity. Described as quick as a ferret and just as lovable, he was not popular, and he soon learned that arbitrary command would not work. He found instead that he needed to put himself across in person to his NCOs and men to get things done. His hard-driving zealotry nonetheless marked him as a professional who really knew his stuff, and his reputation began to snowball. In July 1926 he finally became a substantive major, and before his tour was over his company exercised using live ammunition, including artillery with troops advancing as close as possible behind the fall of shot before it lifted. Montgomery's last innovation was to set up a battalion training cadre of the best-prepared

NCOs to instruct the rest of the battalion in weapon handling and section leading.[6]

Though more pragmatic than academic, Montgomery read widely, enough to complain about lacking books to read in 1942, and possessed a goodly amount of common sense. He nonetheless recognized that practical experience in itself was of little value without thoughtful reflection and serious study. In January 1926 he returned to Camberley as a DS and became a protégé of Colonel Alan Brooke, Director of Studies. Montgomery never lost his admiration for Brooke, who introduced him to larger-scale TEWTs involving artillery and tanks as well as infantry. A veteran artillery officer who would go on to command the British 1st Armoured Division and ultimately become CIGS, Brooke preached the doctrine that corps commanders should be able to command both infantry and armoured divisions that were being established at the time. Promoted brevet lieutenant colonel in January 1927, Montgomery flourished in this environment, testing and refining his already developed theories while expanding his military horizon. Gifted with the ability to take a mass of detail and reduce it to its essentials and possessing a talent for clear and logical exposition in writing and speaking, he soon became an inspiring and unsurpassed lecturer on tactics. Montgomery remained a DS at Camberley until January 1929, knowing enough by then to realize that the teacher learns much more than his students. During this tour he also married the love of his life, whom after ten happy years he would lose to septicemia in October 1937.[7]

In February 1929 Montgomery again returned to his regiment for company command duty, but in October the War Office requested he be attached for six months in the rank of brevet lieutenant colonel as secretary of the committee struck to revise the *Infantry Training Manual, Volume II*. Montgomery leapt at the opportunity and in short order produced a draft that resulted in heated arguments and haggling with higher-ranking members of the committee. In the end they became so exasperated that they agreed to let him take their amendments and write the entire manual by himself in his own unpaid time. This he did with unbounded enthusiasm and vigour, acknowledging criticisms from tank advocate Liddell Hart, who had largely been responsible for the 1921 version, but disagreeing with them. Montgomery accepted that there would be cases where tanks would be employed as the primary arm of assault, instead of serving as infantry support, but he remained unshaken in his belief that future war would still be won by combined arms in which infantry worked in conjunction with artillery and armour. In any case, the manual received a generally favourable reception, especially for what Montgomery penned on leadership. Above all, a leader must have the confidence of his men gained by commanding their respect for his determination and ready acceptance of responsibility; for the clarity and simplicity of his orders and the firm way in which he insists that they should be carried out; for his thorough knowledge of his profession; for his sense of justice; for his common sense; for his keenness, energy, and habit of forethought; for his sense of humour; for his indifference to personal danger and readiness to share his men's hardships; for his persistent good nature in the face of difficulties; and, for the obvious pride he takes in his command.[8]

In this respect, Montgomery should have gone back to his regiment well prepared to practise what he preached in July 1930. After a few weeks he became second in command (2IC), and on promotion to substantive lieutenant colonel in January 1931 replaced the CO to take the 1st Battalion, The Royal Warwicks, overseas to Palestine. Owing to his extreme insistence on professional competence, however, he almost immediately he got off on the wrong foot, nearly to the point of causing mutiny. In a departure from the policy of NCOs being promoted by long service, he instituted promotion based on merit with a view to encouraging younger NCOs to try harder. As the normal tour of an overseas battalion lasted twenty-one years and promotions were few, this understandably caused an uproar among sergeants and generally lowered unit morale. Montgomery's popularity may have been further eroded by the nature of the Palestine deployment in which keeping peace between religious groups necessitated dispersing sub-units to virtually permanent battle outposts. This largely precluded Montgomery from focusing on collective unit training. As senior officer commanding all British troops in Palestine, his first experience at high command, he was also unable to spend much time with his battalion. Besides the Warwicks, he had another infantry battalion under command and was responsible for effecting liaison with Transjordan and the French in Syria and Lebanon.[9]

The subsequent move of the Warwicks to Alexandria, Egypt, in 1932 saw a reduction in Montgomery's authority, but enabled him to concentrate fully on training his battalion for war according to his principles. Now part of Brigadier Sir Frederick Pile's Suez Canal Brigade, he made his mark as an outstanding CO and one of the finest trainer of troops in the British army. His approach gave trusted leaders their heads, telling company commanders to go out in the desert far from Alexandria and work out their logistical and exercise arrangements on their own. He stipulated that they do most training by night and spend not less than forty-eight hours away from camp. They were then to get on with it, after submitting their training plan to him. Montgomery himself would later show up unannounced in the middle of the night or in daylight to observe the training. His heavy emphasis on tactics produced a fit and operationally excellent battalion, with NCOs trained to run the unit in case all officers were casualties. Supremely confident, he handled the night fighting Warwicks with boldness and verve in brigade manoeuvres. He also delivered riveting tactical summations while not refraining from telling Pile, an artilleryman, how to conduct operations. Without question Montgomery was respected if not loved, and he looked after his soldiers well. He ensured the cleanliness of Alexandria brothels by having his medical officer inspect them, thus lowering the venereal disease rate from what he called "horizontal refreshment." He also abolished compulsory church parades.[10]

At the end of 1933 Montgomery's battalion trooped to Poona, which lay within the Southern Command of the Indian Army. The emphasis within the command stressed internal security operations often ensured by overawing unruly crowds with smartly drilled troops. Montgomery had never been a stickler for drill and the 1st Battalion, The Royal Warwicks, arrived plainly incapable of performing ceremonial drill, to the displeasure of his new brigadier. That the battalion CO had supported brothels and abolished compulsory church parades further raised eyebrows. Since the 1857 Indian Mutiny had broken out on a Sunday when the British were at church, battalions had to attend church collectively, armed with weapons. Montgomery's solution of posting a platoon guard outside church each Sunday in case a second mutiny broke out infuriated headquarters. To make matters worse, the General Officer Commanding (GOC) Southern Command, General Sir George Jeffreys, had written the *Infantry Training Manual, Volume I*, on drill. Jeffreys, a guardsman, was as obsessed about drill as Montgomery was about tactical training and considered the latter an opinionated upstart. Fortunately for Montgomery, he received permission to take leave and go on a cruise to the Far East. On the sea journey to Japan he lost little time in seeking out fellow passenger and architect of the new German army, General Hans von Seeckt, whose company and conversation he obviously much preferred to that of "old fogey" Jeffreys.[11]

Yet, despite their mutual animosity, Jeffreys reported favourably upon Montgomery, rating him well above average in knowledge, energy, and power of imparting knowledge. He urged him, however, to bear in mind the frailties of average human nature and to remember that most others had neither the same energy, nor the same ability as he did. With this perhaps in mind and having likely learned something from Jeffreys, Montgomery accepted an offer from Army Headquarters Simla to take up a GSO1 post at the Staff College Quetta. On commencement of duties in June 1934, he also received a promotion to full colonel, backdated to

1 January 1932 for his Palestine service. The Commandant at Quetta, Major General G.C. Williams, capitalized upon Montgomery's skills by appointing him Chief Instructor of the junior division, which enabled him to influence the DS and teach first-year students the techniques of battle command and staff duties. Here he shone as an outstanding instructor, extemporaneously dispensing his tactical concept of war in spellbinding expositions. Under his guidance students learned how to produce a simple plan from a mass of detail and respond in timely and accurate fashion to solve tactical problems. While exhorting his students to make themselves professional and prepare for major war, however, Montgomery trained himself to be a general officer well versed in all facets of combined arms operations. He also saw that the challenge of field generalship was to be clear, decisive, and above all, practical.[12] Quetta punctuated the happiest years of Montgomery's life, and by the time he left in 1937, at the relatively older age of fifty, he went armed with a comprehensive and well-thought-out theory of training and tactics for waging war.

Chapter Two

Canadian Corps Legacy and Loss of Professionalism

Montgomery's first contact with Canadian soldiers occurred during the Battle of Passchendaele in which the four divisions of the Canadian Corps suffered roughly 16,000 casualties between 26 October and 11 November 1917. In lunching with his brother who was serving with the 29th (Vancouver) Battalion, Montgomery gained the impression that the Canadians seemed to think they were the best troops in France and the ones always called upon to do the most difficult jobs. At the time he reminded them that the Third Battle of Ypres had begun on 31 July with a fourteen-division attack by two British field armies and that the Canadians had only fought for Passchendaele Ridge during the last ten days. At plain straightforward fighting they are magnificent, Montgomery observed, but he was less than impressed with their blind heroism and costly gallantry. They forget, he noted, that the whole art of war is to gain your objective with as little loss of life as possible. Though he accepted the inevitability of casualties in war, he considered unnecessary casualties unforgivable. This basic precept, possibly reinforced by the sacrifice of Canadians at Passchendaele, came to characterize Montgomery's later approach to battle, which emphasized that thorough planning, rigorous training, exercise rehearsals, and well executed operations could reduce casualties.[1]

The Canadian Corps commander, Lieutenant General Sir Arthur Currie, would have agreed with Montgomery and actually protested, almost to the point of insubordination, at having to undertake such a potentially costly operation as Passchendaele. Plumer likewise vainly opposed the operation, which aimed to exploit his three earlier successes achieved with low casualties, as rain had now turned the ground into a porridge of mud. Momentum had additionally been lost after a subsequent failed Australian attempt. Currie later categorized Passchendaele as an unproductive effort, unaware that it arguably possessed some strategic merit given the unpalatable circumstances of 1917. Currie had assumed command only in June 1917, by which time the Canadian Corps constituted one of the most formidable fighting formations on the Western Front. Under the inspiring and highly innovative leadership of British Lieutenant General Sir Julian Byng during the Battle of Arras, the Canadian Corps attained its most celebrated victory at Vimy Ridge on 9 April 1917. Shining through as a faint ray of hope in the darkness of revolution in Russia, peak shipping losses from unrestricted submarine warfare, and futile French offensives that would lead to mutiny, the Canadian Corps victory at Vimy produced cheers in the British House of Commons. Shortly thereafter a resolution of the Imperial War Conference formally recognized Canada as an autonomous nation within an imperial Commonwealth. The battlefield success of the Canadian Corps had not come easily, however, as it took years of trial by fire to streamline ramshackle training and have military merit displace political patronage in the selection of commanders.[2]

Essentially, the Canadian Corps adopted and refined British methods to become a professional field force, adept at mounting operations, massing artillery and machine-gun fire, and employing a matchless corps counter-battery organization. Counter-battery fire organized by then Lieutenant Colonel McNaughton played a key role in Canadian Corps success at Vimy. McNaughton had visited the French and formed a low opinion of their gunnery, but became an advocate of British 5 Corps measures developed by Lieutenant Colonel A.G Haig, who had made a name for himself suppressing German artillery in the 1916 Battle of the Somme. These measures resulted in the establishment of counter-battery cells in every corps headquarters and incorporated new techniques such as aerial reconnaissance, flash spotting, and sound ranging. As Canadian Corps Counter-Battery Staff Officer, McNaughton refined these measures for the attack on Vimy, in which he also fired gas shells in an attempt to neutralize German batteries. In tandem with counter-battery efforts, Byng ensured the softening up of German defences with a two-week-long artillery bombardment that increased in intensity as zero hour approached. In all, he deployed 245 heavy and 618 field guns and howitzers on 9 April to support the attack, but as the shell rather than the gun was the weapon of artillery, the true strength of Canadian Corps artillery lay in its massive ammunition dumps and supply delivered over light rail and plank roads. Impact detonating shells fired by heavy guns also cut barbed wire, thus enabling the infantry to get through obstacle belts. Advancing soldiers were further protected by a creeping barrage of artillery fire that moved ahead at a set rate and dwelled as a standing barrage when an objective was taken. This technique had, of course, been developed earlier in actions on the Somme.[3]

As Montgomery and Canadians had learned, in a war of entrenchments that left little room for manoeuvre, tactical innovation effected through diligent staff work was critical to the effective execution of operations. Detailed planning, thorough preparation, and exhaustive training came to characterize Canadian Corps operations. Much of the fighting effectiveness of the Canadian Corps, in fact, sprang from the superior knowledge and skill of attached British staff officers who effected the necessary coordination and checks to translate battle plans into action. At one point a third of all staff officers in the Canadian Corps were British and three of them – John Dill, Edmund Ironside, and Alan Brooke – rose to become CIGS. Currie himself leaned heavily on his British Brigadier General, General Staff (BGGS), or principal operations staff officer, and on his British Deputy Adjutant and Quartermaster General, principal administration and logistics staff officer. He adamantly refused to replace either with Canadians, and in his report on the Hundred Days of 1918 he singled out his BGGS, Brigadier General N.W. Webber, for particular praise. At the divisional level, the first Canadian GSO1 was not appointed until November 1917, and, by the time of the Armistice, one of Canada's four fighting divisions still had a British GSO 1. Happily, the War Office sent only the best and brightest British staff officers to the Canadian Corps.[4]

The Canadian Corps possessed a further advantage in having permanently allocated Canadian divisions that enabled it to develop a uniquely Canadian military cohesion and operational capacity. This was out of the ordinary as corps were not permanently structured formations, but rather headquarters capable of directing the operations of several divisions allocated according to the task assigned to the corps. This made for the more efficient allotment of troops to task in large armies. The only fighting formation permanently structured was the division, which, with minimal artillery and supporting services, could fight on its own for a limited period. To ensure the optimal use of army resources, corps headquarters were in addition allocated sufficient artillery and other supporting troops and services to undertake intended tasks. This task orientation of corps also meant that it made good military sense to alter their composition as the operational situation demanded. Thus, one corps might be given two divisions to defend a position while another might be allocated four to attack an enemy strongpoint. In the case of the Canadian Corps, however, Currie was able to keep it out of the line during the devastating 1918 German March offensive because he insisted that it be fought only as a complete entity.[5]

This ensured that an untouched Canadian Corps was rested and fresh to participate in the Hundred Days of Victory from 8 August to 11 November 1918. Here the Canadian Corps cracked open some of the toughest and most vital points of the German defence, thereby creating the conditions and opportunities that allowed the Allied armies to drive the German military machine to the point of collapse. From the surprise attack at Amiens on 8 August 1918, "the black day of the German army," the BEF advanced over 100 kilometres to break the back of the German army on the Western Front. The Canadian Corps spearheaded this last British offensive of the war that in terms of planning, preparation, and execution, was thoroughly modern in nature and involved the use of tanks, indirect fire, tactical air support, chemical weaponry, electronic deception, and command, control, and intelligence systems. In a series of all-arms actions from early September to the capture of Mons on 11 November, the German army was sent reeling back, to be saved from ultimate destruction only by the eleventh hour-armistice. That this was not easily accomplished without hard pounding was abundantly evident, for the Canadian Corps incurred 45,830 casualties, 45 per cent of total strength, and almost 20 per cent of all Canadian casualties sustained during the entire war.[6] Such a loss was also twice what the First Canadian Army would suffer in the eleven-month campaign in northwest Europe from D-Day to war's end.

Before the war was over, Canadian Corps casualties triggered a conscription crisis in 1917–18 that turned violent in Quebec, which remained at odds with the rest of the country. Out of some 100,000 conscripts, around 47,500 served overseas and about 24,000 at the front. By war's end, Canada had incurred 212,688 combat casualties, including over 60,000 dead. From a population of around eight million souls this was a high price indeed and enough for citizens of the time to bury their dead in Europe and turn away from all thought of war. In 1919 with farm discontent and labour strife rising, Canadians just wanted to deal with the domestic issues of the day. The economy improved after 1921, but collapsed with the onset of the 1929 Great Depression, which many attributed to the blood price paid in war. In this environment, reduced defence budgets coupled with political neglect ensured that efforts to preserve the legacy of the Canadian Corps foundered. In keeping with a policy of retrenchment, the government placed all Canadian services under a single Department of National Defence in 1922. This did not prevent inter-service battles for budget slices, however, which all but eclipsed interest in professional issues. The lessons of the Great War pertaining to the operations of major formations received scant attention as did matters related to military preparedness generally. During this period the army focused mainly upon peripheral activities that included aid of the civil power call-outs in 1922–23 to deal with domestic disturbances sparked by war disenchantment and labour unrest.[7]

From a purely military standpoint, Canadians as British subjects remained tied to the empire with the Great War cementing an even closer association of Canadian and British forces at the working level. At the Colonial Conference of 1907 and Imperial (Defence) Conference of 1909, uniform standards organization, training, equipment, and stores had been agreed and accepted within the empire. For the most part, Canadian doctrine reflected that promulgated by the British War Office. As staff college training was considered key to maintaining uniformity of doctrine following the war, Canadian officers were also nominated to attend Camberley and Quetta courses. The practice of attaching Canadian officers to the War Office recommenced in 1925, and up to 1937 a direct channel for exchanging military information existed between the CIGS in London and the CGS in Ottawa. By the 1920s the Canadian General Staff received on a regular basis a veritable flood of documents from the British War Office, Army Headquarters in India, and other imperial and dominion entities. As the practical assimilation of the Military Forces of the Empire was viewed as desirable, the Canadian regular officer received training similar to that given to his British counterpart. Both were expected to pass promotion examinations set by the War Office, with candidates having first to pass practical portions before attempting associated written examinations in tactical problems set for company and battalion commanders. Other subjects covered included military organization and administration, military law, geography, military history, tactics, map reading, and field works.[8]

In January 1929 Major General McNaughton became CGS after a meteoric rise in rank following his brilliant performance in the Canadian Corps. By war's end he briefly commanded the Canadian Corps Heavy Artillery and in 1920 assumed the appointment of Director of Military Training and Staff Duties in the regular force. In 1921 he attended Staff College Camberley, one year after Montgomery, and two years later became Deputy CGS in the rank of brigadier general. By way of comparison, Montgomery remained a major until January 1927, in which year McNaughton attended the newly founded Imperial Defence College (IDC) along with Colonel Alan Brooke. On return to Canada, McNaughton briefly commanded Military District No. 11 in Victoria, British Columbia, before being promoted to major general at the age forty-one and assuming the appointment CGS. Despite marked lack of field command experience on his way to the top, McNaughton as CGS dominated his colleagues in the military establishment as a great oak dominates a scrub forest. No one could match his qualifications or rival his reputation as a foremost gunner and, given his bureaucratic savvy, he was always three steps ahead of his committees. Blessed with a magnetic personality utterly bereft of pomposity, he also exuded an abiding warmth that endeared him to his troops.[9]

McNaughton also developed a close relationship with Prime Minister R.B. Bennet and helped edit his campaign speeches for his successful run in the 1930 election. Given this association and not content to confine his attention to purely military matters, McNaughton became the most powerful civil servant in the nation. His background in science and engineering nurtured, among other scientific pursuits, a keen interest in furthering northern communications and aerial mapping and charting. In response to the depression and at his personal instigation the army between 1932 and 1936 additionally ran relief camps for unemployed single men. Intended to increase the visibility of the army in the public eye, this endeavour unfortunately turned into a public relations nightmare, rendering McNaughton a political liability. Not surprisingly, such civil undertakings consumed much of McNaughton's time and largely contributed to the almost total neglect of training commanders and soldiers for war. Troops were again deployed in aid of the civil power in 1932–33, but never for permanent force collective field training. Keeping alive the art of war fighting, especially against a first-rate enemy, received low priority. This reflected McNaughton's view that military knowledge was mainly a matter of technical proficiency that scientifically educated civilians and successful businessmen could master better than military professionals. While this approach appealed to academics who showered honours upon him, the Canadian army languished under McNaughton and politicians who could not envision another major conflict. He thus left the army in worse condition than it was when he assumed the appointment of CGS. Before retiring in 1935 to become president of the National Research Council, he produced a memorandum showing equipment deficiencies and the sorry state of the Canadian army, for which several of his former military comrades held him directly accountable.[10]

Despite equipment shortages and the challenge of Canadian geography, McNaughton had he been so inclined could have done more in the area of training through professional studies using cloth model demonstrations, tactical exercises without troops, and skeleton communications exercises. Military leadership rather than the public and political disinterest prevailing during the interwar years thus bears most responsibility for the failure to remember that an army's first role in peace is to prepare for war and to be able to fight it well. In the absence of equipment and field manoeuvres, dedicated officers turned to personal study as the only means by which to ensure professional improvement. Many sought to learn more about military operations through the *Canadian Defence Quarterly (CDQ)*, which disseminated information related to British military developments, giving specific British exercises comprehensive coverage and highlighting selected excerpts from British defence journals. In 1937 the *CDQ* published Montgomery's "The Problem of the Encounter Battle as Affected by Modern British War Establishment," described by the editor as the most thoughtful and valuable tactical discussion that had appeared in any British service journal for some considerable time. That there was a receptive audience eager to learn about the latest thinking on field operations is evident from the number of published articles by Canadian officers, including a tactical debate between Lieutenant Colonel E.L.M. Burns and Captain G.G. Simonds, both future corps commanders.[11] Part-time soldiers like Brigadier P.A.S. Todd, who rose to command 2 Canadian Corps artillery, also took it upon themselves to use every opportunity to learn all that they could about their particular branch, so that when war came they would actually know something about how to fight.[12] But such focus was not actively promoted by the military establishment itself, which left the onus on individuals.

Montgomery in Command of British Formations

Canada commenced limited rearmament in 1937, in May of which year Montgomery departed Quetta to take command of the 9th Infantry Brigade at Portsmouth in the temporary rank of brigadier. On his passage from India he wrote "The Problem of the Encounter Battle," which appeared in the *CDQ* in the same year. This article stressed getting a good start in the execution of a battle plan to avoid having a unit or formation drift aimlessly into action, which, with time at a premium owing to modern transport and air, risked losing the initiative and having to conform gradually to the enemy plan. A bad start because of a poor plan or faulty dispositions could only be pulled out of the fire by the gallantry of troops bound to suffer heavy casualties. Although information may be lacking or incomplete, he wrote, a commander still must make a plan and begin early to force his will upon an enemy. To do this, he and his headquarters had to be well forward to gain the earliest possible information and see the ground, and thereafter pulling back so as not to become unduly influenced by local actions at the front. During battle the commander also had to be prepared to go forward at critical junctures, since waiting at headquarters for information that might never arrive could be fatal. To facilitate forward planning, he also had to have his artillery and engineer commanders in his pocket. Montgomery further advocated planning to fight at night and exercising direct control of armoured mobile forces rather than leaving it to specialized cavalry commanders.[1]

This article formed the basis of his first policy document issued by 9th Infantry Brigade headquarters in August 1937. Montgomery's intent was to make his brigade the best in the army, and he started by cancelling one-day exercises and holding four over three nights each. After the death of his wife in October he immersed himself even more in training, holding a study week in December and another in March 1938 emphasizing defence in depth, the use of reserves, the concentration of artillery fire, the stage management of battle in night attack and withdrawal, defence organization, and river crossings. Although Montgomery recognized that solving tactical problems could not be made subject to fixed rules, which led him to encourage new ideas through study, he insisted that the broad plan of operation had to be known by commanders at every level so that all officers would know the general intention and thus be enabled to think for themselves and act on their own initiative. In July 1938 Montgomery in conjunction with the navy planned and carried out a brigade amphibious assault on Slapton Sands supported by light tanks and air under a joint service command headed by himself.[2]

For his field performance Montgomery received several glowing recommendations for promotion. In October he once again left for Palestine to assume command of the new 8th Division formed to deal with a growing Arab rebellion. Upon arrival he received a further notification that he had been selected to succeed the commander of the 3rd Division in December 1939. In the interim Montgomery contributed to crushing the organized backbone of the insurrection brought on by Arab resistance to Jewish immigration. Following Adolf Hitler's seizure of Czechoslovakia in March 1939, however, he was called back to take 3rd Division command earlier than anticipated. At this point Montgomery took seriously ill and had to be medically evacuated to England in July 1939, not to be declared fit by medical board until 10 August. Previously a moderate smoker and drinker, he vowed from this time onward never to smoke or drink again. Several days later the War Office ordered him to take command of the 3rd Division with effect from 28 August. On 1 September Hitler invaded Poland and the mobilization of the British army began. At the end of the month the BEF deployed to France under the command of Field Marshal Lord Gort, who relinquished his previous appointment of CIGS.[3]

In early October Montgomery's 3rd Division established an anti-tank defensive line south of Lille as part of Brooke's 2 Corps. Over the next six months, during the "Phoney War" lull that followed the German conquest of Poland, Montgomery conducted five major divisional exercises and posted out doubtful officers to rear area jobs. The exercises practised counter-attacks supported by tanks, artillery, and air, and disengagement by night from close contact with the enemy. The latter included rapid withdrawal by motorized movement, in one case over sixty miles, to occupy defensive positions staked out by advance reconnaissance parties. To facilitate night transport movement Montgomery fitted his vehicles with shaded tail lights that shone forward onto rear axles painted white. Route marking drills and guides further aided the movement of main bodies. As radio and even line communications were not always reliable, he backed them up with messengers and liaison officers. Montgomery also planned to fight the 3rd Division as a division from a forward tactical headquarters that included artillery and engineer commanders, leaving his main headquarters to be run by his COS, whom he empowered to make decisions. As he considered it unsound to march soldiers twenty-one miles at night with nothing to eat between 1900 and 0600 hours, and no food on them in case something went wrong, he additionally instituted a system for ensuring his men were well fed, provisioned, and rested.[4]

When the Germans violated Belgian neutrality on 10 May, the 13,000 strong 3rd Division spearheaded Brooke's 2 Corps drive into Belgium, taking up a defensive position west of Louvain from where it counter-attacked the Germans on 15 May. Fear of encirclement, however, prompted a general withdrawal, which 3rd Division adhered to on 16 May, employing concentrated artillery fire to effect a clean breakaway. As the situation continued to deteriorate, Lord Gort on 26 May ordered evacuation through the Dunkirk-Nieuport perimeter. That evening Brooke instructed Montgomery to side-step his division from south to north behind the 4th, 5th, and 50th Divisions and take up a shielding position on the Yser Canal north of Ypres. This involved making another clean break with the enemy on the night of 27 May and, *in total darkness,* crossing three divisional lines of communication behind a fluctuating fighting front to occupy an unreconnoitred defensive position before dawn. Thanks to previous exercises and rehearsals, the 3rd Division executed this twenty-five-mile manoeuvre in superb fashion, drawing from Brooke the comment that Montgomery, as usual, accomplished almost the impossible.[5] From that point on Brooke became the strongest supporter of Montgomery, whom he deemed to be his tactical, but not strategic, superior.

With nerves of steel and full confidence in his subordinates, Montgomery did not miss a night of sound sleep during this taxing period, unlike several other senior commanders who faltered under the strain and went to pieces for lack of sleep. Indeed, he appeared to thrive in the atmosphere of fear and danger, which reputedly sharpened his mind. The experience also taught him the importance of being able to persevere and withstand setbacks when things were not going well. On 28 May the Belgian army surrendered and the next day the 3rd Division withdrew to the eastern flank of the Dunkirk perimeter. Here Montgomery tirelessly inspected his front with a cheerful cockiness and contagious confidence that inspired his troops. On the evening of 30 May Brooke left for England, having chosen Montgomery, his most junior

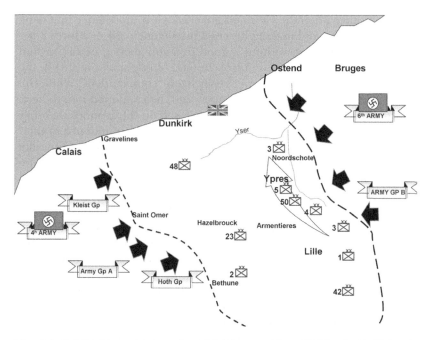

Map 3.1 3rd Division withdrawal to shielding position, 27 May 1940 (John A. Macdonald)

division commander, to be his replacement as 2 Corps commander. After organizing the final extrication of 2 Corps, Montgomery gave his last orders on 31 May and corps perimeter defences disengaged in the early hours of the next day. At 0330 hours, after personally directing traffic toward Dunkirk, Montgomery embarked for England, having achieved Helmuth von Moltke's ultimate measure of a great captain: being able in the face of adversity to carry out a successful retreat. Montgomery saw clearly, however, that Dunkirk was not a victory, but a colossal military disaster and a crushing defeat to be avenged.[6]

On 2 June 1940 Montgomery requested and obtained a private interview with the new CIGS, Sir John Dill, telling him that Lord Gort and certain of his subordinates had proven unfit for field command. Indeed, Gort appeared a model of how not to command, his love of detail precluding him from seeing the woods for the trees. Never once during the Phoney War had he conducted a signals, administrative, intelligence, or movement exercise designed to prepare the BEF for battle. He had furthermore failed to rehearse his headquarters in maintaining communications. Split into three distant parts, they thus remained out of touch with each other when the Germans attacked. Gort's insistence on taking his COS with him and making his chief intelligence officer a force commander left him blind without a good decision-making capability and unable to exercise effective control. In fact, Montgomery told Dill, the BEF had since its inception never really been "commanded." While Dill agreed with much of what Montgomery said, he cautioned him to keep his criticisms of BEF high command to himself on the grounds that they might adversely affect morale and shake the troops' confidence in their leaders. That Montgomery did not do so, and persisted in asserting that military bungling had produced a humiliating defeat, did not earn him many friends in certain places. This did not cost him his command, however, and on 19 June the 3rd Division assumed responsibility for defending the Sussex coast between Brighton and Bognor as part of 12 Corps.[7]

Fear of German invasion now lent a sense of urgency and Montgomery, convinced of the need for ruthlessness in getting the right man for the right job, announced that he would henceforth unilaterally fill key command and staff posts as there was no time for bureaucratic approval by the War Office. Among the first to recognize German tactical superiority, he noted their excellent concealment capability while coming into action, quick establishment of effective observation and sniping coverage, and employment of heavy mortar fire to shake infantry morale. Their ability to infiltrate and exploit success was also first rate, along with their direction-finding means of accurately locating sources of wireless transmissions. He also noted that they conducted operations mainly by day, putting patrols out only by night, and that they highly disliked concentrated artillery fire, which, unlike their Stuka dive bombers, could attack by night as well as day in any weather. His own Dunkirk experience at the same time confirmed the value of tactical exercises and training by rehearsal, the vital importance of communications, the need for mobile headquarters, the worth of night operations, and the requirement to fight a division as one cohesive force. He at once set off to instil these lessons, while preparing to defeat any possible German assault landing by evacuating civilians, requisitioning houses, and demolishing buildings to improve defences. To ensure the tactical upper hand, he deployed minimum force forward to break up lead German elements, which allowed him to hold maximum force back in reserve as a mobile counter-attack body. To practise this role Montgomery slated his first divisional exercise for 25–6 July.[8]

On 21 July 1940, however, Montgomery received word that he was to assume command of 5 Corps in the rank of lieutenant general. His new command comprised the 4th and 50th Infantry Divisions covering 215 miles of coastal front from Bognor to Lyme Regis, including the Isle of

Wight and the garrison of Portsmouth. After his arrival on the morning of 22 July, heads began to roll in the afternoon among corps headquarters staff and services. Poaching calls also went out to the War Office for more intelligence officers and motor contact officers specially trained to receive, query, and ultimately deliver clear verbal orders, even unpleasant ones. On 23 July he visited the 4th Division and found its general condition to be far from satisfactory owing to a lack of firm guidance from the top that a strong commander could have provided. This left Montgomery in no doubt that the division would incur a lot of casualties in action. It lacked the finer points of conducting battle that would save lives, among other things, inadequate anti-aircraft measures, no organization for observation and sniping, no proper vehicle lighting that would enable large-scale night movement avoiding detection from air, and no night driving practice. Even worse, there was no understanding of how to handle mortars and the battle-winning power of artillery. Why no one knew what was required in such areas reflected a serious lack of knowledge at division headquarters. He accordingly recommended the removal of the artillery commander, two field regiment commanders, the service corps commander, and the GSO2 at headquarters. The division commander apparently agreed, with Montgomery noting that he himself should have taken action before on his own. Montgomery concluded that the division would need a lot of help, but that this should be done kindly and tactfully through the commander and his GSO1, who, while out of his depth, was trainable.[9]

The Portsmouth Area under operational command of 5 Corps fared even worse, with Montgomery calling for the removal of the area commander and a number of his staff officers. While a nice person who was trying his best to put things right, by sacking his adjutant for example, the area commander failed to supervise adequately and put things on a proper basis. Medical arrangements hardly existed and reserve supplies remained centrally held rather than dispersed to units in two- to three-day lots. In the end, the area commander failed to stand up under cross-examination by Montgomery who after listening to him talk finally assessed him as ineffective, extremely idle, and lacking in energy and drive. Quite unfit to be a major general, he deserved to be removed. His chief administrative officer, an old retired officer of the 60th Rifles, received similar disparagement. Described as idle and taken to drink, he in Montgomery's opinion should never have been given the job. A director of a brewery who farmed his own estate, he warranted being sent back to his farm. Montgomery placed the commander of the Royal Engineers in the same category. Completely and utterly useless, he had served many years in India and had also taken to drink. A regular officer unable to explain anything clearly, he gave Montgomery the impression of being mentally deficient.[10]

The defenders of the Isle of Wight also failed to impress Montgomery. He insisted on the immediate removal of the CO of the 50th (Holding) Battalion, Hampshire Regiment, as he was far too old and quite unfit to command an operational unit. The 8th Battalion of the same regiment was also officered by old men originally recruited for the Home Guard, but now commanding companies of eighteen-year-old soldiers. Montgomery described the CO, aged sixty-three and a Boer War veteran, as a pathetic sight – old, frail, and looking ill – and recommended his removal so he could live out his life in peace somewhere. He further suggested getting rid of the old and decrepit 2IC and replacing fifty-five-year-old platoon commanders with younger officers.[11]

On 28 July 1940 Montgomery rendered another report that stated the standard of training of the 50th Division was low because all energies had been directed to work on beach defences. Some rifles companies had been in the same place for a month doing nothing but dig and work on defences. Their soldiers had done no PT or field training and did not appear to be on their toes. He did not see the light of battle in their eyes. The net result was that all the finer arts of how to compete with the Germans in battle had been relegated to the background. Some soldiers had never even fired more than five rifle rounds, while others had never fired the Bren light machine gun. None had been taught how to destroy a tank. Without well-trained troops capable of energetically carrying out offensive operations, Montgomery insisted, the best defences in the world were in themselves of little value. Seeing clearly that the eighty-mile front of the 50th Division would inevitably result in fluid operations, he ordered the 4th Division to take over some of that frontage and directed that no more than 50 per cent of forces be allocated to beach defence. A major lesson of the Great War, in Montgomery's view, was that it was not won by tanks, guns, aircraft, trenches, or barbed wire, but rather by the creation, marshalling, and commitment of reserves.[12]

By the beginning of October 1941 all battalions, brigades, and both divisions had been exercised in the field in accordance with Montgomery's pattern of undertaking collective training after the completion of individual and sub-unit training and cloth model and brigade signals exercises. He viewed all minor training as critical in enabling units to carry out large-scale exercises, at least once a week in the case of battalions and brigades and once a month for divisions. In all, Montgomery conducted five division and corps headquarters exercises that practised night movement, traffic control, and the value of demolitions in mobile operations. He also experimented with RAF support and tank–infantry cooperation with an attached army tank brigade. In post-exercise wrap-ups and study weeks he consistently stressed that while artillery was deployed and allotted from above, detailed fire control plans were built up from below by the vital combination of infantry company command-ers and artillery forward observation officers (FOOs). To conceal artil-lery fire capability from the enemy and reduce motor traffic congestion, he further recommended keeping the bulk of artillery in reserve under the divisional artillery commander and allotting but one field regiment per brigade. Upon the conclusion of his fifth major exercise Montgom-ery expressed confidence that commanders could deploy a reinforced division a distance of seventy miles by night into action without confu-sion. He later pronounced the 5 Corps, now including the 3rd Division exchanged for the 50th, as a first-class fighting formation fit in every way to engage the Germans.[13]

Montgomery's concentration on training from section level to divi-sion highlighted his concerns about man management and physical fitness. To facilitate productive training a soldier had to have a good breakfast, a haversack ration with full water bottle during the day, and a hot meal after dark. Troops had to be able to march a minimum of twenty-five miles as a group and then be ready to fight in action. In Octo-ber Montgomery ordered his 5 Corps headquarters staff, including all officers up to captain rank and all majors up to age forty, to complete two cross-country runs weekly. To keep his hand on the pulse of training, he devoted at least half of every working day to visiting units and talking to everyone from CO to NCOs and individual soldiers. He also spent time with non-divisional personnel seeking to train them in the same manner that he did with his 5 Corps troops. Over the months this led to the cre-ation of Home Guard brigades that he deployed to man beach defences, which enhanced his ability to deploy his two divisions and corps troops behind them and form an offensive striking force for a true defence in depth.[14]

In May 1941 Montgomery sidestepped to command 12 Corps respon-sible for the defence of the southeastern coast, considered the most likely German landing area in event of invasion. In his first direction to the commanders of the Kent Area and the 43rd, 44th, and 56th Divi-sions, he stressed that the empire was fighting for its life. Noting that, "In theory we are supposed to be fighting for democracy; I do not know what this means and I doubt if anyone else does," he went on to deal with military practicalities. On finding wives and families living in the 12 Corps area, he immediately called for their removal even though he had no power to order such an evacuation. To ensure that family life would not interfere with soldiering, he directed that no officer or other rank in the corps would be allowed to sleep away from his appointed billet, even for a weekend unless on leave or pass under established rules. Montgomery favoured officers and men being given the opportunity to see their families, but he opposed allowing a situation to develop in which family concerns would detract soldiers from performing their duties. In his view, field army elements had to be prepared to take rapid action in case of invasion, moving instantly to deployment areas from which to carry out their battle roles. As such an invasion would undoubtedly be accompanied by heavy bombing of towns and villages, he wished to avoid placing his troops in a crisis of conscience. To demand that a soldier deploy while his wife and children might be wounded as a result of enemy bombing was to place an unfair strain upon him.[15]

As in the case of 5 Corps, Montgomery found much to his dislike in 12 Corps. Among his major concerns was the low standard of minor tactics that he observed in the infantry throughout the corps. Field craft skills were definitely not up to the standard of the Germans, and junior leadership and fire discipline left much to be desired. Since it was the sub-unit that in the end wins the battle, Montgomery insisted, the standard of minor tactics had to be high, or you will fail – however good the higher plan. Montgomery saw the company commander as key to addressing this issue, but concluded that few officers and NCOs possessed sufficient grounding in the subject, let alone the instructional ability to teach it with any authority. To put the matter right, he suggested that company commanders and junior officers be taught what to teach and how to teach, starting with the basics. This meant tackling first field craft, to make it instinctive of the individual soldier, and the bedrock essentials of section tactics, such as controlling formations, movement using ground, and fire discipline, before progressing to platoon tactics. He further recommended that officers, NCOs, and men be assumed to know nothing of minor tactics until they demonstrated that they did know. While Montgomery pointed out that the required high standard could be achieved only if a CO personally interested himself in minor tactical training, he called on all brigade commanders to get involved and conduct weekly day-long model and ground studies on how to properly practise and teach field craft and section and platoon tactics.[16]

Montgomery further found the physical fitness of troops to be below the standard of that required in war. Troops were too road bound and commanders and staff spent too much time in offices to the detriment of field activity. It was not enough just to be fit to compete successfully in battle against the Germans, troops had to be mentally fit and "hard" with powers of endurance capable of lasting weeks under rough conditions. Montgomery observed that men could march twenty-eight miles along a road, but showed signs of distress when operating in the field. Nor was he convinced that officers were as fit as they could be, which was unacceptable as both officers and soldiers in battle had to perform their duties in fighting order at the double. The answer was regular assault training with troops moving by sections and platoons over a tough course in full battle order with rifle and ammunition. As it was particularly necessary for brigadiers, COs, and company commanders to be really hard with great powers of endurance, he suggested that officers get up at 0630 hours, do physical training at 0700, and run five to seven miles cross country each week. He later suggested substituting battle order for running kit. In this manner Montgomery sought to get officers physically and mentally fit. By his measure, if the men of a unit appeared sluggish and lacking in mental alertness, the unit had a bad CO.[17]

On a higher plane, Montgomery advocated the study of the contact battle, operations by night, and the conduct of offensive operations in mobile war, including the decentralization of supporting arms and weapons when the battle was fluid and recalling them when it was necessary to strike a hard blow. He directed that these subjects should be studied on a model and that every division, brigade, and unit headquarters should have a good indoor instruction room capable of having a good model displayed on the floor. For his corps study week 15–20 December he requested that divisions study the problem of dealing with hostile tanks by an ordinary infantry division. The aim was to evolve within the corps a good technique that would enable every sub-unit, even if comprised of clerks or cooks, to know exactly how to destroy an enemy tank. To get the study started he suggested that as infantry could not deal with tanks in the open by day, a panzer division had to be stopped and made to suffer before taking counter-action. He therefore advocated that the infantry division take up a position astride the most likely enemy axis of advance, ideally straddling an obstacle, and invite the panzer division to run its nose into mutually supporting anti-tank localities sited in depth. Such a deployment would prevent the enemy from reconnoitring the obstacle and taking steps to cross it, while at the same time enable anti-tank localities in front of the obstacle to cut off enemy infantry following panzers. The panzers themselves would then be left alone in the open, exposed to the direct fire of concealed anti-tank and field artillery guns, and, in the darkness of night, vulnerable to destruction by foot infantry anti-tank teams sallying forth from defended localities. The challenge set by Montgomery was for divisions and brigade groups to develop techniques for rapid deployments into anti-panzer defensive areas so as to avoid being caught in the open or on the move by enemy armoured formations.[18]

The defence of the 12 Corps area meanwhile reflected such thinking. Montgomery's first tactical instruction, based on his reading of translated German documents from Libya, altered 12 Corps dispositions that strung out the 43rd, 44th, and 56th divisions in linear entrenchments and pillboxes along the coast. There was no depth to this defensive layout with few reserves earmarked for counter-attack. Rather than defend every yard of beach front that necessitated force dispersal, Montgomery hinged his defence on strong well-wired and entrenched forward localities capable of all-round defence. Panzers were to be lured, trapped, and destroyed in depth between these strong points set up to be mutually supporting and collectively able to hold out until the arrival of reserves. He further condemned the unsound tendency of reserves being dispersed in order to be able to cover all suitable places for enemy airborne landings. In his view, such dispersion could only negate effective offensive action and lead to disaster. His solution was to keep companies and battalions concentrated and reserve infantry brigade groups so assembled that combined action, with full cooperation between the arms, could be taken rapidly in any direction to deal with situations that might arise. Montgomery's Exercises "Binge" and "Morebinge" tested the use of corps reserves in defeating invasion and examined how forward infantry brigades might deal with enemy landings by sea and air. By fortifying the garrison towns of Dover, Folkestone, Ashford, and Canterbury and preserving the concentrated power of mobile reserves, Montgomery was confident that his 12 Corps sector could be held against German seaborne and airborne assault.[19]

To ensure that soldiers would be ready for battle, Montgomery directed every commander to overhaul his training methods with the aim of eliminating troop monotony and boredom. In his view, the high standard of intelligence within the ranks called for creativity and brains and cutting out all unimaginative and soul-destroying training methods. To encourage interest, he recommended introducing the competitive element whenever suitable and basing all individual training on "piece work," that is, dismissing a man who showed proficiency in weapons training or another subject, and not just keeping him training to fill in the time. He further urged concentrating dispersed units once a week so that COs could assert direct influence and control over them as units. Here he also saw high value in a CO handling his unit in close order drill as this allowed him to impress his personality upon his troops, while enabling them to see each other acting in unison with their officers. In similar fashion, divisions were to be concentrated once a month and trained for three days in the field so as to avoid losing their edge in developed techniques. To introduce realism and foster further interest in training, Montgomery also recommended the use of live ammunition, especially in the coastal areas. He additionally sought to capitalize on the Germans being twenty miles away across the Channel by having division, brigade, and unit headquarters collect and compile information on enemy deployments, organization, equipment, and tactics. In this manner, he also aimed to get troops to think offensively about meeting the Germans in battle in other circumstances than defeating invasion.[20]

In November 1941 Montgomery announced that South-Eastern Command had been authorized to carry out small raids on the French coast. The objects of such raids in order of priority were to bring back German prisoners, obtain information about enemy coastal defences, and to inflict casualties and damage. Montgomery had pressed for this opportunity as it enabled commanders and staffs to plan and conduct actual battle ventures that would better condition troops for war. He cautioned, however, that such operations could be tricky and hazardous with disappointments and even reverses liable to result, which meant developing in officers and men the robust mentality that would help them withstand the buffeting of war. He therefore recommended starting small and building up confidence through the achievement of success by limiting first ventures to gaining information by reconnaissance patrols that avoided fighting. Pointing out that taking a patrol to France and bringing it back was in effect a naval operation, which called for close cooperation with the RN and training in landing craft, he stressed the initial need for patrols to get there safely and back with few casualties to personnel and naval vessels. Setting the coast ablaze in a larger fighting venture risked incurring substantial casualties and was thus better left to when more was known about mounting such inter-service operations. In this regard, Montgomery saw the stage management and organization of patrol activity as the purview of the battalion commander under brigade oversight, but coordination with the navy as the responsibility of the division commander. In approaching raiding, which he likened unto traditional army patrolling activity with the addition of naval delivery and return, Montgomery urged divisional commanders to let their subordinates handle their own affairs and avoid cramping their initiative and style by a rigid and centralized control. At the same time, he accepted a division developing its own raiding technique as there was no point in adhering slavishly to what others did if the division had discovered a better way itself.[21]

Montgomery's insistence on training subordinate commanders reflected his strong belief that the first essential of a first-class army was a good corps of officers in which commissions were granted only to the right material. If higher commanders do everything themselves, he warned, we shall only fail when we start fighting. For this reason he was not under any circumstances prepared to accept mediocre unit commanders and old majors who lacked vitality. While the men in the ranks of units were very fine material, they could only prevail in battle if well led. In Montgomery's view, inspiration and leadership had to come from above and any officer who lacked character, drive, and energy, and inspired no confidence was next to useless in any type of military employment. In this regard, it was absolutely essential for unit COs to possess qualities of leadership and the drive to get things done. Any CO who failed to inspire confidence and lacked training ability had therefore to be weeded out and not just transferred to an administrative position. In addition to having commanders check over their subordinate officers, Montgomery also suggested carrying out rigorous and thorough inspections of units to ruthlessly expose all faults and inefficient methods. Within 12 Corps itself, he cleaned house by relieving three brigadiers and six commanding officers.[22]

Montgomery's success in conducting 5 and 12 Corps field exercises so impressed Brooke, new Commander-in-Chief (C-in-C) Home Forces, that he was selected to be the Chief Umpire for full-scale army manoeuvres in Exercise "Bumper" 29 September–3 October 1941. "Bumper" involved nine infantry divisions and the equivalent of four armoured divisions in a two-sided exercise that pitted a superior invasion force against a home defence force. Following a masterly summing up of lessons learned from the exercise, Montgomery returned briefly to 12 Corps before being promoted on 17 November 1941 to head South-Eastern Command comprising both 12 Corps and the Canadian Corps. In keeping with his focus on war fighting, and now with two corps under him, he immediately redesignated his command "South-Eastern Army" and styled himself army commander. On 28 November he issued his first Army Commander's Personal Memorandum setting out an operational policy that covered the individual training of the soldier, field exercises with troops, and the handling of formations in battle.

Montgomery's new command brought him into contact with Canadian troops for a second time, but the Canadian Corps he encountered merely sought to emulate the one that he had visited during the battle of Passchendaele. As has been suggested in chapter 2, years of neglect between wars had taken a toll on Canadian military professionalism. The challenge once more was to turn an army of civilian volunteers into an effective fighting machine. Montgomery would have a soft spot for Canada's willing soldiers, but could hardly have known what went on within the strategic realm of Canadian war planning to field them as a corps. In fact, the Canadian government would have much preferred to send air forces rather than ground troops overseas to fight. To a large extent Canada stumbled into war with a makeshift war machinery that placed the most senior army generals in command of overseas field formations with de facto precedence over the CGS. This approach, which left McNaughton and Crerar heavily involved in time-consuming administrative, personnel, and non-operational matters,[23] ultimately caused Montgomery some professional concern as he held that field command was a full-time job in itself. From this standpoint, that of leaving field commanders to focus principally upon operations, Canada marched to war to a different drummer than either Britain or the United States, and it is to this difference and strategic background that attention will now be turned.

Chapter Four

Canada's Erratic March to War

In 1935, the year in which Montgomery lived through the great Quetta earthquake and McNaughton retired as CGS, the Liberal government of Mackenzie King swept to power in Canada. A consummate politician who sought national harmony and unity above all, King had no interest in military matters and disliked the army in particular. A devoted supporter of former Prime Minister Sir Wilfrid Laurier, a loyalty that helped him rise to power, he never forgot that his political base was firmly anchored in Quebec. He accordingly harboured an obsessive fear of conscription for overseas service, which Quebec had strongly opposed during the Great War, for its potential threat to national unity and his retention of political power. As late as March 1939, King asserted that the days of great expeditionary forces of infantry crossing the oceans were not likely to recur, hence negating any need for conscription. Earlier at the 1937 Imperial Conference, he had also refused to agree to defence commitments in advance, to the extent that British Prime Minister Neville Chamberlain's government interpreted his policy of no commitments as meaning Britain could no longer count on Canada. Yet King, in searching for a foreign policy that would not jeopardize his Quebec base, never doubted that Canada would ultimately go to the aid of Britain in a pinch. His constant insistence on exercising Canadian autonomy within the Commonwealth, however, ensured that the country backed erratically into the Second World War and closed the one avenue by which Canada might have gained a strategic voice.[1]

King and his Undersecretary of State for External Affairs, O.D. Skelton, both supported Chamberlain's appeasement policy in the late 1930s and later planned for a moderate war effort because of financial and domestic considerations. In 1936 the government refused a British request to establish a training school for airmen on Canadian territory, stating that Canada intended to establish air training schools of its own.

This accorded with the view that an air commitment would produce fewer casualties and preclude any requirement for conscription. The 1937 Canadian rearmament program thus gave top priority to the Royal Canadian Air Force (RCAF), which by 1939–40 garnered nearly half of all service appropriations. On 24 August 1939 Skelton proposed guidelines for Canadian war policy in a cabinet paper. Assuming that there would be immediate consultations with Britain and France and discreet discussions with Washington, he advocated giving primacy to the defence of Canada. He saw offering aid to Newfoundland and the West Indies as also within Canadian capability. Skelton further recommended that any overseas military action be undertaken by the air service rather than ground forces. He added that an intensive program of building planes and training men for air service with an RCAF contingent operating in France would be effective from the military standpoint and satisfy public opinion. Beyond this, Skelton envisioned Canada making its greatest contribution in the economic field through the provision of munitions, raw materials, and foodstuffs, which amounted to a variant of Britain's 1937 limited liability war policy abandoned six months earlier.[2]

Skelton's paper, presented to the cabinet without consulting the CCOS, received general approval. On 1 September the cabinet also considered a CCOS submission entitled "Canada's National Effort (Armed Forces) in the Early Stages of a Major War." This submission noted that Britain intended to dispatch an expeditionary force to France and advocated raising a Canadian army corps of two divisions and ancillary troops for overseas service. On 5 September the Cabinet Defence Committee chaired by King informed the CCOS that pending Parliament's decision, the government would adopt measures only for the defence of Canada. King further expressed irritation with their recommendations, pointing to their dissimilarity with Defence Scheme Number 3, which had been amended in 1937 to provide for the direct defence of Canadian territory. This defence scheme dating from 1932 had originally called for the mobilization and overseas deployment of an expeditionary force. Owing to the King government's opposition to such a deployment, however, the general staff modified the plan to provide a force of one mobile and two infantry divisions primarily for the defence of Canada, but quietly added the caveat that the same force might be deployed overseas. The Canadian general staff, in short, saw more clearly than the government that public opinion would ultimately demand the overseas commitment of ground forces.[3]

Unfolding events decided the issue. On 1 September, the day Germany attacked Poland, the entire force mobilized. Two days later, when Britain declared war on Germany, a secret cabinet order directed

Canadian coastal commanders to take all necessary defence measures that would be required in a state of war. While the ferocity of the Nazi assault on Poland lent urgency to the situation, the spectre of overseas conscription also loomed large. On 3 September King nonetheless sent a message to Chamberlain asking how Canada might lend assistance. In reply the British requested naval and air support and the immediate dispatch of a small Canadian fighting unit to take its place alongside British formations. They also requested technical units such as engineers, ordnance, medical, transport, and signals units for attachment to British forces. Five days after Canada declared war on 10 September, the cabinet appointed a subcommittee chaired by the Minister of Finance J.L. Ralston to draft a war program for the nation that gave priority to the provision of supplies and financial aid. On 16 September, however, the government instructed the CCOS to dispatch the 1st Canadian Infantry Division overseas to fight with the BEF in France. Three days later the formation of a second division was announced. On 26 September Chamberlain made an additional appeal for Canada to participate in a grand British Commonwealth Air Training Plan designed to train dominion pilots for service with the Royal Air Force (RAF). King jumped at the proposal, but expressed deep regret that it had not been made earlier so that Canada's war effort could have been formed along this line rather than the dispatch of an expeditionary force.[4]

During the Phoney War, the period between the conquest of Poland and the German invasions of Denmark and Norway in April 1940, Ottawa displayed little interest in influencing the higher direction of a conflict expected to last three years. The Anglo-French Supreme War Council created in 1939 to coordinate the Allied war effort, remained a distant forum in which the prime ministers of France and Britain plus ambassadors of Allied powers determined war policy. King also continually discouraged Chamberlain's proposals to convene a conference of Commonwealth prime ministers. Canada's reluctance to take part in such strategic deliberations, several observers warned, risked rendering the country little more than a supplier of soldiers and pilots. There is no indication, however, that King sought membership on the Supreme War Council, even though orders-in-council passed in 1939 under the Visiting Forces Act of 1933 and the War Measures Act of 1914 authorized Canadian troops to serve under the C-in-C, BEF. Greater voice in the higher direction of the war, of course, might have sparked demands for an increased Canadian war effort, which King, preoccupied by political challenges at home, desperately hoped to avoid. King's outburst on 31 October 1939 that "This is not our war" confirmed his government's intent to keep Canadian involvement limited to financial, economic, and imperial garrison assistance if possible. This policy eventually led to Canadian troops reinforcing the doomed Hong Kong garrison, a deployment strongly recommended by Crerar.[5]

In January 1940 the Ontario provincial government passed a resolution condemning King's war effort as lackadaisical. In response, he called a snap federal election that caught his political opponents off guard and resulted in a landslide Liberal victory on 26 March 1940. While campaigning in February, King also made known that he did not wish to be consulted by the British on policy towards Norway, which he labelled a distinctly European question that should be kept between France and Britain themselves. When the Germans attacked Norway in April, barely two weeks after his election win, he did not even bother to call a meeting of the Cabinet War Committee. The Allies' humiliating defeat in the Norwegian campaign, in contrast, toppled Chamberlain's government, leaving Winston Churchill to take the helm on 10 May as the Germans unleashed their lightning war in the west. Holland surrendered four days later, and Belgium capitulated on 28 May. On 10 June Italy rushed to the aid of Germany and seven days later the French government sued for peace. These cataclysmic events shook Canadians to the core, and the Cabinet War Committee, having not met regularly before May 1940, met eight times before the month was over. On 17 May 1940 King declared the empire to be in extreme danger and the cabinet agreed to raise a third division and form a Canadian corps overseas. During the Dunkirk evacuation of the BEF, the government announced that a fourth division would also be recruited. In June Parliament passed the National Resources Mobilization Act, empowering the government to mobilize all material resources and conscript manpower for home defence. Emphasis also shifted to imperial defence, with Canada consenting to British requests to provide garrisons for Iceland, Bermuda, and Jamaica.[6]

From the fall of France in June 1940 to the invasion of the Soviet Union in June 1941, a dark period when the British Empire stood alone against the Axis powers, Canada was Britain's greatest ally. Yet despite Canada's relative geographical security, the King government refused to take an active part in the higher direction of the war. Ever fearful of compromising Canadian autonomy, King opposed any equivalent of the 1917 Imperial War Cabinet of the Great War. When Australian Prime Minister Robert Menzies proposed such a body to consider strategic matters, King countered that he would require advice from his CCOS on the matter. He also expressed fear about potential separation from his cabinet colleagues and being unable to deal with domestic divisions and conscription issues at home. That Canadian participation could lead to commitments without any real authority further concerned King. He

therefore recommended that individual ministers raise matters as necessary with their British counterparts. On 29 July 1941 the Canadian Cabinet War Committee formally rejected Menzies's proposal. This action
all but ensured that the Anglo-French Supreme War Council would be
replaced not by a Commonwealth body modelled on the Imperial War
Cabinet but, rather, by the British War Cabinet and the British COS
(BCOS), with Churchill as overlord.[7]

Unlike King, who assumed the External Affairs portfolio in addition
to his position as prime minister, Churchill donned the mantle of minister of defence, a new post unencumbered by a working department
like the War Office, the Admiralty, and air ministry. He thus not only
chaired his small War Cabinet, but also acted as ex-officio chairman of
the BCOS committee, which, in his view, for the first time assumed its
proper place in daily contact with the executive head of government,
and in accord with him had full control over the conduct of the war and
the armed forces. Using military members of the cabinet secretariat as
his staff and making their superior, General Sir Hastings Ismay, his personal COS and a member of the BCOS committee, Churchill achieved
a degree of political-military integration unmatched in America or Canada. Other War Cabinet ministers meanwhile shouldered substantial
parliamentary responsibilities and heavy wartime administrative duties
associated with their respective departments. As the war progressed, the
British War Cabinet became decreasingly important in directing strategy,
which became almost exclusively the purview of Churchill and his BCOS.
Churchill thus became the primary channel through which the dominions received strategic information. When the Australians finally won
the right to have their high commissioner attend War Cabinet meetings,
they found that he gained little information on the actual conduct of the
war. Canada, which did not seek the right to be heard in the formulation
and the direction of policy, continued to rely on its high commissioner
receiving daily briefings from the British dominions secretary, a practice
that King had forbidden before the war.[8]

In contrast with Britain's war machinery, that of Canada operated
almost bereft of professional military advice. The Emergency Council
established on 30 August 1939, which replaced the Canadian Defence
Committee originally set up in 1936, considered questions of general
policy and coordinated wartime activities. In a further reorganization on
5 December 1939, the Cabinet War Committee superseded the Emergency Council. Chaired by King, the War Committee comprised the
most experienced and influential ministers of the cabinet and, unlike its
British equivalent, continued meeting throughout the war. While these
ministers were highly competent, honest, and dedicated to winning the

war, they collectively possessed little military experience. The result was that the War Committee tended to examine Canadian military affairs in microscopic detail from a domestic perspective. The CCOS, King's senior military advisers, never attended on a regular basis until the war was nearly three years old. Between 26 December 1943 and 3 May 1944 the post of CGS was also left vacant. This reflected both the low esteem in which the CCOS were held and the eternal tension that existed between them and the overly influential Department of External Affairs. Unfortunately, the CCOS were too often ignored when they should have been consulted. They were rarely invited to attend the War Committee before 17 June 1942, when the committee agreed that they should attend the first and third meetings of each month. The CCOS thus attended only about forty-five of the 167 War Committee sessions until this body dissolved in April 1945. To the end, King, the complete civilian, never appreciated their presence.[9]

After Pearl Harbor ushered in a truly global war in 1941, it was too late for Canada to claim a voice in the higher direction of the war. Secret American-British Conversations (ABC) held in Washington between 29 January and 27 March 1941 had produced a war plan known as ABC-1 that with the congressional passage of the Lend-Lease Act on 11 March 1941, marked the beginning of the great Anglo-American wartime coalition termed the Grand Alliance. The exclusion of Canadian and dominion representatives from Anglo-American military staff conversations indicated the degree of deference that Americans were prepared to show small powers. Although British representatives carefully referred to themselves as the United Kingdom delegation, the Americans deliberately called them British, considering them representatives of the Commonwealth. In short, ABC-1 reserved unto the American and British high commands the power to formulate and execute strategic policies and plans should the United States enter the war. The Americans were also responsible for a decision not to allow dominion officers to attend ABC sessions even as observers. They preferred that the dominions be represented by service attachés through the medium of the British Joint Staff Mission (BJSM) in Washington. When Ottawa eventually remonstrated against this aspect of ABC-1, suggesting a separate Canadian military mission in Washington, the Americans refused to receive it.[10]

The "Arcadia" Conference held in Washington from 22 December 1941 to 14 January 1942 put the final stamp on the issue of strategic direction. Here Churchill and Roosevelt created the Combined Chiefs of Staff (CCS) committee with responsibility to determine the strategic direction of the Allied war effort. Basically, the CCS consisted of the BCOS and the American Joint Chiefs of Staff (JCS) set up in imitation of the former. Their most important decisions were taken during a series of major conferences at which Roosevelt and Churchill presided. Permanent CCS headquarters were located in Washington, where the JCS met in regular session with the heads of BJSM service delegations in Washington representing their respective British chiefs. The head of the BJSM, Field Marshal Sir John Dill, represented both Churchill as minister of defence and the BCOS collectively. Given such a structure, a Canadian military mission appeared extraneous to the Americans.[11]

The Canadian government was neither consulted nor informed about the establishment of the CCS. Such information as was received came through informal contacts with the BJSM. Perhaps because of the firmness with which the JCS rejected Australian and New Zealand pleas for representation, Mackenzie King never lodged a formal protest. A January 1942 suggestion by the CGS, Lieutenant General K. Stuart, to form a joint Commonwealth staff also encountered the accepted External Affairs view that anything short of separate Canadian representation would constitute a reversal of policy. The CCOS contended, on the other hand, that a joint staff would provide a practical basis for more effective representation of the Canadian services in joint planning and allocation than would the establishment of a separate Canadian staff group. Roosevelt and Churchill eventually agreed to allow one Canadian officer to represent the Canadian War Committee before the CCS, but this officer represented a Canadian political authority in front of an Allied military authority. In July 1942 the Americans finally agreed to accept the Canadian Joint Staff (CJS) in Washington, but it was not officially designated a "mission" or paralleled by any American equivalent in Ottawa. Although the JCS in August 1942 advised their staff planning agencies to maintain liaison with the CJS, the BJSM remained the main avenue by which Canadians received information on the higher direction of the war.[12]

Canada received little information from strategic conferences at Casablanca in January 1943, Washington in May, and Cairo and Teheran in November–December. At the "Quadrant" conference held in Quebec City from 14–24 August 1943, Canada acted only as host. Churchill's earlier proposal for Mackenzie King and his CCOS to attend all plenary sessions, and for the CCOS to attend all plenary meetings of the CCS, was vetoed outright by Roosevelt on the grounds that a Canadian presence would provide a precedent for admitting China, Brazil, Mexico, and the other dominions. When Roosevelt informed King that rather than risk potential embarrassment, he would prefer not to come to Canada at all, King wilted. Still, King could record "that Churchill and Roosevelt being at Quebec, and myself acting as host, will be quite sufficient to make clear that all three are in conference together and will not only satisfy but will please the Canadian feeling, and really be helpful to me person-ally."[13] The reality, however, was different. At a Cabinet War Committee meeting on 11 August 1943, attended by Churchill, King stated that his government had accepted the higher direction of the war by the British prime minister and the president of the United States.[14] King's govern-ment was thus left to project the best possible image it could to a public clamouring for a larger Canadian role in the war.

Canada's exclusion from higher Allied planning left the King gov-ernment in a strategic void. Ottawa received no advance warning of Anglo-American landings in North Africa. Neither was the decision to invade Sicily conveyed to King after the Casablanca conference. Most humiliating of all, the Canadian prime minister was actually roused from his sleep in the early hours of 6 June to be told that the invasion of Nor-mandy had commenced. Churchill had chosen not to share the closely guarded secret of the exact date of D-Day. The irony of this situation is that, while an oversight by Churchill, King's difficulty was of his own making. His persistent refusal to expand traditional Commonwealth channels of communication for fear of compromising Canadian auton-omy ensured the primacy of a personal connection to Churchill with its inherent shortcomings. In accepting the exclusion of his government from the 1943 Quebec conference, King may have also given the British prime minister the impression that he could speak for Canada, as Roo-sevelt evidently wished him to do. Having failed to project a strategic voice through Commonwealth machinery before the United States had entered the war, Canada was unable to change the situation after being effectively silenced at "Arcadia."[15]

The upshot was that Supreme Headquarters Allied Expeditionary Forces (SHAEF) set up under the Supreme Allied Commander, Eisen-hower, had only one Canadian on staff and he was only remotely con-nected with operations. Later efforts to establish a Canadian Joint Staff Mission (CJSM) in London to serve as a channel of communication between the CCOS and Allied Supreme Commands in Britain and the Mediterranean received short shrift from the Americans. The appropri-ate channel of communication between the CCOS and the Supreme Commands, Roosevelt and the JCS insisted, had to be through the CCS and not directly through the CJSM to the Supreme Commands. Supreme Commanders derived their authority from governments con-cerned through the CCS and not directly from governments. If Canadi-ans wished to establish a CJSM in London, that was an Anglo-Canadian affair. The British, who knew that the Americans had blocked the scheme, were more accommodating in their reply. To complicate matters further, Crerar, then commanding First Canadian Army, argued that he as senior

Canadian commander operating under SHAEF retained responsibility for liaison with the Supreme Commander through Montgomery's 21st Army Group. Since commanding an army in the field was a full-time job, however, this solution was less than satisfactory militarily for the onerous added responsibility. Crerar's insistence on exercising his presumed authority in this area, despite cautioning by a recent CGS, eventually created friction with Montgomery, who assumed that Canadian field command arrangements would follow British and American lines. The mistake of the King government, in light of American refusal to deal with lesser powers, was in rejecting closer Commonwealth integration that would at least have given Canada a stronger voice at the strategic level. Allowing External Affairs mandarins to quash the formation of a Commonwealth military staff was simply short-sighted.[16]

Chapter Five

Dagger Pointed at the Heart of Berlin

By the time Montgomery took command of South-Eastern Army the build-up of the Canadian Army overseas had been more than half completed. The sheer speed of the German attack on Poland had initially led to the urgent dispatch of the 1st Canadian Infantry division to join the BEF in France. Commanded by McNaughton, called back to service by Mackenzie King to head Canada's volunteer army overseas, the division disembarked in Scotland in December 1939 and moved south to concentration areas in England. In keeping with the terms of the Visiting Forces Act of 1933, Canadian army organization, doctrine, and training generally conformed to that of the British Army. Canadians were, of course, British subjects, there being no such thing as a Canadian citizen until 1947, and few envisioned the end of empire. Since raw recruits made up more than half the strength of the 1st Division, plans called for completing individual training by the end of February 1940 and unit collective training by April. Brigade and divisional all-arms collective exercises were then to follow. This training plan suffered a setback, however, owing to an exceedingly bitter winter, lack of transport and clothing, and the German lightning attack on Norway on 9 April. Nine days later two battalions of the 2nd Brigade deployed to Scotland for a proposed raid on Trondheim, which failed to materialize because of excessive risk. The British War Office in late May also opted not to send the 1st Division to join the beleaguered BEF, but to employ it with Canadian support units as an independent reserve formation called Canadian Force under direct General Headquarters (GHQ) Home Forces control.[1]

Initially during the Phoney War, when French forces in the Maginot Line faced the Germans in the Siegfried Line, many senior British and Canadian commanders expected to fight a protracted war, opening with a trench warfare phase that would enable the gradual development of mobile operations. McNaughton even visited the French front to examine the possibility of retaking German captured Maginot Line defences with Canadian Tunnelling Company diamond drillers in countermining operations. During April 1940, each unit of the 1st Canadian Infantry Division spent an overnight period in a model trench system that had been specially constructed for training in trench routine and relief, patrolling, and raiding. Divisional Training Instruction No. 3 of 27 April 1940 further slated infantry brigade groups to attend the Imber Trench Warfare Training and Experimental Centre. As detailed in an instruction of 2 May 1940, they were each to undergo training in trench warfare for eight to ten days between 11 May and 2 June. The training program called for entrenched units to practise patrolling, night raids, and dawn assaults against each other, employing tanks as available. Trials were also conducted to assess the effect of supporting smoke on direct and indirect friendly fire. Additional experimentation aimed at developing procedures for laying minefields and clearing gaps in them for the passage of tracked vehicles.[2] Essentially, the army trained to refight the middle years of the Great War.

While the 1st Canadian Infantry Brigade Group prepared to conduct patrolling and trench attacks supported by smoke, Montgomery's 3rd Division fought a deadly rearguard action against German panzer forces that on 10 May broke through the French front west of the River Meuse and set out on their drive to the English Channel. Between 27 May and 4 June the Royal Navy in Operation "Dynamo" evacuated some 220,000 British soldiers from the Dunkirk perimeter with huge losses of weapons, ammunition, and equipment. This left McNaughton's 1st Canadian Division one of the best equipped and manned formations on the British home front. In response to the looming threat of invasion, Canadian Force now emphasized training battalion mobile columns in rapid motor transport movement by day and night for possible action against German diversionary or paratroop assaults. In the event of a major enemy seaborne landing, British coastal defence forces were also to be speedily reinforced. To effect such deployments McNaughton split the division into nine battalion groups, each with field artillery and anti-tank troops under command. All battalion groups subsequently practised dawn attack exercises with limited armoured and air cooperation, but there was scant opportunity for exercising as a division against a mobile enemy. The fervent activity and dashing about that characterized Canadian Force during this period earned the formation the name of "McNaughton's Flying Circus." On 8 June 1940 a confident McNaughton cabled the prime minister of Canada that he now considered his Canadian Force to be battle worthy.[3]

The trouble was that no serious attention had been paid to officer train-ing, which pretty much created a situation of the blind leading the blind. McNaughton himself set the pace by being more interested in technical and administrative aspects than field operations, which received short shrift and then mainly the broad brush treatment. The result was that conscientious company commanders like Hoffmeister of the Seaforths were left to flounder with no idea of how to go about leading 130 men in battle. Hoffmeister apparently did not even know the format for an operation order, let alone know how to write one and give orders to his troops. Worse still, he could not seem to get any instruction in this regard and ended up going to local book shops to buy what he presumed to be relevant military pamphlets. The pressure on Hoffmeister was substan-tial, since training under company and platoon arrangements tended to be the norm. In such circumstances, collective training skills did not advance much above section level. As company commanders occupied critical leadership positions within infantry battalions, higher-level com-manders would have profited from ensuring their proper training so that they could have trained their subordinates. During the second half of 1940, prefaced by McNaughton's "battle worthy" assertion, Hoffmeister felt that he was not learning a thing about how to do his job. Apart from small arms range work, map reading, and physical fitness, Canadian army training suffered from a general neglect in which there was little focus on training officers for middle- and higher-level command. The occasional brigade lectures held were also of limited value as officers and other ranks had to learn by doing. What lectures offered were addition-ally given by instructors who often did not know much more about their subject than those whom they tried to teach.[4]

On 17 May 1940 the Canadian government, shaken by the fall of France and peril of the BEF, decided to deploy a Canadian corps and raise a third division in addition to the 2nd Canadian Infantry Division proceeding overseas that summer. On the day of the Dunkirk evacua-tion, the government announced that a fourth division would also be recruited. In July 1940 GHQ augmented Canadian Force with British and New Zealand formations to create 7 Corps under the command of now Lieutenant General McNaughton with British Brigadier M.C. Dempsey as his Brigadier, General Staff (BGS) or principal operations staff officer. The arrival of the 2nd Canadian Infantry Division under Major Gen-eral V.W. Odlum in September 1940 enhanced the Canadian character of the 7 Corps, but not the requirement for continued field exercises. By that date McNaughton considered his troops so highly trained that further intensive training during the winter would make them stale. He deliberately chose not to turn training into a "fetish" as he maintained that given the limitations of creating realism in field exercises, only the shock of battle was needed to drive lessons home. He instead introduced educational training to occupy troops over the winter months on the grounds that such would be of great benefit to them upon cessation of hostilities.[5]

On Christmas Day 1940 the 7 Corps was officially redesignated the Canadian Corps with the British 1st Armoured Division, the 1st Army Tank Brigade, and 53rd Light Anti-Aircraft Regiment under temporary command. As Canadian troops acted "in combination" with British forces for operations under terms of the Visiting Forces Act of 1933 and adhered to similar organization and training practice, both armies were so closely integrated that some Canadian gunners gained the impression that "there were not two armies, British and Canadian, but one."[6] The formation structure of the Canadian army also reflected a successfully transplanted British regimental system, but with divisional composition giving proportional representation to the major territorial regions of Canada. Thus, within the 1st Canadian Infantry Division, regiments from Ontario made up the 1st Brigade, units from the West the 2nd, and units from Quebec and the Maritimes the 3rd Brigade. Similarly, in the 2nd Division, Ontario regiments made up the 4th Brigade, Quebec units the 5th, and Western units the 6th Brigade. The 3rd Division, which arrived in Britain in July 1941 under Major General C.B. Price, reflected roughly the same pattern of Canadian geographic representation. The complexion of the French-speaking 5th Brigade changed, of course, when the Royal 22nd Regiment joined the overseas-bound 1st Division to ensure francophone regular force representation in the first contingent. A critical shortage of qualified staff officers and commanders subsequently ended the 5th Brigade as a French-speaking formation. McNaughton also thought it unwise to lump French-speaking units together in one formation given the political difficulties that might arise from a heavy incidence of francophone casualties.[7]

The Canadian Army Programme for 1941 called for a Canadian Corps of three divisions and an independent armoured brigade. A Canadian Armoured Corps was accordingly authorized on 13 August and the 1st Canadian Army Tank Brigade formed. Shortly thereafter, the British War Office announced its intention to form five armoured divisions plus the equivalent of three more in armoured brigades. At the same time it requested Canada and Australia each to provide one armoured division. Unable to compete with the enemy in manpower, the British reasoned that compensation might be found in armoured fighting vehicles, which were given the highest priority. Subsequent agreement stipulated that the Canadian Corps would by the end of 1941 comprise, in addition to three infantry divisions and ancillary troops, an armoured division equipped with cavalry role cruiser tanks and an army tank brigade of three tank regiments equipped with heavier tanks for infantry support. Personnel for the Canadian armoured division were taken from the 4th Infantry Division, which, in the wake of British victories over the Italians in Africa, had been allowed to run down. Following major successes by German forces in North Africa and Greece, however, the 4th was reconstituted. The 1st Armoured Division was in the meantime formed in accordance with a war establishment that called for two armoured brigades, each of three tank regiments and a motor battalion of infantry, a field artillery regiment, an anti-aircraft regiment, an anti-tank regiment, and one infantry battalion. Two experienced British officers were also taken on strength to fill the key staff appointments of GSO 1 and Assistant Adjutant and Quartermaster General (AA&QMG). Redesignated the 5th Canadian Armoured Division, this formation first commanded by Major General E.W. Sansom followed the 1st Canadian Army Tank Brigade and the 3rd Canadian Infantry Division to the United Kingdom in November 1941.[8]

McNaughton by this time had been built up into a major national figure by a publicity drive launched from the start of the war. There was even agitation to get him back to Canada to lead what some thought to be a flagging war effort. Hailed in the press as a soldier-scientist and the best soldier in the British Empire, he had appeared on the cover of *Life* magazine in December 1939 and basked in a greater popularity than most other generals. In the darkness of defeat, he also appeared to be a natural choice to lead the Allied invasion of the Continent, and he personally envisioned the Canadian army eventually spearheading the assault on Germany. In this regard, McNaughton faced many challenges related to organization, equipment, and training, but he was further burdened by virtue of his status as Senior Combatant Officer Overseas with policy and constitutional issues that consumed much of his time. As was the case when he was CGS, his broad scientific and engineering interests and inclinations drew him more into equipment and weapons development than actual training for war. Shortages of Bren guns, light mortars, 40-mm Bofors, two-pounder anti-tank guns, and tanks throughout 1941 certainly warranted attention, but arguably not to the extent that they precluded training as realistically as possible for higher-level operations.[9]

McNaughton's involvement in wide-ranging fields such as psychological testing, ammunition design, wireless communications, flame throwers, and anti-tank obstacles diverted his attention from field operations. His heavy schedule of attending conferences, ceremonial parades, and meetings with top British scientists and war production authorities, as well as greeting visitors, meant leaving much training in the hands of his staff. As he presented no seriously thought-out guidance for field operations, however, they functioned without the requisite commander's direction. Thus, despite McNaughton's claims to the contrary, his Canadian Corps was not adequately trained for the role envisioned. During Exercise "Fox" conducted west of Dover, the first divisional level anti-invasion scheme, held 11–13 February 1941, problems with motor vehicle movement managed to tie everyone in knots from platoon to corps. Directed by McNaughton, "Fox" aimed to practise the 1st Canadian Division in a vehicular move to a concentration area, an advance to contact with a simulated enemy, and battle procedure and deployment for attack. To manoeuvre large bodies of troops effectively by day and night over narrow, winding English lanes, however, required good staff work and a high standard of map using, especially as most roads were unsigned as an anti-invasion precaution. In the event, poor divisional planning that resulted in inadequate traffic control led to monumental road congestion that blocked artillery from getting forward to support infantry attacks. Livid with rage on seeing his directed exercise turned into a fiasco, McNaughton admitted that "Fox" had shaken the complacency of everyone participating, from the corps commander down to the lowest private soldier.[10]

Similar road movement problems surfaced during Exercise "Dog," 26–8 February 1941, which tested the 2nd Canadian Division along the lines of "Fox." Once more, McNaughton directed the exercise, recommending in his sum-up that participants read and absorb the appropriate pamphlets and formation standing orders dealing with the subject of mechanized movement by roads. The 1st Canadian Division and corps troops again practised road movement between 9–11 April in Exercise "Hare" and showed some improvement. When Brooke, C-in-C Home Forces, visited the exercise on the morning of 10 April, dealing with Dempsey as McNaughton was in bed, he went away depressed by the low standard of efficiency of indifferent brigade and division commanders. The 2nd Canadian Division also practised road movement on Exercise "Benito" during 16–19 April, but in Exercise "Waterloo," directed by Lieutenant General Bernard Paget's Headquarters South-Eastern Command during the period 14–16 June, the division manifested an inability to get moving although on two-hours' notice to move. "Waterloo," the first major exercise in which the entire Canadian Corps participated under McNaughton's command, practised the formation in a mobile counter-attack role within an anti-invasion scenario on the south Sussex coast. Again, serious shortcomings in road movement came to the fore, with Paget additionally charging that too many conferences, held in lieu of issuing brief directives and verbal orders, marred efficient battle procedure.[11]

On 29 September 1941 McNaughton proclaimed the Canadian Corps to be "a dagger pointed at the heart of Berlin."[12] From that date to 3 October he commanded the Canadian Corps in Exercise "Bumper," the biggest manoeuvres ever to be held in Britain. Involving two armies of four corps of 12 divisions, three of them armoured, plus two army tank brigades and ancillary troops, "Bumper" practised the field army in Britain in an anti-invasion role. The Canadian Corps comprising the 1st and 2nd Canadian Infantry Divisions formed part of Lieutenant General H.R.L.G. Alexander's British force in a two-sided exercise against a fictional six-division German invading force. At the conclusion of the exercise Montgomery as Chief Umpire singled out Odlum's 2nd Canadian Infantry Division and the British 6th Armoured Division for missing opportunities. Other criticisms concerned army and corps headquarters being too far back and the use of the brigade group system in fighting divisions. The major lesson was that all corps commanders had to be able to handle armoured divisions. Following the conclusion of "Bumper," Montgomery replaced Paget as commander of South-Eastern Command on 17 November 1941. On the same day the Canadian Corps took over the British 4 Corps defensive sector on the Sussex coast, which placed it directly under his operational control.[13]

In Ottawa meanwhile, Crerar, who had assumed the post of CGS in July 1940, worked to father a Canadian field army overseas. Early in August 1941 he estimated that Canada possessed enough manpower to form an army of eight divisions, two of which would remain in Canada, for a war period of six years. He envisaged an overseas field army of two corps, each of one armoured and two infantry divisions, sustained by voluntary enlistment. The Overseas Army Programme for 1942, however, confirmed converting the 4th Infantry Division to armour and creating a field army headquarters to command and administer a Canadian Corps of three infantry divisions and a Canadian Armoured Corps of two armoured divisions and two independent armoured brigades. The Canadian cabinet, hastened by the Japanese attack on Pearl Harbor, approved the program on 6 January 1942. This resulted in the formation of Headquarters First Canadian Army on Easter Monday 6 April with McNaughton named commander, which gave rise to his title "Father of the Canadian Army," though the original suggestion had been Crerar's.[14]

By the end of 1941 the Canadian Army overseas totalled 124,472 all ranks. The following year the 4th Canadian Armoured Division landed in Britain between 31 August and 4 November while the 2nd Canadian

Army Tank Brigade arrived in June 1943, five months after the formation of 2 Canadian Corps on 15 January. In October and November, respectively, 1 Canadian Army Group Royal Canadian Artillery (AGRA) and 2 Canadian AGRA came into being. By the end of 1943 the Canadian Army overseas reached a strength of nearly a quarter of a million men. Despite its national designation, however, the First Canadian Army was never able to operate entirely as a Canadian field force, for it required the permanent commitment of upwards of 9,000 men per division from British resources. This completed its rearward support services and saved Canada 45,000 men. As the Canadian Army possessed no heavy artillery, this too had to be provided by the British.[15]

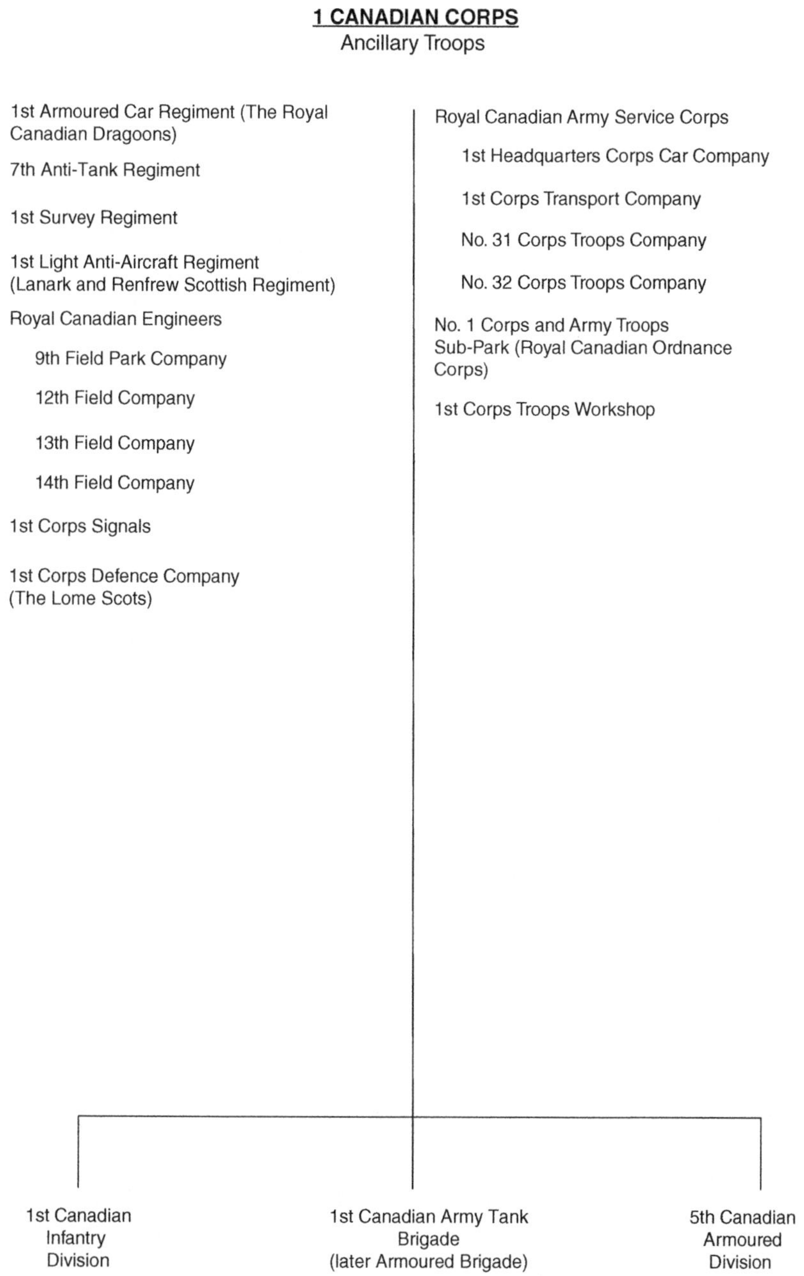

1 CANADIAN CORPS
Ancillary Troops

1st Armoured Car Regiment (The Royal Canadian Dragoons)

7th Anti-Tank Regiment

1st Survey Regiment

1st Light Anti-Aircraft Regiment (Lanark and Renfrew Scottish Regiment)

Royal Canadian Engineers

  9th Field Park Company

  12th Field Company

  13th Field Company

  14th Field Company

1st Corps Signals

1st Corps Defence Company (The Lorne Scots)

Royal Canadian Army Service Corps

  1st Headquarters Corps Car Company

  1st Corps Transport Company

  No. 31 Corps Troops Company

  No. 32 Corps Troops Company

No. 1 Corps and Army Troops Sub-Park (Royal Canadian Ordnance Corps)

1st Corps Troops Workshop

1st Canadian Infantry Division	1st Canadian Army Tank Brigade (later Armoured Brigade)	5th Canadian Armoured Division

Figure 6.1 1 Canadian Corps Ancillary Troops (John A. English)

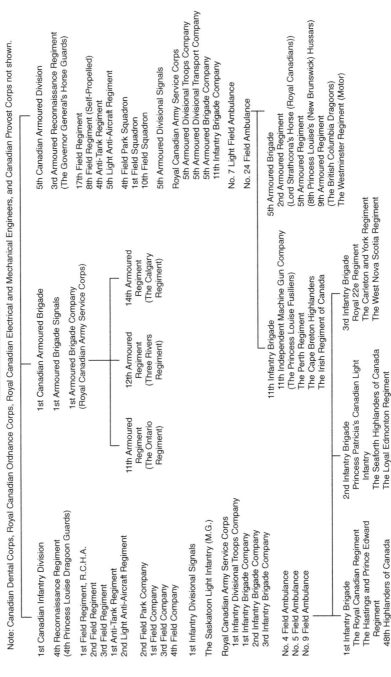

1 CANADIAN CORPS

Note: Canadian Dental Corps, Royal Canadian Ordnance Corps, Royal Canadian Electrical and Mechanical Engineers, and Canadian Provost Corps not shown.

1st Canadian Infantry Division

4th Reconnaissance Regiment
(4th Princess Louise Dragoon Guards)

1st Field Regiment, R.C.H.A.
2nd Field Regiment
3rd Field Regiment
1st Anti-Tank Regiment
2nd Light Anti-Aircraft Regiment

2nd Field Park Company
1st Field Company
3rd Field Company
4th Field Company

1st Infantry Divisional Signals

The Saskatoon Light Infantry (M.G.)

Royal Canadian Army Service Corps
1st Infantry Divisional Troops Company
1st Infantry Brigade Company
2nd Infantry Brigade Company
3rd Infantry Brigade Company

No. 4 Field Ambulance
No. 5 Field Ambulance
No. 9 Field Ambulance

1st Infantry Brigade
The Royal Canadian Regiment
The Hastings and Prince Edward
   Regiment
48th Highlanders of Canada

2nd Infantry Brigade
Princess Patricia's Canadian Light
   Infantry
The Seaforth Highlanders of Canada
The Loyal Edmonton Regiment

11th Infantry Brigade
11th Independent Machine Gun Company
(The Princess Louise Fusiliers)
The Perth Regiment
The Cape Breton Highlanders
The Irish Regiment of Canada

3rd Infantry Brigade
Royal 22e Regiment
The Carleton and York Regiment
The West Nova Scotia Regiment

11th Armoured
Regiment
(The Ontario
Regiment)

12th Armoured
Regiment
(Three Rivers
Regiment)

14th Armoured
Regiment
(The Calgary
Regiment)

1st Canadian Armoured Brigade

1st Armoured Brigade Signals

1st Armoured Brigade Company
(Royal Canadian Army Service Corps)

5th Canadian Armoured Division

3rd Armoured Reconnaissance Regiment
(The Governor General's Horse Guards)

17th Field Regiment
8th Field Regiment (Self-Propelled)
4th Anti-Tank Regiment
5th Light Anti-Aircraft Regiment

4th Field Park Squadron
1st Field Squadron
10th Field Squadron

5th Armoured Divisional Signals

Royal Canadian Army Service Corps
5th Armoured Divisional Troops Company
5th Armoured Divisional Transport Company
5th Armoured Brigade Company
11th Infantry Brigade Company

No. 7 Light Field Ambulance

No. 24 Field Ambulance

5th Armoured Brigade
2nd Armoured Regiment
(Lord Strathcona's Horse (Royal Canadians))
5th Armoured Regiment
(8th Princess Louise's (New Brunswick) Hussars)
9th Armoured Regiment
(The British Columbia Dragoons)
The Westminster Regiment (Motor)

Figure 6.2 1 Canadian Corps Formations and Units (John A. English)

Chapter Six

Inspecting the Canadian Corps

At the time Montgomery took over South-Eastern Army, command of the Canadian Corps was in a state of flux. In November 1941 McNaughton suffered what Crerar termed a "breakdown" that resulted in his return to Canada for extended leave. The senior divisional commander, Major General G.R. Pearkes, assumed temporary command of the Canadian Corps on 14 November 1941. Although he had not commanded a battalion in peacetime, Pearkes had taken the 2nd Brigade overseas in 1939 and been promoted to command 1st Division following McNaughton's appointment as 7 Corps commander in July 1940. A graduate of Camberley Staff College and the IDC, Pearkes enjoyed a considerable reputation as the most experienced Canadian field commander, one enhanced by his having won the Victoria Cross in the Great War. If Pearkes is to be believed, McNaughton told him that he hoped the temporary appointment of corps commander would be made permanent upon formation of the First Canadian Army. This was not to be, however, as Crerar stepped down from CGS to supplant him in command. A protégé of McNaughton, Crerar had taken over from him as Counter Battery Staff Officer in October 1918 and attended Camberley Staff College in 1924 and the IDC in 1934. From 1935 he served as Director of Military Operations and Intelligence in Ottawa and from 1938, on promotion to brigadier, as commandant of the Royal Military College. In October 1939 he proceeded to Britain as the Senior Officer, Canadian Military Headquarters, London, returning to Ottawa in July 1940 to take up the post of CGS, which position he used to fulfil his ambition of getting field command.[1]

Crerar lamented that whereas Pearkes had commanded at three formation levels and acquired a reputation, he had none. He nonetheless pressed the Minister of National Defense to allow him to relinquish his appointment as CGS and replace the too old and inflexible Odlum in command of the 2nd Canadian Infantry Division. Crerar's subsequent promotion to the corps command rank of lieutenant general in the fall of 1941 did not dissuade him from this ambition, and he proclaimed his willingness to accept a reduction in rank in exchange for divisional command. When it appeared that McNaughton would not be able to return to duty before March 1942, however, Crerar abandoned his altruistic stance and turned over CGS duties to Major General K. Stuart. Arriving in England ostensibly to take over the 2nd Division, with his cabinet appointment dating from 19 November, Crerar in fact never served a day as division commander. As a result of his machinations, he instead replaced Pearkes in acting command of the Canadian Corps officially from 31 December 1941. After only a few weeks and enduring a stormy relationship with the resentful Pearkes, he became convinced that a good many shifts in unit and brigade commanders would have to be made if the command element was to be brought up to an adequately high standard. On discussing this aspect with Montgomery, Crerar readily accepted the latter's offer to visit each of the Canadian formations and give his personal views.[2]

During February and March 1942 Montgomery in a series of informal visits inspected all nine Canadian infantry brigades and twenty-seven infantry battalions, employing a highly effective approach he had devised and set forth in his "Some General Notes on What to Look for When Visiting a Unit" (see Appendix). Based on his brigade visits, Montgomery offered a number of constructive and critical comments that on the whole presented a reasonably accurate picture of Canadian field leadership at the time. To Canada's official army historian, Montgomery's reports provide a fascinating glimpse of a great trainer of troops at work. One of Montgomery's greatest assets in the exercise of command was his ability to listen, which he did patiently and attentively during his interviews with key personnel, quietly taking in information that gave rise to his conclusions. Given the seriousness of the military situation during this period, there was scant time for niceties or second-guessing, but a compelling need for expedient direction and decisive leadership. In these circumstances, Montgomery did not hold back or mince words in making his assessments, which in most cases were spot on. A reasonably sound judge of military ability with a practised eye born of long practical command experience, he most of all evinced an abiding concern for the welfare of the common soldier who would face the firestorm. In his view, there were no bad soldiers, only bad officers, and he was not prepared to take chances with the latter, even though some might be borderline. To err in favour of the troops was always better than to give the benefit of the doubt to questionable officers who might possibly let them down in combat.[3]

What Montgomery principally identified was a fundamental weakness at the top. Two brigadiers, in his estimation, were not fit for brigade command, though it is significant that out of eight observed, Montgomery considered three divisional command material and another three as more than satisfactory. In his judgments he differentiated between those who were "completely useless" and those who were "teachable" and worth retaining. Of twenty-five COs observed, Montgomery considered seven to be unacceptable, but there were more who were keen and able, some even potential brigadiers. Montgomery somewhat more severely named nine out of sixteen battalion seconds-in-command (2ICs) as unsatisfactory, but many company commanders as adequate through excellent. He considered all but three of seventeen adjutants encountered to be in the same category, but unnecessarily tied up with paperwork. As for NCOs, he recommended the removal of eight Regimental Sergeant Majors (RSMs) for reasons of age or incompetence. He also expressed concern that the majority of COs did not seem to realize the immense importance of having a really first-class cadre of NCOs. Some did not even see or talk to their NCOs on promotion. He further discovered that within several units, NCO training was hardly conducted at all, noting that there was no system for teaching privates how to be NCOs before they were promoted. Of all ranks commented upon, Montgomery seems to have been least impressed by Canadian company sergeant majors (CSMs).[4]

Montgomery carried out his first inspection on 28 January 1942 with a visit to the 6th Canadian Infantry Brigade. Observing that its commander, Brigadier W.W. Southam, was first class and likely to be a division commander before the end of the war, he further assessed Lieutenant Colonel Sherwood Lett, commanding officer of the South Saskatchewan Regiment, as excellent and doing very well. He was one of two COs who really understood how to organize training properly. Montgomery also considered Lieutenant Colonel A.C. Gostling of the Queen's Own Cameron Highlanders of Canada to be very keen and imbued with good and sound ideas, adding that the regiment had first-class men and good officers, though they had not been properly taught in the past. In contrast, Montgomery rated the Fusiliers de Montréal (FMR) as the weakest regiment in 6 Brigade with a number of old NCOs quite unfit to serve in a fighting battalion, including the RSM whom he recommended for removal. In Montgomery's view, Lieutenant Colonel Paul Grenier and his adjutant were both very poor and the acting 2IC not up to the job. Though Grenier, nearly fifty years old, had commanded the FMR for over five years, he possessed neither the military knowledge not the professional ability to produce a well-trained unit. In particular, he had no proper plan for training his officers. Montgomery accordingly recommended that he be replaced with a better and younger man, but, if not, at least be provided with a first-class 2IC.[5]

The following day Montgomery inspected the 8th Infantry Brigade and found it to be in a very backward and untrained state largely because it had suffered severely from a completely useless brigadier who knew nothing whatever about how to train troops. Not only did he do no good, he did a great deal of harm, with the result that there was no system, no method, and no guidance from brigade headquarters. The relief in the brigade at seeing the last of Brigadier J.P.U. Archambault was patently evident to Montgomery, who considered his replacement, Brigadier K.G. Blackader, to be first class and a future division commander capable of bringing 8 Brigade along. Montgomery similarly assessed Lieutenant Colonel H.C. MacKendrick, CO of the Queen's Own Rifles of Canada, as a good man who with troop training guidance from above would do well. His 2IC, Major J.G. Spragge, and adjutant, R.D. Medland, were also rated as good, though the RSM was too old and warranted removal. Montgomery placed Lieutenant Colonel J.R. Calkin of the North Shore Regiment in the same category as MacKendrick, but his 2IC, Major W.D. Anderson, as quite useless. His adjutant, Lieutenant R.B. Forbes, received a good grade. Montgomery also had kind words to say about Lieutenant Colonel J.J. Chouinard, CO of the Régiment de la Chaudière, whom he described as a very good little chap who commands his battalion in his own queer way. Although lacking in knowledge and training ability, he was teachable and with firm guidance could be expected with supervision to produce a good show. He just needed a better adjutant and a younger RSM. Overall, Montgomery considered all three COs to be a good lot and a very willing team who would pull well together under Blackader. With a lot of hard work and effort the brigade could be made fit by 1 June.[6]

On 2 February Montgomery inspected the 1st Infantry Brigade in the absence of its commander, Brigadier R.F.L. Keller, who was away sick. He was escorted around by Lieutenant Colonel H.D. Graham, CO of the Hastings and Prince Edward Regiment, whom he considered a very good CO with good and sound ideas. Graham knew what he wanted and ran well-organized training, which he admitted had been introduced by his predecessor, newly promoted Brigadier H.L.N. Salmon of 7 Brigade. Montgomery reserved his highest praise, however, for the CO of the Royal Canadian Regiment (RCR), Lieutenant Colonel T.E.D'O Snow, whom he rated the best CO yet met and a potential brigade commander. Only Snow and Lett knew how to properly organize training. At an opposite pole, Montgomery found Lieutenant Colonel W.B. Hendrie of the

48th Highlanders the worst and most ignorant CO he had ever met in his army service. All "bluff and eye-wash," he did not do the things he ought to do, nor how to do them. His officers and men were intelligent and some of his officers extremely good, but Hendrie, utterly ignorant as to how to train a battalion, did not train his officers or his NCOs, including the RSM identified for removal. What training there was, by his own admission, bored the troops. With no method, no system, he left everything to his company commanders, who carried him. As he did not know his stuff, Montgomery wrote him off as useless and quite unfit to command a battalion of 1,000 men and 45 officers.[7] Crerar, in thanking Montgomery for his candid first three brigade reports, stated that they largely confirmed the opinions that he had already formed in the time that he had been Canadian Corps commander.[8]

On 23 February Montgomery inspected the 7th Infantry Brigade and recorded that Harry Salmon was a really high-class commander. A far better and more knowledgeable brigadier than any other in the Canadian Corps, he was fit to command a division. Montgomery described the new CO of the Regina Rifles, Lieutenant Colonel H. Sharpe, as a good, keen, earnest type. Though slow and lacking in imagination, he appeared teachable and with much help and guidance from his brigadier could be expected to do well. His adjutant, while not impressive, was possibly adequate. All company commanders, in Montgomery's view, were good material, but the 2IC and useless RSM were both far too old. Age also presented a problem in the Royal Winnipeg Rifles, where Montgomery recommended a good clean-out at the top, removing at once the 2IC, two company commanders, the RSM, and two CSMs. On the other hand, he found Lieutenant Colonel T.G. Gibson, a regular soldier who had just taken over as CO, to be a very good type capable of making a first-class commander. In contrast, Montgomery assessed the Canadian Scottish CO, Lieutenant Colonel J.R. Kingham, as lacking in character, drive, and determination. "Commanded a battalion for four years in peace," he wrote, "and is now doing it again." In Montgomery's view, the battalion suffered from aging officers whose old ideas were clearly in evidence. Only one company commander was under forty, while three subalterns were over forty. Montgomery's suggested solution was to appoint a young and vigorous CO and reduce the age of platoon commanders by ten years. He nonetheless gave good grades to the adjutant, quartermaster, and RSM, who was young.[9]

On 25 February Montgomery inspected the 9th Infantry Brigade and to his delight found Brigadier E.W. Haldenby to be a keen, enthusiastic, and mentally lively commander running a good show under great difficulties. He also ventured that the somewhat dour and serious CO of the Highland Light Infantry of Canada (HLI), Lieutenant Colonel R.J. McPherson, was made of good solid stuff that would see him do well despite his conservative ideas and limited imagination. His 2IC, Major R.E. Bricker, on the other hand, lacked character and drive, and his company commanders, though a good level lot, were not fit for anything more. Montgomery deemed the adjutant, R.D. Hodgins, to be a good officer who would do well, and he was particularly impressed with the HLI subalterns whose average age was around twenty-three to twenty-four. The RSM, in contrast, was much too old and needed to be replaced. With a new 2IC and RSM the battalion, in his view, would do well.

The CO of the North Nova Scotia Highlanders, Lieutenant Colonel H.W. Murdock, though slow and cautious, also ran a good show. A CO for six years in peace from 1930 to 1935, he was apparently thought by Haldenby to be fit to command an infantry brigade. Montgomery disagreed, however, stating his lack of imagination and military ability rendered him entirely unsuitable to command a brigade. That said, Montgomery rated North Nova company commanders as excellent, and the adjutant and RSM as good and very good. He also assessed the acting 2IC, Major K.R. Mitchell, as very good. With an average age of thirty-five, most subalterns were too old and some did not look like officers. Along with a very poor 2IC, three CSMs were also judged to be of no use. Thus while North Nova senior commanders were good, junior officers were too old. Montgomery recommended reducing the average age of the subalterns by ten years.

Montgomery was most impressed with the Stormont, Dundas, and Glengarry Highlander's Lieutenant Colonel W.S. Rutherford, whom he described as a first-class young CO full of character, drive, and vitality. At age thirty-four he knew what he wanted and did it very well. "We could do with some more COs like Rutherford," Montgomery wrote, suggesting that he would make a good brigadier in six months. The problem with his battalion was that it suffered from an old and decrepit RSM and four old and useless majors, including the 2IC and three company commanders – E. Cockburn, C.A. Beattie, A.R. MacNab, and J. Turnbull – who were quite unfit for the rank and clogging the machine at the top. Getting rid of them was the key, and early in March three of their number returned to Canada. Subalterns with an average age of thirty-two were at the same time assessed as good.[10]

On 27 February Montgomery inspected the 4th Infantry Brigade commanded by Brigadier C.B. Topp. Pegged as an extremely nice person, but very poor brigadier, owing to his deafness, Topp did not hear a great deal and, in consequence, did not know a lot of what went on in his brigade.

Montgomery recommended his immediate removal and replacement with a younger, more energetic officer who had commanded a battalion. This was not the case with Lieutenant Colonel G.H. Basher, CO of the Royal Regiment of Canada (RRC), who at age forty-eight gave the impression of being over fifty, but, being of strong character, ran a good show. With exception of a fat and idle RSM, the RRC in Montgomery's opinion was a very good battalion with first-class company commanders and fine junior officers and NCOs. Yet, while Basher was a good battalion commander, Montgomery disagreed with Topp that he could command a brigade, faulting his general military ability and pointing out that it did not necessarily follow that because he was a good battalion commander he would make a good brigade commander.

The Essex Scottish Regiment earned a similar assessment of being a good and well-commanded battalion. Montgomery ventured that its new CO, Lieutenant Colonel F.K. Jasperson, aged forty-three, should do very well and found his 2IC, Major E.H. Williams, and company commanders all to be good. He singled out Captain K.W. MacIntyre as an excellent young adjutant who would make a good staff captain or GSO3 and thought all subalterns with an average age of twenty-five to be a very good lot. He also assessed the forty-three-year-old RSM to be good.

Montgomery found thirty-seven-year-old Lieutenant Colonel R.R. Labatt of The Royal Hamilton Light Infantry (RHLI) to be the weakest CO in the brigade. Just adequate, he needed a great deal of help to produce a really good battalion. While his subalterns at average age twenty-five were rated a good lot, his company commanders were not up to the standard of those in the other two battalions. In Montgomery's view, the officers of the RRC and Essex were on the whole definitely better than those in the RHLI. This made the RHLI the weakest battalion in the brigade. As Labatt was a nice person who appeared to be teachable, however, Montgomery felt that with help and given a good lead he would be capable of producing a good show. A great deal of attention from a new brigade commander was nonetheless required. Montgomery further noted that Captain W.G. Sharmbrooke had been a good adjutant for fourteen months, which was "long enough in war time" in his view.[11]

On 28 February Montgomery inspected the 2nd Infantry Brigade and pressed the point that Brigadier A.E. Potts may have done good work in the past, but was beyond it now. He knew his officers, but aside from that very little of what was going on. Potts had commanded a brigade for six years in peace, and Montgomery in December 1941 had informed General McNaughton that he was definitely unfit to command a division. Montgomery now held the view that Potts was not even fit to command and train a brigade. A young and knowledgeable brigadier like Snow could, however, make it quite first class. Montgomery had a higher opinion of Lieutenant Colonel J.M.S. Tait, CO of the Seaforth Highlanders of Canada, remarking that he ran a good show with a good adjutant. His company commanders, aged around twenty-nine, were excellent, the best Montgomery had seen in the Canadian Corps, and his subalterns, with an average age of twenty-eight, were also a good lot. Two bad CSMs needed replacing, but the RSM was good and tough in what Montgomery thought was a first-class battalion.

Montgomery also described Lieutenant Colonel R.A. Lindsay of Princess Patricia's Canadian Light Infantry (PPCLI) as the best CO in the brigade. Young and keen, he was direct and frank with no bluff or eyewash about him. His 2IC was away, reportedly because he was of no use, but Montgomery found Major C.B. Ware, the Acting 2IC, along with the adjutant and RSM, all to be good. The company commanders, though adequate, were not up to the standards of the Seaforths. With the exception of two bad CSMs, he rated the NCOs first class. This resulted directly from the sound and proper PPCLI system for the selection, instruction, and promotion of NCOs, which the other two battalions left to companies, with COs not even seeing and talking to them on promotion.

Montgomery did not interview Lieutenant Colonel E.B. Wilson, CO of The Loyal Edmonton Regiment, as he had been away sick for two months, but found the 2IC, Major G.M. Beaton, acting in his place, to be totally unfit to command a battalion. Nor would Montgomery have accepted him as a 2IC. The company commanders were likewise a very poor lot, as were unit officers generally. The adjutant alone looked promising. While Montgomery rated the RSM poor and the NCOs merely adequate, he found the men to be first class. In summary, he described the 2nd Brigade as most interesting, with the best officers in the Seaforths, the best NCOs in the PPCLI, and the best men in the Loyal Eddies.[12]

On 2 March Montgomery inspected the 3rd Infantry Brigade and observed that Brigadier H.N. Ganong was a hard and tough commander who knew his own mind. Although exhibiting no great training ability, he looked to be a grand fighter (an assessment later reversed on observing Ganong's field performance). Lieutenant Colonel L.D. Tweedie, CO of the Carleton and York Regiment, recently appointed and somewhat inexperienced, likewise knew his mind and exhibited plenty of character that suggested he would do well. Montgomery rated his 2IC, W.B. Carson, as good and his company commanders as very good. His subalterns, with an average age of twenty-five, were also judged a good lot. Montgomery noted that his poor adjutant was rightly being replaced and singled out his RSM as the best that he had seen in the Canadian Corps. But battalion NCOs in general struck Montgomery as being not very good largely because they were promoted within companies and no proper system of instruction existed to ensure a good foundation in the lance corporal rank. Montgomery nonetheless thought the battalion a good one that would become quite first class.

Montgomery also had good things to say about the Royal 22nd Regiment (R22eR) and especially its young, keen, and very alert CO, Lieutenant Colonel J.P.E. Bernatchez, who at age thirty-one was first class. While his adjutant was not impressive, but adequate, his company commanders, subalterns, and RSM were all good. No officer in the whole battalion was over thirty-four, and NCO training was handled properly. Montgomery's only criticism was that the RSM did not ensure enough grip and supervision over NCOs, whom he nonetheless rated as much better than those of the Carleton and Yorks. A good battalion, he concluded – to say exactly how good, one had to see it in the field.

The West Nova Scotia Regiment did not fare so well under Montgomery's scrutiny. The CO, Lieutenant Colonel A.A. Ernst at age forty-seven appeared to require precise orders and seemed unable to carry on if given only general instructions. This battalion, Montgomery wrote, "gave me an uncomfortable feeling from the start. The guard was filthy, and the men appeared dejected. The officers, including the C.O., were badly turned out and dirty." While he judged the 2IC, Major J.A. Hebb, and adjutant to be good, only one company commander received this rating. All others were considered very poor along with three bad CSMs who deserved to be removed. Montgomery sympathized with the RSM who appeared to be a very good type who obviously tried to carry on in the face of great difficulty. With subalterns of an average age of twenty-six, the battalion in Montgomery's view required a young, smart, keen CO who knew his job. Given this, the battalion would soon become very good.[13]

Montgomery's last inspection occurred on 3 March 1942 with his visit to the 5th Infantry Brigade. Brigadier G.V. Whitehead impressed him as a good commander. Although manifesting no great training ability, he had a good brain and knew what he wanted; firm and decisive, he inspired confidence. Lieutenant Colonel S.D. Cantlie of the Black Watch, who had commanded for only one month, was another story. After talking to him for an hour and a half, it became quite clear to Montgomery that he knew nothing whatever about how to command and train a battalion. Possibly a good company commander, he had not had the training to enable him to command at a higher level. Montgomery considered it a great pity that he was given command of so fine a battalion. In April Cantlie returned to Canada. In contrast, the 2IC, Major J.B. Weir, received a good rating, while the adjutant, all company commanders and the RSM were graded as very good. NCOs generally were very patchy, recorded Montgomery, as promotion was again determined by company, a practice quite unsuitable in war.

Montgomery was similarly critical of Major D.G. MacLauchlan commanding the Calgary Highlanders. Having been in command for only two weeks after three months in a holding unit, he was completely out of his depth as a battalion commander. Although a decent chap and possibly a good company commander, he was so completely at sea that he inspired no confidence at all. Montgomery expressed only sorrow for him as he just knew nothing whatever about how to command and train a battalion. His 2IC, Major D.K. Robertson, appeared to be capable of running the administration adequately, and Montgomery described his company commanders as a decent lot without being outstanding. He rated the RSM as good, frowned upon NCO promotion by company, and found the men he encountered all first class.

As Montgomery went to see the Régiment de Maisonneuve doing an exercise in the field, he had no opportunity to talk at length with the CO so as to find out how he ran his battalion. He nonetheless found Lieutenant Colonel J.R. Roche to be very alert and keen, but gained the impression that he knew very little about how to train a battalion. Montgomery met all his company commanders, none of whom impressed him, and concluded that what he saw was an amateur show.

In summary, Montgomery wrote that Brigadier Whitehead had a difficult task with three new COs, none of whom was really fit to command and train a battalion. Only Roche, having been to Senior Officers School, knew something about it; Cantlie and MacLauchlan were completely unfit, with which assessment Whitehead agreed. Montgomery went on to state that the art of training was not well understood in 5 Brigade. The COs seemed to think that division and brigade commanders would train their companies for them, which is what, he suspected, actually happened. The result was that no proper company training had been done at all. Companies had not been trained to operate as companies in operations of war. The Calgary Highlanders, for example, spent their company training periods working on defences and doing battle drill. They did not seem to understand that battle drill was not the whole art of war, but merely a procedure, applicable to unit and sub-unit action; a company still had to be taught how to carry out the various operations of war.[14]

On 7 May 1942 Montgomery additionally reported on the 1st Canadian Army Tank Brigade, finding Brigadier R.A. Wyman to be a vigorous young commander with the right ideas, including the recognition of sound administration as a necessary basis for good training. If given good, sound advice and assistance on how to train, Wyman could be expected to produce a really first-class fighting brigade. With no divisional commander to train him, however, Montgomery recommended that corps headquarters provide the necessary guidance and supervision to bring him on. Wyman's BM, R.W. Moncel, received a very good grade, but his service company commander at age fifty-three was too old to fight overseas. The CO of the Ontario Regiment, Lieutenant Colonel G.Y. Masson, would also be very good if taken in hand and properly taught how to train and make war. Montgomery thought his squadron commanders all very good and strongly suggested that Major H.R Schell was the best one to fill the vacant position of 2IC. In contrast, the Three Rivers Regiment did not stack up so well. The CO, Lieutenant Colonel J.G. Vining, was not "in the first flight" and, with the exception of a good adjutant, officers generally were poor. The unit soldiers, 30 per cent francophone, were good, but there was no system for teaching officers and NCOs. The Calgary Regiment fared better as it had a young, alert, and first-class CO in Lieutenant Colonel J.G. Andrews. He had very sound ideas and his system for teaching officers and NCOs was excellent. The officers were a good lot and the NCOs particularly good. Montgomery admitted to being highly impressed.[15]

During this period Montgomery had a Canadian aide-de-camp (ADC), Captain Trumbull Warren, who accompanied him on his inspections. Warren made a great impression on Montgomery who told him that he was by far and away the best ADC he had ever had. When Warren went to the Canadian staff college in Kingston, Ontario, Montgomery struck up a regular correspondence with him. In a reply to Warren's letter of 6 March 1942, Montgomery asked the former to consider him a real friend and not just a British general whom he had served. Montgomery trusted Warren completely, to the extent that he discussed confidential matters with him that he would never have done with any ADC before, and never did after. In April Montgomery told Warren that his objective was to make the Canadian Corps the finest war machine ever and that he was not going to fail in this endeavour. In the same letter he told Warren that he hoped to be sending Pearkes, Potts, and Ganong back to Canada shortly, allowing the good young chaps a chance to emerge. In a letter dated 1 June Montgomery brought up Exercise "Tiger," remarking that the Canadians under Crerar performed splendidly, but that he hoped to send Price, GOC 3rd Division, back to Canada, where his business knowledge of the milk industry would be of great value in helping the national war effort. He added that he felt he was gaining the confidence of Canadians who might have been a bit suspicious at first.[16]

In a July letter Montgomery wrote that he had told McNaughton that if Warren had been a British officer he would have been made a BM long ago. In the same letter Montgomery expressed continued disappointment with the performance of higher commanders in collective training exercises and dismay at getting rid of Potts by promoting him to general rank. After two and a half years the Canadian Corps was nonetheless beginning to become a good corps, though he detected a considerable amount of jealousy from a certain quarter, inviting Warren to read between the lines. He further related how he had established fitness standards for Exercise "Tiger" by turning out all his headquarters staff officers and making them march with full kit in a test. Of 52 officers paraded, 30 did six miles in an hour, 40 did ten miles in two hours, 48 did ten miles in two hours and ten minutes, and four fell out. If staff officers could perform like this, he concluded, it was obvious that soldiers in a fighting battalion should be able to meet the standard of marching six miles in one hour and a further four miles in the second hour, covering ten miles in two hours. In a later July letter Montgomery wished Warren good luck in finishing the staff course in a blaze of glory and mentioned that he had arranged for his highly regarded replacement, Don Mackenzie, to go on the next course at Kingston. On 10 August Montgomery wrote that he was off to Egypt to fight Rommel and that he often wished that Warren were his own son.[17]

Chapter Seven

Military Godfather of the Canadian Army

For his efforts in inspecting Canadian brigades Montgomery acquired a better understanding of Canadian field operational capabilities than the inexperienced Crerar. As Chief Umpire on Exercise "Bumper," Montgomery had earlier noted that Canadians, as well as the British, placed too much faith in the brigade group as a tactical formation. This development reflected the recommendations of the Bartholomew Committee struck to examine the lessons of Dunkirk. The committee concluded that fighting by divisions was too unwieldy and slow, and that artillery had failed to carry out its role owing to the vast array of towed field guns being rendered impotent by Stuka action and fast-moving German panzers. The committee therefore recommended basing the tactical handling of the division on brigade groups of all arms as the lowest self-contained fighting formation. While this yielded more mobile groupings, however, it resulted in "penny packeting" divisional engineers, artillery, and attached tanks. Permanently allotting artillery regiments to brigades further undermined the system for massing artillery fire under the Commander, Royal Artillery (CRA) at divisional level and the Commander Corps, Royal Artillery (CCRA) at the corps level. Both artillery commanders now came to be considered redundant and little more than staff officers.[1]

Montgomery, who had fought his division as a division at Dunkirk, considered this unsound doctrine and set about correcting it. At Canadian Corps Study Week, 19–23 January 1942, attended by all senior formation commanders and staff officers, as well as unit commanders, the division as a fighting formation received emphasis. Here on a large cloth model the headquarters of the three Canadian infantry divisions, the army tank brigade, and the Canadian Corps made presentations on the division in the approach march to contact, infantry–artillery cooperation, infantry–tank cooperation, all-arms coordination in defence, and movement, organization, and new equipment. After discussions that followed, Montgomery did his customary summing up, stressing in particular the importance of massed concentrated artillery fire and the vital necessity for adequate logistical support.[2]

In the area of administration Montgomery expressed misgivings about the vast amount of paper circulating within Canadian units and formations. Brigades literally foundered under paper, which by making everyone office bound had the effect of cramping initiative, stifling training, and generally impairing military effectiveness. He found adjutants sitting in their offices all day long trying to deal with paper; when being responsible for unit discipline, they should have been out with their RSMs every afternoon to keep in touch with companies, keep their fingers on the NCO pulse, and generally see that the unit was running properly. Citing his experience with 12 Corps, Montgomery advocated assembling a corps headquarters committee chaired by a brigadier to review means by which paperwork could be reduced and unnecessary returns eliminated. He estimated that it would be immediately possible to cancel at least twenty of the latter. All units, for example, sent five copies of their training programs to corps headquarters for little purpose that he could see. Crerar agreed with Montgomery on the need to cut down paper and indicated that he already had the matter in hand.[3]

As in the case of his British corps commands, Montgomery also observed the inability of most Canadian commanders to conduct proper troop training. While a great deal of time was spent in teaching people how to fight, little time was spent in teaching officers how to train troops. The real trouble, Montgomery noted, was that officers generally had never been taught "training" as distinct from fighting in battle and they did not really understand it. Company commanders who had never been taught how to train companies thus employed old-fashioned training methods that were in use thirty years earlier, with the result that much time was wasted and many men bored. His solution was to introduce live fire and mix training, exercising as a company at least once while conducting weekly platoon training, and exercising as a battalion at least once while conducting company training. Fewer exercises lasting more than twenty-four hours from dusk to dawn were also better than more exercises conducted for shorter periods. From his observations Montgomery concluded that commanders appeared quite content just to know that training was happening. There was little supervision to ensure it was properly organized and run on sound lines and scant interest in investigating exactly how a CO might be training his officers or NCOs. Noting that many Canadian officers did not even understand "skeleton force" exercises such as telephone battles and signals exercises requiring minimal manning, he ventured that they would likely welcome definite instruction about training principles and methods.[4]

Officer training in particular tended to be conducted in haphazard fashion with little attention paid to shaking out battalion and brigade headquarters, which seldom seemed to go out for a headquarters exercise. Montgomery further noted that few battalions since November 1941 had actually exercised for any extended period as a unit, some having not operated as a battalion in the field, which he thought necessary once a month. When collective training did take place, moreover, it often suffered from improper organization and wrong methods that wasted much energy. In many instances there was no testing of companies in turn by COs and brigade commanders. COs also allowed company commanders to "direct" their own exercises, which usually saw 2ICs rather than company commanders being exercised in the hot seat. This was clearly anathema to Montgomery, who chastised COs for not setting surprise exercises that would have forced company commanders to take command themselves.[5]

Montgomery also expressed serious concern about the amount of time being devoted to training, an aspect that apparently disturbed several Canadian COs as well. Whereas the 1st Division allocated four days per week for construction of beach defences and anti-boat and anti-tank scaffolding, half a day for recreation, and one day off duty, only one and a half days were set aside for training. In Montgomery's view, this system merely served to dash any hope of serious accomplishment. He suggested as a far better solution separating work from training and concentrating on each for longer periods of time so that more profitable results could be attained – for example, putting all hands to work on finishing field defences, then committing all solely to their training. Crerar responded by directing that three days a week be devoted to tactical training.[6] As he did in 5 and 12 Corps, Montgomery additionally prescribed what he termed "piece work," an incentive-oriented training approach that allowed individuals and groups to be dismissed from instruction the minute they fully grasped what had been taught. [7]

In his training and tactical approaches Montgomery stressed the offensive spirit. In respect of field defences, he disapproved of the 4th Brigade digging and wiring defensive positions in its Stand to Area, pointing out that as a divisional reserve its purpose was to deal blows, not receive them. He similarly criticized the 3rd Division digging within its Stand to Area when it was unlikely to fight a defensive battle there. To start any battle sitting in prepared trenches, behind barbed wire, Montgomery warned, encouraged a defensive mentality. He could not emphasize too strongly that the first requirement in the successful defeat of invasion was not good defensive works, but rather a good and well-trained soldiery imbued with the offensive spirit. In this regard it is clear that Montgomery reshaped Canadian tactical thinking. Whereas 2nd Division Operation Instruction No. 12 issued 27 November 1941 was entitled "Defence of Sussex," it had by 3 January 1942 been amended to "Plan to Defeat Invasion."[8]

Montgomery took copious notes during his observations of field exercises and concluded that the collective training of the Canadian Corps revealed first-class troops, but a high command found seriously wanting. In May 1942 he advised Crerar that the training of commanders, such as brigadiers, CRAs, and unit commanders had not matched the progress of the lower levels owing to neglect and not being tackled properly. In Montgomery's view, the weak point in the Canadian Corps was the lack of knowledge of commanders in the stage management of battle and the technique of fighting on their own level. He had remarked after observing Exercise "Flip," part of the "Flip," "Flap," "Flop" series conducted by 2nd Division in April 1942, that none of the operations attempted would have succeeded against a good enemy, because commanders did not know their stuff. During Exercise "Conqueror" in the same month he again expressed concern about brigade and unit commanders' lack of knowledge in how to lay on a battle. He had greater concern about generals, noting that, if they could only learn how to put their divisions into battle properly, and how to keep firm control over "the ship in a rough sea," then the corps would be unbeatable.[9] In short, training generals was the key to getting an army ready for battle. It was no good having battle schools for officers and NCOs, he later wrote, concentrate on generals; if they know their stuff they will teach the soldiers.[10]

In respect of stage management, Montgomery asserted that against an enemy as good as the Germans it was difficult, almost impossible, for a formation or unit to recover if it was put into battle badly in the first instance. Initial errors resulting from blundering forward without balanced dispositions were increasingly difficult to rectify owing to the great firepower available, speed of movement, use of armoured fighting vehicles, and air power. The days were past when good troops could save a battle that had been badly "teed-up." Henceforth, victory would go to that side put that was into battle properly and that could retain control throughout the fight. Nowhere was this more important than in the advance to contact or encounter battle, which subject Montgomery had addressed with great perception in 1937. Stressing that mechanization increased the significance of ground, he argued that the initial encounter between opposing forces was likely to develop into endeavours to secure such ground that would enable the subsequent battle to be staged successfully. He concluded that even when faced with a paucity of information about the enemy, a commander had to decide *before* contact how he would fight to impose his will and attain his object. The absence of any plan to do so would inevitably mean drifting aimlessly into battle piecemeal and conforming gradually to the enemy's plan.[11]

Montgomery considered it vitally important that commanders be taught how to deal with situations in which little was known about enemy dispositions or intentions. His solution was to reconnoitre widely, recognizing that information on the enemy would become progressively urgent and, from a certain stage, be obtainable only through fighting. He accordingly recommended reinforcing reconnaissance units with forces of all arms, including artillery, from the start. Such "forward bodies," or advanced guards, besides being strong enough to deal with minor opposition, could additionally hold any ground secured. He saw the main body, in the meantime, directed towards some area the possession of which would give a commander the advantage in operations after gaining contact. Montgomery later termed this the first golden rule of battle, the second being that commanders think two levels down so as to avoid assigning lower-level tasks impossible to carry out. This meant division commanders thinking in terms of battalions before giving orders to brigade commanders, and battalion commanders thinking in terms of platoons before giving orders to company commanders. Whatever the circumstances, commanders had to be trained to be in the right place at the right time. In the advance this meant being well forward so as to be able to influence the battle on the basis of first-hand information and give orders to subordinates in proximity to relevant ground, yet, after gaining contact, not so far forward as to become unduly influenced by local situations to the detriment of effective planning ahead.[12]

Montgomery incorporated these concepts in a policy directive promulgated in December 1941. The directive listed fourteen points essential to success in battle. The stage management of battle headed the list followed by "sub-unit efficiency," which recognized that once battle was joined the issue passed to the junior leader and his sub-unit; the infantry company and its platoons; the tank squadron and its troops; the artillery battery and its troops; and the field engineer company and its sections. If these groups lacked the requisite skills, initiative, and leadership, the best plan was unlikely to succeed. Third on the list came high standards of physical fitness, endurance, and fighting spirit. Planning the contact battle, seizing and retaining the tactical initiative, and maintaining control through correctly positioning headquarters with good communications followed in order. The necessity for the cooperation of all arms came seventh, which stressed in particular the advantage of using the divisional artillery as a seventy-two-gun battery under the CRA, who also acted as gunner adviser to the divisional commander.

The eighth lesson emphasized the decisive influence of armoured forces and suggested using them to create opportunities for the employment of ordinary divisions. Anti-panzer defence, on the other hand, aimed to strip enemy tanks of their infantry protection and destroy as many as possible, not merely stop them. The role of anti-tank guns was to kill tanks, not protect infantry. Montgomery's ninth and tenth lessons referred to the crucial importance of commanders and staffs thoroughly understanding the technique of road movement and holding the enemy in the grip of their observation and sniping from the beginning, and not vice versa. No enemy movement was to be allowed and any enemy seen was to be shot. Lessons eleven and twelve dealt with the requirement for protection against surprise enemy ground and air attack. The thirteenth lesson pointed to the need for sub-units, using concealment and deception, to continue to fight the battle on a locality basis, taking under their command all small and isolated sub-units of other arms in the vicinity, until such time as reserves came into action. The last lesson highlighted the value of achieving surprise and urged that it be included as an essential part of every battle plan.[13]

Montgomery stamped his tactical approach upon the Canadian Corps at every turn. Much of what he dispensed was practical in nature and reflected detailed knowledge of the nuts and bolts of field operations. During Exercise "Flip" he reminded formation commanders of the importance of directing subordinate headquarters to move on axes near their own headquarters in order to facilitate control. Seeing artillery as the key to battlefield success, he also stressed the vital importance of the infantry company commander–artillery forward observation officer (FOO) relationship in producing simple artillery fire plans, without which no attack could be well launched. The primary role of field artillery was to "neutralize" or paralyze enemy soldiers for a short period of time by forcing them to keep their heads down. A good fire plan could additionally restore lost impetus and give a good "kick-off." He strongly criticized the Canadian practice of assigning a task to a battalion, stating it would be supported by a field regiment, and leaving the battalion CO, who possessed few artillery coordination means, to work out details alone. In all such cases he found no proper fire plan laid on and precious artillery resources wasted as COs had neither the time nor the staff to do so.

To Montgomery, it was the duty of the higher headquarters to assist the lower, which meant the fire plan had to be done by brigade headquarters that had an artillery staff. Providing brigade staff organized the fire plan, a reserve battalion near to its start line with a supporting battery already deployed could mount a fresh attack supported by a field regiment in one and a half hours. Montgomery further calculated that a brigade attack supported by three field regiments could be "teed-up" in three to four hours if participating units were in reasonable proximity along the axis of advance. To speed up the execution of fire plans, he insisted that all artillery reconnaissance parties include one "pistol" gun to register anticipated targets so that the bulk of the guns, usually arriving after dark, could incorporate pistol gun data. Again, Montgomery underscored the war-winning capability of artillery and the need for thinking ahead at all levels, warning that hurrying units into battle without giving them time to make their preparations just added to casualties.[14]

The practice of treating CRAs as staff officers and permanently allotting artillery regiments to brigades ceased with Exercise "Bumper." Here artillery command and control turned into a shambles, unable to rectify situations where if one brigade of a division was attacking or defending against attack, none of the guns of the others could be switched to its support. The sin of letting guns sit idle much of the time was thus committed over and over again. As a result of "Bumper," artillery command was restored. Commanders of reserve artillery formations were reintroduced and the positions of CRAs and CCRAs buttressed within a dedicated artillery chain of command. Henceforth artillery was to be commanded at the highest level for deployment and allotment, with control of fire decentralized to the lowest level. Much of this was due to the influence of Montgomery, who stressed that the business of artillery COs was first to train their regiments and then to train infantry brigadiers to use them properly. Here again, he saw the infantry company commander–FOO relationship as key to building up the detailed fire plan to quickly overcome organized enemy resistance encountered during decentralized offensive mobile operations. He also left no doubt as to the ultimate responsibility of infantry commanders, despite being advised by their gunners, for fire planning.[15]

Largely through the efforts of Brigadier H.J. Parham, the Royal Artillery perfected a matchless gunfire control system capable of producing a massive blow in a matter of minutes. As Parham realized, improved radio communications circumventing the normal chain of command enabled faster responses to requests for gunfire. Forsaking extreme accuracy further allowed overwhelming fire to be brought rapidly to bear. Under the Parham or "Uncle" target system, designated artillery officers could order the fire of all guns within range. To a radio call prefaced by "Uncle target" repeated three times, the entire seventy-two-gun divisional artillery responded. Likewise, "Mike target" drew a twenty-four-gun regimental shoot, "Victor," a corps response with 200 guns or more, and "William," all army guns within range. Fully evolved by mid-1943, this system saw artillery commanders integrated at every level and linked together by their own radio network. At the front, troop commanders serving as FOOs could be authorized to order the full weight of available artillery fire. Eventually, artillery batteries of two four-gun troops were intimately affiliated with armoured regiments and infantry battalions, and artillery regiments with brigades, the gunner CO acting as artillery adviser to the brigade commander from whom he was inseparable. At higher levels, the CRA and CCRA dealt with the movement and allotment of guns, the principal tenet of the Parham system being that every gun within range be laid, loaded, and ready to respond to a request for fire.[16]

Behind the divisional and corps artilleries stood army-level artillery brigades, which sought "destruction" more than "neutralization." These brigades, called Army Groups, Royal Artillery (AGRA) had no fixed composition, but usually consisted of three medium and one or two field and heavy regiments in proportions considered most suitable to the mission assigned. To gain maximum effect from the longer range and greater throw weight of medium and heavy guns, they were best employed as single-fire entities and not in "penny packets" along a front. The purpose of the AGRA was to give an army commander a wide measure of flexibility in the rapid allotment of artillery resources to smash unexpected enemy resistance or repel counter-attacks. In practice, they were almost invariably used as affiliated corps troops to reinforce divisional artilleries. With CCRAs each retaining a basic element that included an anti-tank regiment, a light anti-aircraft regiment, and a survey regiment, a corps could expect to be strengthened by one or more AGRA for bombardment, harassing fire, or counter battery tasks. The requirement for reinforcing artillery also increased as the enemy attempted to stabilize the battle. An AGRA or one of its medium regiments might further be placed in support of a division during fluid operations. Always, however, the guiding principle was that decentralization of artillery firepower should not preclude its concentration in the greatest possible strength when required.[17]

Montgomery saw the stage management of the tactical battle as the key to making the best use of artillery firepower and getting it into action quickly, but without undue haste likely to produce casualties. Artillery enabled a commander to dominate the forward areas and retain the initiative. In exercises "Conqueror," "Beaver III" (22–4 April), and "Beaver IV" (10–13 May), however, Montgomery repeatedly noted the hesitancy of Canadian divisional commanders to seize the initiative, without which they could not possibly win in battle. He attributed this to "criminal" indecisiveness and reiterated that vague and imprecise information about the enemy need not preclude quick and aggressive reaction by a division to regain the initiative and tactical advantage. The main thing was to start reconnoitring, and at the same time set the division in motion to meet the threat from a position favourable to launching offensive operations. Again, there remained a requirement for a simple but definite plan aimed largely at securing such ground with balanced dispositions so as to avoid having to react to the enemy. The enemy on first clash was to be hit, thrown on the defensive, and subjected to fresh blows. In advancing to contact, he again advocated the employment of "forward bodies" moving in rear of reconnaissance troops prepared to act offensively as soon as the latter were held up. [18]

Montgomery's repetitive emphasis on "forward bodies" reflected his assumption that there would always come a time when further and more detailed information could not be obtained without fighting. It does not seem to be understood, he lamented, that complete information about the enemy will never be gained by the use of reconnaissance troops and air alone. To attack the enemy and make him dance to your tune, he stressed, you have to gain contact with him and obtain by fighting the further and more accurate information that will enable you to plan the offensive battle successfully. In "Beaver III" and "Beaver IV" such a system of reconnaissance in force, which also called for divisional commanders to be forward, was not employed by Canadian formations in the advance. Consequently, when reconnaissance elements were held up, divisional commanders in headquarters tended to wait for information that was slow in coming, while brigades consolidated and settled in.[19] Valuable time was thus lost, which enabled the enemy plan to interfere with the progress of the friendly-force plan, even to the point of forcing change upon it, which amounted to losing the initiative.

Montgomery thought Pearkes's 1st Canadian Infantry Division badly handled in Exercise "Beaver III" for advancing on its objective without flank protection reconnaissance. When a threat developed on his right flank, Pearkes persisted in attacking the objective without protecting against this blow, which would have destroyed his division under real war conditions. Ever conscious of the time factor, Montgomery also faulted Pearkes for leaving out critical timings and coordination details in his order to conduct a withdrawal. Nor was he impressed with Pearkes's peacetime habit of trying to confuse the enemy by changing battalions between brigades. To hazard the loss of good formation teamwork on the possible chance of misleading the enemy did not strike him as sound practice in war. To Montgomery, it was not the fault of regimental officers and men that the 1st Division failed badly, but the fault of the divisional commander, who got the bit between his teeth, put on the blinkers, and drove blindly ahead. For the fine material of the 1st Division to perform well in battle, Montgomery asserted, it had to have a commander other than Pearkes, who seemed unable to grasp the essentials of a military problem and formulate a sound plan. A gallant soldier without brains, Pearkes would fight his division bravely till the last man was killed, and, he added, the last man would be killed all too soon. Noting that there was good replacement material to hand, such as Salmon for division command and Snow and Mann for brigades, he recommended relieving Pearkes and two of his brigade commanders, Potts and Ganong, the last initially assessed favourably.[20]

Montgomery's severe criticism of Pearkes could not but have pleased Crerar, whose strained relationship with the latter continued to deteriorate with overtones of open insubordination. That Pearkes remained the most obvious choice for command of 2 Canadian Corps also concerned Crerar, who discussed his reservations with McNaughton, pointing out that Pearkes's lack of foresight and broad vision constituted disabilities. On 25 April, the day after "Beaver III" ended, he told senior diplomat and friend Mike Pearson that while Pearkes was a forceful leader and able trainer, he was a man of limited scope who would be better as a battalion commander than a brigadier or better as a brigadier than a division commander. Crerar felt that Pearkes possessed a narrowness of vision that left him able to see only one thing at a time. Nor did he exhibit any interest in long-term planning. Although a first-class fighting soldier who would handle his men with determination, Crerar allowed, he might also produce negative results. The upshot was that McNaughton appealed to Pearkes's sense of duty and posted him back to Canada to take over the Pacific coast command. On 15 January 1943 command of newly formed 2 Canadian Corps thus fell to a dubious McNaughton choice, Lieutenant General E.W. Sansom, first commander of the 5th Canadian Armoured Division.[21]

Price had replaced Sansom as commander of the 3rd Canadian Infantry Division on 14 March 1942 and during Exercise "Beaver IV" received an adverse assessment from Montgomery. Montgomery found Price's performance as a divisional commander simply lamentable and completely ineffective. He did not possess the military ability, professional knowledge, forceful determination, and drive to get things done – the essential qualities of a commander in war. In addition, he failed to inspire, instilled no confidence, and generally forfeited his grip on the activities of the division in the field. The earlier marked indecisiveness of his senior brigadier, Haldenby, also prompted Montgomery to have second thoughts about his suitability for brigade command. Though a delightful person, Price was a complete amateur, totally unable to train his division, which was behind the others in readiness for war. Montgomery, having first expressed doubts about Price in February, concluded that he was unfit to command a division in a field army.[22]

Crerar agreed, even though he as CGS had appointed Price to divisional command. Indeed, he had written to McNaughton on the occasion, also referring to the appointment of Sansom to command the 5th Armoured Division, "I think these are good appointments and should result in credit to the Commands as well as to their Commanders."[23] He later roughly parroted Montgomery in a letter to McNaughton, saying that he had come to the definite conclusion that Price as a divisional commander was "handicapped in two important respects. He does not possess what might be termed a 'sense of tactics.' He is unable quickly to appreciate a military situation and to dominate it with the requisite speed and decision."[24]

As was his customary practice, Montgomery intentionally came down harder on officers than men, and he did not think it possible to produce good divisions unless they had good division commanders. Without a first-class general officer commanding, the 3rd Division had little hope of becoming the very fine division it could be. He further considered it quite impossible to make progress in the stage management of battle unless divisional commanders were themselves fully conversant with the handling of a division in battle and competent to train their subordinates. Since time was at a premium and men's lives were at stake, Montgomery insisted that plain speaking was necessary. Those commanders known to be bad had to be told they were bad, but they also had to be taught so that they would become good. Significantly, Montgomery believed that most Canadian brigadiers and unit commanders were excellent material and needed only to be taught. Many lower-level officers also appeared to be "teachable," willing, and of reasonable, if not always outstanding, calibre. In Montgomery's view, the 2nd Canadian Infantry Division performed well in "Beaver III" under Major General J.H. Roberts, whom he described as sound, but "not in any way brilliant." Montgomery noted, however, the very positive influence of Roberts's GSO 1, Lieutenant Colonel C.C. Mann, and concluded that Roberts would always do well if he had a good GSO 1.[25]

Apparently, McNaughton at one point considered Roberts a better choice for permanent corps command than Pearkes. Montgomery, however, could hardly have agreed that Roberts was ready for corps command. Indeed, his critical assessment of the state of training of Canadian troops contrasted sharply with McNaughton's claim that "ceaseless training by day and night in all the intricacies of armoured warfare, through all the phases from teaching skill at arms to the individual, to the combination of units, divisions and larger formations" had ensured that the Canadian Corps was thoroughly prepared for battle by the end of 1941.[26] Montgomery could not have more strongly disagreed and warned that "We live in a sort of peace-time atmosphere" where such things as courts of inquiry, traffic accidents, reports and returns, inspections, work on coast defences, and the paper and routine of peace conditions – "all tend to leave little or no time for the study of the things that really matter in war. And so it often happens that officers forget the things that really matter."[27] Montgomery viewed the fit and tough soldiers of the Canadian Corps as probably the best material in any army of the empire but were doomed to be killed in large numbers unless commanders learned how to launch them properly into battle.[28] The problem was that the Canadian high command did not know how to train them for such action and, but for Montgomery's intervention, would have left them totally unprepared for modern war and vulnerable to incurring unnecessary casualties.

Crerar retained all of Montgomery's 12 Corps directives and for the rest of the war attempted to imitate his military approach, echoing his emphasis on stage managing the battle, seizing the initiative, fighting for information, retaining control, and forcing the enemy to dance to your tune. His speaking notes on "Conqueror" and later directives essentially dispensed Montgomery's teachings. The army was not a mutual congratulation society based on popularity, and bad work had to be stamped upon. [29] Crerar further intimated that Montgomery's views on Canadian commanders very largely corroborated his own conclusions.[30] Crerar's handling of the Canadian Corps during Exercise "Tiger," which pitted 12 Corps operating with new experimental divisional structures against 1 Canadian Corps with old organizations in an eleven-day encounter battle scenario in 19–30 May 1942 also earned Montgomery's praise. "You did splendidly," he told Crerar, "and when I say you did well, I mean it." Of course, Montgomery again recognized the importance of the staff officer behind the commander when he said, "you have a first class BGS in Simonds ... I thought he was very good."[31]

This was high praise indeed as Exercise "Tiger" proved a tough challenge that tested formation fighting organization, doctrine, and troop capabilities to the limit. One of the most important lessons stressed by Montgomery was that a corps of one armoured and two infantry divisions constituted a well-balanced formation for all normal operations. Corps commanders therefore had to be able to handle efficiently both types of divisions, whether grouped as three infantry, three armoured, or any combination of the two divisions. Tanks alone were never the answer, and the punches they were capable of delivering had to be supported by the maximum effort of artillery, infantry, and all other arms. The broad plan of battle had to be made at field army level, with the RAF brought into planning from the start and divisions grouped appropriately within corps intimately concerned with fighting the tactical battle. As divisions could not operate on a wide front, division commanders had to be trained to launch attacks on a narrow front, the "schwerpunkt" and, from penetrations made, work outward to attack intervening enemy positions from the flanks and rear in "aufrollen" action. The primary function of the artillery in the attack was to neutralize enemy localities holding up the forward movement of friendly forces. Encountering strong enemy resistance thus called for field regiments placed under the command of forward brigades for mobile operations to revert to command of the CRA, who then could bring the fire of the entire divisional artillery to bear on the selected front of attack. In this instance, artillery regiments would remain in support of their affiliated brigades. To practise the cooperation of all arms in battle emphasizing concentration, control, and simplicity, Montgomery slated all-arms brigade exercises with live ammunition for July, August, and September.[32]

Montgomery visited eight Canadian brigades during Exercise "Tiger," which saw most units march over 150 miles and fight simulated battles in the severest test of endurance experienced by Canadian arms. More than a few wore out a pair of boots. To meet the standards set, a marching battalion in full battle order had to be able to cover six miles in an hour and ten miles in two hours. The soldiers travelled light as Montgomery stressed that a soldier's weight should not exceed 40–50 pounds, including ammunition, which left room only for a dry vest, dry shirt, cardigan, and pair of socks. He further insisted that Canadian soldiers had to learn how to live on hard rations, practice water bottle discipline, and go without a greatcoat or blanket for short periods. He considered it absurd that some Canadian units allowed a soldier to carry both a greatcoat and blanket and decreed that only one or the other be taken for purposes of sleeping.[33] For his tough approach and insistence upon standards, many regarded Montgomery as an "overbearing martinet – a proper bastard." When he left to take command of the Eighth Army in North Africa the prevalent attitude was good riddance. Once in action, however, they realized that his training methods had been the best preparation for war and they were more than happy to fight under his command.[34] Montgomery may not have been the "father of the Canadian Army" in the organizational fashion of either McNaughton or Crerar, but he was most certainly its military godfather.

Chapter Eight

Montgomery and Dieppe

Montgomery has been criticized for his involvement in planning the disastrous Canadian assault on Dieppe, even though the raid occurred after he had left England to take command of the Eighth Army. His April 1942 approval of the attack plan, which bore traces of being hastily conceived by too many masters, constitutes the crux of this criticism, especially as the operation eventually unfolded essentially unchanged. Montgomery did not originate the plan, the roots of which lay in the strategic realm of trying to mollify the Russians after Brooke convinced the Allies to abandon Marshall's highly questionable idea of opening a second front in France in 1942. Brooke agreed, however, to a proposal of the newly appointed Chief of Combined Operations, Lord Louis Mountbatten, to mount a large-scale cross-Channel raid that would give heart to the sorely pressed Russians. As early as February 1942 Mountbatten selected Dieppe as a possible target, and by 25 April his Combined Operations staff and a GHQ Home Forces representative had agreed on an outline plan for Operation "Rutter." As Dieppe was flanked by hard-to-scale cliffs with a beach dominated by headlands, the "Rutter" plan called for preliminary bombardment by heavy bombers in darkness, medium and fighter bomber strikes, parachute drops against coastal gun positions, flank landings, and a frontal attack on the town supported by tanks. Mountbatten also promised naval gunfire direct support. On 13 May the BCOS accepted the plan owing largely to interest in the capture of a defended port and strong RAF desire to entice the Luftwaffe into air battle on favourable terms. Since South-Eastern Army lay directly opposite Dieppe, GHQ Home Forces, previously charged with sole responsibility for raiding, agreed to yield troops for "Rutter" and nominated Montgomery as army representative in Combined Operations planning.[1]

Montgomery first learned of Mountbatten's secret plan when he visited GHQ on 20 April. The plan then called for flank landings seven miles west and twelve miles east of Dieppe, both supported by tanks, with the aim of capturing the airport and the dominating high ground southeast and west of the town. When Montgomery learned that the navy could provide shore support only for fifteen hours, however, he pointed out the impossibility of flank forces carrying out their tasks within that time frame, especially in the face of German opposition and the need to cross two rivers in the west. He suggested instead that the only way the town and seaport could be seized quickly was to deliver a surprise frontal attack supported by tanks and closer-in flank landings at Pourville to the west and Puys to the east. He additionally proposed parachute and glider assaults on heavy coastal gun batteries located near Berneval and Varengeville-sur-Mer. All of this, of course, was predicated on the promise of effective naval gunfire direct support and heavy air bombardment. Montgomery's advocacy of a frontal attack on Dieppe has been criticized, but his logic in condemning the initial Combined Operations plan as unworkable given the time restraints can hardly be faulted. Using tanks for the first time in amphibious operations also offered prospects of success.[2] Then, too, amphibious operations by their very nature have always involved launching frontal attacks against hostile shores. With the exception of Dieppe and a handful of other attempted landings from the sea, moreover, nearly all modern amphibious landings since Gallipoli have been successful.[3]

Montgomery sent a representative to the 25 April planning meeting at which the foregoing changes were incorporated, but he himself attended only one Combined Operations meeting on 5 June, three months after the conception of the operation. On 30 April he confided details of the operation to McNaughton after first conferring with Crerar, who had for some time been strongly agitating for Canadian troop participation in raids. On 5 February he had complained to Montgomery that his Canadian troops had been unjustly denied any opportunity for combat, to the detriment of their morale and pride. Montgomery replied vaguely that he would try to make landing craft available so that Canadians could practise raiding operations, but this was not good enough for Crerar, who suspected, with reason, that Montgomery remained lukewarm to "Rutter" largely because he was not calling all shots in what was essentially a naval operation. Montgomery also knew that raids, the tactics of the weak, were not going to win the war and refused to cancel any of his exercises related to his main mission of training a field army for major warfighting operations. In these circumstances Crerar on 1 March went over Montgomery's head to appeal to his old friend Brooke, who responded by offering to arrange a meeting between top Canadian commanders and the Combined Operations staff to discuss a leading role for Canadians in raiding operations. Mountbatten, who preferred Royal Marine commandos forming the major element rather than Canadians, reluctantly agreed to include them in the next big raid, which turned out to be Dieppe. To clinch this arrangement, which promised to keep the Canadian army concentrated in the decisive theatre while incurring light casualties in limited raids, McNaughton visited Mountbatten several times in April and obtained the authorization of the Canadian government.[4]

Before Montgomery first informed McNaughton about the Dieppe operation on 30 April, he had consulted Crerar on troop selection. Pressured to field a composite Anglo-Canadian force, he recommended instead the 2nd Canadian Infantry Division commanded by Roberts as best suited for such a task. This reflected Crerar's advice and accorded with his aim of carrying out "Rutter" as an entirely Canadian operation. Although McNaughton, kept in the dark, may have been more interested in raids against northern Norway, Crerar worked behind the scenes to ensure Canadian participation in the Dieppe raid. There is also good reason to believe that ever since his 1 March personal discussion with Brooke and 6 March meeting with the Deputy CIGS, he had a hand in tactical planning for the operation as he attended Combined Operations meetings. He quite correctly insisted on Canadians being brought into the planning on the principle that the actual commander must possess intimate knowledge of the plan to be executed. Roberts and his GSO 1, Lieutenant Colonel Mann, thus took a leading part in the detailed planning, reporting two to three times a week to Crerar on their progress. In assessing the feasibility of the outline plan in May, Mann concluded that the plan was "almost a fantastic conception of the place most suited to land a strong force" of armoured fighting vehicles. Mann also noted that using tanks to support the beach frontal attack might necessitate cancelling the air bombardment for fear that this would cause craters impeding armoured advance and seal off exits from the beach thereby trapping the tanks. The only alternative would have been to bomb the flanks.[5]

Montgomery has been blamed for accepting the cancellation of the heavy bomber preliminary bombardment, which remains mystifying as he originally viewed it as one of the essential elements of the plan. The devastation wreaked on Dieppe by bombing promised to reduce effective enemy opposition to the minimum, but concerns about compromising surprise and Bomber Command reluctance to take on such a task also factored in the cancellation. Indeed, arranging heavy-bomber support posed such a challenge to planners that Mountbatten at his 13 May briefing to the BCOS even suggested that if force commanders did not insist on such bombardment it could be dispensed with. The major obstacle was Air Marshal Sir Arthur Harris, who did his best to keep heavy bombers out of the Dieppe operation as he did not wish to waste them on what he termed "side shows." While promising only token bombing effort, he at the same time supported the RAF intention to destroy Luftwaffe fighters, the nemesis of his bombers, in an air battle showdown above Dieppe. Around 4 June Mountbatten also announced that Churchill, for political reasons related to protecting French civilians, had decided it inexpedient to undertake the bombing of Dieppe. In fact, Churchill and his Foreign Minister had already authorized bombing the town. For whatever reason, Mountbatten in a Combined Operations planning meeting on 1 July suggested abandoning the aerial bombardment by heavy bombers. In a following meeting on 5 July presided over by Montgomery in Mountbatten's absence, Air Vice-Marshal Leigh-Mallory, commanding No. 11 Fighter Group RAF, accentuated the positive side of the cancellation on the movement of tanks and downplayed the now limited support of Bomber Command. Roberts supported Leigh-Mallory, saying that bomb damage would prevent tank movement, but that there was a good chance of surprise compensating for lack of air bombardment. That Montgomery expressed no concern on hearing this presumably indicated that he already knew no major bombing effort would be forthcoming from Harris. Possibly because he banked on Mountbatten's promise of heavy naval gunfire support, he confirmed the decision, much to his later expressed regret. Other evidence indicates that he did not like the cancellation as it left the entire plan dependent on surprise, which he thought problematical, but when he expressed this reservation to Paget, the latter answered that he was powerless as the matter lay outside his authority.[6]

Meanwhile, Crerar during July oversaw the training of the 2nd Canadian Infantry Division until its deployment with the Calgary Tanks to the Isle of Wight for Combined Operations exercises. Although no longer in the operational chain of command directing Roberts, he also observed dress rehearsals for the raid. His desire to be involved in all aspects of the Dieppe operation further manifested itself when Montgomery, heading army participation, excluded both him and McNaughton from the "Rutter" coordination centre at No. 11 Fighter Group headquarters in Uxbridge. Crerar objected to being denied access on the grounds that neither he nor McNaughton could be divested of responsibility to the Canadian government for the employment of Canadian troops. This responsibility included the power to withdraw a Canadian force acting "in combination" with British forces if its commitment to action appeared to be unsound and not "a practical operation of war." Roberts as senior Canadian officer in the Combined Operations chain of command also possessed such power. In pointing out this implication, Crerar advised Montgomery that he was making a mistake in attempting to treat the problem of command of Canadian troops as a simple military chain of command issue, when in fact it was a complicated problem involving national policies and imperial constitutional relations.[7] Faced with Crerar's threat to politicize the issue, Montgomery backed down and invited both Crerar and McNaughton to accompany him to the headquarters of 11 Group. What Crerar may not have realized, however, was that the British in addition to trying to avoid the perception of using dominion troops as cannon fodder were also aware of the withdrawal threat to the point of being reluctant to plan operations on the basis of using Canadian troops for raids.[8]

In run-up training for the Dieppe raid, approved by McNaughton and Crerar, Roberts began to have misgivings. This struck Montgomery as wavering that risked eroding the confidence of commanders and troops, and he passed his concerns on to Paget. The latter, in turn, alerted McNaughton, who immediately sent Crerar to brace Roberts. Ever keen on the operation, Crerar allayed Roberts's fears by telling him that 100 per cent accuracy could never be expected in any human endeavour and that some error was bound to happen. Having reassured Roberts, Crerar concluded his report to McNaughton with the assertion, "I would have no hesitation in tackling it, if in Roberts' place," which he was not. While the assault troops loaded onto their landing craft and ships for "Rutter" on 2 and 3 July, Montgomery himself began to have second thoughts about the dangers involved. These were prompted by the arrival of the 10th Panzer Division in Amiens on transfer from the Eastern Front. Bad weather further resulted in the postponement of the operation planned for 4 July. It persisted until 7 July, the same day Luftwaffe planes bombed the assembled raiding craft, when Montgomery abruptly cancelled the operation for all time much to the chagrin of Combined Operations staff and Canadian troops. To some, this action marked him as a trouble maker, and when Mountbatten within a week managed to revive the raid on Dieppe as Operation "Jubilee," Paget eased Montgomery out of the chain of command. He replaced him with McNaughton, who now headed a purely Canadian chain that ran down to Crerar as "responsible military officer" for coordination and Roberts, whom McNaughton on 16 July ordered to execute "Jubilee." Much of this reflected Crerar's machinations in support of Mountbatten to resurrect the Dieppe raid as a Canadian operation, and he knew before McNaughton that the operation had been revived.[9]

The story of Operation "Jubilee" launched on 19 August 1942 has been recounted many times. Despite the benefit of fleeting local surprise, the operation proved a disaster. German air power degraded the effect of naval gunfire support, which turned out to be much less than promised, while the RAF essentially fought a losing air superiority battle to the detriment of fighter support for ground troops taking withering fire from strong enemy defences. In the space of some nine hours Canadians incurred 3,367 casualties, over 900 of whom were killed or died of wounds. The Germans took more prisoners at Dieppe than the Canadian Army lost in the entire eleven-month campaign in northwest Europe. To have remounted the Dieppe operation after Montgomery cancelled it was clear folly, but Crerar, the Canadian primarily responsible for reviving the raid as a Canadian operation, defended the sacrifice of "Jubilee" to the end. He also downplayed his role in the revival of the raid, claiming it was a British plan. Yet, as has been shown, Crerar was more closely connected with planning and training than is generally believed. As "responsible military officer," the plan was definitely his to adjust to fit the circumstances, but this he chose not to do.[10]

When McNaughton honourably opted to shoulder total responsibility for the disaster, Crerar advised him to make no such admission, but rather to take a positive line in concert with Mountbatten, stressing that although the raid had been tragically costly, it had been worthwhile for valuable lessons learned. This, of course, became the official party line for public consumption, which for political, strategic, security, and propaganda reasons could hardly admit that eager and willing soldiers had died for nothing. Crerar even suggested that had Dieppe turned out to be a "cheap success," real problems facing invasion would never have been unearthed. Failure, on the other hand, made a positive strategic contribution and raised morale and fighting spirit. Such rationalization after the fact ensured that he was neither blamed nor held responsible for the Dieppe raid, the treatment of which in the official history he deemed "quite first class." Yet, apart from beach cobblestones breaking tank treads, few lessons were learned that were not known beforehand or which could have been learned far more easily at less cost by other means.[11]

Far more than Dieppe, the highly successful amphibious assault against Sicily orchestrated by Montgomery laid the framework for the invasion of Normandy. Here he objected to the proposed invasion plan formulated by diverse staff agencies and committees after seven earlier versions, rightly insisting that a commander must never allow a battle plan to be forced upon him by his staff.[12] He has to do the hard work of thinking things through himself. Leaving staffs to spin their wheels in coming up with options in the absence of command direction was also a wasteful and inefficient use of staff officers. In this case, Montgomery courageously prepared a new plan in the face of powerful opposition, rejecting two widely separated landings in favour of one concentrated effort with corps and divisions in supporting distance of each other. Dempsey later called this Montgomery's finest hour, and to him belongs credit for Operation "Husky," the invasion of Sicily, which involved more ships and troops than the initial Normandy assault, making it by such measure the largest amphibious assault in history.[13] Montgomery's experience of Sicily uniquely qualified him from a practical perspective to take charge of 21st Army Group for the invasion of Normandy.

With the possible exception of Brooke, no other British or American commander could have conducted the Normandy landing, since none possessed a better understanding or grasp of the intricacies and challenges of land–air warfare than Montgomery did. After the war Eisenhower's COS offered that "no one else could have got us across the Channel and into Normandy."[14] Again, Montgomery rejected the staff plan that had been developed as it called for only three assault divisions and a complicated transference of command in the face of enemy opposition. His replacement plan reflected simplicity and provided a strong foundation for retaining the initiative and avoiding serious setbacks, both considered essential to eventual success. Montgomery also displayed great forbearance and perseverance in withstanding numerous criticisms from many quarters as the Normandy battle progressed to a dramatically successful ending. Unlike in Sicily where the bulk of the German army escaped, Montgomery masterminded the most successful invasion in the history of warfare and delivered a crushing defeat to the enemy.[15]

Chapter Nine

Monty's Eighth Army and Canadians

On 8 August 1942 the War Office ordered Montgomery to take command of the Eighth Army in Egypt. He was not a first choice and had only been selected after Churchill's preferred designate, desert veteran Lieutenant General W.H.E. Gott, was killed when the airplane carrying him was shot down. A prevailing attitude, best expressed by Roberts before Dieppe, was that Montgomery was a great trainer of troops, but rather too old to lead them in battle.[1] Nor was Montgomery a desert veteran, but he came strongly armed with his theory and doctrine of war developed over the years and honed in South-Eastern Army through exercises like "Tiger." Although looking thinly small and white-kneed on arrival, he was not cowed by the bronzed desert warriors of the Eighth Army. Finding the situation completely unsatisfactory, he prematurely took charge on 13 August and ordered the immediate creation of a powerful reserve corps of armoured divisions. He also put a stop to fighting the enemy with brigade groups and smaller "Jock columns" in pin-prick operations. Henceforth divisions would fight as cohesive divisions and not be split up in bits and pieces all over the desert. He further confirmed the collocation of army headquarters with that of the Desert Air Force so that they could fight one coordinated battle instead of drifting apart fighting two separate efforts. That evening he addressed all army headquarters officers, instituted his COS system, and stated unequivocally that if the Germans attacked, the Eighth Army would stand and fight – there would be no withdrawal, no surrender. "If we can't stay here alive," he said, "then let us stay here dead."[2]

The Eighth Army that Montgomery took over was a mainly Commonwealth force of two armoured divisions and five infantry divisions, one each from Australia, New Zealand, South Africa, India, and Britain, the last immediately hastened from the Egyptian delta on his order. The 10th Armoured Division with three brigades contained the mass of British armour, including all Grant tanks, while the 7th Armoured Division had a motor brigade and light or cruiser tanks. With this force Montgomery intended to hold the line against expected attack by Field Marshal Irwin Rommel and, in the interim, lay plans for a great offensive. He had absolutely no intention of attacking before he was ready, however, especially as reinforcements were on their way. With two weeks breathing space, Montgomery felt confident that he could blunt any attack Rommel launched. Having further recognized that Rommel's technique was to lure British armour into attacking him, then have his panzers withdraw behind a hidden anti-tank screen that accomplished the main destruction of British tanks, Montgomery had no intention of dancing to his tune. He instead put a leash on his armour, the preferred tactics of which he equated to the cavalry hunting the fox, and ordered the GOC 13 Corps, Lieutenant General Brian Horrocks, to dig in his tanks and anti-tank guns on Alam Halfa Ridge and entice the Germans onto them. Over the protests of the commander of the 7th Armoured Division, he refused to consider unloosing armour against Germans who excelled in all-arms manoeuvre. As expected, the Axis attacked within seventeen days of Montgomery's arrival and were met with massive artillery and anti-tank fire plus air attacks that forced them to withdraw by 7 September having not managed to either break in or breakthrough.[3]

Having stopped Rommel in his tracks, Montgomery now had to fight off intense pressure from Churchill to launch the offensive in September. In doing so, he made the audacious promise that he would guarantee victory if he could be given until 20 October to reorganize and train his forces, as well as institute deception measures and practise vital minefield clearance. With the arrival of reinforcements, the Eighth Army finally began to comprise a majority of British divisions. For the planned offensive, Montgomery grouped 10 Corps with the British 1st, 8th, and 10th Armoured divisions, 13 Corps with the British 7th Armoured and 44th and 50th divisions, and 30 Corps with the 9th Australian, 51st Highland, 2nd New Zealand, 1st South African, and 4th Indian divisions. Following large-scale rehearsals and detailed briefings down to unit level, the Eighth Army finally counter-attacked supported by massive artillery bombardment on the moonlit night of 23 October, with 30 Corps in the north and 13 Corps in the south breaking into heavily mined Axis defences and methodically destroying enemy infantry divisions through local flank and rear attacks in a "crumbling" process and "dogfight." The task of 10 Corps was to pass armour through cleared lanes in 30 Corps and destroy enemy panzers drawn

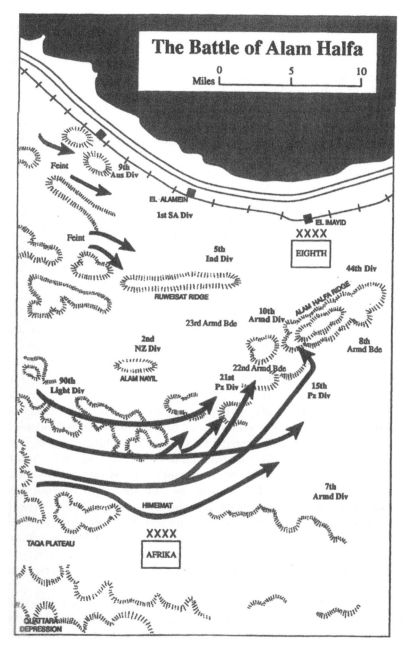

Map 9.1 The Battle of Alam Halfa, 31 August–6 September 1942 (John A. English)

in to prevent the destruction of Axis infantry. The inability of armour to get through, however, forced Montgomery to mount an alternative coastal thrust with the 9th Australian Division, which delivered three night attacks that drew the weight of Rommel's reserves onto it. Finally, in Operation "Supercharge" launched at 0100 hours 2 November at the junction of Italian and German forces south of the 9th Australian, the 2nd New Zealand Division with 9th Armoured Brigade and two British infantry brigades under command achieved a breakthrough that forced Rommel to withdraw. His next serious stand was made 1,500 miles farther west four months later.[4]

The Battle of El Alamein ended on 4 November after eleven days of hard pounding in what Montgomery termed a "killing match." While the battle did not play out according to initial plan, Montgomery adapted quickly to changing circumstances and never lost the initiative. With a firm grip and grim determination, he fought a flexible army–air level battle using methods that he had taught and preached to the Canadian Corps in South-Eastern Army. Here concentrated artillery fire coordinated by CRAs and CCRAs proved to be a battle-winning factor that enabled him to develop new thrusts very quickly and support these thrusts with such overwhelming fire that nothing could stop them. In fact, the artillery arm in support of hard-fighting infantry compensated for the disappointing performance of British armour in 10 Corps commanded by Lieutenant General Herbert Lumsden, whom Montgomery had not wanted in the first place.[5] In contrast, Dunkirk veterans Horrocks and Oliver Leese, whom he had brought in to command 13 Corps and 30 Corps, respectively, had proven quite first class. Montgomery also heaped praise on the commander of the 2nd New Zealand Division, Lieutenant General Bernard Freyberg, VC, calling him "superb" and the best fighting division commander that he had ever known. The next best fighting division commander, in Montgomery's view, was Major General L.J. Morshead of the 9th Australian Division. On 4 November, with victory assured, he went straight to the latter's headquarters to thank him for his leadership and the performance of his troops who had done so much to redeem the failure of British armour between 5 October and the 2 November launching of "Supercharge." Morshead's division alone sustained as many casualties at Alamein as the entire 10 Corps.[6]

Alamein unquestionably turned the tide in North Africa and propelled Montgomery into the limelight. Next to Churchill he became the figure most associated with victory. By February 1943 the Eighth Army reached the enemy Mareth Line on the border of Tunisia. Montgomery's advance coincidentally reinforced his influence upon Canadians

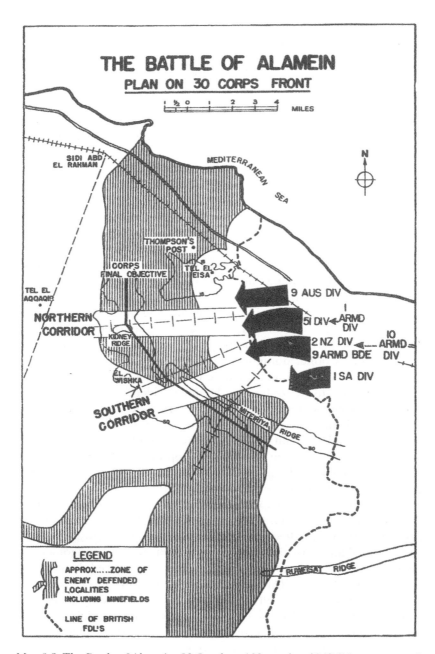

Map 9.2 The Battle of Alamein, 23 October–4 November 1942 (Montgomery of Alamein, Field Marshal the Viscount, *Memoirs* [London: Collins, 1958])

and especially Crerar, who in a congratulatory letter related how all Canadian troops applauded his victory over Rommel, adding that "our money has been on you all the time." In a subsequent exchange of letters Montgomery stressed how important it was to have good commanders down to brigade level as "you just cannot win battles if the generals are no good." He further pointed out that administration in the rear was also commensurate with what a commander wished to achieve in front. Montgomery also sent Crerar a copy of his pamphlet "Some Brief Notes for Senior Officers on the Conduct of Battle," which laid down Eighth Army doctrine of how to fight. In commenting on the pamphlet, Crerar noted that Montgomery had "not lost his power of clear and forcible expression."[7]

In his "Brief Notes for Senior Officers on the Conduct of Battle" Montgomery stressed that a commander had to be quite clear, before the start of an operation, as to how he intended to fight the battle. His intention and his plan to achieve it had to be impressed upon every commander right down to and including unit commanders. To attain the best results at army level, the commander *himself* had to explain his intention *personally* to all corps commanders in turn, emphasizing the most vital points. Regimental officers and men in the ranks had also to be told relevant details and the part they were to play in achieving what was wanted. If such things were done, Montgomery noted, every officer and man would enter the fight knowing how his actions would influence the whole battle and then be able to give of his best. Having decided how he would fight the battle, a commander had to persevere in relentlessly carrying out his intention and impressing his will upon the enemy. If he started with the initiative, he had to retain it; if the enemy started with the initiative, it had to be wrested from him at the earliest opportunity through offensive action. Every commander at every level had to be made to understand that without the initiative he could not win.[8]

In response to Crerar's expressed desire to learn more about the practical side of war, Montgomery extended an invitation to visit. Thus, in February 1943 Crerar flew to Tripoli with a group of British generals and attended an instructive study period conducted by Montgomery at Eighth Army headquarters. Here Montgomery emphasized the value of joint planning with the RAF and the war-winning capability of centrally controlled artillery, especially in overcoming and smoking off enemy anti-tank gun screens. He also confirmed the wisdom of fighting as divisions, the importance of the proper grouping of fighting elements, and the need for all-arms cooperation as no one arm could prevail in battle by itself. Other points mentioned included the importance of tactical surprise and deception, the requirement for decisive leadership, and simplicity in the development of battle plans so that as many troops as possible could easily understand what was required. Complexity, in contrast, risked sowing chaos. In his visit report Crerar observed that he saw nothing new in Montgomery's tactics, but he recirculated the latter's "Some Lessons Learnt during the First Two Years of War" and asked that they be thoroughly absorbed. In his covering memorandum he offered that the title might better read "Some Lessons Learnt during Two Thousand Years of War."[9]

Yet, there was much new in Montgomery's method as Crerar's own notes reveal. Foremost, Montgomery accentuated the need to train *in* war as few other generals had. Unlike Gort, who never even held a signals exercise in the period before Dunkirk, Montgomery mandated that while fighting was going on at the front, all unengaged formations and units were to discuss lessons recently learned and carry out training to perfect themselves in still better techniques. He also introduced permanently for the first time the "J" service in which his staff officers listened into the wireless communications of forward divisions and brigades to gain quicker information than that coming up the chain of command. This service coupled with "Y" interception of enemy communications enabled Montgomery to acquire a better feel for what was actually was going on at the front. The manner in which the Eighth Army integrated its staff organization to synchronize operations with the RAF was additionally new compared with previous practices. Phantom units, originally formed by the RAF to pinpoint forward troop locations and immediately report this information back, were also integrated with "J" service.[10]

Dealing with minefields on an unprecedented scale likewise called for new approaches that had been carefully studied and worked out in detail by the Eighth Army. This included the development of minefield gapping and clearance drills by engineers and infantry covered by artillery fire. Another relatively novel idea of Montgomery was the need to train subordinate commanders to work on verbal orders based on good standard operating procedures and delivered personally by higher commanders at all levels. He further emphasized forward command, which meant never calling front-line commanders back to receive orders. Never forgetting that he commanded an army of civilians in uniform, Montgomery also insisted that any plan of operations had to be in accordance with the standard of training reached by one's troops, which limited the scope of operations to what was possible. Introducing new and untried troops to battle had to be done carefully, initially assigning them easy-to-achieve tasks in order to build confidence. Launching new troops on tasks for which they were not trained, on the other hand, risked producing lasting harm. To ensure optimum all-arms coordination in drawing up a battle plan, he further suggested that a brigade commander required the advice of the CRA, CRE,[11] and the supporting tank commander. At a higher level, Montgomery displayed remarkable foresight in pioneering the integration of tactical air power with ground operations. The emphasis he placed on troop morale as "the big factor in war" and the efficient organization of supply and transport services likewise exceeded the norm.[12]

Montgomery also abandoned the practice of army commanders remaining with their main headquarters and exercised personal command and control of the Eighth Army from a small mobile Tactical Headquarters (Tac HQ) located well forward in the battle area. Apart from allowing closer control of the battle, this arrangement, which required good communications, saved him from getting immersed in the detail and enormous paperwork of main headquarters and allowed him to plan in an atmosphere of calm and tranquillity. Operating from a couple of caravans, the Tac HQ consisted chiefly of signals and cipher specialists, liaison staff, defence troops, and a very small operations staff for keeping in touch with the battle situation. Montgomery gave verbal orders to his subordinate commanders from Tac HQ, leaving the staff work required to execute those orders to main and rear headquarters. Main headquarters was the core of the headquarters system, and the COS and chief administrative officer both lived there. The chief administrative officer's deputy headed the rear headquarters where the administrative ("A") and quartermaster ("Q") branches and service heads were located. When necessary, the COS, chief intelligence officer, artillery commander, and chief engineer, and would come forward to Tac HQ for briefings or orders groups. Montgomery took this system with him to the 21st Army Group when he left the Eighth Army. While he cautioned that a corps commander required the full machinery of his main headquarters around him in order to fight the tactical battle, the concept of forward command from a Tac HQ caught on and trickled down to lower levels, where commanders and COs sallied forth daily from their main headquarters with artillery and engineer advisers in tow to exercise command from the front.[13]

The only permanent staff stationed at Tac HQ with Montgomery consisted of a couple of junior staff officers, two or three aides-de-camp, and three or four liaison officers (LOs). The LOs were Monty's eyes and ears in keeping in daily touch with the battle. In his selection of these LOs Montgomery was most discriminating as he gave them wide-ranging authority in carrying out one of the most difficult and dangerous jobs in the battle area. Each day he demanded that the LOs go as far forward as possible to various sectors of the fighting front and make contact with the lead infantry companies, armoured squadrons, or even scout-car patrols in order to give him before nightfall a clear, first-hand report of the battle situation. Churchill in his memoirs described this system of daily operational intelligence, likening these few LOs to homing pigeons returning from their dangerous mission by late afternoon to give Montgomery up-to-date accounts of the front, independent of the official and routine situation reports that came in later. The responsibility of Montgomery's LOs was widely appreciated throughout the battle zone, and unit commanders gave them all possible help and whatever transport they needed. Monty later described his LOs as young officers of character, initiative, and courage who had seen much fighting and were able to report accurately on battle situations. It was dangerous work – some were wounded and some were killed. They were a gallant band of knights. Two Canadians served as LOs: former Montgomery ADC Major Warren during the Sicilian campaign and Major R.S. Malone from the invasion of Italy onward. Warren served as GSO 1 of the 1st Canadian Infantry Division after Sicily and became Montgomery's personal assistant for the invasion of Europe.[14]

On 8 November, four days after the first decisive victory at Alamein, the Allies launched Operation "Torch" with American amphibious landings in Morocco and Algeria, where the kernel of the First British Army also went ashore. That "Torch" saw American troops in action before Canadian soldiers, with the exception of the disastrous Dieppe raid, caused much consternation in Canadian public and political circles. McNaughton nonetheless maintained his focus on cross-Channel operations and remained averse to Canadian divisions fighting separately. Although opposed to sending substantial forces to support the campaign in North Africa, he did accept that Canadian soldiers needed combat experience and seized upon "Torch" as an opportunity to loan individual Canadian personnel to British fighting units. In December 1942 after the Allied advance into Tunisia, McNaughton convinced the War Office to allow Canadian troops to be loaned to the British First Army for three months. Spaces were apportioned on a pro rata basis to the various arms of Canada's four available divisions and army ancillary troops, as well as to reinforcement units in Britain. The men selected were to be the most capable officers in the rank of major and below and NCOs above the rank of sergeant that units had to offer, with two staff spaces reserved for lieutenant colonels. In all, 201 officers and 147 NCOs were inserted into First Army's reinforcement pool and used to fill positions as if they were British soldiers. Their task was to gain first-hand combat experience and pass on the lessons they learned to their units upon their return.[15]

The push to get Canadian fighting formations into action had mean-while gained traction largely owing to duplicitous manoeuvring behind the scenes by Crerar, partly for his personal desire to gain operational experience. This brought him into conflict with McNaughton, whose attempts to reserve unto himself the politics of high command increased Crerar's latent resentment. Disenchantment with McNaughton's exag-gerated insistence on Canadian autonomy and associated reluctance to make major splits off the First Canadian Army also grew in Ottawa, where Stuart, the CGS, shared Crerar's views. So, too, did the defence minister, J.L Ralston, once described by McNaughton as "small potatoes" in whom he had no confidence. There was little love lost between the two men, with their animosity dating back to the late 1920s when then defence minister Ralston accused McNaughton of exceeding his authority as CGS on matters of policy. Ralston now believed that getting Canadian formations into action was necessary for political reasons, a stance sur-reptitiously supported by Crerar while feigning loyalty to McNaughton. In conversations with the British, who long questioned McNaughton's approach, Crerar agreed with Ralston, but also for reasons of morale and battle experience. In the fall of 1942 during a visit to England, Ralston openly advocated getting Canadian formations into action at the earliest opportunity, contrary to McNaughton's advice. McNaughton responded by venting his displeasure on Crerar, and their relationship deteriorated from there.[16] After the "Torch" landings, however, McNaughton's stance could not be sustained against growing public pressure to get Canadian troops in action.

Crerar now connived with Ralston, Stuart, and the British to remove McNaughton from command. In this endeavour he received support from the latter's questionable field performance in Exercise "Spartan" conducted 4–12 March 1943. Although McNaughton had performed brilliantly as a counter-battery officer in the Great War, he had never felt the need to prepare himself for higher command as had Montgomery. In assuming that military expertise would flow naturally from scientific knowledge, and preferring to focus on constitutional and administrative issues, McNaughton neglected the practical side of training command-ers and staff for operations. An insatiable dabbler who had to have a finger in every pie, he was forever having "attacks of the gadgets" and fiddling with vehicle and gun modifications that any ordnance officer could have handled. For not taking army command seriously as a full-time job that required attention and study, McNaughton floundered in deploying his formations during "Spartan." In hastily ordering one corps to pass through another at night, which proved a challenge at divisional level for Montgomery at Dunkirk, he demonstrated gross ignorance of large-formation operations. His time estimates for having corps execute tasks exposed him as a rank amateur. On 6 March at 2335 hours he ordered 2 Corps to advance east through 1 Corps in darkness, only to issue a counter-order at 1615 hours the next day for a westward deployment that night. At 2130 hours on 10 March he issued orders to 2 Corps for operations the following day, and at 2255 hours 11 March he issued orders for operations on 12 March. He had no idea that a corps required at least 24 hours' and a division 12 hours' warning in order to execute a major task.[17] The result of such short-fuse orders and counter-order not surprisingly produced disorder marked by huge traffic jams and fighting elements intermingled with administrative echelons.

Staff officers charged with coordinating details at all levels had little time to react to such command direction. As a rule, the GSO 1 of a division called upon to make a decision had to make one that could be put into operation that day, while a corps COS had twice that time and an army COS about four days.[18] Crerar in his 1 Canadian Corps after-action report pointedly referred to command failure to appreciate the time required between ordering a brigade or division attack and launching battalions supported by coordinated firepower. He stressed that all commanders had to have a realistic appreciation of the time factor in operations as coordination could not be effected unless sufficient time were allowed for orders to be translated into action. This called for thinking two levels down; speed was desirable, but not unorganized haste. Citing battle experiences of the Eighth Army, Crerar emphasized that tactical knowledge had to be acquired through study, thought, and practice, and that the duty of every commander was to train not only himself, but his subordinates and staff as well. He also warned that the stage management of battle had to be right from the beginning to avoid operations being badly launched. Other points mentioned by Crerar further reflected Montgomery's teachings, including keeping headquarters well forward, reconnoitring widely, concentrating main forces on ground of importance while being prepared to fight for information if required, and consolidating after attacks as it was dangerous to halt and defend on a broad front.[19]

McNaughton failed to appreciate that a field army commander should be looking and planning well beyond the close battle in progress to the distant one he intended to fight. This meant thinking two or even three operations ahead, which roughly translated into four or more days in advance, compared with three for a corps commander, and forty-eight hours for a division commander. To Brooke, who visited "Spartan" on 7 March as CIGS, the performance of McNaughton confirmed his inability to command a field army and certainly not one that included

British troops. Brooke knew first-hand the passage of lines challenges faced by Montgomery's division at Dunkirk and rightly concluded that McNaughton had no idea how to deploy large formations and "was tying up his force into the most awful muddle." Sir James Grigg, British Secretary of War, was appalled at McNaughton's indecision as "he stood in front of his situation map hesitating as to what to do and what orders to issue."[20] According to Crerar, both Grigg and Ralston personally observed McNaughton's inability to sum up the situation and issue clear and precise orders. Crerar later recalled that it became patently obvious to all during Exercise "Spartan" that McNaughton was totally unsuitable for high operational command. In Crerar's view, McNaughton was primarily an administrator, organizer, and technician, but one apt to get immersed in detail and unable to stand back and view the whole picture as a senior operational commander must. Though competent in mobilizing, equipping, and preparing an army, he could not give it or its senior commanders the higher training that was essential.[21] An experienced Canadian field commander would later write that McNaughton was "a clever man in some spheres, but a military ignoramus, conceited and obsessed with misguided Canadian nationalism."[22]

In April 1943, largely owing to pressure exerted by Ralston and the CGS, partly in response to public calls to get Canadian soldiers into action for reasons of honour and post-war prestige, and partly to reduce the presumed adverse effect of continued inaction upon troop morale, the 1st Canadian Infantry Division and the 1st Canadian Army Tank Brigade replaced equivalent British formations in the order of battle for the invasion of Sicily set for July. As a sop to McNaughton, who reluctantly approved, the stated intention was to have them return to disseminate battle experience for the invasion of Europe, but this was definitely not the real reason for their deployment. In any event, on 10 July the 1st Canadian Infantry Division supported by the Three Rivers armoured regiment from Wyman's tank brigade went ashore as part of the Eighth Army assault force in Operation "Husky," the invasion of Sicily. Simonds commanded this Canadian field formation, but like Montgomery he was not the first choice for the job. Simonds had trooped to Britain as GSO 2 (Operations) with the 1st Canadian Infantry Division and after a brief tour as CO of the 1st Field Regiment, Royal Canadian Horse Artillery, conducted the first Canadian staff college course in 1940. He subsequently served as GSO 1 of the 2nd Canadian Infantry Division and later as BGS of the Canadian Corps, where he earned Montgomery's praise. Early in 1943 he relinquished command of the 1st Canadian Infantry Brigade and assumed the position of BGS, First Canadian Army. Shortly after witnessing the Eighth Army victory at Wadi Akarit in early April

1943 as a staff observer, he replaced Roberts in command of the 2nd Canadian Infantry Division. Only two weeks later, he transferred to command the 1st Division on the death of Major General Salmon in a plane crash.[23]

After landing against light resistance, the 1st Canadian Infantry Division supported by Three Rivers' tanks, advanced smartly inland on the left flank of Lieutenant General Oliver Leese's 30 British Corps to seize Modica. As the division was the only one in the Eighth Army unaccustomed to Mediterranean heat, Montgomery on 13 July directed the Canadians to rest for a day and half at Giarratana, where he visited every unit and received an enthusiastic reception. On 15 July Canadian troops experienced their first major encounter with Germans at Grammichele, where the rearguard of the retiring Hermann Goring Panzer Division ambushed them. By noon the 1st Canadian Infantry Brigade had cleared the town, but Simonds, dissatisfied with progress, delivered a tongue lashing to the brigade commander, Brigadier Howard Graham, for not advancing aggressively enough and being too lenient on his battalion commanders. There was doubtless some truth to this, but Simonds in his first test of battle was also too prone to intervene in brigade and even battalion operations, second-guessing their commanders. Graham later claimed that he resigned his command because Simonds reprimanded him in front of his driver and signaller, but there is reason to believe Simonds fired him on the spot, as he told his GSO 1, Lieutenant Colonel George Kitching, to take over the 1st Brigade the next morning. When Simonds reported the incident to Leese, the latter replied that while he did not wish to interfere in a Canadian affair, he would be inclined to give Graham another chance.[24]

When Montgomery first learned of this affair he wrote to Leese stating what a great pity it was as Graham was a splendid fellow beloved in his brigade. Suspecting that Simonds had lost his temper, Montgomery observed that he had much to learn about command, and sacking brigadiers like Graham would upset his division. He added that Simonds would be well advised to consult his superiors before taking violent action in which he might not be backed up. Stating that he would see Simonds, Montgomery also made a point of personally interviewing Graham, opening with, "Now, what's this trouble between you and Guy Simonds?" After listening patiently to Graham's side of the story, Montgomery told him that he would go back with Leese and resume command of his brigade. There will be no problem, the army commander added, both of you are to blame – just get on with the battle. In a 17 July note to Simonds Montgomery wrote, "I hear you had a row with Graham. I have seen Graham at Corps HQ. The corps commander will

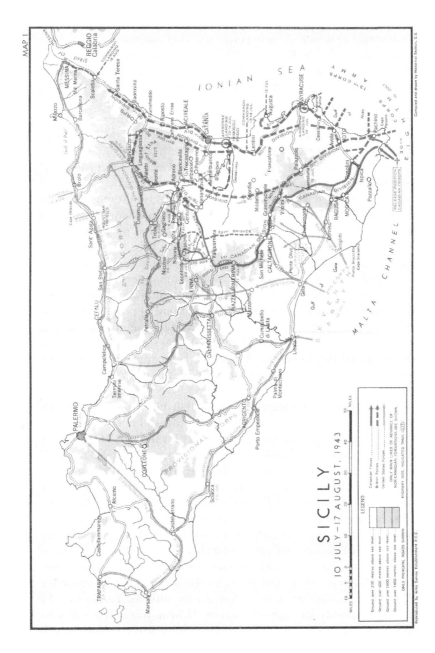

Map 9.3 Sicily, 10 July–17 August 1943 (G.W.L. Nicholson, *The Canadians in Italy*, 1956)

tell you my views about it, and my general views on the whole question of command in war. I want you to do the big thing and take Graham back, giving him a warning and a last chance. Difficult subordinates have to be led and not driven, and the higher commander has got to keep calm and collected and not be too ruthless." In the same note Montgomery congratulated Simonds on how well he was handing his division and how well it was fighting.[25]

Around this time, with the expectation that Canadian formations would be returning to First Canadian Army after the Sicilian campaign, however unrealistic for reasons related to shipping availability, McNaughton requested permission to visit Canadian troops. In mid-July, he and a party of staff officers had arrived in Malta with this purpose in mind, only to be told by the C-in-C Middle East, General Alexander, that permission was denied. Montgomery, true to form, never wished to be bothered by visitors whom he understandably always found to be a nuisance and unnecessary distraction in the execution of operations. In this instance he had also decided that the young and inexperienced Simonds commanding a division for the first time would not be disturbed during his Canadian formation's baptism by fire. To confirm this, he went to see Simonds and asked him if he would like McNaughton to come to Sicily. Simonds, who had earlier requested that the visit be postponed, responded with an unequivocal "For God's sake, keep him away." McNaughton, of course, had the constitutional right to visit Canadian troops, but his timing was bad. Although later able to visit in August, he remained livid at his first refusal and made an issue of it with Brooke, little knowing that plans had been laid to get rid of him. Montgomery played no part in these, but on meeting McNaughton in Italy was quick to point out the difficulties of being both senior Canadian officer and army commander, suggesting clairvoyantly that McNaughton concentrate on the former and become a government minister. Defence minister Ralston, no friend of McNaughton, enjoyed a happier meeting with Montgomery in November and thanked him for his cordiality, adding that "our boys membership in the 8th Army under your dynamic leadership is an honour indeed."[26] The ruckus over the Sicily incident nonetheless cloaked McNaughton's army command shortcomings in the eyes of the Canadian public.

Brooke saw things in a more balanced light despite his opinion that McNaughton and his government had made more fuss than all the rest of the Commonwealth together concerning the employment of Dominion forces. In Brooke's retrospective view, the McNaughton incident provided an excellent example of unnecessary clashes caused by failings in various personalities. In the first place, he considered it typical of Montgomery to try to stop McNaughton's visit for no valid reason, and to fail to realize, from the Commonwealth perspective, the need for McNaughton to visit the Canadians under his orders the first time they had been committed to action. Second, it was typical of Alexander not to have the strength of character to sit on Montgomery and stop him from being foolish. Third, it was typical of McNaughton's ultra-political outlook always to look for some slight to his position as a servant of the Canadian government. The bulk of the troubles that occurred in this area, Brooke ventured, did not emanate from Canada, but were born in McNaughton's brain. He was devoid of any kind of strategic outlook, and would rather have risked losing the war than agree to splitting Canadian forces. As Brooke correctly noted, the move of the 1st Canadian Division to the Mediterranean in place of the 3rd British Division had not been achieved without the application of considerable pressure on him from Canada, and it was therefore doubly unfortunate that through Montgomery's foolishness he had been prevented from visiting Simonds's division.[27]

Canadian operations in the Sicilian campaign ended on 10 August. In the course of the campaign the 1st Division group had acquitted itself well in overcoming German rearguard actions at Grammichele, Caltagirone, Piazza Armerina, and Valguarnera and going on to capture Assoro through surprise manoeuvre and Leonforte by hard fighting. The Battle for Agira, however, proved to be the greatest challenge to Canadian arms. Here Simonds insisted on having the divisional artillery fire a series of concentrations on specific targets and lay a smoke screen lifting 1,000 yards every twenty minutes. Unfortunately, attacking troops advanced only to see the fall of shot and smoke move forward too quickly, leaving them prey to fire from surviving enemy. Simonds later blamed this failure on Graham's troops for not following the artillery fire closely enough. Graham blamed an inflexible plan, but there was blame enough to go around as Graham committed only one battalion initially, then two more piecemeal, one behind the other, and finally ordered the withdrawal of the first battalion that had achieved some success. In contrast, the 2nd Brigade then attacked with properly coordinated artillery fire supporting two battalions up and a third right flanking to take Agira. On 5 August Simonds compensated for this controversial battle by unleashing an armoured-infantry strike force down the Salso valley to seize the high ground overlooking the Simeto River in a classic exploitation evincing all arms cooperation, speed, and surprise. Montgomery was more than pleased with his Canadians, writing that they are willing to learn and that they learn very fast. In due course Simonds would be a first-class division commander of one of the best divisions.[28]

For the invasion of Italy across the Strait of Messina, Operation "Baytown," the 1st Canadian Division supported by the Calgary tanks came under the British 13 Corps now commanded by Lieutenant General M.C. Dempsey. Dempsey had been BGS of the Canadian Corps and had gotten on well with Canadians. On 3 September 1943 his 13 Corps assaulted across the strait with the 1st Canadian Division on the right heading for Reggio Calabria and the British 5th Division supported by the Ontario armoured regiment on the left heading for Villa San Giovanni. The 1st Division then advanced eastward inland while the 5th Division followed the western coastal highway northwards. Five days later Italy capitulated, but the Germans continued to fight using the tactics they employed in Sicily against the British subsequent advance up both coasts of the Italian boot. Following "Baytown" the US Fifth Army on 9 September launched Operation "Avalanche," an amphibious landing at Salerno, which for lack of proper planning and timidity proved a disaster with the beachhead coming close to being eliminated. Alexander rejected Fifth Army plans to evacuate the beachhead on 11 September, and five days later advanced guards of the Eighth Army, having covered 300 miles in 17 days, made contact with Fifth Army elements 40 miles south of Salerno. In light of the mounting threat from the Eighth Army, the Germans loosened their cordon around Salerno. The slow pace of Montgomery's advance northwards to relieve Salerno has been criticized, but long supply lines and rugged terrain intervened and he remained determined not to increase Eighth Army casualties through poor planning and wasteful haste. More to the point, no effort had been made to synchronize "Baytown" with "Avalanche," thus leaving the initiative to the Germans whether or not to oppose "Baytown," which rendered it unreliable as a diversionary operation and too distant, if unopposed, to support Salerno 300 miles away. [29]

After Salerno the Eighth Army shifted its main axis of advance to the east coast, leaving the western axis to the US Fifth Army. The slog up the mountainous boot of Italy now became a matter of crossing one defended river line after another. Montgomery overcame the successive obstacles of the Fortore, Biferno, Trigno, and Sangro rivers in a methodical manner by building up superiority in every arm, amassing ammunition and supplies, and employing preliminary air and artillery bombardments aimed at obliteration. Infantry then assaulted in deliberate fashion, often under cover of darkness, with tanks following to provide direct fire support. By mid-November the Eighth Army reached the German winter defensive Bernhard Line across the narrowest part of Italy and based in the east on the Sangro. Montgomery proposed to crack this line with a left feint by Dempsey's 13 Corps and a main attack

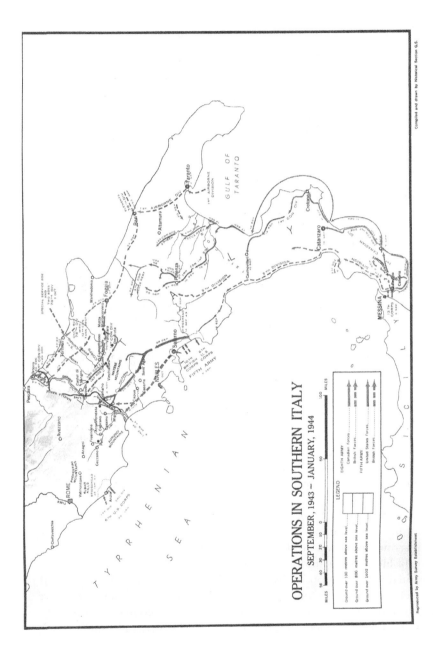

Map 9.4 Southern Italy, September 1943–January 1944 (C.P. Stacey, *The Canadian Army, 1939–1945,* 1948)

on the right by Lieutenant General C.W Allfrey's 5 Corps, to which the 1st Canadian Division now led by Major General Chris Vokes had passed under command. On 28 November the Eighth Army delivered a colossal crack that by darkness two days later secured the ridge overlooking the Sangro River, breaking the backbone of the winter line and driving the Germans back to the Moro River. As always in such operations, the object was to limit casualties through good planning and execution. Montgomery's soldiers knew that casualties were inevitable, but they went into battle fully confident that he had done everything in his power to cut down losses. Yet he couldn't control the weather, and in the flood and mud that prevailed in December casualties mounted. The subsequent advance by the 1st Canadian Division from the Moro to the Riccio Rivers, which controversially included urban warfare in Ortona, accounted for nearly one-quarter of Canadian casualties in the Italian campaign.[30]

Still, casualties in Italy appeared light compared with Dieppe and those anticipated for the invasion of France, and this assessment factored largely in the political calculus of Mackenzie King, who desperately wished to avoid a conscription crisis as happened in the Great War. Heavy casualties in France might be avoided by sending more troops to Italy. For this reason, as well as the Canadian public's clamour to see Canadian troops in action, and Crerar's personal quest to command a formation in battle, serious consideration began to be given to sending a Canadian corps to the Italian theatre. In August defence minister Ralston justified such a course to McNaughton on the grounds of gaining troop battle experience, corps headquarters training, and raising the morale of both the army and the Canadian people. The Canadian War Committee in the same month conveyed to Churchill a strong desire to send another division to Italy. In October, after a decision to bring back four divisions and 30 Corps headquarters to Britain for the Normandy invasion, the green light was given to have Crerar's 1 Canadian Corps and the 5th Armoured Division take over their equipment in the Eighth Army. This movement, Operation "Timberwolf," commenced in November and finished in January. McNaughton reluctantly bowed to the inevitable, which left the fate of First Canadian Army up in the air as it now comprised but one Canadian corps. Told that he could stay on as army commander, but not lead it in battle, he resigned in December 1943. McNaughton returned to Canada a bitter man bent on taking scalps.[31]

The dispatch of 1 Canadian Corps and the 5th Armoured Division to Italy came as a surprise to the 15th Army Group commander, General Alexander, who was never privy to what was essentially a political decision of the Canadian government. There was no need for another armoured division in the rugged terrain of Italy or an inexperienced corps headquarters. Major General Chris Vokes had reservations about his 1st Canadian Division serving under a corps commander and staff all inexperienced in the handling of an army corps in battle. The permanent grouping of an infantry and an armoured division under Canadian operational command also limited their useful employment in his view. If the army commander moved one, he had to move the other and employ them under the Canadian Corps commander. Permanently grouping divisions in a corps furthermore ran counter to the operational doctrine that corps were temporary formations in which large numbers of divisions could be concentrated in one corps for an attack and minimized in another for defence. This provided an army commander with maximum flexibility in planning that also called for commanders to think two below their own command level. The commander of a corps in determining tasks thus had to think in terms of brigades, although he would only give orders to the appropriate divisional commander. Unless an officer had practical experience in command of a brigade, of course, he could hardly think in terms of its proper employment in battle. As Crerar had never commanded a brigade or a division, but had been elevated from a senior staff appointment to corps command, Vokes considered it completely understandable that until the former proved himself as a corps commander, the Eighth Army commander was unlikely to place non-Canadian divisions under his command.[32]

Vokes went on to allege that after eight months in Italy the 1st Canadian Division had served in the British 5, 13, and 30 corps and gotten on amicably with their commanders and corps staff, but on 31 January 1944, when it came under command of 1 Canadian Corps things vastly changed. Paper instructions dealing with training and administration descended on the division in a continuous deluge that at times allegedly verged on the stupid. Crerar at the same time proved a stickler for having things done by the book rather than using the book as a guide. He was also obsessed with observing dress regulations to the point where Vokes noted that, "If he was improperly dressed I'm quite sure he felt naked." Crerar's insistence that troops had to be dressed according to regulations at all time contrasted starkly with the Eighth Army attitude of not caring what soldiers wore as long as their fighting efficiency was unimpaired. That Crerar arrived filled with preconceived ideas further irritated Vokes, who gained the impression that he regarded Canadian generals of a younger generation as ignorant upstarts who in spite of considerable operational experience really knew nothing. If Crerar had a sense of humour, it was never in evidence and contrasted sharply with the cheerfulness and ribald humour of General Oliver Leese, who took over command of the Eighth Army on Montgomery's departure to plan the invasion of Normandy. As Leese had commanded at all lower levels, both Vokes and Major General Bert Hoffmeister, GOC 5th Canadian Armoured Division, would continue to favour him over the commanders of 1 Canadian Corps. Vokes regretted leaving his competent British commanders for Crerar.[33]

Montgomery, equally surprised by the deployment of 1 Canadian Corps and the 5th Armoured Division, told Crerar on his arrival in Sicily on 29 October 1943 that another corps headquarters was not required until the new year. Picking up on an earlier McNaughton suggestion, he recommended that Crerar gain operational experience by taking command of the 1st Canadian Infantry Division after the transfer of Simonds, on Montgomery's suggestion, to command the 5th Armoured Division from 1 November. Despite his earlier pleas and expressions of willingness to do so, Crerar declined to step down to divisional command, which would have left him virtually following in the footsteps of Simonds and courting possible failure in field command. He now argued that the situation had changed and that he had been charged by his government to command 1 Canadian Corps to gain experience at that level. To Major General George Kitching, it was a great mistake on Crerar's part to not temporarily command the 1st Division because it would have given him his one opportunity to establish himself as a real commander instead of remaining "just a kindly figurehead."[34] Crerar nonetheless retained Brooke's confidence since his good showing in Exercise "Spartan" and had received approval from Alexander in theatre. Canadian government pressure to keep a Canadian in command of the First Canadian Army, even though it would have an Anglo-Canadian character with the addition of a British corps and up to 50 per cent British staff officers, also reinforced Crerar's position. His betrayal of McNaughton, whom the British had refused to accept, additionally ensured that he was next in line for army command.[35]

The more youthful Simonds, blessed with an incisive mind capable of reducing problems to their essentials in a flash, remained the long-run choice of Montgomery, who wanted to see Crerar tested in battle before determining his fitness for field army command. By now, of course, Simonds was a disciple of Montgomery and had proven himself in command of an infantry division. Crerar, left to observe the rising fortune of his once quite junior subordinate, appears not only to have grown increasingly envious, but also resentful at Simonds's switch of loyalty. The depth of Crerar's resentment manifested itself following his visit to Simonds's headquarters in Cassoria in late 1943. There he took a special interest in the design of Simonds's three-ton caravan office and sleeping quarter and subsequently dispatched a maintenance captain to ascertain its dimensions. The captain was in the caravan taking measurements when Simonds, who had expected the caravan to be readied for an important meeting, returned and brusquely kicked him out. The captain reported the incident to Crerar. who took it as a personal slight. In a letter that clearly sought to put Simonds in his place, Crerar reminded his junior of "a good many reasons, extending over a number of years" that should have induced in him "feelings, for me, of loyalty and appreciation." He then alleged that the episode indicated Simonds's nerves were "over-stretched and that impulse, rather than considered judgement," might begin to affect his decisions. Stating that he would be extremely worried if this were the case, Crerar went on to warn Simonds that he was reaching a position in the army when balance was becoming even more important to his future than brilliance. Incredibly, he then asked Simonds to undertake a self-examination and give him a diagnosis of his mental and physical condition.[36]

The caravan incident brought out the dark side of Crerar's kingmaker role in the selection of senior officers, a role honed by long experience in nasty bureaucratic infighting and behind-the-scenes manoeuvring in Ottawa. On the surface Crerar appeared to be a nice man, as Montgomery once put it, but there was an unpleasant mean streak in him and an element of terror in his handling of juniors.[37] He was also prepared to go to any length to keep a rival down. Not content to deal with Simonds entirely by himself, Crerar broached the issue with Montgomery, stating that he had serious cause to doubt Simonds's suitability for higher command, especially since he was next in line for corps command. Though Simonds possessed all the military brilliance for such command in the field, Crerar wrote, his "tense mentality, under further strain through increased rank and responsibilities," might see him go off the deep end "very disastrously indeed." To reinforce this point, Crerar confided that Simonds had always been high strung "with a tendency to be introspective, rather than objective, when faced with acute problems." Crerar's main concern, however, appears to have been Simonds's lack of deference to him. "Up until now I have always been able to handle Simonds successfully," he complained, "but since my arrival in Italy he gives the impression that he resents any control or direction on my part." In this regard, he pointed to Simonds's arbitrary 11 December removal of the 5th Division CRA, Brigadier R.O.G. Morton, two days after he had asked Crerar for his views and before the latter's response was forthcoming.[38] In his letter Crerar made no mention of the caravan incident.

Simonds defended his decision to relieve Morton on the operational grounds of being ordered to launch 11th Infantry Brigade into action at short notice. As Morton had shielded incompetent subordinates rather than weeding them out, Simonds was not prepared to risk men's lives by having him provide inadequate artillery support for attacking infantry. He consequently asked Crerar's CCRA to provide a more competent replacement, which he did. Simonds strongly disagreed with Crerar that Morton should not have been removed before he was tested in battle. The recalcitrant subordinate also rejected Crerar's allegations about his strained nerves and impulsiveness, maintaining that he was more than capable of keeping a level head and making sound decisions under stress.[39] He additionally saw that Crerar's real intent was to deliver a rebuke. Fortunately for Simonds, Montgomery responded to Crerar in characteristically straightforward manner, stating that he continued to hold the highest opinion of Simonds. Though he had tried to go off the rails once or twice when he first went into action with his division, he had been pulled back and taught his stuff. He further stressed that Simonds was a very valuable officer in the Canadian forces as there was no one else with his experience, adding that he must therefore be handled carefully and trained on. By way of comparison, Major General Chris Vokes, Simonds's replacement as GOC 1st Division, was not even in the same parish. "I am trying hard to teach him," lamented Montgomery, who actually liked Vokes, "but he will never be anything more than a good plain cook."[40]

Montgomery's assessment of Simonds from the perspective of field command in the middle of war was not enough to satisfy Crerar, who now impugned Simonds behind the scenes in the realm of "Canadian policies and business." Gathering all correspondence related to the caravan incident and the removal of Morton into a single file, he sent it off to Lieutenant General Ken Stuart, COS at Canadian Military Headquarters, for safekeeping under lock and key for possible future use in the "potential problem of Simonds." In his accompanying letter Crerar restated his fears that Simonds in an independent Canadian command might conduct "higher policy responsibilities ... very disastrously indeed," though performing well in operations. Crerar expressed particular concern about Simonds taking command of 1 Canadian Corps if something happened to him. In the same letter he remarked that Simonds's "egocentric state of mind" worried him to the extent that he had under confidential arrangements consulted medical and psychiatric authorities to obtain their advice on the fitness of Simonds continuing in command or assuming still higher responsibilities in view of his mental condition. According to Crerar, these authorities on perusing the correspondence related to the caravan incident and the removal of Morton determined that "in spite of marked egocentricity, Simonds ... could be relied upon to function effectively as a Senior Commander though very

preferably *not* as an independent Canadian force Commander." His sus-
picions thus confirmed by a highly questionable judgment by inexpert
authorities on field command, and one possibly aimed at pleasing the
boss, Crerar consigned his bureaucratic file as background to be locked
up, but to be read again at some future time when the employment of
the brilliant and comparatively young Simonds came up for consideration. He nonetheless accepted that Simonds was "the only present bet"
for corps command.[41]

Around the same time Crerar expressed his fears about Simonds as
a Canadian national commander, Montgomery was coming to his own
conclusions about Crerar's suitability for operational command of a field
army in war. On 23 December 1943, the day he learned of his appointment to command the 21st Army Group and Allied invasion ground
forces, Montgomery wrote to Brooke: "The more I think of Harry Crerar
the more I am convinced that he is quite unfit to command an army in
the field at present ... He has already (from Sicily) started to have rows
with Canadian generals under me; he wants a lot of teaching." Montgomery suggested that Dempsey be given command of the First Canadian Army instead, as he was well liked by Canadians, who would gladly
accept a British general whom they knew and trusted rather than have
their troops mishandled by an inexperienced general of their own. Crerar still had much to learn on the practical side of war, in Montgomery's
view, and would receive many shocks before learning this properly. In the
same letter Montgomery recommended to Brooke that Simonds be sent
back to Britain to command 2 Canadian Corps immediately as he was
"quite first class." As soon as the Canadians produce their own general
capable of exercising competent army command, Montgomery added,
he can take over at once.[42] Crerar's earlier refusal during the administrative buildup of 1 Canadian Corps to take temporary command of the 1st
Division to gain operational experience, as Montgomery strongly urged
him to do, likely influenced this assessment.

It is also conceivable that Montgomery heard about troop dissatis-
faction resulting from the excessive paperwork produced by 1 Corps
headquarters and Crerar's obsessive fixation with Canadian soldiers following dress regulations to the letter. Arguably, the only area in which he
felt confident, Crerar clearly disapproved of the Eighth Army's relaxed
approach to dress in the field and forbade the practice of drivers painting
pictures and names of girlfriends on vehicles. When Vokes protested that
this personalization encouraged driver pride, Crerar in bloody-minded
fashion amended his orders to permit the painting of a name one inch
high on the dashboard where only the driver could see it. Montgomery, in contrast, was anything but strict in such matters and boasted that

he only once issued an order on Eighth Army dress. Ironically, this was prompted by the occasion of a naked Canadian soldier leaning out of his truck and doffing a Sicilian top hat in sweeping salute as the army commander drove by. After a good laugh, Montgomery issued the order: "Top hats will not be worn in Eighth Army."[43]

Unlike Crerar, who remained coldly remote to soldiers in the ranks, Montgomery enjoyed a close, almost magical, rapport with his troops. According to US General Omar Bradley, "Even Eisenhower with all his engaging ease could never stir American troops to the rapture with which Monty was welcomed by his."[44] His hold upon the hearts and minds of his soldiers was indeed remarkable and he took pains to visit them at every opportunity. For Canadians the most appealing thing about him was his lack of remoteness. Six levels of command existed between the rifleman and Monty, yet to the private he seemed to be his own personal commander with no one else really in between. This incredible ability of Monty to project his personality over the heads of all his subordinate formation commanders, right down to the forward trench, made him a soldier's general. He was only ever referred to as Monty by one and all. When gathered with his soldiers in an orchard or open field they were completely at ease with him in a simple community of friendship.[45] The drill was always the same, he would arrive in an open car in front of formed-up brigades or units, hold up his hands, and ask troops to break ranks and gather round his vehicle. Pictures of enthusiastic soldiers eagerly running toward him, often thought to be Tommies, were in fact Canadians. Montgomery made every effort to find out the backgrounds of Canadian troops in order to talk with them about their hometowns and provinces. According to Hoffmeister, on some of his visits to units Monty would be talking to a commander but really be more interested in engaging his driver and finding out the name of his hometown. On learning, for example, that it was Saskatoon, Saskatchewan, Monty would produce a Saskatoon newspaper and hand it to the driver. Of course it was a setup, but news of a lowly soldier getting such a personal gift from the Eighth Army commander spread like wildfire, reinforcing Montgomery's image among Canadian troops.[46]

Hoffmeister, who distinguished himself as commander of the 5th Canadian Armoured Division, expressed great pride in being one of Montgomery's disciples and had approved of the latter's housecleaning of the Canadian Corps in 1942. He also marvelled at how his role model could inspire soldiers and get the best out of them. To Hoffmeister, Montgomery was a bit of a showman, but "a darned good psychologist" who had a great flare for dealing with people. Canadian soldiers were always delighted to see him and he had a knack for always saying the right thing at the right time. After meeting him the troops invariably marched back to their areas with their tails in the air. It was always like a breath of fresh air, Hoffmeister related, to have Monty inspect his division. So long as he felt you were giving your utmost, Monty was your best friend. Hoffmeister's loyalty to Montgomery and pride in the Eighth Army ran deep. He also admired Leese and other British commanders under whom he served and sought to emulate their human touch. He further appreciated the informality of the Eighth Army in which verbal orders held sway. Hoffmeister found British units either under command or in support of Canadians to contain tremendous people with whom a great mutual understanding and rapport developed. "We were," he stressed, "very proud to be Canadians fighting with the Eighth Army and somewhat depressed to learn we would be transferred to North-West Europe. In working with Canadians, things were stuffier and a little more formal than they were working with the British."[47]

The 1st Canadian Army Tank Brigade, later 1st Canadian Armoured Brigade, especially saw itself as part of the Eighth Army fabric with its regiments paired with divisions according to their allocated tasks. Thus in Sicily the Three Rivers Regiment supported the 1st Canadian Infantry Division while the Ontario Regiment supported the British 5th Division. This pattern of employment continued throughout the Italian campaign with the 1st Canadian Armoured Brigade seldom serving alongside major Canadian formations. At one point, as part of 13 Corps the brigade served with the Fifth US Army supporting both the 8th Indian and 4th British divisions. As the most experienced armoured brigade in the British order of battle, it remained much in demand. The formation also enjoyed being separated from the main Canadian force and actually preferred fighting alongside British, Indian, and Ghurka troops because it escaped the "chicken shit" with which Crerar's troops were afflicted. For most Canadians serving in Italy the departure of Monty was a severe blow as he embodied the heart and soul of the Eighth Army. When he flew to England on 31 December the army lost some of its spirit. [48] On 1 February 1944 Crerar's 1 Canadian Corps finally took over a static sector on the Adriatic front. On 3 March he turned over his command to his successor. After just a month in the line he returned to Britain without having gained any operational experience in a major corps action.[49] In fact, the 1 Canadian Corps would not even fight a corps battle before the Canadian government commenced agitating in May 1944 for its early repatriation to First Canadian Army.

Chapter Ten

Handling Canadians in Normandy

From late 1942 the First Canadian Army had been earmarked for exploitation operations, breaking out from a bridgehead, in the invasion of France. Indeed, in Exercise "Spartan" it had practised for this spearhead role, which Mackenzie King never really warmed to owing to fear of heavy casualties. On 17 June 1943 General Paget, then C-in-C Home Forces, told McNaughton that the latest invasion plan envisaged the First Canadian Army commanding its own assault divisions and following them in to enlarge the bridgehead. A new plan completed in July by Lieutenant General F.E. Morgan, COS to the Supreme Allied Commander (COSSAC), projected a Canadian army of five divisions centrally deployed after the assault phase between a six-division British army on the left and a seven-division American army on the right. First Canadian Army retained a prominent role as late as December 1943. At that time the COSSAC plan called for a three-division seaborne assault on a thirty-mile front by the First US Army, initially composed of one British and one American corps. Once two British corps were securely ashore, the First Canadian Army was to land and take them under command. Both armies were then to come under the British commander of the 21st Army Group.[1]

Montgomery discarded the COSSAC plan when he assumed command of the 21st Army Group in January 1944. He called instead for an initial assault by five divisions, protected on both flanks by airborne landings, on a frontage sufficient to accommodate two attacking armies, the First US and the Second British, each of two corps and one airborne division. The 1st Infantry Division of the American V Corps was to assault Omaha beach while the 4th Infantry Division of VII Corps landed on Utah beach. The 50th (Northumbrian) Division of the British 30 Corps was to assault Gold beach while the British 1 Corps launched 3rd Canadian Division against Juno beach and the 3rd British Division against

Sword beach. Behind the First US and the Second British armies were to come two "follow-up" armies, the First Canadian and the US Third, also operating under the 21st Army Group. Believing that an eastern breakout as planned by COSSAC was less likely than one farther west, Montgomery as early as 21 January at the first Supreme Commander's Conference stated that the task of Anglo-Canadian forces would be to shield American forces operating against Cherbourg and the Brittany peninsula from the enemy main body approaching from the east. Ideally, Montgomery sought to entice the Germans to counter-attack him on ground of his own choosing as he had done at Alamein, making the enemy commit reserves on a broad front and then hitting him narrowly with husbanded Allied reserves. Above all, he intended to retain the initiative and avoid serious setbacks.[2]

With his elevation to army group command Montgomery became a more distant figure, although he still worked his magic with troops of all nationalities before D-Day. By the end of May 1944 and travelling by special train, he visited over a million soldiers commonly drawn up in hollow-square, ten thousand at a time, speaking to them by loudspeaker from the hood of a jeep. His effect on American troops proved surprisingly effective as they appreciated his friendly manner, lack of pomp, and the news that he had visited every one of their outfits.[3] That said, he now also had to deal with two American generals, Omar Bradley and George Patton, in his group of four field army commanders. Patton had developed a maniacal obsession over rivalry with Montgomery in Sicily, where his fixation on getting to Messina as the price of providing flank protection for the 1st Canadian Infantry Division had left Simonds totally unimpressed. Other Canadians, like Todd, intensely despised his leadership for his slapping of two enlisted men in hospital. Montgomery had his reservations about Patton, but also recognized that he had commanded a field army with flair. In comparison, he found Bradley dull, but conscientious, loyal, and dependable. His British field army commander, Dempsey, though called a yes-man by Patton, possessed a legendary eye for ground, a prodigious memory, and an incisive mind. He also ran a high-calibre headquarters and was, behind his quiet manner, completely unflappable. Crerar, on the other hand, worried Montgomery as he retained grave doubts about him as a battlefield leader. Also, the First Canadian Army had drifted aimlessly for months after McNaughton's departure. Prior to end-January the overstaffed headquarters floundered without command direction.[4] In these circumstances there was no question of giving such an army a leading role.

With the role of the First Canadian Army changed from exploitation to follow up, Canadian participation in the D-Day landing devolved to the 3rd Canadian Infantry Division and the 2nd Canadian Armoured Brigade under the operational control of the Second British Army. That the First Canadian Army had no real commander at the time doubtless influenced the final decision on its operational employment. Between McNaughton's departure on 26 December 1943 and Crerar's arrival as General Officer Commanding-in-Chief on 20 March 1944, the First Canadian Army remained essentially leaderless largely by design. On Crerar's advice, Lieutenant General Stuart had been appointed acting commander on 27 December 1943, but only as a secondary appointment to his principal employ as COS, CMHQ in London. Up to this time Stuart had been as CGS in Ottawa, which senior position, shockingly, remained vacant until 3 May 1944. Stuart refused to get involved in details of operational plans allegedly for security and reasons of ill health, but more likely because he left First Canadian Army command to Crerar in distant Italy and acted only as a caretaker responding to the latter's direction.[5] This odd situation prevailed until Simonds took command of 2 Canadian Corps on 30 January 1944 and temporarily assumed de facto operational leadership of the Canadian Army remaining in Britain. In terms of staff employment and commanding a large formation in action, Simonds was Canada's most experienced general and still Montgomery's favourite for ultimate army command. Not surprisingly, his request for comments on his corps operational policy directive and plan for a study period 13–18 March drew a favourable response from Montgomery.[6]

In assuming command of 2 Canadian Corps Simonds finally replaced Sansom, who, since his dismal performance on Exercise "Spartan," had been protected from removal by McNaughton, in spite of GHQ Home Force recommendations to the contrary. Sansom had commanded 2 Canadian Corps since its formation on 15 January 1943 and led the corps in "Spartan," which practised the First Canadian Army in breaking out from a secure bridgehead in what McNaughton described as a full-scale invasion of the Continent. Oddly, for this exercise, McNaughton grouped his armoured divisions under Sansom, his most inexperienced corps commander. Sansom's 2 Canadian Corps thus comprised the 5th Canadian and Guards armoured divisions, each of one armoured and one infantry brigade. In the event, traffic snarl-ups, gasoline supply problems, and signals shortcomings all contributed to the lacklustre performance of 2 Corps. In a highly dubious move Sansom also split his two armoured divisions, grouping their infantry brigades intended for tank support under the 5th Canadian Armoured Division and their two armoured brigades under the Guards Armoured. Although McNaughton countermanded this highly questionable grouping, his action came too late to prevent it, with the result that Guards Armoured tanks were left without infantry support and notionally destroyed by umpires. This did not prevent Sansom, however, from preparing an adverse report upon Major General C.R.S. Stein, GOC 5th Armoured Division, who was later replaced by Simonds in October 1943 after a medical board diagnosed him as suffering from "progressive anxiety neurosis."[7]

Despite his reputation as a partygoer who gave no direction bordering on incompetence, Sansom retained command of 2 Canadian Corps for over nine months before Simonds took over. Immediately upon his arrival in London, Simonds met personally with Montgomery, newly appointed Allied ground force commander for the invasion of France, after which he swept into 2 Corps like a new broom. Reluctant to deal with unknown quantities and unimpressed by the performance of key 2 Canadian Corps staff officers, he replaced the BGS, the CCRA, and the CCRE[8] with his own team from Italy. This included his CRA, Brigadier A.B. Matthews, and his CRE, Brigadier G. Walsh. He also brought on board a new BGS, N.E. Rodger, newly promoted Brigadier E.R. Suttie to command 2 Canadian AGRA, and Brigadier Wyman to command 2nd Armoured Brigade. Of seven senior staff officers at 2 Corps headquarters only two retained their jobs, the Chief Signals Officer, Brigadier S.F. Clark, and the Deputy Adjutant and Quartermaster General, Brigadier H.V.D. Laing. Within the 4th Armoured Division veteran officers of the Italian campaign assumed command of the 4th Armoured and 10th Infantry Brigades. Simonds's former GSO 1 in the 1st Canadian Infantry Division and later commander of the 11th Brigade, 5th Canadian Armoured Division, thirty-three-year-old Major General G. Kitching, took over the 4th Armoured Division on 1 March.[9]

Crerar did not arrive in England until 16 March 1944 after having turned over command to Lieutenant General E.L.M. Burns thirteen days before. He had commanded 1 Canadian Corps for thirty-six days in static operations. In February, realizing that he was not going to gain any operational experience in major corps action in Italy, and fearful that he would not get command of the now half-British First Canadian Army, he had requested an earlier return to England. Reassured by Stuart and Brooke that a March arrival would be fine, he focused, not just on 1 Canadian Corps in Italy, but on the detailed control of the First Canadian Army from afar. On 9 March Tac HQ First Canadian Army became operational and within hours of landing in England seven days later, Crerar ordered a new caravan and office trailer, specially designed by his staff,[10] to be used as his tactical headquarters. Crerar immediately set about fine-tuning his headquarters for operations, but, true to form, found the pull of policy and personal influence irresistible. Insisting on his rights as a Canadian national commander, he took umbrage at not being informed of Eisenhower's inspection of the 3rd Canadian Infantry Division training as part of the British 1 Corps. For reasons related to casualties and command, he also kept himself abreast of all issues concerning Canadians fighting in distant Italy. Among other non-operational matters, he even dealt with the appointment of the RMC Commandant in Kingston, Canada, and such things as dress standards and car flags for senior officers. That he insisted in getting involved in peripheral issues like these suggests the difficulty he had in focusing entirely upon operations. In contrast to his assurance in handling Canadian constitutional matters, he remained unsure of himself in the operational sphere despite repeating variants of Montgomery's teachings.[11]

Montgomery and other British formation commanders were not plagued by numerous non-operational concerns that Crerar seemingly embraced with relish, since these were mostly handled by army headquarters headed by Brooke. A similar situation prevailed in US Army circles where General George Marshall exercised supreme command. Moreover, in operational matters the British and Americans willingly accepted the intermingling of field formations and commando units despite teething problems. For example, in Operation "Torch" the Eastern Task Force that assaulted under British Lieutenant General K.A.N. Anderson comprised a brigade from the British 78th Division and a brigade from the US 34th Infantry Division. Anderson's First Army eventually consisted of the US II Corps, the British 5 Corps, British 9 Corps, and the French XIX Corps. At Salerno the US Fifth Army under Lieutenant General Mark Clark comprised the British 10 Corps and the US VI Corps, which assaulted with the British 46th and 56th Divisions and the US 36th Infantry Division respectively. At Anzio on 22 January 1944 a similar pattern played out with the invasion force including the US 3rd Infantry Division, the British 1st Infantry Division, the 46th Royal Tank Regiment, the US 751st Tank Battalion, the 504th Parachute Infantry Regiment, the 509th Parachute Infantry Battalion, and British Commando and US Army Ranger units. Montgomery in the Eighth Army had also been used to working with New Zealand, South African, Australian, and Indian divisions, flexibly deploying them as the situation warranted. Indeed, the South Africans did not wish to put all their eggs in one basket by uniting their divisions. While the Australians had earlier tried to keep their forces together, they accepted fragmentation owing to operational imperatives and the practical aspects of field command.[12] The ability to easily regroup divisions increased the effectiveness of major army operations by efficiently matching troop strength to tasks.

Montgomery has been portrayed as persistently refusing to recognize Crerar's constitutional status as a Canadian commander. This is not entirely true as he told Stuart that he agreed that a Canadian commander must have the right of appeal to the Canadian government and be responsible to it for the general welfare of Canadian troops. He disagreed, however, that this officer should be the commander of the First Canadian Army as this was a full-time job in itself with little room for distractions. Non-operational administrative involvements were better handled by Stuart as COS, CMHQ, which had been set up intentionally in the Great War to relieve field commanders of such responsibilities. Crerar saw CMHQ as the rear echelon of the First Canadian Army and the forward echelon of Ottawa army HQ, formerly headed by Stuart as CGS, which position was now left vacant until 3 May 1944. In these circumstances, with Stuart now heading CMHQ, it is quite understandable why Montgomery viewed Stuart as more properly the Canadian national representative than Crerar. Montgomery went on to state that while he would attempt to keep all Canadian formations under Crerar's command, he could give no guarantee as a different operational grouping might be necessary for success. In such a case he promised to consult with Crerar beforehand, admitting that the latter had the right to refer any point to his government whenever he liked through CMHQ, which tacitly acknowledged his different status from a British army commander.[13]

This approach seemed eminently practical and workable to Stuart, who told Crerar that Montgomery "fully recognized the constitutional issues involved," but disagreed on their interpretation. Confessing that he found it most difficult to argue against Montgomery's point, Stuart wrote, "In fact, I did not attempt to do so because I feel that he is probably right."[14] He later suggested that as there always tended to be a conflict between constitutional and military concerns, any such disagreement should be decided in favour of the military side if it risked jeopardizing the success of an operation. Warning against becoming too "bloody minded" about constitutional issues, he added that he knew Crerar would not agree "with Monty's interpretation of our respective jobs."[15] In this he was most certainly right, for Crerar angrily retorted that he did not accept that Stuart was the Canadian national representative, but rather the opposite of the CIGS, despite Stuart no longer being CGS, but the COS, CMHQ. Crerar went on to assert that Stuart had no responsibility to the Canadian government for the tactical and administrative problems of Canadian field formations placed in combination with British forces.[16] This made no sense at all as Crerar had earlier proposed that CMHQ concentrate on policy issues, thus freeing the army commander to concentrate on operations. As Ralston noted, too, Crerar also bristled at the idea of Stuart, who was his junior, occupying any position that might appear superior to his own.[17] One suspects that what Crerar really sought under the guise of constitutionality was to be Supreme Canadian Commander in total control of all aspects of Canada's army overseas as well as in Ottawa.[18] In this regard, Canada was out of step with the British and Americans, whose most senior army generals did not assume field command abroad. The exception appears to have been Lord Gort, who left his position as CIGS to command the BEF, which may have been the model for McNaughton and Crerar. Regardless, it was a mistake to allow field commanders to be saddled with non-operational involvements.

In the lead-up to D-Day, Crerar's headquarters laid plans for taking over the eastern sector and advancing to capture Le Havre and Rouen. This included concurrent planning with headquarters 2 Canadian Corps, which was more likely to be committed to Normandy operations before the First Canadian Army. Although the 3rd Canadian Division and 2nd Canadian Armoured Brigade had been training under the British 1 Corps since July, Crerar made a point as Canadian national commander of following their training activities and getting reports from them. In spite of his having no operational responsibility whatsoever, this appeared to be his first priority, one even taking precedence over army matters. Judging from tensions with Simonds over operational planning, however, it seems that Crerar remained unsure of himself in his role as army commander.[19] He also felt compelled to ask Montgomery for advice about an incident that happened three weeks before D-Day. During a drinking celebration for a medal award, Brigadier Wyman in a raucous conversation overheard by a local milkman may have compromised the secrecy of invasion plans. Unsure as to whether Wyman should be replaced as commander of the 2nd Canadian Armoured Brigade at this late date, Crerar referred the matter to Montgomery, questioning whether he should court-martial Wyman or simply dress him down instead. In the interests of operational continuity Montgomery recommended the latter action, one which a less insecure Crerar could have taken himself. In contrast, Montgomery made decisions easily, even banning Mackenzie King from observing the 3rd Canadian Infantry Division in Exercise "Fabius" on the grounds that non-professional people should not be about. He later made it up to King over lunch on 18 May, gaining his acceptance that winning battles and saving lives trumped constitutional niceties.[20]

On D-Day the 3rd Canadian Infantry Division Group, which included the 2nd Canadian Armoured Brigade, landed as part of Lieutenant General J.T. Crocker's British 1 Corps. The Canadians advanced farther inland than any other Allied formation on the day, but were driven back from Authie for lack of artillery support by a surprise German counter-attack on 7 June. Here the lead 9th Infantry Brigade commander, Brigadier D.G. Cunningham and his artillery adviser, Lt. Col. H.S. Griffin, CO 14th Field Regiment, had not adequately planned artillery support in accordance with Montgomery's teachings.[21] Five days later the British 7th Armoured Division encountered the Tiger tank at Villers-Bocage and after taking heavy tank casualties received an unfortunate order to withdraw. On 14 June Montgomery suspended all offensive operations for forty-eight hours in order to regain balance. Neither were serious setbacks, only lost opportunities, and he intended to retain the initiative. As Caen had not yet fallen as originally planned, he determined to carry it by directing Dempsey to launch a series of "colossal cracks"or alternate thrusts through right and left hooks to shake the city loose. News that 2 SS Panzer Corps had arrived on the front increased the urgency to attack, thereby drawing enemy armour in, rather than let it be committed at a time and place of the enemy's choosing. Montgomery's intention to attract more massive German armoured reserves produced the first major British offensive, Operation "Epsom," which saw the British 8 Corps strike southeast toward the Orne River on a four-mile front between Carpiquet and Rauray with three fresh divisions, the 15th (Scottish), 43rd (Wessex), and the British 11th Armoured.[22]

Assisted by supporting attacks from the British 30 Corps on the right and 1 Corps on the left, 8 Corps had some 550 tanks and over 700 artillery pieces, plus the supporting fire of three RN cruisers and the 2nd Tactical Air Force. Preliminary operations commenced on 25 June with a 30 Corps attack to seize Rauray. The 8 Corps attack that aimed at capturing bridges over the Odon River kicked off on 26 June, but bad weather limited the effectiveness of air support. German resistance also proved so tough that by the end of the first day "Epsom" had gained only four muddy miles. The 30 Corps managed to take Rauray on 27 June, and that same day, after decisively repulsing a panzer counter-attack, 8 Corps seized a bridge over the Odon. Alarmed by the development of the British threat, the Germans strained every sinew to counter it. When 8 Corps seized the bridge over the Odon the commander of Seventh German Army frantically ordered an immediate counter-attack by 2 SS Panzer Corps and committed suicide several hours later. The counter-attack went in on 29 June but foundered under concentrated artillery fire that turned it into a rout. The 8 Corps subsequently consolidated in anticipation of further strong panzer counter-attacks. In the five days of "Epsom" 8 Corps incurred some 4,020 casualties, which led Montgomery to terminate the operation on 30 June largely because he recognized that the

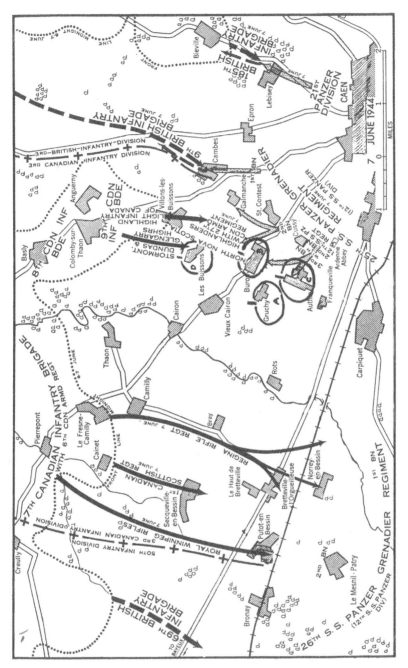

Map 10.1 12th SS counter-attack, 7 June 1944 (C.P. Stacey, *The Victory Campaign: The Operation in North-West Europe, 1944–1945*, 1966)

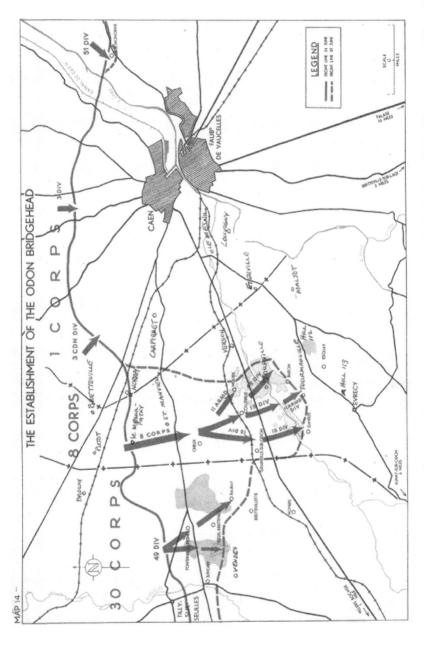

Map 10.2 Operation "Epsom," the establishment of the Odon Bridgehead, 26–30 June 1944 (Mongomery of Alamein, Field Marshal the Viscount, *Memoirs* [London: Collins, 1958])

British Army was a wasting asset and had not the manpower to replace heavy losses.[23]

While "Epsom" did not attain its territorial objectives, the Germans had been forced to use all available reserves to stem the onslaught, which only succeeded in pushing back, but not eliminating, the Odon bridgehead. The hasty and premature commitment of 2 SS Panzer Corps, ordered to France from the Eastern Front, fatally cost the Germans the initiative in Normandy and left them unable to wrest it from Montgomery. From "Epsom" up to the First US Army breakout on 25 July, German reactions saw between 520 and 725 panzers continuously deployed against the British sector, whereas during this same period the Americans rarely faced more than 190.[24] Four of the seven divisions opposing the British and Canadians were also elite SS, which fielded two more infantry battalions than normal panzer divisions. In the Panther battalion of their panzer regiments, moreover, the Germans evinced a qualitative superiority in armour, reflecting Eastern Front experience. The Sherman 75mm could not pierce the frontal armour of a Panther and could deal with a Tiger only from the rear or point-blank from enfilade. The US 76mm tank gun introduced later was not much of an improvement. Fortunately for their offensive capacity, the British possessed the only Allied tank capable of taking on Panthers and Tigers, which also suffered from mechanical unreliability. The Firefly, a Sherman variant in which the British 17-pounder anti-tank gun had been mounted, could easily penetrate the frontal armour of the heaviest German tanks with Sabot shot at 2,000 yards. Although the Firefly was initially issued on a limited scale and had to wait for a good high explosive round, it proved a formidable enough weapon for the Germans to seek it out as a prime target. Despite these disadvantages, crews loved it and the Firefly enabled Second British Army to take on a weight of German panzer might that less well-gunned tanks over open ground could hardly have handled.[25]

Still determined to capture Caen, Montgomery on 30 June directed Dempsey to mount a new offensive, Operation "Charnwood," to take the city. Crocker, in turn, ordered the 3rd Canadian Division to take both Carpiquet village and the airfield as preliminary to a three-divisional assault directly on Caen. For this operation, named "Windsor," the 8th Canadian Infantry Brigade, augmented by the Royal Winnipeg Rifles and supported by Fort Garry Horse tanks, had roughly 760 guns providing artillery support. The 16-inch guns of HMS *Rodney* assisted with preparatory bombardment. Additional support included heavy 4.2-inch mortars, three squadrons of "special armour," and two squadrons of tank-busting Typhoon fighter-bombers on call. Despite this massive firepower, fierce enemy resistance prevented the Canadians from taking more than the village of Carpiquet and a portion of the airfield. Crocker attributed the limited success of "Windsor" to a lack of control and leadership by the GOC 3rd Canadian Infantry, Major General R.F.L Keller. On 5 July 1944 Crocker informed Dempsey that Keller "was not really fit temperamentally and perhaps physically (he is a man who has the appearance of having lived pretty well) for such a responsible command." Crocker expressed regret at having to report that the 3rd Canadian Division, which he had the great privilege to have under his command, had "lapsed into a very nervy state" after the excitement of the initial assault phase had passed. Except for the 7th Brigade, which stood considerable enemy pressure with great fortitude, the division "became jumpy and ... far too quick on the trigger," submitting exaggerated reports of enemy activity and its own problems. In Crocker's view, the "steadying hand required to combat this general attitude of despondency was not forthcoming; indeed the state of the Division was a reflection of the state of its Commander who was obviously not standing up to the strain and showed signs of fatigue and nervousness (one might almost say fright) which were patent for all to see."[26] The trouble with Keller, his CRA, Brigadier P.A.S. Todd, would later say, was that "Keller was yeller."[27]

In Crocker's view, the Carpiquet operation reflected a lack of control and leadership from the top. More divisional guidance should have been forthcoming when things started to go wrong. Dempsey, who earlier observed the 3rd Division's "highly strung state" in the first three or four days ashore and its loss of offensive spirit thereafter, agreed with Crocker. Dempsey had also questioned Keller's performance when his division was sent reeling back by German counter-attack on 7 June and felt compelled to tell him the next day to get a grip of his artillery and armour.[28] In similar fashion, Operation "Windsor" had not been well handled, and Dempsey told Montgomery that it proved quite conclusively Keller was not fit to command a division. At a time when the situation demanded a clear-cut decision, Dempsey wrote, the GOC failed to take a grip. Blaming Keller for failure to properly control and inspire his formation, Dempsey further remarked that had it been a British division he would have recommended his removal at once.[29] Montgomery in a letter to Crerar concurred, giving his opinion that Keller was not good enough to command the magnificent soldiers of a Canadian division, but left official action to be taken by Canadians.[30] In a letter to Brooke, Montgomery observed that Keller had not proved himself fit to command a division as he is unable to get the best out of his soldiers, who are grand chaps. On learning that Crerar had once suggested Keller for corps command, he called it "a quite absurd idea as brigade command was his ceiling."[31] In fact, Crerar actively considered Keller as a

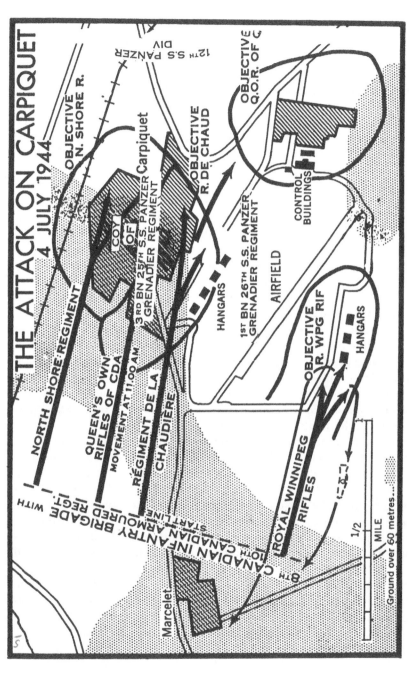

Map 10.3 Operation "Windsor," the attack on Carpiquet, 4 July 1944 (C.P. Stacey, *The Victory Campaign: The Operation in North-West Europe, 1944–1945*, 1966)

replacement commander for 1 Canadian Corps in Italy and remained irritated that the British wanted him fired.

In recommending the firing of a Canadian division commander the British were even-handed. As a result of the lost opportunity and needlessly unsuccessful battle for Viller-Bocage in mid-June, Dempsey had begun to doubt the leadership of both the British 7th Armoured Division commander, Major General G.W.E.J. Erskine, and the 30 Corps Commander, Lieutenant General G.C. Bucknall. Dempsey's concern proved to be well founded as Bucknall's later performance in Operation "Bluecoat" launched on 27 July exposed his lack of personal drive, initiative, and failure to carry out orders. Dempsey sacked him on 3 August along with Erskine and Brigadier Robert "Looney" Hinde of the 7th Armoured Division. Similarly, in the battle for Caen the performance of the 51st (Highland) Division came to be questioned as it did not fight with the required determination. In the considered opinion of Crocker, Dempsey, and Montgomery, the division failed in every assigned operation. To Montgomery, blame for the division not being battle-worthy lay entirely with the divisional commander, Major General D.C. Bullen-Smith. He had neither adequately prepared the division for Normandy operations nor exercised sufficient grip over his subordinates, who as desert veterans thought they possessed superior knowledge of training and tactics. In fact, too little attention had been paid to the tactical training needed to fight the Germans in Normandy. Montgomery not only relieved Bullen-Smith, but actually considered returning the entire division to England for further training. Fortunately, a new commander, Major General T.G. Rennie, revitalized the division in time to take part in battle under the 2 Canadian Corps.[32]

In contrast to his treatment of Simonds, Crerar maintained an almost unshakeable faith in Keller, whom he considered a first-class commander. Keller had graduated from RMC, where, presumably for his toughness or bluster, he had been nicknamed "Captain Blood." He attended staff college Camberley a year ahead of Simonds on the same course as Captain F.W. de Guingand, who later became Montgomery's COS. Crerar in June 1942 had placed Keller first in line within the 1 Canadian Corps for appointment to command a division. For whatever reason, he did not rate Brigadier Salmon, regarded by many as outstanding and the best-qualified officer available to command a division in the field, quite as high as Keller for promotion.[33] Even when in March 1943 he felt compelled to counsel Keller on alleged "misbehaviour in the matter of overindulgence" as reported by British and Canadian general officers, Crerar maintained that he had no doubt as to his abilities as a commander.[34] On 16 May 1944, still convinced of Keller's tactical and man-management skills, he wrote: "I believe that Keller would make a two-fisted and competent Corps Commander in the field."[35] Keller's assault landing training of 3rd Division within the British 1 Corps apparently gave Crerar a certain sense of personal satisfaction. "The technique ... employed by Second British Army of which 1 British Corps was part," he boasted, was "almost in its entirety, that developed by me when 3 Can Inf Div was under my command in 1 Cdn Corps."[36] All that said, the attack upon Carpiquet on 4 July exposed Keller's shortcomings as a division commander and defied Crerar's assessment.

The day after the attack on Carpiquet, Crocker issued orders for Operation "Charnwood" to be carried out on 8 July by the British 3rd Division on the left, the 59th (Staffordshire) Division in the centre, and the 3rd Canadian Division on the right. Crocker's plan unfolded in a five-phase concentric advance: first, an assault by the British 3rd and 59th Infantry Divisions from the north in a sustained drive on Caen; second, an attack by the 3rd Canadian Division from the northwest to secure the area as far south as Authie; third, a general push into Caen and onto the line Franqueville-Ardenne; fourth, the final reduction of Carpiquet and mopping-up to the River Orne; and fifth, consolidation and further divisional thrusts to obtain bridgeheads over the river. Support laid on for the attack included special armour from the British 79th Division, the firepower of 3 and 4 AGRA, and naval gunfire from several ships of the RN. "Charnwood" also saw heavy bombers of Bomber Command employed for the first time in a close support role on the battlefield. Apart from their positive effect upon morale, however, the bombers yielded less-than-expected tactical advantage. Because of a required 6,000-yard troop safety distance, the rectangular target area finally selected (4,000 yards long and 1,500 wide) lay well behind the German forward ring of fortified villages and contained few enemy defensive positions at all. That the ground attack did not commence until 0420 on 8 July, long after 467 bombers dropped 2,562 tons of bombs between 2150 and 2230 the previous evening, further degraded their impact and served to alert the enemy of the imminence of the attack. A series of nasty close-quarter battles for desperately defended villages and suburbs followed, but by 1600 on 9 July Crocker's divisions had cleared the northern portion of Caen. Although the city southern suburbs and the Falaise plain still lay in German hands, the Anglo-Canadians had scored a symbolic victory.[37]

"Charnwood" added another twist to the command situation within the 3rd Canadian Division when Keller on 10 July called on Crerar to discuss the removal of Brigadier Cunningham from command of the 9th Brigade. Keller explained that such a change was necessary and he had so informed Cunningham. His stated reasons were the latter's failure to

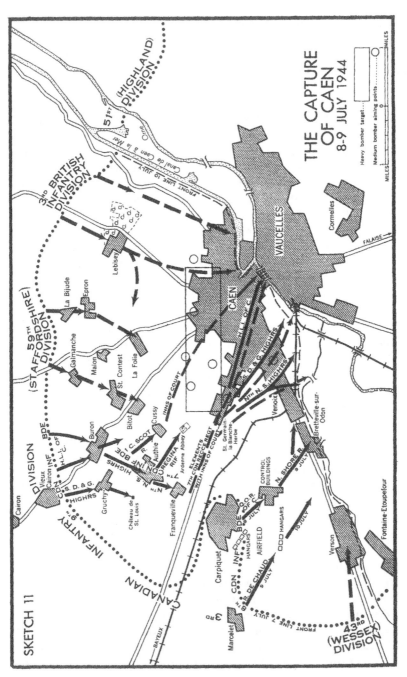

Map 10.4 The Capture of Caen, 8-9 July 1944 (C.P. Staccy, *The Victory Campaign: The Operation in North-West Europe, 1944–1945,* 1966)

get on and hesitancy to use reserves promptly and aggressively, which had squandered opportunities to exploit and increased casualties. Specifically, Keller pointed out the 9th Brigade's failure to take its D-Day objectives, the delayed use of reserves at Authie on 8 July, lack of drive at Caen the next day, and a failure to get patrols swiftly forward to the river line on the night of 9/10 July. In response, Crerar advised Keller to prepare a submission to Simonds, under whose command the 3rd Division was to shortly pass. Crerar had the same day passed to Simonds the adverse letters that had been raised on Keller by Crocker, Dempsey, and Montgomery. Crerar went on to suggest that it was quite possible Keller had not been handled well, perhaps because Crocker preferred to talk to brigadiers, bypassing the divisional commander in whom he had obviously lost confidence. Crerar, though he did not tell Simonds, also seems to have been of the opinion that Cunningham was the fair-haired boy of Crocker and Dempsey before the assault.[38] On 13 July Simonds reported to Crerar that while Cunningham had failed on some occasions to show the speed and determination that might have been expected, he generally appeared to have carried out his instructions intelligently and well. Simonds expressed concern, however, that he had not always received the direction and guidance from above that he was entitled to expect. Simonds further reported that he had shown Keller the comments made on his performance by Crocker, Dempsey, and Montgomery. Although Keller appeared distinctly upset on reading these comments, Simonds was more surprised by his response that he did not feel healthy enough to stand the heavy strain and subsequent request to be medically boarded as he felt that he would be found to be unfit.[39] Crerar approved of the way Simonds handled Keller and Cunningham, admitting for the first time that he would certainly not now consider the former for higher command.[40]

On 11 July Simonds's 2 Canadian Corps took the 3rd Canadian Infantry Division and 2nd Canadian Armoured Brigade under command and, with the 2nd Canadian Infantry Division and 2 AGRA already under command, launched a secondary attack codenamed "Atlantic" on 18 July in support of Operation "Goodwood," an attack delivered by the British 8 Corps. "Goodwood" was the brainchild of Dempsey, who recognized that the Second British Army had reached its manpower peak. With tank reinforcements pouring into Normandy faster than the rate of tank casualties, he proposed utilizing the surplus in tanks to conserve infantry. Greatly impressed by the shock effect of the bomber attack at Caen, he also looked to the employment of heavy bombers to blast a swathe for armoured divisions to deliver a smashing blow to the Germans. The primary aim of the operation was to hit the enemy hard and

FIRST CANADIAN ARMY

Ancillary Troops[1]

25th Armoured Delivery Regiment (The Elgin Regiment)

1st Armoured Personnel Carrier Regiment[2]

1st Army Group, Royal Canadian Artillery (1 Canadian AGRA):
    11th Army Field Regiment
    1st Medium Regiment
    2nd Medium Regiment
    5th Medium Regiment

2nd Army Group, Royal Canadian Artillery (2 Canadian AGRA):
    19th Army Field Regiment
    3rd Medium Regiment
    4th Medium Regiment
    7th Medium Regiment
    2nd Heavy Anti-Aircraft Regiment (Mobile)

1st Rocket Battery

1st Radar Battery

1st Canadian Army Troops Engineers
    10th Field Park Company
    5th Field Company
    20th Field Company
    23rd Field Company

2nd Canadian Army Troops Engineers
    11th Field Park Company
    32nd Field Company
    33rd Field Company
    34th Field Company

No. 1 Workshop and Park Company

1st Field (Air) Survey Company

2nd Field Survey Company

3rd Field (Reproduction) Survey Company

First Army Signals

First Canadian Army Headquarters Defence Battalion (Royal Montreal Regiment)

No. 1 Army Headquarters Car Company

No. 35 Army Troops Composite Company

No. 36 Army Troops Composite Company

No. 81 Artillery Company

No. 82 Artillery Company

No. 41 Army Transport Company

No. 45 Army Transport Company

No. 47 Army Transport Company

No. 63 Army Transport Company

No. 64 Army Transport Company

No. 1 Motor Ambulance Convoy

No. 2 Motor Ambulance Convoy

No. 2 Casualty Clearing Station

No. 3 Casualty Clearing Station

No. 4 Casualty Clearing Station

No. 5 Casualty Clearing Station

No. 6 Casualty Clearing Station

| 1 Canadian Corps | 2 Canadian Corps | 1 British Corps (from 23 Jul 44)[3] |

NOTES:

1. Not listed are elements of the Canadian Dental Corps, Royal Canadian Ordnance Corps, Royal Canadian Electrical and Mechanical Engineers, Canadian Postal Corps, and Canadian Provost Corps.

2. 1st Armoured Personnel Carrier Regiment operated under 79th British Armoured Division.

3. Including from 13 August 1944 the Royal Netherlands Brigade (Princess Irene's) and the 1st Belgian Infantry Brigade. On 9 October the 1st Czechoslovak Independent Armoured Brigade Group also came under First Canadian Army.

Figure 10.1 First Canadian Army Ancillary Troops (John A. English)

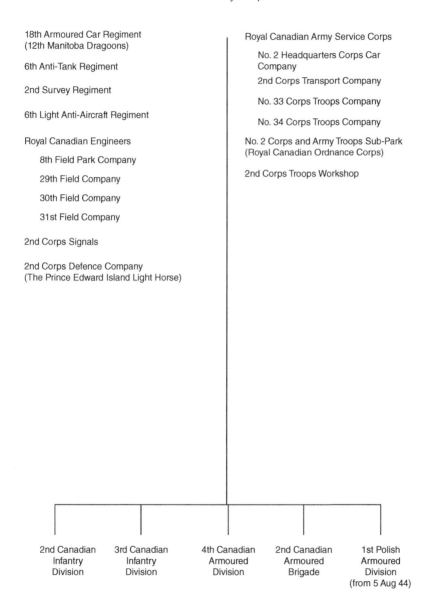

2 CANADIAN CORPS

Ancillary Troops

18th Armoured Car Regiment
(12th Manitoba Dragoons)

6th Anti-Tank Regiment

2nd Survey Regiment

6th Light Anti-Aircraft Regiment

Royal Canadian Engineers

    8th Field Park Company

    29th Field Company

    30th Field Company

    31st Field Company

2nd Corps Signals

2nd Corps Defence Company
(The Prince Edward Island Light Horse)

Royal Canadian Army Service Corps

    No. 2 Headquarters Corps Car
    Company

    2nd Corps Transport Company

    No. 33 Corps Troops Company

    No. 34 Corps Troops Company

No. 2 Corps and Army Troops Sub-Park
(Royal Canadian Ordnance Corps)

2nd Corps Troops Workshop

2nd Canadian Infantry Division	3rd Canadian Infantry Division	4th Canadian Armoured Division	2nd Canadian Armoured Brigade	1st Polish Armoured Division (from 5 Aug 44)

Figure 10.2 2 Canadian Corps Ancillary Troops (John A. English)

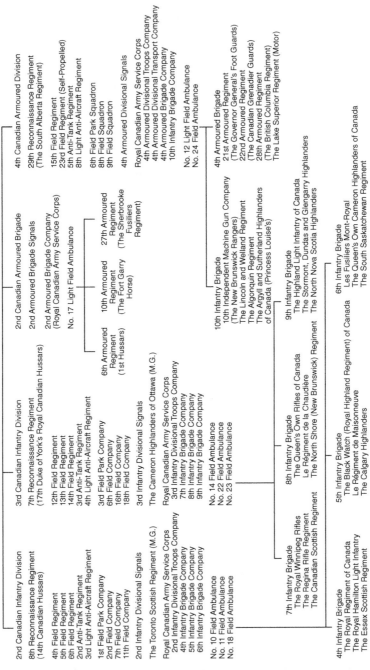

2 CANADIAN CORPS

Note: Canadian Dental Corps, Royal Canadian Ordnance Corps, Royal Canadian Electrical and Mechanical Engineers, and Canadian Provost Corps not shown

2nd Canadian Infantry Division

8th Reconnaissance Regiment (14th Canadian Hussars)

4th Field Regiment
5th Field Regiment
6th Field Regiment
2nd Anti-Tank Regiment
3rd Light Anti-Aircraft Regiment

1st Field Park Company
2nd Field Company
7th Field Company
11th Field Company

2nd Infantry Divisional Signals

The Toronto Scottish Regiment (M.G.)

Royal Canadian Army Service Corps
2nd Infantry Divisional Troops Company
4th Infantry Brigade Company
5th Infantry Brigade Company
6th Infantry Brigade Company

No. 10 Field Ambulance
No. 11 Field Ambulance
No. 18 Field Ambulance

7th Infantry Brigade
The Royal Winnipeg Rifles
The Regina Rifle Regiment
The Canadian Scottish Regiment

4th Infantry Brigade
The Royal Regiment of Canada
The Royal Hamilton Light Infantry
The Essex Scottish Regiment

3rd Canadian Infantry Division

7th Reconnaissance Regiment (17th Duke of York's Royal Canadian Hussars)

12th Field Regiment
13th Field Regiment
14th Field Regiment
3rd Anti-Tank Regiment
4th Light Anti-Aircraft Regiment

3rd Field Park Company
6th Field Company
16th Field Company
18th Field Company

3rd Infantry Divisional Signals

The Cameron Highlanders of Ottawa (M.G.)

Royal Canadian Army Service Corps
3rd Infantry Divisional Troops Company
7th Infantry Brigade Company
8th Infantry Brigade Company
9th Infantry Brigade Company

No. 14 Field Ambulance
No. 22 Field Ambulance
No. 23 Field Ambulance

8th Infantry Brigade
The Queen's Own Rifles of Canada
Le Régiment de la Chaudière
The North Shore (New Brunswick) Regiment

5th Infantry Brigade
The Black Watch (Royal Highland Regiment) of Canada
Le Régiment de Maisonneuve
The Calgary Highlanders

9th Infantry Brigade
The Highland Light Infantry of Canada
The Stormont, Dundas and Glengarry Highlanders
The North Nova Scotia Highlanders

6th Infantry Brigade
Les Fusiliers Mont-Royal
The Queen's Own Cameron Highlanders of Canada
The South Saskatchewan Regiment

2nd Canadian Armoured Brigade

2nd Armoured Brigade Signals

2nd Armoured Brigade Company (Royal Canadian Army Service Corps)

No. 17 Light Field Ambulance

6th Armoured Regiment (1st Hussars)
10th Armoured Regiment (The Fort Garry Horse)
27th Armoured Regiment (The Sherbrooke Fusiliers Regiment)

4th Canadian Armoured Division

29th Reconnaissance Regiment (The South Alberta Regiment)

15th Field Regiment
23rd Field Regiment (Self-Propelled)
5th Anti-Tank Regiment
8th Light Anti-Aircraft Regiment

6th Field Park Squadron
8th Field Squadron
9th Field Squadron

4th Armoured Divisional Signals

Royal Canadian Army Service Corps
4th Armoured Divisional Troops Company
4th Armoured Divisional Transport Company
4th Armoured Brigade Company
10th Infantry Brigade Company

No. 12 Light Field Ambulance
No. 24 Field Ambulance

4th Armoured Brigade
21st Armoured Regiment (The Governor General's Foot Guards)
22nd Armoured Regiment (The Canadian Grenadier Guards)
28th Armoured Regiment (The British Columbia Regiment)
The Lake Superior Regiment (Motor)

10th Infantry Brigade
10th Independent Machine Gun Company (The New Brunswick Rangers)
The Lincoln and Welland Regiment
The Algonquin Regiment
The Argyll and Sutherland Highlanders of Canada (Princess Louise's)

Figure 10.3 2 Canadian Corps Formations and Units (John A. English) force him to either commit reserves or risk a breakthrough. Although Montgomery after Alamein never favoured employing an all-armoured corps over combined arms formations, he acceded to Dempsey's proposal because it offered the best chance of gaining a bridgehead opposite Caen "without undue losses," as he had stipulated after "Epsom" and "Charnwood."[41] Ironically, "Goodwood" foundered owing to the misemployment of infantry integral to armoured divisions. The "Goodwood" supporting attack, "Atlantic," also stalled in the face of dogged German resistance and SS counter-attacks. The 3rd Division charged with clearing the industrial outskirts of Caen east of the Orne incurred 386 casualties, while the 2nd Division advancing south from the city to seize the area of Verrieres Ridge lost 1,149 men. Montgomery expressed his discontent with the performance of the 3rd Division by noting that if Crerar had acted on his advice and fired Keller the progress of the division would have been better.[42]

On 25 July the 2 Canadian Corps struck again, this time at night in support of Operation "Cobra," a major attack delivered the same day by the First US Army. The object of the Canadian attack, Operation "Spring," was to apply pressure to prevent the seven panzer divisions facing the British front from reinforcing two panzer divisions facing the American front. On a strategic level "Spring" elevated German concerns that the British rather than American front posed the greatest threat. Significantly, the C-in-C West, Field Marshal Guenther von Kluge, chose to visit the Caen front that day rather than the opening of Operation "Cobra" during its first critical hours because he considered the US attack diversionary.[43] Unfortunately, with the exception of one highly successful attack by the RHLI, "Spring" turned out to be a tactical disaster and, after Dieppe, the second bloodiest day of the war for Canadian arms. Poor divisional leadership clearly accounted for this, and Simonds considered firing the GOC 2nd Division, Major General Charles Foulkes, for incurring unnecessary casualties because he had no idea of what was going on at the front and made minimal effort to find out the true situation and make the necessary interventions. In making a muddled plan, he also switched battalions between brigades, thus compromising working relationships. Keller's 3rd Division attack on Tilly-la-Campagne by one battalion also foundered against stiff resistance. A second attack never materialized as Brigadier Cunningham and two unit commanding officers refused to continue what they considered to be futile action. While a subsequent board of inquiry into the failure to take Tilly resulted in the relief of these officers,[44] Simonds was far kinder to Keller.

In a 27 July letter to Dempsey reporting on Keller's fitness to command, Simonds pointed out that the division had never been out of contact

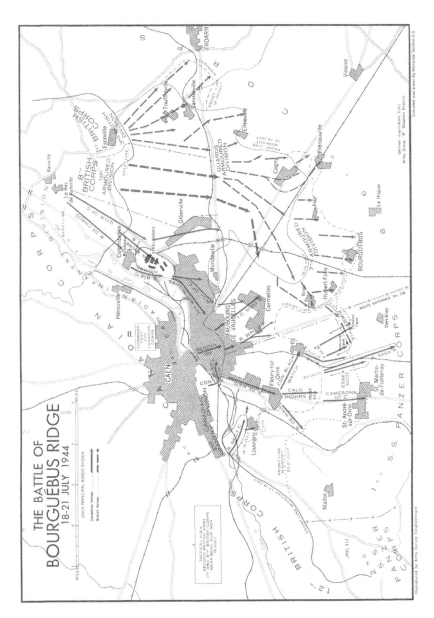

Map 10.5 The Battle of Bourguébus Ridge, 18–21 July 1944 (C.P. Stacey, *The Victory Campaign: The Operation in North-West Europe, 1944–1945*, 1966)

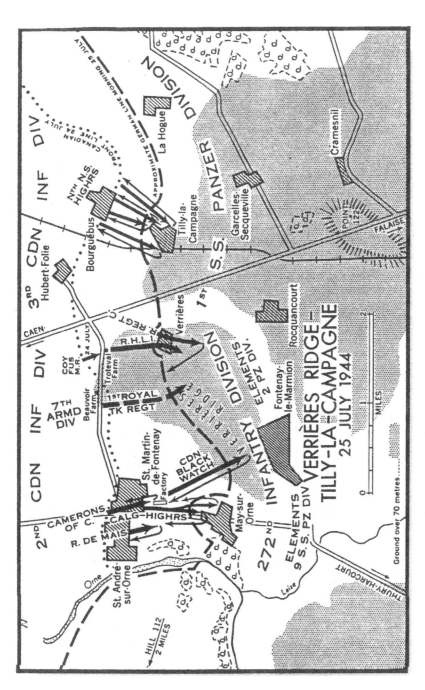

Map 10.6 Verrières Ridge – Tilly-la-Campagne, 25 July 1944 (C.P. Stacey, *The Victory Campaign: The Operation in North-West Europe, 1944–1945*, 1966)

since D-Day and had incurred some 5,500 casualties. Such loss plus the inability of the division to get out of the line and reorganize properly had resulted in a deterioration of its fighting efficiency. Within many sections and platoons the men hardly knew one another or their commanders owing to heavy casualties among junior leaders. In short, sub-units lacked the cohesion of a trained battle team. Simonds also found commanders to be apprehensive about operations because they felt their units were unfitted in their state of training to put up a good show. He further sensed a feeling of resentment within the division that due credit had not been given for hard fighting. Simonds therefore recommended against the removal of Keller on the grounds that it would have a most adverse effect on morale and be regarded as censure on the efforts of the formation. In order to develop the full fighting efficiency of the 3rd Division, it had to be given a period out of the line to reorganize and train and absorb reinforcement personnel. Only after a successful operation could he envision a command change being made without affecting the feeling of the division itself. Compared to the bigger problem of maintaining the morale of the 3 Canadian Division, Simonds considered the individual qualities of Keller to be unimportant. He nonetheless thought that Keller had failed to appreciate the importance of the moral aspects of higher command and the absolute necessity for a commander to be a stabilizing influence in the give and take of active operations.[45] In later years Simonds expressed regret about sacking Cunningham and felt he should have sacked Keller instead.[46] Keller thus continued in command until wounded and invalided home as a result of US bombing in Operation "Totalize" on 8 August.

Meanwhile, Crerar's First Canadian Army had become operational on 23 July 1944, seven weeks after D-Day and twelve days after Simonds's 2 Canadian Corps had deployed under the Second British Army. By this time the 3rd Canadian Infantry Division Group had been in action forty-eight days. The 2 Canadian Corps did not revert to the command of the First Canadian Army until 31 July 1944, however, in accordance with Montgomery's plan to delay the introduction of Crerar's headquarters. Until the Second British Army gained sufficient space to the northeast, east, and southeast of Caen, there was neither sufficient frontage nor depth for the deployment of another army. The Second Army battle area could handle the 2 Canadian Corps as a fifth corps, but not all the ancillary troops that would accompany Headquarters First Canadian Army. Montgomery therefore decided to bring in Crerar's headquarters and army troops after the arrival of the 2 Canadian Corps and have them take over the eastern sector held by the British 1 Corps comprising the British 3rd, 49th, 51st infantry divisions and the 6th Airborne Division, including the 1st and 4th Special Service brigades. In August the 1st Polish Armoured Divison, the 1st Belgian Infantry Brigade, the Royal Netherlands Brigade, and the 1st Czechoslovak Independent Armoured Brigade also joined the First Canadian Army.[47]

With more British troops under command than the Eighth Army had at Alamein, the First Canadian Army was arguably the last great British imperial army, appropriately commanded by a dominion general officer. The multinational nature of the formation also indicated that the bottom of the British manpower barrel had been reached. After it, there would be no more British armies. Casualties had taken their toll on British and Canadian troops. In July the British Adjutant General warned Montgomery that if infantry casualty rates continued at the rate they had, replacements could be obtained only by "cannibalizing" other branches. This resulted in the eventual disbandment of four tank regiments and an armoured and infantry brigade. Indeed, the situation was so dire that the 59th Infantry (Staffordshire) Division secretly disappeared in August, closely followed by the gallant 50th (Northumbrian) Division that had assaulted Gold Beach and saved the Americans by drawing in German reserves that should have been unleashed to extinguish Omaha. Casualties incurred by 2 Canadian Corps also continued to mount, ultimately provoking a conscription crisis that called into question the validity of Crerar's assessment that Canada could deploy and sustain a field army of volunteer soldiers. Simonds advised his troops that casualties were an inevitable part of any operation and that the only hope was to limit their number. Keeping casualties small had been Montgomery's creed all along and he constantly strove to preserve British and Canadian infantry with a view to preserving Anglo-Canadian influence.[48]

Montgomery also continued to harbour reservations about First Canadian Army command, confiding in his personal war diary that "Crerar himself has no real qualifications that fit him to command an Army; he is not a commander and inspires no confidence. The only really good general in the Canadian forces is Simonds."[49] On 7 July Montgomery wrote to Brooke expressing "grave fears that Harry Crerar will not be too good." Although an awfully nice chap, the prosy and stodgy Crerar was definitely not a commander and quite unfit to lead an army. He concluded by saying of Crerar, "I am keeping him out of the party as long as I can."[50] To this Brooke replied, "It is evident that the Canadians are very short of senior Commanders, but it is equally clear that we shall have to make the best use of the material we have." Pointing out that "with McNaughton's dismissal we run the risk of being accused of thinning out Canadians to make room for British commanders," he then stated, "I want you to make the best possible use of Crerar." He must be retained as army commander and given his Canadians under command at the earliest possible moment. "You can keep his army small and give him the less important role," Brooke added. "And you will have to teach him."[51] Montgomery fired back that all Canadian troops in Normandy were under Canadian command, that of Simonds who was far and away the best Canadian general, "the equal of any British corps commander, and ... far better than Crerar."[52] While insisting that it would be wrong to introduce another army into the British sector too soon, he promised that when he did hand over a sector to Crerar he would teach him his stuff and give him tasks commensurate with his capabilities. Montgomery added that personal affection for Crerar should not lead him to do unsound things. He further offered that Canadian commanders were not very good. They had some good officers, but their top commanders were bad judges of men. As shown in the case of Keller, Crerar was no exception and "does not know what a good soldier is."[53]

As if to reinforce Montgomery's reservations, when the First Canadian Army became operational, Crerar almost immediately got into a quarrel with his one and only corps commander. With Simonds's 2 Corps astride the Caen-Falaise road remaining under command of the Second British Army, the First Canadian Army initially assumed responsibility only for the eastern sector of the front held by Crocker's 1 Corps. Crerar's assigned task was to advance First Canadian Army's left flank eastwards so that Ouistreham would cease to be under direct enemy observation and fire in order that use could then be made of the port of Caen. To achieve this, Montgomery suggested pushing the enemy back to the east side of the River Dives and occupying positions that would ensure friendly-force domination of all territory to the west of the river. On 22 July Crerar sent a written instruction to Crocker repeating this general direction and ordering him to draw up the necessary plan, which Crerar indicated he wished to discuss on the morning of 24 July. In the same instruction Crerar stipulated that the immediate task would be to gain possession of the general line of the road running from Breville through Le Marais to the road junction Le Petit Homme.[54] At the 24 July meeting, however, Crocker voiced strong objections to such detailed tactical direction, and, at Crerar's request, put them in writing the same day.

In Crocker's view, Crerar did not consider that the action to be taken was a corps matter to be decided at that level – corps being the highest tactical level. The operation ordered by Crerar would also have required an attack on a narrow front through close and difficult country where the enemy was well posted in some strength and would, in its later stages, have called for clearing an extensive build-up area. Instead of achieving the object of enabling the Ouistreham–Caen Canal to be brought into

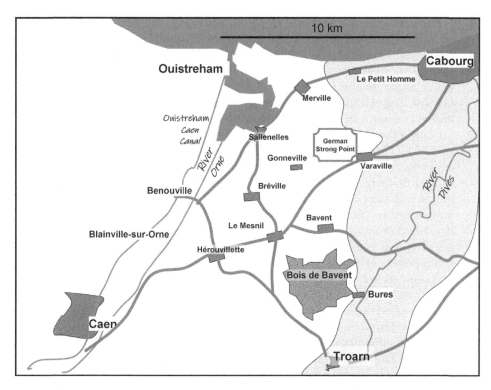

Map 10.7 Area of the Crerar–Crocker dispute, 24–6 July 1944 (John A. Macdonald)

use, Crocker argued, the proposed advance to Breville–Le Petit Homme road would merely result in purposeless losses and an extended front that could be held only with disproportionate daily casualties from the enemy artillery east of the Dives and the undisturbed mortars and short-range weapons in the Gonneville-Varaville-Bavent area. Since the German 12cm mortar and 15cm Nebelwerfer with ranges of 6,500 and 7,000 yards, respectively, could easily reach past the objective line selected by Crerar, Crocker had a point. He accordingly requested Crerar to reconsider his specific direction, adding that he was not prepared, personally, to be responsible for carrying it out. As an alternative to attacking on a narrow front, Crocker proposed earmarking 3rd Division to capture Troarn and Bures as a first-priority task, which he estimated would require a brigade with full air and ground support. On success of this phase, he saw a division again supported by air advancing on a broad front to the line Bavent-Gonneville-Merville, with exploitation to Varaville and towards Cabourg.[55]

Centred on command and tactics, this dispute revealed the nature of working relationships at corps and army levels where disagreements between superiors and subordinates have neither been uncommon nor necessarily viewed as unhealthy. Crerar's defensive reaction, however, was to annotate and forward Crocker's written objections to Montgomery with regret and call upon him "for aid." Crocker allegedly gave the immediate impression that he resented receiving any direction from Crerar either for personal reasons or because he was Canadian. He exhibited no tact or desire to understand Crerar's views. Crocker's substantial experience in command of a corps in action appears to have been the catalyst that triggered this disagreement and pushed Crerar to react the way he did. Crocker's recent attempt to fire the favoured Keller may also have sowed resentment. In any event, Crerar remained quite convinced that Crocker was temperamentally unsuited to be one of his corps commanders and asked Montgomery that he be exchanged for either of the commanders of 12 or 30 Corps, both of whom Crerar had served with and claimed to know well. "They will work with me," he wrote, "Crocker never will." As has been noted, however, the 30 Corps commander, Bucknall, who had been Crerar's GSO 2 when the latter was RMC Commandant, was destined to be sacked by Dempsey and replaced by Horrocks. Crocker on the other hand was a decorated Great War veteran who had fought in France in 1940 and commanded the 6th Armoured Division and 9 Corps in North Africa with great distinction. [56]

On 25 July Montgomery once more interviewed Crerar on the matter of an apparently recalcitrant subordinate. While allowing that Crocker could be somewhat difficult, he reproached Crerar for not using persuasion rather than formal orders to harness Crocker's operational experience and proven ability, especially since he had just come under command. Montgomery also declined to transfer Crocker to another corps on the sensible grounds that such reassignment, besides requiring staff changes during a difficult period in operations, would only restrict future flexibility as it might still be necessary under certain conditions to place Crocker's corps under the First Canadian Army. Crerar acknowledged that he had "not given full weight to this prospective situation" and the next day agreed to go more than halfway toward salvaging the situation, stating, "I'll make a go of it with Crocker."[57] He nonetheless requested Montgomery to speak with Crocker to straighten out the relationship and confirm that what was urgently wanted was the clearance of Ouistreham and the Caen Canal from close enemy observation and mortar fire at an early date, along the lines of Crerar's instructions. Montgomery promised to see Crocker the following morning, advising Crerar to meet his corps commander later that day to go over the tactical problem once more with "the air cleared and good prospects of mutual understanding."[58]

Montgomery wrote to Crerar on 26 July saying that he had instructed Crocker to quit bickering and be a loyal subordinate, "one prepared to lead the way" by stating what an honour it was to serve in the First Canadian Army. Montgomery then counselled Crerar that a field army commander should give his corps commanders a task, and let them decide how to do it. While keeping in touch, the army commander must stand back from the detailed tactical battle, the province of his corps commanders, and intervene only if he thinks it is not going to be a success. To reinforce this point Montgomery warned that in an army of but one corps the higher commander will, if he is not careful, find that he is trying to command that corps himself. With not enough to do, he may also be inclined to become involved in details that are the province of his subordinates. Montgomery further pointed out that Crocker was a very experienced fighting commander who because he knew his stuff had to be led rather than driven. Remarking that it takes all sorts to make a good army, Montgomery went on to stress to Crerar that once you can gain the confidence and trust of your subordinates, you will have "a pearl of very great price." This was not likely to be attained, however, without a very great deal of hard work, and very considerable subordination of self. In the same letter, Montgomery urged Crerar to cut down paper in the field. He also suggested in direct reference to Crerar's written instruction to Crocker that best results were obtained by dealing verbally with corps commanders who could then give their views.[59]

That Crerar also chose to issue a tactical directive to all senior formation commanders on 22 July seems to have caused Montgomery additional irritation. It would be a good thing to tell Crocker, he advised, that you sent him several copies only in case he wished to send them on to his subordinates. In the field, Montgomery explained to Crerar, it was wrong to send tactical directives to anyone except your immediate subordinates – as they are responsible to you, and their subordinates are responsible to them. Stating that he had expressed this opinion many times, Montgomery faulted Crerar's action in this regard, which lesson the latter readily accepted and absorbed. As for the directive itself, the first three pages consisted largely of extracts taken from a translated report by Panzer Lehr Division covering its experiences during the period 6–22 June. The report dealt with German responses to certain British tactical methods, including the attack on a very narrow front. Crerar's assessment that this called for maximum surprise employing maximum firepower bordered on the general as opposed to Montgomery's focus on specifics. The last three pages were also extracts, taken directly from an address given by Crerar on 14 May 1944, itself a patchwork effort taken almost verbatim from paragraphs in previous letters and memoranda. All told, they remain more revealing of a commander short on original ideas of his own. The emphasis he placed upon the employment of barrage fire and the need for infantry, deployed in width rather than depth, to keep close to it during the "break-in battle" was certainly not new. Nor was there mention of the use of armour, except in the most general terms.[60]

Montgomery's advice in the Crocker incident smoothed over relations, though Crerar may have inwardly harboured resentment.[61] There is reason to believe, however, that Crerar's lack of judgment and tactical inexperience were not the only factors at play here. He was not a healthy man. He suffered from severe anemia brought on by bouts of dysentery. An attack in Sicily and a second in Italy had responded to sulfa treatments, but in Normandy he was wracked by attacks during June that did not respond to treatment. Bothered by abdominal pain and stomach distress from late June, he began to suffer noticeable shortness of breath on exertion and increasing fatigue and loss of energy. This condition, aggravated by chain-smoking and stress, also led to outbursts of temper and a defensive edginess that left him tense most of the time. Allegedly, such ill health caused his control of his headquarters to slip slowly, but significantly.[62] Montgomery may not have realized the true state of Crerar's health at the time, but by now conditioned to settling disputes among senior Canadian commanders, he expressed his exasperation in a letter to Brooke on 26 July. "Harry Crerar has started off his career as an Army Comd by thoroughly upsetting everyone," he wrote, "he had a row with Crocker the first day, and asked me to remove Crocker. I have spent two days trying to restore peace; investigating the quarrel, and so on." As always, there were faults on both sides, wrote Montgomery, but the basic cause was Crerar, who "began to throw his weight about" to show that he was a great soldier. He "was determined to show it the very moment he took over command at 1200 hrs 23 July. He made his first mistake at 1205 hrs; and his second after lunch." Montgomery saw each of them separately, telling Crerar that in his opinion the basic fault lay with him, and counselling Crocker to play 100 per cent. Montgomery then expressed the hope that he could "get on with fighting the Germans – instead of stopping the Generals fighting amongst themselves."[63]

Chapter Eleven

Cracking German Lines

Montgomery took over the 21st Army Group with a well-thought-out and practical fighting doctrine for the limitations of a citizen army. He based his planning on seven modern principles of war, starting with winning the air battle before any land operation and ensuring that administration accommodated the needs of the front. Cooperation between armed services, Allies, and the fighting arms came next, followed by tactical surprise that he deemed always possible, in contrast to problematic strategic surprise. The last three were concentration of effort, simplicity in everything, and morale and fighting spirit. He divided combat into fighting and "frigging about," the former dealing with the actual seizure of objectives and the latter with such activities as patrolling. The rules for the stage management of battle included incorporating surprise and, through foresight, forcing the enemy commander to conform and avoiding fighting haphazardly. This called for having the right deployment capable of meeting any threat to the envisioned plan. To retain the initiative, added later as an eighth principle, a commander had to exercise close control with great drive. The plan of battle had also to be communicated down to the soldiers, each to be enthused and told how the battle would be fought. To ensure against morale-sapping failure, he recommended limiting the scope of what was to be achieved successfully.[1]

Montgomery further stressed that commanders at every level had to focus on only the things that matter and direct all their energy and capacity to achieving them. As focus would vary at each level, however, commanders had to stick within their bounds and refrain from getting involved in matters that a lower commander had to take in hand. In this respect, he stated that the division would be the largest fixed formation and that there would be no standard composition of corps. Corps commanders and headquarters had to be trained to handle infantry and armoured divisions, or a number in combination, since grouping divisions under corps might in some circumstances have to be changed during battle. For this reason administration had to be controlled and coordinated at field-army level. Montgomery went on to emphasize the importance of the cooperation of arms, the need to always have a firm base from which to operate, and the battle-winning capability of artillery. To promote operational effectiveness, he mandated that a commander deal with only one gunner adviser; hence CRAs and CCRAs had to be prepared to handle and offer advice on all dispositions of artillery, including anti-tank and anti-aircraft elements. Having all artillery under a dedicated gunner chain of command not only ensured a high standard of technical capability, but made it easier to conduct all arms planning.[2]

Reflecting his experience with the Eighth Army, Montgomery also broached the idea of the main battle tank. British doctrine in the initial stages of the war distinguished between a fast "Cruiser" tank for cavalry style operations and a more heavily armoured "I" tank for infantry support operations. Thus, armoured brigades in armoured divisions were equipped with "Cruiser" tanks and independent armoured brigades with "I" tanks. Montgomery proposed treating both categories as a "Capital" tank and making independent armoured brigades interchangeable with the armoured brigades of armoured divisions. The catalyst for this was the introduction of the Sherman medium tank with a 75-mm gun capable of firing high-explosive, smoke, or armour-piercing rounds, which blurred the distinction between the Cruiser and "I" tank, of which the more heavily armoured Churchill was the last. In a conference on 13 January 1944 Montgomery decreed that henceforth only two types of tanks would be recognized: the light reconnaissance tank and the "Capital" tank, the latter category comprising both the Sherman and the Churchill mounting either a six-pounder or 75-mm gun. In short, whether Sherman or Churchill equipped, there was to be but one category of armoured brigade with "Capital" or main battle tanks being employed in any role, including that of infantry support. As light tanks could not survive in the close reconnaissance role, armoured reconnaissance regiments of armoured divisions were given Capital tanks, thus making four main battle tank regiments per armoured division.[3]

Despite Montgomery's decree, however, Sherman and Churchill brigades in Home Forces trained differently in infantry-tank cooperation. As, the Sherman proved easy prey to the German 50-mm Pak, the greatest killer of Allied tanks, Sherman-equipped brigades preferred to support infantrymen on foot by sitting back in hull or turret-down positions using their very effective high-explosive shells and machine guns to gnaw through a defensive position. Heavier Churchill tanks, on the other hand, proved capable of accompanying infantry in the attack. Another difference in fighting organization was that the armoured brigade in an armoured division included a motorized infantry battalion whereas the independent tank brigade intended to support an infantry division did not. Whatever the case, where an armoured regiment might be placed in support of an infantry brigade in an infantry division, Montgomery stipulated that the armoured brigade commander should conduct planning with the infantry brigade commander and not leave the planning insofar as it affected armour to the tank regimental commander alone. Montgomery's emphasis on tactical planning being done at the brigade level reflected the reality that only that level possessed the requisite staff and communication means to effect the proper coordination of artillery fire support. In this manner, the coordination of all three fighting arms was thus ensured.[4] Sadly, in Operation "Spring" Canadian divisional attacks had been delivered only by battalions with limited and late tank support. Properly mounted brigade attacks employing infantry, tanks, and artillery in concert would most certainly have produced better results.

Long before Alamein, Montgomery had preached that success in battle depended not on tank action alone, which could achieve little, but on the intimate cooperation of all arms. This meant the coordinated employment of tanks, indirect artillery fire, anti-tank guns, infantry, and engineers in tactical combination. When Anglo-Canadian troops employed their weapons properly and used good tactics they had no difficulty in defeating the Germans. He pointed out that the Mark IV panzer was in no way superior to the Sherman or the Cromwell tank, and that mechanically unreliable Tigers and Panthers spent a lot of time in workshops. The Panther had heavier frontal armour than British tanks, but was very vulnerable to penetration from a flank. In close country there were instances where infantry destroyed Panthers with the hand-held PIAT (Projector Infantry Anti-Tank). Tests additionally showed that the 17-pounder gun would go straight through the Panther turret front as would the 6-pounder (sabot) at 400 yds. The 17-pounder using sabot ammunition could easily pierce the heavy frontal armour of any known German tank, including the Tiger, at 2,000 yards. Montgomery sought to pop up tank-gun power and considered increasing Fireflies to two per troop the best way to do so, with a view to eventually increasing numbers even more. So as not to adversely affect the morale of the fighting soldier, he also sought to suppress "alarmist" reports of the inadequate quality of British equipment and weapons, while encouraging informed investigations of where improvements could be made.[5]

Two days after "Spring" Montgomery directed the Second British Army to deliver a strong right-wing offensive in the Caumont area with not less than six divisions. The aim of this operation, called "Bluecoat," was to further the breakout by American forces in Operation "Cobra" to the west. Montgomery deemed it essential that the First Canadian and Second British Armies continue to attack the enemy vigorously in the east to prevent the Germans from transferring forces across to the western flank. The objectives of their operations were to gain ground of tactical advantage and write down German manpower and equipment. Within the 2 Canadian Corps sector this translated into further attacks on Tilly-la-Campagne defended by the 1st SS Division. On 1 August the Calgary Highlanders launched a dawn attack against the strongly held village that stalled in the face of German machine gun and artillery fire. A second daylight assault enabled some Canadians to get into Tilly, but, unable to consolidate, they retired to the area of their original start line. At this juncture the shattered battalion received orders from the 5th Brigade commander to attack again with the support of tanks. The Germans similarly repulsed this effort short of Tilly with withering fire.[6]

As a result of Montgomery's personal appeal to Crerar on the morning of 1 August to keep up the pressure on the 2 Corps front, the Lincoln and Welland Regiment of the 4th Canadian Armoured Division now launched a silent night attack against Tilly. This effort also failed, but despite this reverse the commander of the 10th Brigade, Brigadier J.C. Jefferson, ordered a final company assault on Tilly that foundered as well. Apparently Jefferson, whom Montgomery had rated low in 1942, considered Tilly not more than a two-company target. A further attempt to capture Tilly made by the Argyll and Sutherland Highlanders of Canada backed by a South Alberta tank squadron on 5 August also failed. The same day Montgomery remarked to Simonds, "Congratulations, you've been kicked out of Tilly again!"[7]

In the meantime Crerar had advised Simonds on 29 July to plan a thrust down the Caen-Falaise road to coincide with projected First US and Second British Army operations. Montgomery on 4 August issued formal direction for First Canadian Army to launch a heavy attack from the Caen sector towards Falaise no later than 8 August. He followed this with a call on Simonds for a half-hour conference the next day. The main object of the Falaise operation, code named "Totalize," was to cut off the enemy forces facing Second British Army as it advanced from the west. The promise of this undertaking was not lost on Crerar, who saw an opportunity for Canadian arms to conduct as decisive an attack as that delivered by the Canadian Corps at Amiens on 8 August 1918, the "black day of the German army." On 5 August in an address to senior officers that predicted a turning point in the war had been reached, he stated that "a highly successful, large scale operation, now carried out by one of the Armies of the Allied Expeditionary Force, favourably placed for that

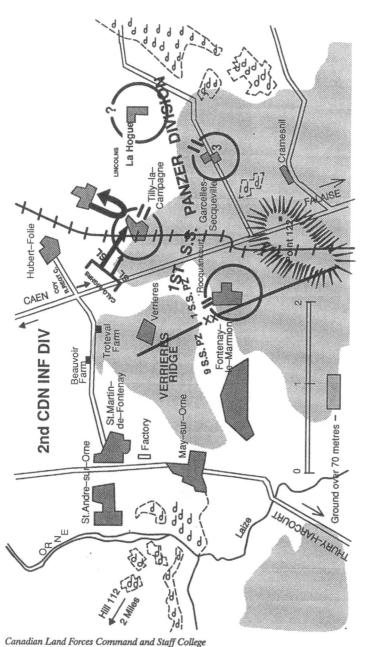

TILLY-LA-CAMPAGNE
0230–1430 HRS 1 AUG 44

Canadian Land Forces Command and Staff College
August 1990

Map 11.1a Tilly-la-Campagne, 1 August 1944 (C.P. Stacey, *The Victory Campaign: The Operation in North-West Europe, 1944–1945,* 1966)

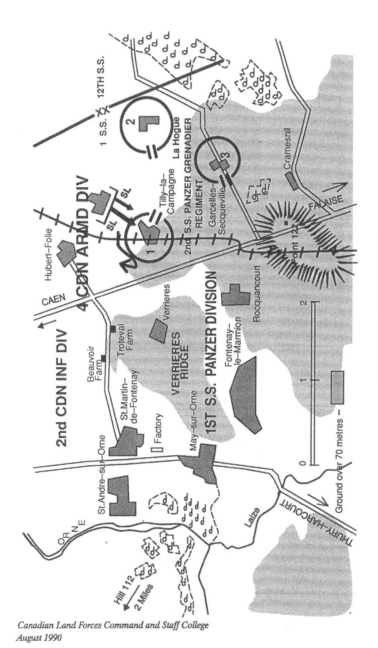

TILLY-LA-CAMPAGNE

FROM 2300 HRS 5 AUG TO 0200 HRS 6 AUG

Map 11.1b Tilly-la-Campagne, 5–6 August 1944 (C.P. Stacey, *The Victory Campaign: The Operation in North-West Europe, 1944–1945*, 1966)

Canadian Land Forces Command and Staff College
August 1990

purpose, will result in the crushing conviction to Germans, even of the S.S. variety, that general defeat of the German Armies on all fronts has become an inescapable fact."[8] Expecting a quick termination of the war to follow, Crerar entertained high hopes that the results of "Totalize" would be historically decisive. Montgomery agreed that the Canadians should be able to fight their way to Falaise, but noted that they would not have the easy time they fancied.[9]

Crerar later claimed to having laid down the basic plan for "Totalize" and that the tactics adopted largely reflected an earlier directive he had issued. He credited Simonds with two innovations: the night employment of strategic bombers on targets close to friendly troops on each flank of the attacking front; and the use of improvised APCs to transport infantry.[10] Crerar stressed that all ranks had to firmly grasp the vital importance of maintaining the momentum of the attack and went on to underscore the importance of keeping the initiative. He condemned the tendency among all ranks to look upon objectives on the ground as an end rather than a means of killing the enemy. He further cautioned that on reaching an objective, preparations had to be made at top speed to ward off quickly mounted small-scale counter-attacks by enemy tanks and infantry. Warning that surrendering to German SS troops invited death, Crerar exhorted the infantry to drive on using their own weapons in the absence of artillery support. He decried as far too prevalent the attitude that, without a colossal scale of artillery, or air support, infantry could not continue to advance.[11] In the event, however, Montgomery observed to Brooke that the desperately anxious Crerar, worried about fighting his first battle at the head of Canada's first field army, had "gained the idea that all you want is a good initial fire plan, and then the Germans all run away!" Montgomery added that Crerar would feel much better when he realized that battles seldom go completely as planned, that you had to be patient and keep at it until the other side cracks, and that worry will only drive you mad.[12]

Despite Crerar's claim to authorship of "Totalize," the weight of evidence shows that it was mainly the conception of Simonds. In response to Crerar's direction of 30 July, Simonds produced a highly creative plan to launch a night armoured attack in the wake of strikes by strategic bombers, using "Kangaroo" APCs to enable infantry to keep up with tanks. As finally crafted, the plan called for a corps attack by two infantry and two armoured divisions, two armoured brigades, two complete AGRA plus the support of two additional ones, four squadrons of flail tanks, engineer assault vehicles, and flame-throwing Crocodiles, and all the available air effort. Noting that the enemy front was manned by the 1st SS Division right and the 9th SS left, each disposed with one infantry regiment back and one forward with all tanks and self-propelled (SP) guns in support, Simonds expected very heavy fighting. The presence of the 12th SS in close reserve also meant that a counter-attack was likely on the eastern flank. Simonds thus envisioned one "break in" phase to penetrate the foremost defensive zone along May-sur-Orne–Tilly-la-Campagne–La Hogue and a second to pierce the partially prepared rear position along Hautmesnil–St. Sylvain. Given the open nature of the ground, which ideally suited the characteristics of German long-range anti-tank weaponry, he deduced that the defence would be most handicapped by bad visibility, smoke, fog, or darkness that impaired long-range fire.[13]

The first phase called for a night attack on the Fontenay-le-Marmion–La Hogue position by two APC-borne infantry divisions, each spearheaded by an armoured brigade, under cover of a rolling barrage. The task of the 2nd Canadian Infantry Division west of the Caen-Falaise road with the 2nd Canadian Armoured Brigade under command was to secure the Caillouet–Gaumesnil line and ensure the "mopping up" of St. Andre, May-sur-Orne, Fontenay-le-Marmion, and Roquancourt. East of the road, the 51st (Highland) Division with the 33rd British Armoured Brigade under command was to capture the areas of Lourguichon Wood, Garcelles-Secqueville, Cramesnil, St. Aignan de Cramesnil, and Secqueville-la-Campagne. There was to be no preliminary artillery bombardment during the first phase, though commencing at H-hour RAF Lancaster bombers were to obliterate the areas of May-sur-Orne, Fontenay-le-Marmion, and La Hogue-Secqueville. The second phase, expected to commence after noon the following day with a massive air strike, called for the 4th Canadian Armoured Division to dash southward along the Caen-Falaise road to seize Point 206 between Fontaine-le-Pin and Potigny. Simultaneously, the 1st Polish Armoured Division was to pass through the 51st Highland Division and advance directly, east of the Caen-Falaise road, to take Point 159 overlooking and dominating Falaise.[14]

Each armoured division was to have one medium artillery regiment under command and the support of medium and fighter bombers, on call, to deal with possible threats from the 12th SS Panzer Division. To enable them to blast their way forward, two AGRA, each of five medium regiments, were also made available, one to each division. The second phase was to be heavily supported by fighter, medium, and US B-17 and B-24 heavy day bombers. While the 2nd Canadian Infantry and 51st Highland divisions secured the right and left flanks around Bretteville-sur-Laize and Cavicourt, respectively, the 3rd Canadian Infantry Division was to remain in reserve north of Caen, prepared to move on Simonds's order to take over the areas of Hautmesnil, Bretteville-le-Rabet, and Point 140

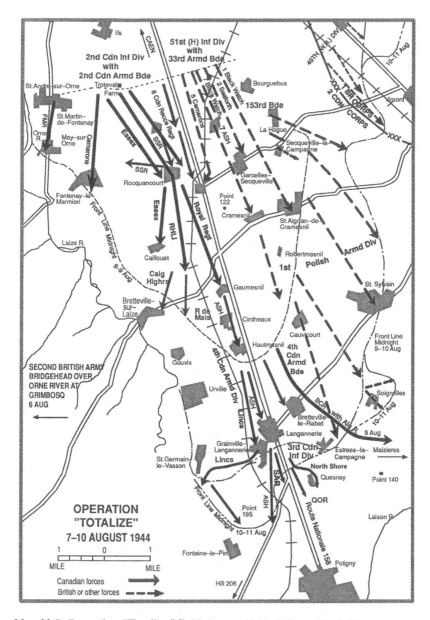

Map 11.2 Operation "Totalize," 7–10 August 1944 (John A. English)

east of the Caen-Falaise road. New intelligence that the powerful 1st SS Division had been relieved by the 89th Infantry Division and fallen back to the second German defensive line served to accentuate the importance of carrying out bomber strikes before launching the ground attack in phase two.[15] In fact, the 1st SS had left to participate in Adolf Hitler's westward thrust against US forces in Mortain and Avranches, but this was not entirely clear at the time.

Crerar, who tired easily owing to declining health, played a passive role in "Totalize." Unable to match the operational expertise of Simonds, he found refuge in his responsibility for arranging air support as it was the one planning area that remained the sole prerogative of the First Canadian Army. As strategic bombing support had to be requested through No. 83 Group, 2nd Tactical Air Force (TAF), and the Allied Expeditionary Air Force (AEAF) headed by Air Chief Marshal Sir Trafford Leigh-Mallory, making the case for the tactical employment of strategic bombers, which many top airmen considered a misuse of air power, required considerable effort. Heavy bomber strikes in darkness also raised troop safety concerns that initially left the C-in-C Bomber Command, Air Chief Marshal Harris, cool to the idea. He would agree to Bomber Command carrying out the task only if his "Master Bombers" were satisfied that red- and green-coloured concentrations fired by 25-pounder artillery gun-howitzers could be clearly identified in the dark. It took a trial on the night of 6 August to confirm that targets indicated by coloured marker shells could be satisfactorily identified in darkness. The H-hour for the commencement of the first phase of "Totalize" thus continued to be 2300 hours 7 August, from which time both flanks of 2 Corps armoured-infantry thrusts would be protected by heavy bombing. Air support for the second phase, now estimated to start at 1400 hours 8 August, was more comprehensive and, owing to a last-minute change, became largely the responsibility of the US Eighth Air Force with coordination still effected through No. 83 Group. Entrenching air support timings, of course, left all land force movement contingent upon bomber strikes.[16]

On 7 August at 1700 hours Montgomery called on Crerar to discuss future operations for the First Canadian Army while Simonds's manoeuvre elements formed up in tight columns of tanks, special armour, and APCs. An armoured and infantry brigade constituted the main assaulting force in both the 2nd and 51st Divisions. After dark all columns rolled closer to the start line, and at 2300 hours 1,020 RAF bombers dropped a total of 3,462 tons of bombs on flank targets identified by red artillery marker shells in the east and green in the west. At 2330 hours both divisional columns crossed the start line, picking up from

2345 hours a rolling barrage fired by 360 guns in nine field and nine medium regiments, advancing in 200-yard lifts to a depth of 6,000 yards. In all, 720 guns each with up to 650 rounds supported the attack with barrage, flanking, and depth fire, including counter-battery. To assist columns in keeping direction, a Bofors tracer barrage coordinated by corps fired over divisional thrust lines. Other innovations, artificial moonlight and wireless radio directional beams, two per divisional front, provided additional guidance.

Although the movement of the armoured columns by night proved a harrowing experience despite all navigational aids, it nonetheless worked brilliantly and, within hours, chaos spawned success. The rapid advance of the 51st Highland Division took it past Tilly to secure Lorguichon by 0445 hours, Garcelles-Secqueville by 0530, and Cramesnil by 0730. With the exception of bypassed Tilly, which held out until 1200 hours, the division had seized all of its first-phase objectives, including St. Aignan-de-Cramesnil, and was ready for the 1st Polish Armoured Division to pass through. Similar success attended the 2nd Division attack, which rolled around Rocquancourt southwards into the debussing area between Cramesnil and Caillouet. By 0600 hours leading elements of the 2nd and 51st Divisions were fighting in the vicinities of their first objectives and had nearly cleared them.[17] While mopping-up operations against rearward enemy pockets continued, the first phase of "Totalize" had cracked a hole in the German front line for the relatively light total of 380 casualties. The road to Falaise also lay open.[18]

The first phase of "Totalize" had also been a resounding success in terms of timing, and Crerar rushed forward to offer congratulations.[19] Simonds's plan to pause for several hours before initiating the second phase proved unfortunate, however, as it guaranteed the very loss of momentum that Crerar had specifically sought to avoid. Indeed, the pause allowed the Germans to mount the very counter-attacks that Simonds so much feared and which, by striking deep into the German defensive depth in phase one, he had hoped to avert. The commanders of the 4th Canadian and 1st Polish Armoured Divisions worried about the potential danger of such a long pause, asked to call off the bombing. Simonds, under the erroneous perception that the formidable 1st SS now defended the second German defensive zone, nonetheless insisted that the armoured divisions await the support of heavy bombers. He understandably did not want a repeat of "Atlantic," where he had deliberately opted to exploit a successful advance by launching further quick offensive action against seemingly light German opposition only to receive a bloody nose from the counter-attacking 1st SS. Similarly, vicious German reactions in "Spring" reinforced his decision to pause. Yet, as

Crerar so correctly pointed out, losing the momentum of the attack was something that should have been avoided at all costs. In this case, moreover, the loss was self-inflicted. The limitation on forward reconnaissance imposed by the bomb line further highlighted the wisdom of Simonds's earlier admonition that there was nothing more dangerous than to sit down in front of the Boche and not know what he was up to.[20]

The best time to have launched a second attack upon the Germans was when they were reeling and disorganized, unable to immediately recover owing to severe disruption. This opportunity presented itself on the morning of 8 August, when the shattered German defence was in turmoil, but it was a fleeting moment that should have been seized upon by continuing to press the attack. The inescapable fact remains that the momentum of the first-phase attack, which exceeded expectations, could have been maintained only by keeping up the pressure in phase two. Every passing minute allowed the Germans time to catch their breath and regroup. That neither Simonds nor Crerar actually knew that the route to Falaise lay open was of less consequence than recognizing the historical reality that breakthroughs have not always been easily discernible. As Montgomery preached, vague and imprecise information about the enemy should never preclude fighting for information or quick and aggressive action by reserves. In Operation "Cobra," American Major General J.L. Collins, VII Corps commander, ordered one division to pass through another despite the risk of congestion and conditions generally described as chaotic. His later decision to commit the 3rd Armoured Division was even based on bad information. Yet, his unleashing of exploitation forces before breakthrough elements had secured their immediate objectives turned out to be one of the vital decisions of the "Cobra" operation.[21]

Maintaining similar momentum in "Totalize" would have necessitated moving the bomb line[22] and launching air strikes farther south, or cancelling the bombing attack altogether to enable the armoured divisions to strike directly toward their objectives. In fact, the Eighth Air Force bomber strike could have been cancelled in flight up to 1100 hours. Earlier arrangements had also provided for postponing the 1400 strike up to 2000 if army headquarters so requested before 0900 hours, but weather predictions mandated that the strike had to start at 1226 and end at 1355. Owing to enemy anti-aircraft fire and heavy clouds of dust and smoke, only 492 of 678 US Eighth Air Force bombers managed to attack, and just three of four targeted areas were adequately bombed. Two twelve-plane groups also mistakenly bombed elements of the 2nd Canadian Armoured Brigade, 2 Canadian AGRA, 9 AGRA, and the 1st Polish and 3rd Canadian divisions, killing 65 soldiers and wounding another 250.

Although this fratricide did not prevent the 1st Polish and 4th Canadian armoured divisions from crossing the start line for the attack on time, the US bombing had not fatally crippled the now-recovered German defence. The bombing was thus hardly worth the wait as it proved largely ineffective and partly counter-productive. In light of what actually happened, moreover, cancelling the bomber strike before it was launched should have been no more difficult than it was after 1245 hours when Simonds went to observe the strike and personally called Crerar asking him to stop all bombing as it was falling on friendly forces.[23]

Had the armoured divisions attacked mid-morning rather than in the afternoon they would have encountered far less coordinated resistance and beaten German counter-attacks to the punch. The road to Falaise lay open and undefended from midnight 7 August to noon 8 August. German counter-moves escalated to serious counter-attacks north of the bomb line between 1230 and 1340 hours that afternoon. Although beaten off in the area of St. Aignan-de-Cramesnil, they served as spoiling attacks that shook Canadian confidence and morale. The German forces so engaged also fell back on cohesive defensive positions along the general line Gouvix–Hautmesnil–St. Sylvain, which had been prepared by rearward German troops frantically digging in and coordinating defensive arcs of fire. Plans to strengthen the German defence further had also been set in motion with the redeployment of the 12th SS Panzer Division's Kampfgruppe Wunsche from fighting the Second British Army in the area of Grimbosq to occupy the heights west and northwest of Potigny and defend the narrow passage between the Laison and the Laize rivers. When Simonds's armoured divisions finally attacked after bomber strikes between 1226–1355, roughly the period of German counter-attacks north of the bomb line, they got nowhere. Within an hour the Poles lost some forty tanks to enemy anti-tank and tank fire, and by 1600 their advance stalled completely with a paltry gain of two kilometres. The badly launched 4th Canadian Armoured Division did not fare much better, barely getting to Hautmesnil for an advance of just under four kilometres.[24] On the basis of the evidence as it relates to German counter-moves and deployments, it is hard to imagine that Canadian arms could have done any worse had they opted to cancel the bombing and attacked earlier. By maintaining the momentum of the attack they would at least have stood a chance of forcing the situation to develop to their advantage, rather than waiting to let it develop to the advantage of the defending enemy.

The performance of Simonds's armoured divisions during the second phase of "Totalize" has been deemed lacklustre for various reasons, inexperience and fighting structure among them.[25] Simonds had decentralized an AGRA of five medium regiments in support of the 4th Canadian Armoured Division to enable it to blast its way forward. The 4th Armoured Brigade spearheaded the division advance, however, with a battle group comprising the Canadian Grenadier Guards tank regiment, the Lake Superior Regiment (Motor), and anti-tank and engineer elements. Called "Halpenny Force" after the Guards CO, Lieutenant Colonel W.W. Halpenny, this battle group set out to capture Bretteville-le-Rabet, but only managed to advance beyond Cintheaux by 1800 hours, at which time the 10th Brigade seized the village and pushed south to take Hautmesnil, the farthest penetration of the 4th Division that day. The missing element in the performance of "Halpenny Force" was artillery, and making the best use of the huge fire resources available called for more artillery staff planning and coordination expertise than units like the Guards possessed. The decentralized battle group idea appears to have been embraced in imitation of German practice by the 4th Armoured Brigade commander, Brigadier E.L. Booth, who correctly reasoned that tanks alone had little chance of success against German mixed groups of all arms. Yet, as so often with imitation, Booth failed to see that the German Kampfgruppe all-arms structure bore greater resemblance to the Canadian brigade than the unit.

The formation of battle groups like "Halpenny Force" without brigade fire planning assistance saddled a single-arm commander with all-arms coordination problems that Canadian brigade staff organization and communications were better equipped to handle. Montgomery had constantly warned against this practice, asserting that leaving unit COs to shoulder responsibility for all arms operations was an abrogation of tactical responsibility. In this case, he was absolutely right, for when the 4th Armoured Division commander, Major General Kitching, irritated over the delay of "Halpenny Force," finally established contact with Booth, he found him nearly two miles away from the battle and fast asleep in his tank. The eventual solution was to form battle groups based on the brigade. Battle organization within the armoured division involved forming two mixed brigades, each of two armoured regiments and two infantry battalions backed up by artillery as required. While all units were completely interchangeable with regimental-battalion groups organized and commanded according to assigned task, a significant aspect of this structure was that the brigades themselves lost their separate armoured and infantry character. Both brigadiers and their headquarters had to be equally competent at executing all arms operations, including artillery planning, which Montgomery held was best coordinated at this level.[26] In this case, "Halpenny Force" could have used more artillery fire planning assistance and stronger direction from Booth and his brigade headquarters to deal with enemy anti-tank screens holding up its advance.[27]

Another major factor affecting armoured division performance was the road congestion that held up the forward deployment of the 1st Polish and 4th Canadian attacking divisions. Knowing that the attack was not to go in until around 1400 after heavy bombing strikes further-more failed to induce any sense of urgency for armoured divisions to move forward aggressively, ignoring and brushing by enemy pockets of resistance. That gunners expected pre-designated gun positions to be perfectly sanitized and clear of all enemy mortar and machine-gun fire was also unreasonable in the circumstances. Artillery incurred but 8 per cent of casualties compared with the infantry's 76 per cent, and SP armoured artillery should have been forced to accept greater risks in gun position areas. The roughly six-hour wait for the start of phase two also contributed to the tendency of first phase assault divisions to tidy up the battlefield and bring their administrative rear echelons forward, thereby increasing congestion that slowed the forward movement of the attacking armoured divisions. Had the air strike been waived and high command attention turned to stopping this and giving absolute priority to getting second phase fighting troops and supporting artillery forward, the tempo could have been sustained. Given the relatively short distances involved, the armoured divisions standing by on notice to move should have been able to run roughshod through first-phase troops ordered to get well out of the way.[28] Focusing solely on driving deeply into enemy territory would also have prevented them from being sidetracked into dealing with enemy pockets of resistance.

As things turned out, it was mainly the 12th SS Division's resourceful handling of limited numbers of panzers that stemmed the 2 Canadian Corps attack. The bulk of roughly eighty 88-mm anti-tank guns, mostly belonging to three Luftwaffe flak regiments, remained deployed south of Potigny with only the divisional batteries forward.[29] Such an anti-tank screen could only have been overcome by artillery. At 1830 hours Simonds attempted to regain the momentum lost during the pause by directing the 4th Armoured to press on through the night to secure Bretteville-le-Rabet and Point 195, the highest feature before Falaise. At 0200 hours 9 August the division's other battle group, "Worthing-ton Force," named after the CO of the British Columbia Regiment and including three infantry companies of the Algonquin Regiment, drove deeply into German territory to arrive by 0700 not on Point 195, but rather, through an error in map reading, roughly four miles almost directly east in the area of Point 140.[30] Here it was annihilated, but the aggressive advance of the battle group demonstrated just what might have been accomplished had it headed in the right direction. If "Worthington Force" had been unleashed in daylight at 1100 hours on 8 August, it might well have been on Point 195 by 1600 hours or even earlier.

Crerar was the only one who could have altered Simonds's plan, and had he been a more experienced field army commander he may have done so, opting to hit the enemy immediately to ascertain his true strength while seeking to shape a more favourable development of the situation. To have overruled Simonds, of course, would have taken a field army commander with the requisite experience and confidence to do so. Crerar was certainly aware of the adverse implications of the loss of momentum in an attack, but he obviously did not think that he could do much to influence matters.[31] Simonds did not therefore receive the prodding that might have been forthcoming from a field army commander like Dempsey. Having expended so much staff effort in arranging strategic bomber support, moreover, Crerar may also have been reluctant to request a cancellation for fear of jeopardizing future support from "Bomber" Harris, with whom he had ingratiated himself.[32] His recent dispute with Crocker could additionally have disposed him not to interfere in corps operations. That he had absorbed Montgomery's advice in that dispute is certain, as he later remarked that, under normal conditions an army commander would not give a direct order to a division or tell Simonds which troops should be employed to carry out assigned tasks, though "he might suggest that, say, the … Polish Armoured Division seemed to be well placed to do the job."[33] Yet the essence of Montgomery's counsel was that a higher commander should interfere to prevent things going badly. Arguably, Crerar could have directed Simonds to use the reserve 3rd Canadian Infantry Division to outflank the Germans from the west via Claire Tizon, as was eventually done by the 2nd Division. Alternatively, it may have been wiser to send this reserve to outflank the Germans to the east.

Failure to break out in Operation "Totalize" dashed Crerar's hope of exploiting a golden opportunity presented to the First Canadian Army. Following the successful breakout of the First US Army from St. Lo on 27 July, the Seventh German Army on 6 August launched a major five-division counter-attack westward toward Mortain with a view to stemming the rapidly accelerating American advance through Avranches. A subsequent Canadian advance to the area of Falaise would thus have caught the Germans in full stride as they struck west, rupturing the right rear flank of the Seventh German Army and sealing off its main body engaged around Mortain. Such a movement successfully executed on 8 August would have led to bagging the entire German force that attacked west on 6 August. Although falling short of this situation, "Totalize" forced enemy logistical elements to withdraw southwards, which deprived the Seventh German Army of its rear installations and necessitated re-supply to be provided by the Fifth Panzer Army. The Commander-in-Chief West, Field Marshal Guenther von Kluge, also quickly grasped that the Seventh German Army risked being cut off at the base by "Totalize." On 8 August he remarked that a breakthrough had occurred near Caen "the like of which we have never seen."[34] He knew then that his head was in a potential noose and that Montgomery still possessed the initiative.

Each day between 9 and 12 August Montgomery conferred with Crerar and Dempsey urging the quick capture of Falaise, and ordering Crerar on 11 August to operate with one division west of the River Laize to take the town in the flank.[35] For the First Canadian Army this required mounting another corps attack, Operation "Tractable," in which the imaginative Simonds used the cover of smoke in daylight to hurl his divisions down the Caen-Falaise road at 1000 hours 14 August. Crerar, for his part, decided to fly back and forth along the west side of the Caen-Falaise road, attempting to "escort" heavy bombers so as to prevent them from bombing short as occurred in "Totalize." Sadly, his efforts failed miserably and seventy-seven bombers mistakenly unloaded on Canadian rearward units, especially 2 Canadian AGRA and elements of the 1st Polish Armoured Division, causing 400 casualties.[36] Attempts to stop the bombing by setting out yellow markers and firing yellow flares and smoke only brought more bombs as the air force used the same colour to indicate targets. Bomber Command remained unaware of a SHAEF directive that authorized using the colour yellow to indicate forward ground troop positions. SHAEF should have advised Bomber Command, but as Headquarters First Canadian Army arranged all land–air coordination, this aspect should have been addressed. Crerar's COS certainly saw it that way and suggested to Crerar, "we (and myself in particular) might be considered as having some responsibility" insofar as First Canadian Army "erred … by not pointing out the use of yellow smoke and flares" to indicate ground troop positions. Crerar, on the other hand, disagreed, stating that it was AEAF's fault in not drawing the attention of Bomber Command to the SHAEF directive.[37] Since higher headquarters have a responsibility to ensure that all aspects of an operation are thoroughly checked and coordinated, however, it is difficult to accept Crerar's shifting of blame for bombing errors in "Tractable."

Although Canadian ground forces broke well into German defences in "Tractable," the operation fell short of expectations. This later prompted Bradley and others to criticize Montgomery for not reinforcing the First Canadian Army drive on Falaise with more battle-seasoned troops from the Second British Army. That Montgomery had forces

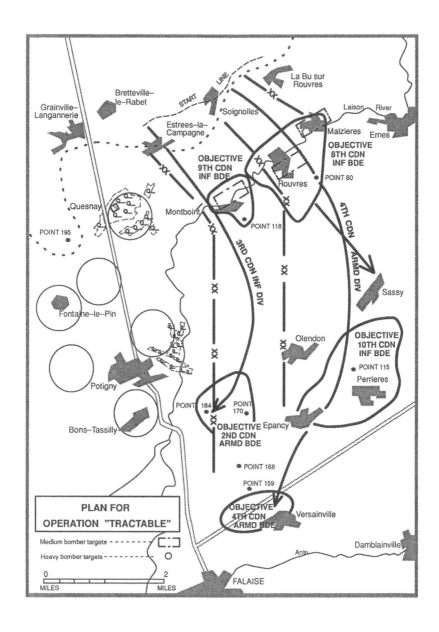

Map 11.3 Plan for Operation "Tractable" (C.P. Stacey, *The Victory Campaign: The Operation in North-West Europe, 1944–1945*, 1966)

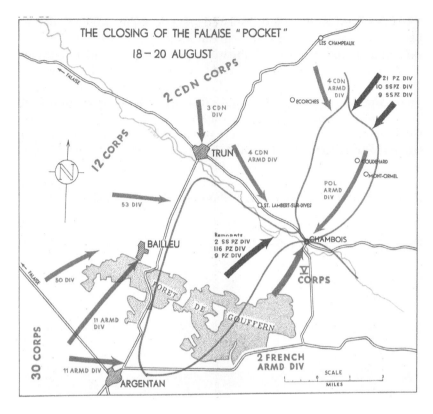

Map 11.4 The closing of the Falaise "Pocket," 18–20 August 1944 (Montgomery of Alamein, Field Marshal the Viscount, *Memoirs* [London: Collins, 1958])

available to reinforce the Canadians, but chose not to do so, has been attributed to his concern that the sensitive Canadians might interpret such a move as a loss of confidence in them. Another explanation is that he was overly optimistic in the ability of Simonds to get to Falaise, though he did add the caveat "if possible."[38] Instead of reinforcing the Canadians, he ordered Dempsey to support them by advancing his left flank on Falaise to join up with the First Canadian Army. A related point is that although Montgomery had accepted Bradley's recently suggested shorter envelopment of German forces at Falaise and Argentan, he remained far more interested in effecting a longer envelopment on the River Seine. As insurance against Falaise not falling, he resorted to generalship, ordering Crerar to take Trun in the realistic expectation that the shorter envelopment could be better effected farther east in the Trun-Chambois sector leaving the Germans to run a gauntlet of fire.

In this regard Montgomery displayed great flexibility, accommodating a late change in plan suggested by an American ally and not showing lack of confidence in Canadians, all the while looking days ahead to trapping the Germans on the Seine.[39] The 2nd Canadian Division ultimately outflanked the enemy from west of the Laize, entering Falaise on 16 August and completely clearing the town two days later when the withdrawal of German forces through the Falaise Gap reached full flood. By 25 August Montgomery's four field armies were on the Seine, ten days earlier than originally envisioned in D-Day planning,[40] after having inflicted a crushing defeat on the German army in the west. In this greater context, the importance of the capture of Falaise did not loom so large, leaving Montgomery's faith in the Canadians undiminished and well placed.

Chapter Twelve

First Canadian Army's Greatest Contribution to Allied Victory

On 20 August Montgomery ordered the First Canadian Army to ensure that the Trun-Chambois bottle remained tightly corked, while simultaneously developing a strong thrust toward Lisieux and eastwards toward Rouen. In his order he also expressed the expectation that the 2nd Canadian Infantry Division would deal very suitably with Dieppe.[1] Montgomery's order saw Crocker's northernmost 1 Corps drive on Honfleur and the Seine north of Rouen, and, after the end of organized resistance in the Trun-Chambois area, Simonds's 2 Canadian Corps advance through Bernay toward Elbeuf and the Forêt de la Londe southwest of Rouen. On 26 August the Canadians made their first crossing at Elbeuf, establishing contact with enveloping First US Army forces already there. In the Forêt de la Londe, however, the 2nd Canadian Infantry Division battled stiff German rearguard resistance for three days. The 2nd Division had suffered exceptionally heavy losses in Normandy and was still deficient 1,910 other ranks despite receiving numerous reinforcements. The shortage was mainly in trained infantrymen, but this did not stop Foulkes, the division commander, from throwing in battalion after battalion. By the end of the fighting in the Forêt de la Londe, the South Saskatchewan Regiment's four rifle companies mustered only sixty men. The 1st Corps had meanwhile closed up to the Seine only to find on crossing at Caudebec-en-Caux and Duclair that the enemy had withdrawn. By 30 August, the 3rd Infantry and 4th Armoured divisions of 2 Canadian Corps had pushed north and east out of the Elbeuf bridgehead, enabling the 9th Canadian Infantry Brigade to take Rouen from the east.[2]

On the same day, Crerar issued a new directive to his corps commanders, giving 2 Canadian Corps the immediate task of capturing Dieppe while advancing along the main army axis running through Neufchatel to Abbeville on the Somme River. This was in keeping with Montgomery's 26 August direction that stressed moving quickly in an all-out effort to hasten the end of the war and protect England from rocket attacks by overrunning flying bomb sites in the Pas de Calais area.[3] He listed the tasks of the 21st Army Group as follows: to operate northwards and destroy enemy forces in northeast France and Belgium; secure the Pas de Calais area and airfields in Belgium; and secure Antwerp as a base with the eventual aim of advancing on the Ruhr. Montgomery specifically directed Dempsey's Second British Army to cross the Seine with all speed and drive through the industrial region of northeast France into Belgium. He also ordered Crerar's First Canadian Army to seize the ports of Le Havre and Dieppe and quickly destroy all enemy forces in the coastal belt up to Bruges, especially V1 rocket sites used to strike Britain since 12 June. Accordingly, on the morning of 31 August, 2 Canadian Corps commenced a pursuit through the zone of German flying bomb launch sites from Rouen to the Pas de Calais while 1 Corps turned north to besiege Le Havre. Crerar's headquarters followed along the main army axis, collocating from 2 September with headquarters No. 84 Group, RAF for the remainder of the campaign in Europe.[4]

Meanwhile, the Second British Army, after crossing the Seine at Vernon on 23 August 1944, raced 250 miles to the east in one week, demonstrating, as had Patton, that spectacular exploitations reflected light enemy resistance. Indeed, Dempsey went all out to bring up fuel at the expense of ammunition and other stores. He also employed 8 Corps transport to enable Horrocks's 30 Corps to move swiftly in a spearhead role, with the British 12 Corps close behind. His order to Horrocks was simple: "You will capture (a) Antwerp (b) Brussels."[5] Early on 31 August 30 Corps arrived in Amiens on the Somme, having moved so fast that they captured German General Heinrich Eberbach, who had just taken over as Seventh Army commander. Downstream on the Somme Ritchie's 12 Corps reached Pont Remy and Abbeville in the front of 2 Canadian Corps. That afternoon Montgomery conferred with his army commanders, directing Crerar to drive on that night to relieve British forces in these locations the next day so that Second Army would be free to push on to Arras and St. Pol. Crerar told Montgomery he would assign this task to 2 Canadian Corps, using the 4th Armoured Division with the 1st Polish Armoured Division following up. In his diary Montgomery noted that Crerar had grouped his army badly for what was wanted. This perhaps reflected Simonds having to cancel his plans to refit the 4th Armoured Division, which resumed the advance and despite colliding with British elements reached the outskirts of Abbeville early on 2 September.[6]

As earlier suggested by Montgomery, the 2nd Canadian Infantry Division had been deliberately earmarked to capture Dieppe, where those killed in the costly raid of 19 August 1942 lay buried. In anticipation of a

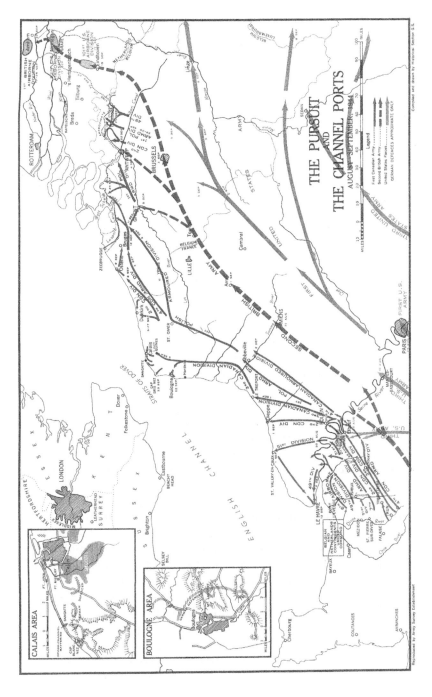

Map 12.1 The pursuit and the Channel Ports, August–September 1944 (C.P. Stacey, *The Canadian Army, 1939–1945*, 1948)

strong German defence of the town, a divisional attack plan that included heavy bombardment by Bomber Command had been prepared. On finding that the enemy had withdrawn, however, the air strike was cancelled with twenty minutes to spare. On 1 September the 2nd Division entered Dieppe without opposition, and the following day the 51st (Highland) Division, in a similarly symbolic action, took St. Valery-en-Caux, where the division's main body had been surrounded and forced to surrender in June 1940. On learning that the 4th Armoured Division intended to refit east of Abbeville while the 2nd Division remained in Dieppe, Montgomery signalled that with the Second Army over one hundred miles ahead nearing the Belgian frontier this was not the time to stop for maintenance. He therefore urged Crerar to push his two armoured divisions, the 1st Polish and 4th Armoured, forward with all speed to St. Omer and beyond. Although the 4th Armoured was at half strength in tanks and at three-quarters strength in infantry, which Montgomery likely did not know, his direction to press on regardless made good military sense as at this juncture operations involved the pursuit of a fleeing enemy. Failing to note that Montgomery referred specifically to the two armoured divisions, which were ideally suited to pursuit operations that called more for fuel than ammunition, Crerar guardedly replied that reinforcement was essential for the 2nd Division and that there was "no lack of push or rational speed" on the part of his army.[7]

Montgomery, promoted Field Marshal[8] on 1 September for his resounding victory in Normandy, had not objected to the 2nd Canadian Infantry Division halting at Dieppe to absorb a thousand reinforcements, but he did think that since crossing the Seine the First Canadian Army had been badly handled and slow. Part of the problem may have been Crerar's personal involvement in non-operational administrative issues that diverted his attention from field army command. In September alone he actioned twenty-nine pieces of substantial correspondence dealing with such matters. Other factors affecting his performance included his impression that the war was ending, his persistent attacks of dysentery, and his guilt-ridden fixation with Dieppe, for which disaster he was largely responsible. On 2 September he met with Foulkes to discuss ceremonial arrangements for the Dieppe commemoration and the next day attended the ceremony at which he took the salute. In doing so he missed a conference called by Montgomery to discuss maintaining momentum in future operations with his army commanders, including Bradley, Dempsey, and Hodges. He had replied to Montgomery's request to attend the conference by asking that it be postponed from 1300 to 1700 hours, but then went off to Dieppe without waiting for confirmation. There he received a hand-delivered message from

Montgomery requesting his presence. When Crerar arrived at Montgomery's tactical headquarters on the afternoon of 3 September he received a "ticking off" to which he responded that he had acted as Canadian national commander and was prepared to take the matter up with his government if necessary. For Crerar not to have sent his COS, however, was unprofessional and could well have reflected his admitted deteriorating powers of decision. In the end, on finding that Crerar had not received his last message in sufficient time, Montgomery solicited the advice of his Canadian personal assistant who told him to apologize. This Montgomery did, accepting full blame. He nonetheless privately noted that Crerar was not fit to general a field army, but that he would have to put up with him.[9]

If the capture of Dieppe was personally important to Crerar, it was also logistically important to the Allied effort. From 7 September the First Canadian Army received 60 per cent of the tonnage offloaded at the port, which eliminated serious Canadian army supply problems by mid-September.[10] This accorded with "Overlord" plans that originally reserved the Channel ports for the British and Canadians. The exception was Le Havre, later earmarked for the Americans, whose far more serious supply problems ultimately determined the employment of First Canadian Army. Much responsibility for this lay with Eisenhower and SHAEF, which in the hope of attaining Channel ports, and even Rotterdam and Amsterdam, decided on 3 September to abandon plans to use the Brittany ports of Lorient, Quiberon Bay, St. Nazaire, and Nantes. On 14 September a similar decision was made regarding Brest, which like Cherbourg on surrender yielded a thoroughly demolished port that from a planning perspective could only have been expected in the case of Antwerp.[11] This did not happen because the rapid capture of Antwerp by Dempsey's Second British Army on 4 September had caught the Germans completely off guard with the result that the dock facilities of Europe's second-largest port remained entirely intact. Unfortunately, the British had not acted fast enough to prevent the build-up of German forces in the heavily dyked "polder" country of Walcheren, Beveland, and the west bank of the Scheldt estuary from Knocke-sur-Mer to Terneuzen. This left Antwerp some 50 miles inland inaccessible from the sea, and hence of limited logistical value to the Allies. Montgomery's fixation with the Ruhr and his desire to establish a bridgehead over the Rhine before winter further complicated the opening of the port. With the German army reeling all along the Allied front in early September, his preferred choice was to thrust immediately into the German heartland rather than risk being be drawn into a casualty intensive protracted struggle with a cornered enemy on a flank.

The result was "Market Garden," one of the most imaginative operations of the war, which Eisenhower enthusiastically approved, allowing Montgomery to defer the clearance of the Scheldt.[12] The epic story of "Market Garden" has been the subject of heated debate, but aspects of Montgomery's desire for a bridgehead across the Rhine have been overlooked. On 12 September the CCS drew attention to the importance of the northern thrust toward Germany and emphasized the need to open Antwerp and Rotterdam before bad weather set in. Antwerp remained closed as the Germans held the mouth of the Scheldt, but an Arnhem bridgehead would have left 21st Army Group within striking distance of the great port of Rotterdam, which was closer to the sea and had far shorter channel access than the long Scheldt estuary leading to Antwerp. In his "Market Garden" order of 14 September Montgomery stressed that the real objective remained the Ruhr, to be isolated, surrounded, and occupied "as we may desire," but "on the way to it we want the ports of Antwerp and Rotterdam."[13] Advancing northeast from Eindhoven to Arnhem would also have left Montgomery in a position to rope off the whole of Holland, including the 150,000 fleeing troops of the German Fifteenth Army and the V2 sites in the area of Rotterdam and Amsterdam, another great seaport close to Arnhem. On 17 September as Allied airborne forces winged their way to parachute and land near Arnhem, Montgomery's chief plans officer, Brigadier C.L. Richardson, put before him a plan to advance via Utrecht, 35 miles from Arnhem, to seize either Rotterdam 30 miles distant or Amsterdam 20 miles distant.[14]

Montgomery has been chastised for his "Market Garden" operation after the fact. On 5 October Brooke recorded in his diary that instead of carrying out the advance Montgomery "ought to have made certain of Antwerp in the first place."[15] Other voices nonetheless defended Montgomery, including US General James M. Gavin, who argued that if Eisenhower had stopped Patton and thrown full support behind Montgomery, which he did not, "the operation in Holland could have been an overwhelming triumph."[16] Tank pioneer and military theorist, Major General J.F.C. Fuller, similarly maintained that despite the blockage of Antwerp Montgomery "vigorously urged an all-out advance northwards, and we think that the dictum of history will be that he was right."[17] Like Montgomery, both Gavin and Fuller believed that a single powerful thrust north of the Ardennes could have ended the European war in 1944. In a related vein, Montgomery could hardly have been expected to take American supply problems into account as these remained the province of Eisenhower.[18] The British maintained a separate supply system from the Americans and had less need for Antwerp. As previously mentioned, there was no serious supply problem in the First Canadian Army after the capture of Dieppe. Yet, on 2 September formations in the US First and Third armies ran out of gas. Clearly, it was also easier to maintain the 21st Army Group along the northern seaboard than the US 12th Army Group farther inland. Unfortunately, the much-touted one-way Red Ball Express route, which delivered almost 90,000 tons to US armies between 25 August and 6 September, ultimately failed to live up to its hype and proved to be grossly wasteful and inefficient. Arguably, American supply shortages stemmed less from a lack of harbours than from mismanagement in the US Communications Zone. In any case, Eisenhower on 10 September specifically authorized Montgomery to put off clearing the Scheldt until after "Market Garden."[19]

Anticipating the green light, Montgomery signalled Crerar on 6 September that he wanted Boulogne badly for the rapid development of his plan, since Antwerp looked to be unusable for some time. By 7 September he had also calculated that it would be possible to advance to Berlin on the basis of the ports of Dieppe, Boulogne, Calais, and Dunkirk and supplemented by 3,000 tons of cargo per day through Le Havre. He further estimated that with Boulogne and another Pas de Calais port producing 5,000 tons a day, plus an extra 1,000 tons of airlift per day, and twenty companies of motor transport, it would be possible to reach the Rheine-Munster-Osnabruck area. The tasks assigned to the First Canadian Army on 9 September thus gave priority to the capture of Boulogne, Dunkirk, and Calais, and then the capture of the islands at the mouth of the Scheldt. On 12 September, however, Montgomery received a message from Brooke stating that the early opening of Antwerp and clearance of the Scheldt appeared to be of great importance. That morning Montgomery signalled Crerar requesting his views on how he would go about tackling such an operation. The next day Montgomery advised Crerar that while the capture of Boulogne, Calais, and Dunkirk remained desirable, operations to open Antwerp were probably more important. As a helpful hint, he further suggested that to ensure maximum concurrent activity and speed Crerar use one of his corps headquarters to control operations from Boulogne to Dunkirk and the other to plan and execute the opening of Antwerp. In a supplementary message the same evening Montgomery added that the early use of Antwerp was so urgent that he was prepared to give up operations against Calais and Dunkirk and be content with Boulogne. He also asked "if we do this will it enable you to speed up the Antwerp business?"[20]

Crerar referred the matter to his staff and the same day offered the tentative conclusion that, on the basis of staff analysis, he needed more resources. Specifically, he asked for the temporary transfer of the British 12 Corps currently in the Antwerp area or, alternatively, for his British 1

Corps to take over the 53rd (Welsh) Division from 12 Corps and assume responsibility for the city of Antwerp. He further suggested that the development of operations along the axis Breda–Tilburg would then become a Canadian Army responsibility with the inter-army boundary adjusted as necessary.[21] Crerar's proposal of the latter role for Crocker's 1 Corps, rather than following Montgomery's advice and designating it to control operations from Boulogne to Dunkirk, while selecting Simonds's 2 Corps headquarters for opening the Scheldt, appears to have been a mistake on Crerar's part. This would have been a simple solution that presented an opportunity to *commit* elements of the First Canadian Army, which Montgomery would have had difficulty in extracting for other tasks later. In any case, special armour used in the 1 Corps siege of Le Havre had to be moved to support Boulogne operations. As neither 12 Corps nor the 53rd Division could be spared from "Market Garden," Montgomery now seized upon Crerar's alternative suggestion and ordered him to move 1 Corps and its subordinate 49th (West Riding) Division, using 51st (Highland) Division transport, to relieve the 53rd Division in Antwerp as soon as possible. The 51st Division thus remained grounded without vehicles at Le Havre, which had been captured by 1 Corps on 12 September after a brilliant two-division attack launched forty-eight hours earlier.[22]

At a conference of army commanders on 14 September, Montgomery issued his directive on the Arnhem operation, which also formally assigned the clearance of the Scheldt, specifically the capture of the Walcheren group of islands, to the First Canadian Army as a first priority. The next day Crerar forwarded his own directive to his two corps commanders allotting the Scheldt operation to 2 Canadian Corps. With several assigned tasks hinging on the success of others, his directive was not an easy read. As a first step, he ordered the 2nd Canadian Infantry Division to turn from the task of taking Dunkirk, leaving it to be masked by the 4th Special Service (Commando) Brigade,[23] and take over the city of Antwerp from the 53rd Division of 12 Corps by 18 September. Crerar initially detailed two alternate tasks for the British 1 Corps: first, to mount a deliberate attack on Calais in the event it did not fall easily to 2 Canadian Corps; and, second, in the event Calais did surrender quickly, to take over the right front of First Canadian Army to protect the right flank of 2 Canadian Corps while it engaged in the operations to open Antwerp. On 19 September, perhaps reflecting his attack of dysentery that day, Crerar in another directive decided to make 2 Canadian Corps exclusively responsible for the eventual reduction of Calais. At same time, he ordered Crocker's 1 Corps minus the 51st Highland Division to take over the British 12 Corps sector near Turnhout, east of Antwerp, with a view to developing operations northward toward Breda and Tilburg east of

1 Monty summoning troops to gather round (LAC PA 132891).

2 Prime Minister Mackenzie King and General McNaughton (LAC PA 68246).

3 Montgomery training visit with Simonds in background (LAC PA 142272).

4 Monty addressing soldiers of the Calgary Regiment in Sicily, August 1943
(LAC PA 168548).

5 Major General Chris Vokes, GOC 1st Canadian Division (left), with Brigadiers B.M. Hoffmeister, 2nd Infantry Brigade (centre), and R.A Wyman, commander 1st Canadian Armoured Brigade (LAC PA 131064).

6 Monty briefing Prime Minister Winston Churchill on the Normandy situation, 22 July 1944, with Lieutenant General G.G. Simonds, GOC 2 Canadian Corps, holding map and Lieutenant General Sir Miles Dempsey, GOC-in-C Second British Army, looking on (Imperial War Museum TR2047).

7 Major Generals R.F.L. Keller, GOC 3rd Canadian Infantry Division, and C. Foulkes, GOC 2nd Canadian Infantry Division (LAC PA 116519).

8 General M.C. Dempsey, GOC-in-C Second British Army, Monty, and Simonds (LAC PA 142101).

9 Major General R.F.L Keller and Lieutenant General Sir John Crocker, 25 June 1945 (LAC PA 129170).

10 Panther tank destroyed by hand-held PIAT (Projector Infantry Anti-Tank),
Normandy (LAC PA 130149).

11 Sherman Firefly 17-pounder (LAC PA131391).

12 Master and Disciple (LAC PA 129125).

13 Simonds's Armoured Personnel Carrier. M7 self-propelled 105mm howitzer with main armament removed (LAC PA 177352).

14 Forming up for Operation "Totalize" (LAC PA 132904).

15 Preparing for Operation "Tractable" (LAC PA 116525).

16 This photo captures the essence of Monty's close relationship with Simonds and more distant one with Crerar (LAC e010796910).

17 Simonds and J.L. Ralston, Minister of National Defence in Belgium (LAC PA 136762).

18 Brigadier John Rockingham, commander 9th infantry Brigade, and Lieutenant General Brian Horrocks, GOC 30 Corps (LAC PA 145101)F.

19 First Canadian Army senior commanders May 1945. Left to right, seated, Major General H.S. Maczek, Simonds, Crerar, Foulkes, Hoffmeister; standing R.H. Keefler, A.B. Matthews, H.W. Foster, R.W. Moncel, S.B. Rawlins (LAC PA 132281).

20 Eisenhower and Polish troops. His only visit to First Canadian Army, 29 November 1944 (LAC PA 128052).

21 Lieutenant General Howard Graham, CGS
1955–58 (Canadian Army Journal).

22 Lieutenant General Findlay
Clark, CGS 1958–61 (Canadian
Army Journal).

23 Lieutenant General Geoffrey
Walsh, CGS 1961–64 (Canadian
Army Journal).

Roosendaal. Although the reasons for this change were not apparently recorded,[24] it is possible that given the exigencies of "Market Garden" Montgomery may have taken Crerar up on his earlier suggestion that 1 Corps assume responsibility for operations against Breda and Tilburg.

The effect of Crerar's direction left the four divisions of 2 Canadian Corps stretched between Boulogne and Antwerp.[25] On 12 September Simonds had directed the 1st Polish Armoured Division to clear the Ghent-Antwerp-Terneuzen triangle up to the West Scheldt. The 4th Canadian Armoured Division was at the same time directed to clear the area west of the Ghent–Terneuzen Canal up to Breskens, making its main thrust eastward from just below Bruges. The 8th and 9th Infantry Brigade Groups of the 3rd Canadian Infantry Division in the meantime prepared to attack Boulogne on 17 September. The remaining brigade of the division, the 7th, supported by the 7th Reconnaissance (capital tank) Regiment, continued to invest Calais and the great German cross-Channel gun batteries at Cape Gris Nez. After the reduction of Boulogne on 22 September, the 8th Brigade joined the 7th to participate in an assault upon Calais while the 9th captured Cape Gris Nez. Following the capitulation of Calais on 1 October, Crerar expected 2 Canadian Corps to thrust northwards toward Roosendaal and Bergen op Zoom in order to establish a firm base to the east of South Beveland, from which that objective could be attacked.[26] That Crerar held a protracted series of conferences to effect these actions left several commentators to observe that the clearance of the coastal belt and ports by the First Canadian Army was ponderous and slow. To one commentator, the Canadians on the Channel coast were investing Boulogne and Calais as though there was all the time in the world, and without a trace of imagination.[27] Two Canadian military historians have even charged that operations were conducted so poorly that had Crerar been a British rather than Canadian general, he would most surely have been sacked.[28]

The sixteen days that passed between Montgomery's 6 September request to get Boulogne and its eventual capture are at particular issue. Although the German garrison defending the port city was only slightly smaller than the one defending Le Havre, Boulogne was attacked not by two divisions, but by two brigade groups at a higher cost in both time and casualties. It took six days and 634 casualties to take Boulogne compared to two days and 388 casualties to take Le Havre.[29] Using two divisions at Le Havre versus two brigade groups at Boulogne only went to show once again the truth of the old military adage: "the more you use the fewer you lose." The fact that the assault on Boulogne had also to be delayed until after the fall of Le Havre, so that special armoured fighting vehicles could be released from 1 Corps for use by the 3rd Division, also begs the question as to whether it would have been wiser to have had 1 Corps execute a second forty-eight-hour operation to reduce Boulogne. This would have released 2 Canadian Corps for operations along the Scheldt. Moreover, the final attack on Calais, which had to await the fall of Boulogne, may have been unnecessary. It may have sufficed simply to capture Cape Gris Nez and the gun emplacements west of Calais to permit the free use of Boulogne harbour.[30]

Crerar later defended his actions by citing the difficulties of the coastal terrain, from a tactical and administrative point of view,[31] but it is also clear, as he informed Montgomery on 13 September, that rather than risk failure at Boulogne after the rapid fall of Le Havre, he wanted Simonds "to button things up properly, taking a little more time, if necessary, in order to ensure a decisive assault."[32] Simonds, on the other hand, had supposedly protested giving priority to the Channel ports and made an earlier suggestion to Crerar that 2 Canadian Corps instead conduct a relentless pursuit along the coast to Breskens, masking German coastal defences encountered, and then turn east to cut the Fifteenth Army off from the Scheldt. To ease transport difficulties, Simonds further proposed provisioning his corps with ammunition, fuel, and bridging by beaching preloaded landing craft at designated intervals during the advance. He was also confident that had he been allowed to explain his concept to Montgomery, it would have been quickly approved, permitting an earlier opening of the Scheldt. Crerar, in contrast, was less inclined to analyze the intent behind orders received from Montgomery and his planning conferences tended to be indecisive and inconclusive. Trying to solve the problem of the Scheldt simply seemed beyond him.[33]

As previously mentioned, Crerar was also far less healthy than commonly supposed, his medical condition allegedly contributing to the impairment of his command ability and powers of decision. A chain-smoker with a persistent cough, he suffered from a severe anemia brought on by recurring bouts of dysentery that left him both fatigued and irascible. During the planning stages for the Battle of the Scheldt he suffered attacks severe enough to be recorded on 1, 19, and 21 September. After a final attack of dysentery that failed to respond to the usual medical treatment, he checked himself into hospital for a thorough examination. On 26 September at a conference of army commanders Crerar told Montgomery that he had to go back to England for further diagnosis and tests. Montgomery, who observed that Crerar looked very ill, reported this development to Brooke and suggested that he might possibly like to assure Canadian authorities that the First Canadian Army would be in good hands with Simonds in charge. The elevation of Simonds to army command called, in turn, for Foulkes to take over the 2 Canadian Corps. The medical evacuation of Crerar followed on 27 September.[34]

Before his departure Crerar handed over command to Simonds, whose arrival was described as electrifying and a breath of fresh air. Whereas Crerar often appeared stymied by the problems facing him and thus relied heavily upon his G (Plans) Section for devising operational solutions, Simonds rose to the challenge of personally thinking things through, then giving orders.[35] To use Chester Wilmot's categorizations, if Montgomery was an expert implementer, Simonds was a radical innovator forever seeking new solutions.[36] Lack of resources, such as being denied the use of airborne troops, merely called for greater creativity. Even before assuming army command he had exposed the weaknesses of G (Plans) recommendations related to the opening of the Scheldt estuary that had been endorsed by Crerar. In particular, Simonds pointed out that the aim was not simply to capture Walcheren and South Beveland so the port could be used, but to destroy, neutralize, or capture enemy defences that denied Allied free passage through the West Scheldt to the port of Antwerp.[37] The critical appreciation that Simonds produced himself remains one of the most striking and original tactical documents of the campaign.[38]

Simonds also fought the Scheldt campaign as an army-level joint service battle in which he earmarked naval and military forces for amphibious assaults upon the fortified island of Walcheren, the Breskens Pocket, and the South Beveland peninsula. Over strong expert objections, he additionally insisted on flooding the island, much of which lay below sea level, by breaching the sea dykes through heavy bomber attacks in order to isolate German forces and leave them open to amphibious attack. In so doing, Simonds turned the tables on the Germans, who would undoubtedly have flooded the island themselves in a last-ditch stand to counter any Canadian ground force attack. Simonds further envisioned the 2nd Canadian Division pushing northward from Antwerp to seal off South Beveland and exploit the land approach leading to Walcheren as far as possible. The 4th Canadian Armoured Division, having encountered fierce opposition, was meanwhile tasked to probe the area north of the Leopold Canal up to the West Scheldt until relieved by the 3rd Canadian Infantry Division from the Boulogne–Calais area. Both the 4th Canadian Armoured and Polish Armoured Divisions would then be available to move east of Antwerp on Bergen op Zoom and Roosendaal.[39]

For the most part, Simonds's plan superseded an earlier elaboration produced by Crerar's (G) Plans Section, which based its conclusions on the dubious assumption that the whole of the south shore of the West Scheldt from Antwerp to the sea had been cleared. First Canadian

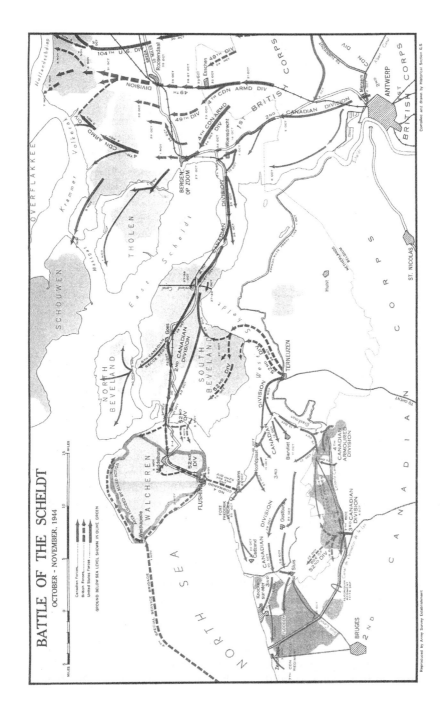

Map 12.2 The Battle of the Scheldt, October–November 1944 (C.P. Stacey, *The Canadian Army, 1939–1945*, 1948)

Army intelligence apparently did not believe, despite Ultra decrypts to the contrary, that the Germans would choose to defend south of the West Scheldt. On the day Simonds took charge of the First Canadian Army, and two days after the remnants of the 1st Airborne Division had withdrawn from Arnhem, Montgomery issued his M527 directive. In it he stated his intention to open up the port of Antwerp and destroy, in conjunction with the First US Army, all enemy forces preventing the capture of the Ruhr. To accomplish both, he instructed Simonds to shove his right wing forward in a northeasterly direction along the Tilburg–Hertogenbosch axis so as to assist the Second British Army in a continued drive on the Ruhr. Simonds, in turn, issued his own directive that assigned the thrust on Hertogenbosch to Crocker's 1 Corps. The tasks assigned to 2 Canadian Corps to open Antwerp included the clearance of the Breskens Pocket fronting the Leopold Canal south of the West Scheldt in Operation "Switchback," the clearance of South Beveland in Operation "Vitality," and the capture of Walcheren in Operation "Infatuate." Within 2 Corps the 3rd Canadian Infantry Division received the task of clearing the Breskens Pocket and the 2nd Canadian Infantry Division, then under operational command of 1 Corps but due to revert to 2 Corps on 7 October, responsibility for the isolation of the Beveland peninsula.[40]

The Battle of the Scheldt began in earnest on 2 October when the 2nd Canadian Infantry Division advanced north from Antwerp to close the isthmus exit from South Beveland. After rapidly crossing into the Netherlands on 6 October, which day also saw Montgomery confer with Simonds, the division encountered bitter German opposition in the area of Woensdrecht, a farming village astride the entrance to the isthmus of South Beveland. The Canadians, with their right flank now exposed owing to the commitment of the Polish Armoured Division to the British 1 Corps, had run into elements of "Battle Group Chill." This "emergency" counter-attack formation commanded by Lieutenant General Kurt Chill comprised remnants of the 84th, 85th, and 89th infantry divisions formed around the formidable 6th Parachute Regiment and had been committed from the Nijmegen salient expressly to deal with the Canadian threat to South Beveland.[41] In the extremely savage fighting that followed, the 4th Canadian Infantry Brigade nonetheless managed to partly sever the isthmus on 10 October. Six days later the 4th Brigade's RHLI supported by tanks of the Fort Garry Horse executed a well-orchestrated attack in darkness behind a heavy barrage and fought their way into Woensdrecht and onto the low ridge above the village. And there they stayed, despite fierce counter-attacks and mounting casualties. The nature of the fighting saw platoon strengths established at around thirty-four fall to an average of sixteen men, with a few companies mustering only twenty-five. Such losses eventually compelled the Canadian Parliament to approve the dispatch of 16,000 conscripts overseas as replacements.[42]

The vicious three-week struggle to isolate the South Beveland peninsula typified the pattern of fighting in the Scheldt. The 4th Canadian Armoured Division encountered similar resistance in the Breskens Pocket when it failed to establish a bridgehead across the Leopold Canal northeast of Bruges on 13 September. The boggy polder country criss-crossed by five-metre-high dykes further hindered the use of tanks. By mining roadways on top of dykes and burrowing mortar pits and machine gun slits along their length, the Germans managed to create a formidable defensive grid of fortified intersections that could be breached only by fighting men on foot. For the most part, attacking Canadian infantry had either to struggle through flooded fields, often up to two metres deep, or crawl alongside dykes in narrow, exposed lines of advance "between the wind and water, eating, sleeping, fighting, and dying in sodden uniforms and squelching boots."[43] Here Montgomery methods ensured success: attacks had to be deliberately planned, preferably with an element of surprise; coordinated in detail, often through the use of sandbox models; and adequately supported, especially by direct and indirect fire. Where they were not, disasters occurred, such as that which befell the Black Watch at Woensdrecht on "Black Friday" 13 October when the unit attacked a strongly defended enemy position. In this action a poorly conceived daylight frontal assault across an open thousand-metre polder "killing zone" foundered for lack of effective supporting fire by stationary tanks, artillery, and air. A second attack using the cover of smoke also failed, and a third accompanied by Wasp flame-throwing carriers merely increased the casualty toll that included four company commanders wounded.[44]

On 7 October, the day after the 3rd Canadian Division attacked across the Leopold Canal in Operation "Switchback," Dempsey informed Montgomery that he could no longer in the aftermath of "Market Garden" defend the Nijmegen bridgehead gained, eliminate the enemy on his right flank, and continue to attack between the Rhine and the Meuse "at one and the same time." On accepting Dempsey's judgment, Montgomery reported to SHAEF that while he could possibly carry Antwerp and maintain the Nijmegen bridgehead, he could not do both and deal with the enemy on his right flank west of the Meuse, which the First US Army stalled before Aachen had been unable to clear with its 7th Armoured Division. Montgomery felt that his only option was to commit the British 8 Corps to assist the US 7th Armoured, which left attacking toward the Ruhr out of the question. He therefore decided to postpone offensive operations until Antwerp was opened and the enemy pushed back over the Meuse.[45] At this point Montgomery weathered the essential truth behind the saying that victory finds a hundred fathers, but defeat remains an orphan. The knives were now out for him over "Market Garden" failure to gain a bridgehead over the Rhine, though it had bored a long hole in German defences with relatively light casualties, and would have succeeded had drop zones been closer to the bridge at Arnhem.[46]

Another factor that weighed against Montgomery was relative Allied troop strength. On 1 July 1944, the Anglo-Canadians fielded thirteen divisions, including one Polish, which equalled the number deployed by the Americans. By September 1944, however, there were twenty-eight American divisions on the Western Front compared with eighteen Anglo-Canadian and Polish. This contributed to the waning influence of Montgomery, who nonetheless persisted in his request to have the First US Army placed under his command to help force a Rhine crossing that he still thought to be possible well into October. Instead, a by now disappointed Eisenhower transferred only the US 7th Armoured Division, which had been unable to clear the Nijmegen flank, and the newly arrived US 104th (Timberwolf) Infantry Division to the 21st Army Group sector. Simonds assigned the latter, the first American formation to fight under the First Canadian Army, to Crocker's 1 Corps then advancing northwards on Roosendaal and Breda. He also made a point of visiting every US regiment and personally briefing American troops. He further provided them with 18,000 Canadian army blankets and eased the division into battle with attainable operational tasks designed to foster confidence. Following progressively tougher battles, they emerged as veterans. The experienced commander of the 104th Division, Major General Terry de la Mesa Allen, had led the US 1st Division in North Africa and Sicily, where Bradley, who resented his aggressive command style and focus on field operations to the exclusion all else, took credit for relieving him. Under Allen, a firm believer in intensive field training, the 104th served with distinction to the end of the war. In a thank-you letter to Simonds he expressed his appreciation for the combat introduction of his division by the First Canadian Army from 23 October to 8 November.[47]

Earlier on 9 October Montgomery had issued his M530 Directive calling for the Second British Army to drive the enemy back to the east side of the Meuse. The First Canadian Army, reinforced by the US 104th Infantry Division and the 52nd British (Lowland) Division arriving through Ostend, remained responsible for the opening of the Scheldt as a priority. A signal from Eisenhower to Montgomery the same day, however, alleged on the grounds of a Royal Navy report that the Canadians would not be able to begin clearing the Scheldt until 1 November because of a shortage of ammunition. Angered by such accusations and SHAEF's recent refusals to provide airborne and bombing support for Simonds's operations, Montgomery shot back that attacks were already in progress. He then went on to offer another missive on what by now were his well-worn opinions on high command. Eisenhower thereupon fired back in some exasperation that the main issue was not one of command, but simply one of opening Antwerp harbour. In a four-page letter written on 13 October, the Supreme Commander also explained that he had the unequivocal backing of both Marshall and Brooke on this matter. Finally, citing Montgomery's own admission that his army group could no longer continue attacking, Eisenhower stated that he intended to give Bradley primary responsibility for mounting an attack on the Ruhr. The 21st Army Group would be in support. Montgomery, who had just the day before reported that the ammunition situation within the First US Army was so bad that it had not the slightest chance of reaching the Rhine, accepted this ultimatum with uncharacteristic grace. In a new directive dated 16 October he gave the opening of Antwerp "complete priority over all other offensive operations in 21 Army Group, without any qualifications whatsoever."[48]

The Second British Army now closed down all other large-scale offensive operations and threw its weight north and westwards along the Hertogenbosch–Breda axis to assist the First Canadian Army. The 3rd Canadian Infantry Division had meanwhile commenced Operation "Switchback" against the tough 64th German Infantry Division defending the moated "island" of "Scheldt Fortress South" northeast of the Leopold Canal in the flooded polder country of the Breskens Pocket. Here the fighting proved every bit as fierce and costly as that around Woensdrecht. The opening attack on 6 October by the 7th Brigade, supported by Wasp flame-throwers and diversionary feints by the 4th Canadian Armoured Division, yielded only two shallow toeholds across the Leopold Canal south of Aardenburg. In the miserable close-quarter struggle that ensued, Canadian infantrymen nonetheless managed to consolidate their bridgehead by hanging on grimly against countless German counter-attacks that could not be blunted solely by artillery or air strikes. Fortunately, Simonds had devised a highly innovative plan for the 3rd Division "Water Rats" to take the Breskins Pocket in the rear by launching a secondary amphibious attack on its eastern mudflats from the vicinity of Terneuzen.[49]

Difficulties in transporting landing craft, however, delayed the attack until 9 October when the 9th Brigade, supported by the 4th Armoured

Division artillery, finally crossed the mouth of the Braakman inlet in troop-carrying "Terrapins" and "Buffaloes"[50] to assault east of Hoofd-plaat. Shielded on the south by the clever use of smoke "floats," this remarkably successful first use of amphibians in Europe caught the Germans completely off guard and permitted the establishment of a firm bridgehead through which the 8th Infantry Brigade now passed. Although the Germans reacted with their customary speed and fury, even ferrying reinforcements across from Walcheren, the cohesion of their defence disintegrated. At last light on 18 October the Lowland Division's 157th Brigade, now under command of the 3rd Canadian Division, relieved the 7th Canadian Infantry Brigade in the Leopold bridge-head and occupied Middelbourg and Aardenburg without opposition. On 21 October Breskens fell and on 1 November, the same day amphibious assaults captured Flushing and Westkapelle, the German divisional commander surrendered at Knocke-sur-Mer. Two days later all resistance ceased in "Scheldt Fortress South."[51]

Crocker's 1 Corps advancing on Roosendaal and Breda had in the interim taken the 4th Canadian Armoured Division under command and assumed responsibility for preventing enemy interference on the right flank of the 2nd Canadian Infantry Division. This enabled the 2nd Division to complete the final clearance of the Woensdrecht area and advance into South Beveland on 24 October, thus beginning Operation "Vitality." The 4th Armoured Division concurrently moved on Bergen op Zoom, which it entered on 27 October. By 31 October the enemy hold on South Beveland loosened, especially after the 156th Brigade of the 52nd (Lowland) Division on 26 October executed a second amphibious assault near Hoedekenskerke, outflanking German defences on the Beveland Canal. The 157th Brigade followed, linking up with the 2nd Canadian Infantry Division advancing on Walcheren, where sea dykes had been breached by RAF heavy bombers, leaving German defences flooded and vulnerable to amphibious assaults. [52]

On the afternoon of 31 October the 5th Canadian Infantry Brigade launched company attacks across the 1,200-yard Beveland-Walcheren causeway in the mistaken belief that there was no other way over the mudflats. In succession the Black Watch, Calgary Highlanders, and Maisonneuve regiments attacked, the last managing in the face of fierce enemy resistance to secure a tiny western bridgehead by morning 2 November. In contrast, the 52nd (Lowland) Division sought another solution, eventually finding a path through salt marshes two miles south of the causeway that allowed the 156th Brigade to cross the Sloe channel to Walcheren. By nightfall 4 November it held a bridgehead that expanded with the entry of the 157th Brigade. Meanwhile, the 155th

Brigade had crossed from Breskens to Walcheren on 1 November in the train of a No. 4 (Army) Commando amphibious assault on Flushing and advanced to capture Middelburg on 6 November. Four hours after the assault on Flushing, the main body of the Royal Marine Commando 4th Special Service Brigade landed at Westkapelle, and on 8 November all organized enemy resistance on Walcheren ceased.[53]

With the capture of Walcheren, the Royal Navy in Operation "Calendar" commenced minesweeping the 50-mile-long estuary from the sea to the docks. On 28 November the first Allied supply convoy arrived. The struggle for the Scheldt cost the First Canadian Army 12,873 casualties, of whom 6,367 were Canadian.[54] This was a high price to pay, but without the port of Antwerp Eisenhower's broad front advance of American armies into Germany could not have been logistically sustained. From this Allied perspective, the Battle of the Scheldt was definitely the most important action fought by the First Canadian Army. Ranking among the most arduous and unglamorous military operations of the Western Front, the battle also demonstrated that Canada's front-line soldiers were second to none. In junior leadership and the stage management of battle, which reflected the rise of more competent division and brigade commanders, the performance of the First Canadian Army bordered on the brilliant. Simonds distinguished himself as a dynamic field army commander in dealing with a daunting military challenge that would have confounded lesser generals. In his insistence on flooding Walcheren despite the doubts of many; in his innovative use of amphibious assaults to turn flanks and gain surprise; in his employment of floating smoke screens; and in his detailed coordination of complex bombing and artillery firepower, he demonstrated superior generalship in what was clearly his finest hour. On 3 November Montgomery expressed his admiration for the way in which Simonds and his army had conducted joint operations under the most appalling conditions. In extending his personal congratulations, he added that it was an inspiring performance that could only have been carried out by first-class troops. [55]

Chapter Thirteen

Canadian Army Triumph

Crerar recovered from his illness during the Battle of the Scheldt and on 22 October signalled Simonds that he would be resuming command at the end of the month. Two days later, however, Brooke requested Crerar not to return from sick leave until after Simonds had completed operations in the Scheldt. The reason given was that Montgomery did not want the disruption that would result from a change of command in the midst of a battle, but the evidence also suggests that Montgomery wanted to keep Crerar away so that his more operationally brilliant subordinate could be given his head. Foulkes, who had taken command of 2 Canadian Corps in Simonds's place, later recollected Montgomery telling him that Crerar would not be returning to field army command. Montgomery revealed his preference for Simonds when he told Ralston on 8 October that Crerar was neither "a ball of fire" nor "in the same parish as Simonds" as a field army commander. He went on to say that he would like to see Crerar come back, but not before he was in good shape. Montgomery may have inadvertently heightened Crerar's national value, however, by stoking Ralston's fears that Canadian command of the First Canadian Army might conceivably be lost as it was an Anglo-Canadian field army. If Simonds became a casualty, Montgomery said, he would most likely have to be succeeded by an experienced British corps commander as no Canadian, including Foulkes, possessed the requisites.[1]

On 18 October Montgomery reiterated to Brooke his concern about Crerar's health, stressing the high importance of the latter not being allowed to return to army command until he was capable of withstanding the rigors of a winter campaign in a damp and cold climate. In the event, Crerar received a clean bill of health from two specialists and returned to First Canadian Army headquarters on 7 November. After completing a two-day handover with Simonds, he resumed command of the First Canadian Army. On 16 November he was also promoted to the rank of general, which prompted Montgomery to request that Brooke not convey the impression that the promotion was in any way linked to distinguished service in the field. This, of course, could have gone without saying as the promotion buttressed Crerar's old habit of getting involved in time-consuming, non-operational matters. Fortunately, combat conditions now allowed for such attention. The 2 Canadian Corps by this time had relieved the British 30 Corps in the Nijmegen salient gained by "Market Garden," while the British 1 Corps held the line of the lower Maas as far eastward as Maren. For the next three months, largely because of the Battle of the Bulge, the First Canadian Army wintered on the Maas, enjoying a static period in which it was not involved in any large-scale operations. This was just as well, because at the end of Scheldt operations all formations of the army, and its three Canadian infantry divisions in particular, were thoroughly exhausted.[2]

In the meantime, plans had been made for the Second British Army to attack southeast between the Maas and the Rhine. The aim of this operation, then called "Valediction," was to clear the west bank of the Rhine opposite the Ruhr. Apparently Montgomery preferred the Second British Army to conduct the operation owing to his suspicion of Crerar's abilities. Yet stripping the First Canadian Army bare of divisions as required by "Valediction" would have bordered on being politically unacceptable. In the end, because the Second Army holding the Nijmegen salient was unable to muster sufficient attacking forces in the Grosbeek area and at the same time defend its long southern front down to the boundary with the Ninth US Army, Montgomery had no choice but to assign First Canadian Army the task of attacking out of the salient. He therefore decided to reinforce Crerar strongly with British formations, leaving a truncated Second British Army in static positions for the first time. For what he termed the "great winter offensive effort of the British Empire," Crerar received nearly two-thirds of 21st Army Group's entire resources and some 470,000 troops, including Horrocks's 30 Corps of five divisions. Although Montgomery courteously left the decision to Crerar, the deployment of 30 Corps on the right of First Canadian Army logically dictated that it should spearhead the offensive. This was announced on 7 December during a conference at First Canadian Army headquarters where the code name "Veritable" now superseded "Valediction."[3]

Detailed planning for "Veritable" followed, with the target date being set for 1 January, or as soon after as conditions permitted. The operation as planned called for the British 1 Corps to deceive the enemy by feigning a northern attack to liberate Holland. The main attack was to be initiated in the opposite direction on a narrow front by 30 Corps and subsequently widened to two corps with 2 Canadian Corps attacking on the left. Owing to Simonds's observation that it would be a shame if no Canadian troops participated in the opening stages of this important battle expected to end the war, Crerar transferred the 3rd Canadian Infantry Division to 30 Corps for the main attack. Simonds may also have wanted to see his own corps, rather than a British one, play the leading role in "Veritable." Indeed, the tacit assumption since his 2 Canadian Corps relieved 30 Corps in the Nijmegen salient had been that the Canadian corps would undertake the operation. Canadian planners had also made use of a 30 Corps outline plan called "Wyvern" that had been prepared back in October for this eventuality and handed over to them when they relieved 30 Corps.[4]

When Montgomery issued what was expected to be his final directive on "Veritable" on 16 December, however, the First US Army received the full shock of a German offensive by eight panzer and seventeen infantry divisions that aimed at splitting US and British forces to produce another Dunkirk. On 19 December Montgomery instructed Crerar to release 30 Corps to the Second British Army so that it could shore up the 21st Army Group right flank. The First Canadian Army's most important responsibility now became the defence and consolidation of the Nijmegen salient.[5] As the German penetration ballooned between Lieutenant General Courtney H. Hodges's First Army headquarters and Bradley's poorly positioned distant 12th Army Group headquarters in Luxembourg, Eisenhower on 20 December placed both the First and more northern Ninth US armies, eighteen divisions in all, under the operational control of Montgomery. Despite the vehement objections of Bradley, who had not visited either army or sent senior staff officers to them, this was a prudent decision and many in Hodges's beleaguered staff, to whom the 12th Army Group appeared remote and even uncaring, saw benefits in the change. When Montgomery first arrived at Hodges's headquarters on 20 December he also provided a degree of direction and support that had not been forthcoming from Luxembourg. In addition, the British provided the First Army with 250 medium tank replacements, enough 25-pounder guns and ammunition to equip four artillery battalions, and thirty 6-pounder anti-tank guns to replace US 57mm models lost in combat. Throughout the battle Montgomery visited Hodges's headquarters daily in the afternoon to talk over the situation and lend support.[6]

On the whole Montgomery approved of most First Army dispositions, including the necessity for V Corps to hold Elsenborn Ridge on the northern shoulder at all cost. He then requested that the Ninth US Army take over Major General J.L. Collins's VII Corps frontage to enable him to assemble a counter-attack force of at least three new divisions.[7] Montgomery retained personal control of this force to prevent a Liege–Namur

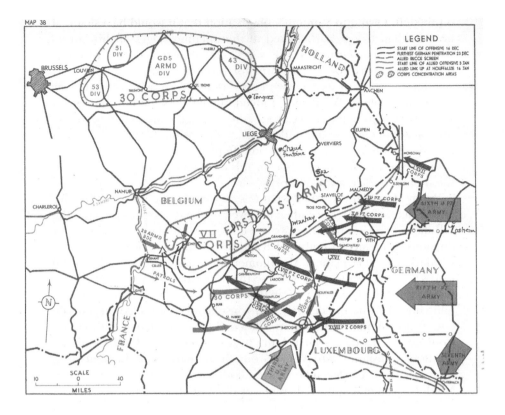

Map 13.1 The Battle of the Bulge (Montgomery of Alamein, Field Marshal the Viscount, *Memoirs* [London: Collins, 1958])

crossing of the River Meuse, as he did not think that Hodges had an adequate grip on the situation. He recorded that he dealt mainly with Brigadier General William B. Kean, the tough First Army COS, and that Hodges looked worn and anxious.[8] Montgomery's intelligence chief was less kind and remarked that the First Army commander looked as if he had been poleaxed. Eisenhower's Deputy G-2, Brigadier General Thomas J. Betts, sent to investigate conditions at First Army headquarters on 21 December, reported the place a mass of confusion and recommended that Hodges be relieved.[9] Although Eisenhower gave Montgomery permission to do so, which he would doubtless have done had Hodges been a British general, he chose instead to exercise close supervision over First Army. Through his "J" Phantom service and liaison officer "gallopers" he was also able to offer information on low-level developments that

Hodges's system was unable to acquire. American corps commanders were at the same time informed of Montgomery's intentions long before written orders could be passed down the chain of command.[10] In accordance with his practice of never calling front-line commanders back for orders, Montgomery further carried out numerous personal visits to divisions and corps,[11] the only senior commander to do so.

By 21 December Hodges was on the mend and two days later felt well enough to travel to discuss counter-attack planning with Collins at Marche. The gravest threat at this juncture appeared to be an enemy thrust in the vicinity of Manhay between VII Corps and Major General Matthew B. Ridgway's XVIII Corps fighting in the centre on the right of V Corps holding the northern shoulder. In the face of mounting enemy pressure Montgomery had granted permission for the beleaguered 7th Armoured and 106th Infantry to withdraw from St. Vith where their vigorous six-day defence had helped the 101st Airborne hold out at Bastogne. In doing so he saved a grateful 7th Armoured from ultimate destruction. By Christmas Eve German penetrations as far west as Celles, but four miles from Dinant on the Meuse, compelled VII Corps to side-step and, although designated a reserve, engage to blunt the enemy spearhead. At this point, in response to Hodges's request for more 21st Army Group troops to back up his line, Montgomery gave him the 51st Highland Division as a reserve while reconstituting Collins as an uncommitted reserve.[12] Meanwhile, on the southern flank of the German salient, Patton's Third US Army had launched a drive to relieve Bastogne.

As early as 19 December Hodges's staff had wanted to counter-attack, but Montgomery believed in rolling with the punches. He looked upon ground as "something to be fought over, not for" and insisted that the main German effort be allowed to run its course, ideally past its culminating point when a counter-attack would have maximum effect. The most critical actions, in the meantime, were to shore up the northern shoulder and channel the enemy penetration to prevent the Germans from crossing the Meuse and advancing on Liege and Antwerp, Hitler's main objective. On 26 December Patton broke through to Bastogne in the south and middle of the salient and on 3 January Collins's VII Corps attacked to link up at Houffalize, with Ridgway's XVIII Corps protecting its left flank and advancing towards St. Vith. To ensure absolutely that here would be no repeat of Dunkirk, Montgomery deployed 30 Corps as a backstop to VII Corps. Hodges, plagued with a cold since 30 December, exercised little influence in the slugging match that ensued. Unlike Montgomery, who went forward to visit Collins and Ridgway,[13] he remained for the most part at his headquarters recuperating until 9 January. Seven days later the First and Third US Armies linked up and Montgomery called for a farewell chat. Unfortunately for the First Army, Patton's dash to the relief of Bastogne during 22–6 December captured the imagination of the press as the hard fighting of Hodges's long-suffering army had not. Bastogne and its relief came to symbolize the entire Battle of the Bulge. Although it was primarily First Army doggedness and redeployment that won the day, Patton and his Third Army stole the glory to the understandable resentment of many First Army officers.[14]

On 17 January Hodges's First US Army reverted to Bradley's command. Unfortunately for Montgomery, his well-intentioned but ill-chosen words at a press conference on 7 January gave the impression that the British had saved the day for the Americans, when in fact he had held his troops back for "Veritable." Bradley, who had been caught out and humiliated by the surprise attack, seethed with anger. Sadly, because of the disastrous press conference, few remembered Montgomery's superb generalship in the Battle of the Bulge,[15] but he carried on undaunted. Quite possibly, after observing the abysmal performance of Hodges, he may even have looked more favourably upon Crerar as a field army commander. In any case, planning for "Veritable" had continued throughout the Battle of the Bulge and intensified on the return of 30 Corps from 18 January. On 20 January Montgomery worked all day on plans for operations "Veritable" and "Grenade," a northerly converging thrust to be conducted concurrently by Lieutenant General William H. Simpson's Ninth US Army still under Montgomery's command. The next day he issued his M548 directive, stating his intention to destroy all enemy in the area west of the Rhine between Nijmegen and Julich-Dusseldorf. His plan still called for converging attacks by the First Canadian and Ninth US armies, but the latter army's slow build-up and the threat of the Germans unleashing Roer dam waters prevented the Americans from attacking concurrently. With the target date for "Veritable" set for 8 February, Montgomery could only urge Simpson to make every effort to launch "Grenade" by the 15th of the month.

On 25 January Crerar issued his own directive to 2 Canadian and the British 1 and 30 corps. The directive advocated the technique used at Amiens in 1918 and stressed achieving surprise by eliminating prolonged preliminary bombardment and substituting, instead, overwhelming air and ground fire as the operation commenced. As in "Totalize," Crerar also emphasized keeping the initiative and maintaining the momentum of the attack by driving on and through the enemy without let-up. The disposition of enemy defences in three zones in depth and an initial seven-mile attack frontage that roughly widened to twenty at the final objective line, Xanten–Geldern, led Crerar to break the operation into three distinct phases dealing with each zone. Phase 1 called for 30 Corps to clear the Reichswald and secure the line Gennep-Asperden-Cleve, from which point on the battle would be conducted on a two-corps front with 2 Canadian Corps operating between the Rhine and the Cleve–Xanten road inclusive. The tasks of both corps in Phase 2 were then to breach the enemy's second defensive Seigfried system east and south-east of the Reichswald and secure the Weeze–Udem–Calcar–Emmerich line and routes between these localities. Finally, in Phase 3 they were to break through the Hochwald "lay-back" defensive line and advance to secure the general line Geldern–Xanten.[16] Meanwhile, the British 1 Corps would conduct a feint attack into Holland.

For Phase 1, Horrocks's 30 Corps had been built up to over 300,000 troops comprising seven divisions, three independent armoured brigades, eleven regiments of special armour from the British 79th Division, and five AGRA. Faced with three strong German defence lines and no room for manoeuvre against them, Horrocks decided to blast his way through. As the Germans had flooded the ground on his left flank and continued to dominate the Mook–Goch road on his right from the Reichswald, the only promising line of attack lay north of the forest along the road through Kranenburg lapped by the southern edge of the flooded plain. Hoping for favourable going over frozen ground, Horrocks aimed to break through the Materborn Gap between the Reichswald and Cleve before it could be blocked by German reserves. His plan accordingly called for three phases, the initial attack to be delivered on the seven-mile front between the Maas and the Waal by five tank-reinforced infantry divisions: from right to left, the 51st (Highland), the 53rd (Welsh), the 15th (Scottish), and the 2nd and 3rd Canadian. The first four divisions were to attack simultaneously at 1030 hours 8 February and the 3rd Canadian Infantry Division at 1800 hours in the evening. After the 15th (Scottish) Division had secured the Materborn feature, Horrocks intended in Phase 2 to send the 43rd (Wessex) and Guards Armoured divisions through the gap into the open country south of Cleve, with the 43rd driving on Goch and the Guards Armoured on Udem. In Phase 3, the villages of Geldern, Issum, and Bonninghardt were to be taken.[17]

On 6 February Montgomery visited Headquarters 30 Corps where Horrocks outlined his plans for "Veritable." As artillery could bring fire to bear regardless of weather, a total of 1,034 guns, one-third of them mediums, heavies, and super-heavies, had been deployed to carry out the initial bombardment from huge ammunition dumps holding 700 rounds per gun. In all, seven divisional artilleries, five AGRA, and two anti-aircraft brigades supported Horrocks's 30 Corps attack on 8 February. Contrary to Crerar's original direction to dispense with preliminary bombardment, the 30 Corps fire plan for "Veritable" as devised by Horrocks and his artillery commander, Brigadier S.B. Rawlins, constituted one of the greatest preliminary bombardments ever. Indeed, with densities of 650 to 2,000 shells bursting per kilometre, the artillery fire delivered on "Veritable" was probably not equalled on any front during the entire war in the West. Horrocks accepted the resultant loss of tactical surprise in order to take advantage of the increasingly sophisticated application of artillery firepower that, in this case, proved ingenious as well as flexible with excellent target discrimination.

The artillery preparation that started at 0530 hours showered enemy headquarters and communications with harassing fire and pounded enemy locations in order to destroy and demoralize as many personnel as possible. At 0740, after laying down a smoke screen across the entire front, firing stopped. Thinking the smoke and lull signalled imminent attack, the Germans rushed to their guns to return fire, thereby enabling British survey teams equipped with sound-ranging devices to locate their gun positions. After ten minutes the bombardment resumed, delivering accurate counter-battery and counter-mortar fire on the located positions. The preliminary bombardment also included an innovative "Pepperpot" in which all Bofors, tank guns, anti-tank guns, mortars, and machine guns that could be spared fired on specially selected targets to impede local reinforcement, ammunition supply, and movement. Rocket salvoes from the 1st Canadian Rocket Battery's twelve projectors additionally saturated thirteen targets with 4,000 rounds in German forward positions.[18]

Although air support, unlike artillery, depended on good weather and had been planned as a bonus, plenty had been laid on. The air plan called for both pre-planned and impromptu air strikes. Before D-Day railways, bridges, and ferries were to be hit so as to isolate the battle area without indicating the true direction of the attack. Air forces assigned to the operation included heavy bombers of RAF Bomber Command and the US Eighth Air Force, medium bombers of No. 2 Group, 2nd TAF, and fighter bombers of the US Ninth Air Force and 83 and 84 RAF Composite Groups supporting Second British and First Canadian field armies. To effect close coordination, a representative authorized to make decisions on behalf of Bomber Command was attached to No. 84 Group, affiliated with First Canadian Army, while requests to SHAEF for the support of the US Eighth Air Force went through Headquarters 2nd TAF.

On the night of 7 February the towns of Cleve and Goch were to be obliterated by Bomber Command, with Horrocks accepting cratering as unavoidable. The main air task on 8 February was to destroy and demoralize the enemy blocking the northern corridor against 30 Corps. While Horrocks agreed to accept shallow cratering on the Materborn feature, he insisted on airbursts at Nutterden, between Kranenburg and Cleve, so movement would not be impeded. Responsibility for coordinating close air support over the battlefield rested with 84 Group, while 83 Group focused on countering the Luftwaffe and maintaining the isolation of the battle area by interdicting enemy rear areas across the Rhine. To ensure effective impromptu air strikes, the 1st Canadian Air Support Signals Unit laid down the procedure for engaging targets of opportunity by wireless and line. At 30 Corps headquarters an air force Forward Control Post (FCP) operated a "cab rank" of fighter bombers overhead, dispatching them as necessary to strike approved targets. A Mobile Radar Control Post capable of directing aircraft in bad weather supplemented this arrangement. Contact cars deployed at divisional headquarters additionally served as mobile wireless links and stood ready to provide visual control of aircraft if authorized by the FCP.[19]

Horrocks's 30 Corps ground attack commenced at 1030, covered by a creeping barrage 500 yards deep. The barrage began slowly on the opening line at 0920 and thickened up to full intensity by 1000, after which it moved forward from 1030 in 300-yard lifts every twelve minutes. Barrage fire supported the attacks of the 2nd Canadian, 15th (Scottish), and 53rd (Welsh) divisions between 0945 and 1600. A smoke screen blanketed the northwestern edge of the Reichswald, but the enemy, sensing perhaps another ruse, proved reluctant to retaliate. The guns had in fact so surprised and shocked the enemy that the initial attack met only light opposition. The 51st (Highland) Division, which had opted for concentrations and stonks[20] in lieu of barrage support, encountered the stiffest resistance from the southwest corner of the Reichswald. The attack of the 3rd Canadian Infantry Division at 1800, reminiscent of the Scheldt, saw infantry mounted in "Buffaloes" fighting their way across the flooded plain on the northern flank.

In the first day of battle 30 Corps broke through the enemy's strong outpost screen and closed to the main Siegfried system defences. On 9 February, however, low-hanging clouds and heavy rain put an end to the air support that to this point had been excellent. With the 2nd Canadian Infantry Division now pinched out of the battle, four divisions continued the advance to crack the Siegfried defences. By the end of the second day, the 53rd (Welsh) Division had reached the northeastern edge of the Reichswald overlooking Materborn. The 51st (Highland) Division had meanwhile fought through the southern half of the forest as far as the Kranenburg–Hekkens road. While the 3rd Canadian Infantry

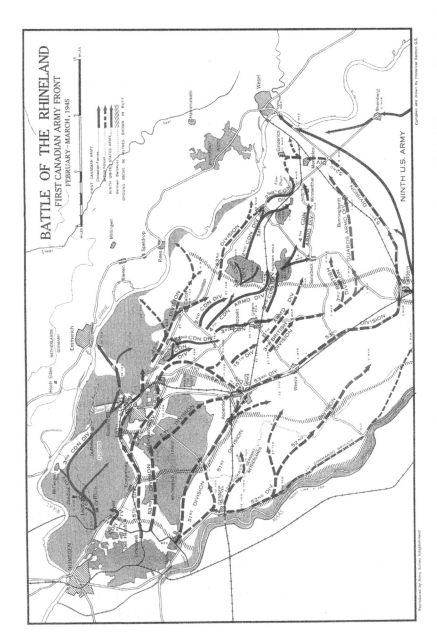

Map 13.2 The Battle of the Rhineland, First Canadian Army Front, February–March 1945 (C.P. Stacey, *The Canadian Army, 1939–1945*, 1948)

Division seized village after village in its huge flooded sector, the 15th (Scottish) Division achieved even more spectacular progress in the corridor between the Reichswald and the Canadians, taking first Nutterden and then the heights to the west of Cleve. Although initial divisional reconnaissance reports indicated that the enemy in Cleve appeared disorganized and unlikely to offer resistance, patrols seeking an eastern route south of Cleve found their way blocked by a coordinated German defence in Materborn village.[21]

Horrocks's 30 Corps had done well in taking virtually all of its Phase 1 objectives in two days, but the Phase 2 tasks of capturing Goch, Udem, and Calcar, were to prove more difficult. Flooding induced by the rapid thaw that set in at the end of January plus heavy precipitation turned routes into quagmires. Although planners had anticipated the possibility of muddy conditions, the weather encountered in "Veritable" set seasonal records for adversity, including the highest flooding in fourteen years and extremely bad icing and freezing rain. This development saw some twelve engineer, twenty-nine pioneer, and three road construction companies fully employed in maintaining roads. To make matters worse, the Germans on the night of 9/10 February opened the sluice gates of the Roer River dams, which caused the river to overflow its banks across the entire Ninth US Army front. The flood level of the Roer, high enough to prevent a Ninth US Army crossing, did not recede for two weeks. Operation "Grenade," planned for 10 February, had consequently to be postponed with the dire result that no southern pincer movement would now be launched to draw off enemy opposition facing the Canadian drive from the north. The Germans were thus free to deploy their reserves against the First Canadian Army without fear of having to contend with the Americans in their rear. On 10 February, having deemed the Canadian offensive to be a strategic move demanding the commitment of all available reserves, the German High Command decided to commit the 47 Panzer Corps to reinforce the elite 1st Parachute Division already deployed against the Canadian front. During the night of 11 February the Panzer Corps moved into an assembly area at Udem in preparation for a counter-attack the next day.[22]

The momentum of the 30 Corps attack could not be reversed by German counter-attack, however. On the evening of 9 February Horrocks ordered the reserve 43rd (Wessex) Division to break through the Materborn gap, which he erroneously thought had been seized by the 15th (Scottish). Although this decision produced heavy road congestion all through 10 February, it was not necessarily the mistake he later said it was, since the British did manage to secure Materborn and Cleve the next day. By daybreak 12 February the 15th (Scottish) had cut across the

Cleve–Goch road to take Hau, west of Bedburg, and by 0930 the 43 (Wessex) Division was advancing on Bedburg and southward along the Cleve road to Goch. Resistance began to stiffen, however, as the Germans took up a defensive line running from Bedburg to the west end of the Cleve Forest.[23]

Operations on the left and right flanks made comparatively better progress. On his 11 February visit to the flooded left-flank sector Montgomery noted that the "Water Rats" of 3rd Canadian Infantry Division were running amphibious operations. The next day they seized Griethausen and Kellen northeast of Cleve without opposition and two days later secured the towns of Warbeyen and Hurendeich west of Emmerich across the Rhine. On 15 February he visited the Canadians and travelled to Cleve in a DUKW.[24] On the right flank the night before the 51st (Highland) Division had taken Gennep on the Maas and Kessel on the Mook–Goch road slated to become the new main supply route and axis for 30 Corps. The 53rd (Welsh) Division meanwhile continued mopping up pockets of resistance in the Reichswald itself. By this time the left flank of the First Canadian Army had been pushed well ahead of the projected limit of the "Veritable" first phase laid down by Crerar. Still, the going had been tough for 30 Corps, and whereas it had faced but one enemy division at the start of "Veritable," it now faced nine. The chance of achieving an opening through which to launch the reserve Guards Armoured Division now seemed remote even though the front had widened from six to fourteen miles.[25] "Veritable" had turned into a close-quarter infantry slogging match under the worst possible weather conditions with air support rarely available.

At this point Crerar sought to maintain momentum by adding the weight of a fresh corps and stretching the enemy to the breaking point by attacking on a broad front. Although Goch had not been captured or a maintenance route yet established for 30 Corps south of the Reichswald, both viewed as preconditions to the commitment of 2 Canadian Corps, Crerar on 14 February ordered Simonds to take over the 30 Corps' left sector the next day. He set the main axis of 2 Canadian Corps along the road running southeast from Cleve to Udem and that of 30 Corps along the line Cleve–Goch–Weeze–Kevelaer. By taking charge through this direction, Crerar reasserted himself in the operational realm that up to now had been pretty much Horrocks's show, even in the planning of air support coordinated at army level. Yet, according to one senior staff observer, when Montgomery sat next to Horrocks at 30 Corps tactical headquarters for a few days during "Veritable," Crerar merely looked on, playing virtually no direct role in the proceedings. The immensely popular Horrocks, nonetheless liked Crerar and later wrote that he was much underrated, noting in particular that he possessed common sense and was always prepared to listen to the views of his subordinate commanders.[26]

Horrocks, of course, commanded with a flair and style that few others could match. Brigadier J.A. Roberts, commander of the 8th Canadian Infantry Brigade, described him as a born leader such as he had never met before, which made him wonder why Canadian senior officers did not exhibit similar leadership traits. He was not alone in asking this question, for official army historian Stacey also queried why so many Canadian generals and politicians were as grimly cold as codfish on a slab. He went on to allege that whereas Churchill gave Britain the roll of drums and the flash of steel, Mackenzie King gave Canada cold porridge. For the most part, in his view, senior Canadian army commanders from Currie through Crerar, Simonds, and Foulkes were cold fish. Montgomery nonetheless ranked the creative and innovative Simonds equal to Horrocks as a corps commander. Although Simonds lacked a warm and attractive personality like McNaughton and failed to inspire his troops like Montgomery, they manifested immense respect for him as a field commander. As Roberts related, however, when the confident and amusing Horrocks finished delivering his Operation "Veritable" orders and briefings outlining his plans and intentions "most Canadian commanders felt like cheering."[27]

Horrocks observed that Crerar operated by very different command methods than either he or Dempsey. Whereas Dempsey visited Horrocks fairly frequently during battles, Crerar visited him almost every day. Although Horrocks, like Dempsey, often travelled by light aircraft to make quick personal contacts, he stressed that flying had the disadvantage of making it difficult to get a feel for the battle in the same way as travelling forward by jeep. Stopping and speaking to people, and seeing the look on their faces, in Horrocks's view, better enabled him to "smell the battlefield." In contrast with both Dempsy and Horrocks, Crerar made a practice of flying over the fighting area almost daily hoping to gain a clear picture of the front. From 8 February until bad weather prevented flying on 15 February, Crerar went aloft every day to conduct reconnaissance and regularly visit Horrocks. Between 21 February and 10 March he flew forward some dozen times to exercise what he may have thought was a modern, progressive method of command. Yet, apart from nagging subordinates about road traffic congestion, there was little in practical terms that a lone airborne army commander, bereft of artillery and air advisers, could do to influence the close battle unfolding or effectively plan the distant one that was more properly his purview. One can only surmise that this questionable command approach developed during the long-strung-out largely static operations to clear the Channel ports, in which he travelled by air on fourteen days out of twenty.[28]

Apart from aerial excursions, Crerar occupied himself with the enormous administrative and logistical preparations for "Veritable," which he may well have relished as he was more of a quartermaster general than field commander.[29] Plans addressed requirements for food, fuel, equipment supply, force movement and assembly, ammunition dumping, field engineering tasks, communications, and medical support. He once briefed his corps staff that given comparable equality in men, means, and morale, the "successful waging of war is mainly a matter of the more effective movement of tonnage ... made up of men, their weapons, ammunition, motor transport, fighting vehicles and essential supplies of all kinds." The commander "who can move the right mixture of this tonnage, in the right amounts, to the decisive point, in the quickest time, and launch it in a manner unexpected by the enemy, has victory in its grasp."[30] Largely on the basis of tonnage and the grounds that he now commanded almost half a million troops, Crerar recommended the promotion of his COS to the rank of major general.[31]

The staff work involved in "Veritable" unquestionably demonstrated the proficiency of First Canadian Army headquarters, which dealt with numerous challenges with a high degree of efficiency and creativity. Detailed staff calculation, in short, gave form to the commander's plan by ensuring that troops arrived in the correct order with the necessary equipment at the right place and time. While the magnitude of "Veritable" is difficult to encapsulate, the scale of the operation can be partly illustrated with a few rough figures. The build-up for the operation required some 22,200 tons, of which ammunition accounted for 16,000 in addition to 7,000 already dumped. Over eighteen nights under closely controlled movement arrangements 35,000 wheeled and tracked vehicles travelled an average of 100 miles into concentration and assembly areas along deteriorating routes with many detours. Some 400 miles of road were repaired and 100 miles constructed, widened, and improved. In addition, around 10,000 feet of bridging spanned the River Meuse at five sites. Daily maintenance alone required some 7,250 tons per day.

Other indicators of scale included the British 1 Corps feigned attack into Holland plus the army-wide deception plan involving controlled and camouflaged movement, clandestine reconnaissance, as well as the use of dummy tanks, guns, and positions. All of these proved exceptionally effective and resulted in the complete operational surprise of the Germans. The smoke screen operations carried out under the auspices of First Canadian Army headquarters were also cleverly implemented on an impressively large scale. To shield the left flank of the 3rd Canadian

Division from enemy observation as it advanced along the Rhine, a curtain of dense smoke from zinc chloride and fog oil generators was laid down from the river bend northeast of Nijmegen along the south bank to progressively cover successive divisional forward positions. At its greatest extent it constituted an almost continuous smoke screen 30,000 yards long.[32]

With the Reichswald cleared, the most immediate operational challenge facing Crerar, now commanding two corps in line, was to capture Goch and Calcar, both of which Hitler decreed were to be held at all costs. By this time it was also becoming clear that although not more than half of the "Veritable" second phase had been completed, a new offensive would have to be mounted. Heavy fighting continued, however, and on 16 February the 43 (Wessex) Division outflanked the Cleve Forest, cut the Goch–Calcar road, and in a brilliant night attack seized the eastern escarpment overlooking Goch. The next day Montgomery visited Crerar and impressed upon him the need to go on fighting hard.[33] That night in his final act of "Veritable," Horrocks launched the 15th (Scottish) and 51st (Highland) divisions against Goch in a coordinated corps attack that included elements of the 43rd (Wessex) and 53rd (Welsh). Although the garrison commander surrendered on 19 February, German troops of the 2nd Parachute Corps continued to resist until the evening of 21 February.

The German defence of Moyland Wood proved equally tenacious. On 15 February the 3rd Canadian Infantry Division, reverted to command of Simonds's 2 Canadian Corps, assumed responsibility for clearing the wood. It took six days of intense close combat, however, before the division was able to declare the wood clear on 21 February. That afternoon Crerar also held a conference to outline the details of the new offensive designed to complete the second and third phases of "Veritable." Christened "Blockbuster," the operation was to be executed by Simonds's 2 Canadian Corps, which effectively shifted the weight of the First Canadian Army effort to the left. The primary responsibility of Horrocks's 30 Corps was now to protect the right flank of the Canadian corps. In the meantime, preliminary operations called for the 15th (Scottish) Division to capture a wooded area northeast of Weeze on 22 February and the 53rd (Welsh) Division, on 24 February, to drive south from Goch to take Weeze and exploit southwest. This was to be followed by "Blockbuster" two days later.[34]

On 21 February Montgomery ordered the Ninth US Army to commence Operation "Grenade" at 0330 hours 23 February. As operations now entered a critical stage in which the next blow by First Canadian Army had to be carefully staged and "be exactly right," he proceeded to

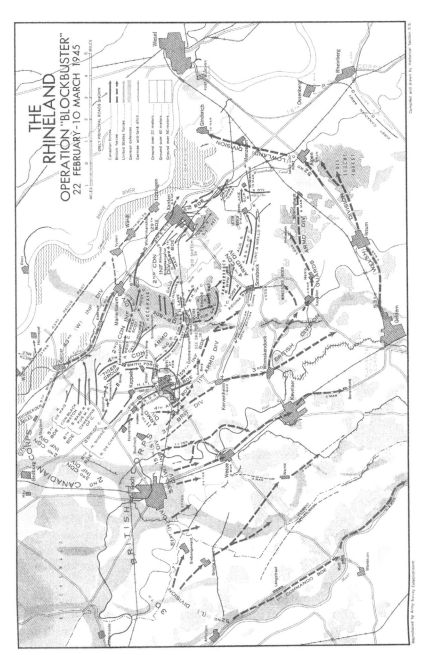

Map 13.3 The Rhineland, Operation "Blockbuster," 22 February–10 March 1945 (C.P. Stacey, *The Victory Campaign: The Operation in North-West Europe, 1944–1945*, 1966)

Crerar's tactical headquarters for a two-night stay during which he met with and presented medals to troops. He spent most of 22 February with 30 Corps visiting the 15th (Scottish), 43rd (Wessex), and 51st (Highland) divisions. He also on that day issued his "Memorandum on British Armour." Following the launch of Operation "Grenade" he spent the whole day with the Canadian Corps, visiting the 2nd Canadian Infantry Division, 3rd Canadian Infantry Division, 4th Canadian Armoured Division, 2nd Canadian Armoured Brigade, and most of the infantry brigade headquarters in those divisions. What prompted Montgomery to spend time with the First Canadian Army was the impression he had gained that Crerar was not too good at fighting an army-level battle and, consequently, his operations were liable to become disjointed. Even with two corps in line, Montgomery noted, Crerar still inclined to fight two corps battles rather than one army battle as Simonds had done in the Scheldt. This was a most perceptive observation as Crerar's command approach left Horrocks to fight his 30 Corps battle and Simonds to fight his 2 Canadian Corps battle.[35] A battle at army level, on the other hand, would have seen Crerar regrouping formations and changing inter-corps boundaries as necessary, creating new reserves after the commitment of existing ones, and mounting alternate thrusts as the situation demanded.

Crerar allotted Simonds five divisions to conduct "Blockbuster": the 2nd and 3rd Canadian, the 43rd (Wessex), the 4th Canadian Armoured, and the British 11th Armoured. Simonds briefed his divisional commanders on 22 February, highlighting the value of having two fresh armoured divisions in reserve and stressing the need to commit them in mass rather than piecemeal. The plan called for launching a deliberate attack across the Calcar–Udem ridge, smashing through the enemy's strong Hochwald defences, and exploiting toward Xanten and Wesel. The Calcar–Udem ridge had first to be secured against enemy counter-attack from the east, however, in order to provide a firm base from which armour could advance over the open fields leading up to the Hochwald feature.

In Simonds's view, the road maintenance difficulties that had slowed the initial advance of the 30 Corps in "Veritable" underscored the need to secure a good main supply route along which to sustain the momentum of the offensive. The embankment of the Goch–Xanten railway line running east-west through the gap between the Hochwald and the smaller Balberger Wald struck him as highly suitable for this purpose since the track, reportedly free of mines and demolitions, could be torn up by engineers and developed into a major road as the attack progressed. To get to this point Simonds gave verbal orders for a continuous operation in four phases. First, at 0430 on 26 February the 2nd Canadian Infantry

Division was to secure the north end of the Calcar–Udem ridge with the aim of attracting enemy attention and reserves. Then, in the second phase, the 3rd Canadian Infantry Division would seize Keppeln to the west, while the 4th Canadian Armoured Division passed between the two infantry divisions to extend the Canadian hold on the ridge as far as Todtenhugel. In phase three the 3rd Division was to take Udem, enabling the British 11th Armoured Division to pass south of that town to seize the southern tip of the ridge near Kervenheim. Finally, the 4th Canadian Armoured was to seize the railway line in the Hochwald gap while the 11th Armoured captured Sonsbeck and the high ground between it and the Balberger Wald. With the two infantry divisions following to protect their flanks, the armoured divisions were then to be prepared to exploit toward Xanten and Wesel.[36]

The "Blockbuster" plan was a sound one, and the proposed end run of the 11th Armoured Division around the Hochwald–Balberger Wald via Sonsbeck looked especially promising. The problem was Simonds's fixation on seizing the Hochwald gap to gain logistical use of the Goch–Xanten railway as a main supply route to sustain operations to beyond the Rhine. The so-called Hochwald Layback that extended from Rees on the Rhine to Geldern was anchored in the Hochwald and Balberger Wald. Called the Schlieffen Position by the Germans, giving some indication of its importance, it was the First Parachute Army's last prepared position on the Rhine's left bank. Constructed to protect the Wesel bridgehead, it was strongest on the northern end, where three successive lines roughly 500 yards apart extended from Kehrum along the western front edge of the Hochwald and Balberger Wald to a wooded area one and a half miles west of Sonsbeck. Reinforced with 88m gun emplacements covering anti-tank minefields in the north, the Schlieffen Position was manned by some of the best troops on the Western Front, including the 47 Panzer Corps in front of Marienbaum and the 2 Parachute Corps in the Weeze-Udem sector. The 6th Parachute Division defended the Calcar sector and the 116th Panzer Division the Keppeln area. South of Udem, held by the 2nd Parachute Division, the 2 Parachute Corps retained a hefty reserve comprising the tough 7th Parachute Division, elements of the 8th Parachute Division, and remnants of the 15th Panzer Grenadier and 84th divisions. As might have been expected, the Germans were also able to bring a massive amount of artillery into play from across the Rhine. In fact, fire from German artillery eight miles north behind a river bend on the other side of the Rhine actually came in behind the Canadians. In all, the Germans were able to concentrate some 1,054 artillery pieces, 717 mortars, plus an unknown number of self-propelled guns, effectively matching Anglo-Canadian numbers.[37]

Crerar must have known that 2 Canadian Corps would be attacking where the enemy was strongest, which is probably why he warned Simonds and Horrocks on 25 February that if the armoured breakthrough on the left had not been achieved by 27 February, he would transfer the main effort of First Canadian Army to 30 Corps on the right.[38] As the weakened 86 German Corps held the area from Weeze south to Venlo in the Ninth US Army sector, this made some sense. The launching of "Grenade" by the Ninth US Army on 23 February also took some pressure off "Blockbuster" in this area, but made it even more imperative for the Germans to reinforce the northern shoulder of the Wesel bridgehead[39] against a 2 Canadian Corps breakthrough that would have cut off the German line of retreat. Crerar's allocation of the main effort to 2 Canadian Corps may have had less to do with enemy strength, however, than with the concern that British troops had spearheaded Rhineland operations and shed the most blood to this point. Whether for reasons of national pride, a willingness to share equitable casualties, or both, Crerar and Simonds seem to have deemed it the Canadian turn. The perception that the Battle of the Rhineland might prove to be the most important terminal action of the war, as earlier suggested by Simonds, may have further disposed Crerar to accept a major participation by Canadians, even though it meant committing them against the strongest point in the German defences. Simonds, driven by Crerar's threat to give the main effort to Horrocks, did not object.[40]

To some degree "Blockbuster" resembled "Totalize," with the 2nd Canadian Infantry Division delivering an all-armoured attack at night on a 3,000-yard front behind an artillery barrage. The difference was that whereas "Totalize" opened in oppressive heat with heavy air support, "Blockbuster" unfolded in miserable conditions of driving rain, icy cold, and sodden fields with no air cover during the critical first two days. A similar artillery program fired by some 700 guns commenced at 0345 on 26 February and infantry mounted in Kangaroo APCs followed tanks across the start line at 0430 under the "artificial moonlight" of searchlights playing on low hanging clouds. By 1700 the first-phase objectives of "Blockbuster" had been successfully attained by the 2nd Canadian Infantry Division. The 3rd Canadian Infantry Division had meanwhile seized Keppeln, while the advance by elements of the 4th Canadian Armoured as far as Todtenhugel that afternoon marked the completion of the second phase. The assault on Udem by the 3rd Canadian Infantry Division at 2100 and completed by the afternoon of the next day, opened the way for the British 11th Armoured Division to advance from Stein to the Gochfortzberg feature a mile northeast of Kervenheim.

"Blockbuster" to this point had cost some 100 tanks and 1,000 casualties, but both Simonds and Crerar could look with some satisfaction upon the continuous operations of 26 February. Their hopes for a quick advance through the Hochwald gap in the fourth and final phase quickly faded, however, in the face of an unprecedented heavy weight of enemy artillery fire and fierce resistance by German parachute forces defending their Wesel bridgehead. The attempt by the 4th Canadian Armoured Division to clear the northwest corner of the Balberger Wald and dash through the gap to the east was bloodily repulsed on 28 February. There was to be no armoured breakthrough, and the battle quickly devolved into a grim infantry struggle, with the 2nd Canadian Division attacking the Hochwald and the 3rd Canadian Division the Balberger Wald. Although the weather broke on 28 February to allow the only large-scale close air support received during "Blockbuster," it was of little avail in close-quarter fighting in woods. Not until nightfall of 4 March were the Hochwald and Balberger Wald reported clear of enemy.[41]

Crerar's reluctance to switch the main effort of the First Canadian Army away from the bloodletting in the Hochwald Gap remains puzzling. During this time the advance of 30 Corps had picked up speed, with the British 3rd Division next to the boundary with 2 Canadian Corps pushing forward three miles a day, capturing Kervenheim on 1 March and Winnekendonk the next day. By 3 March it had reached the deserted Schlieffen line in front of Kapellen, the same day on which Ninth US Army troops linked up with 30 Corps elements at Berendonk, three miles northwest of Geldern. That Crerar should have adhered to his stated intention to intervene in the battle after the failure of the armoured breakthrough seems perfectly clear, and it would have saved Canadian casualties. Again, this would have involved overruling Simonds, this time by stopping him from trying to force the Hochwald Gap in a desperate battle of attrition. Here Crerar would have been on operationally firm ground as the bitter experience of Moyland Wood had already indicated just how costly in lives it would be to clear the two larger forests flanking that gap.

Crerar did not necessarily have to transfer the main effort to 30 Corps since he had another option that might have enticed Simonds to outflank the woods from the south and take the gap in the rear. Apparently, Simonds had ruled out using the good road that skirted the woods some three miles south as he feared that it would have to be shared with 30 Corps and hence become too congested to support all the supplies needed for the forthcoming assault across the Rhine. In fact, 30 Corps was already looking to fulfil its maintenance requirements by bridging the Maas in the area of Well and Wanssum. The 53rd (Welsh) Division captured a deserted Weeze on 2 March, and the Well locality across the Maas from Wanssum fell to the 52nd (Lowland) Division on the night of 3 March. A bridge was completed three days later.[42]

As field army commander, Crerar could have nudged Simonds to conduct a right flanking by placing the British 3rd Division under his command and adjusting the inter-corps boundary to the Neirs River. This would have had the effect of leaving the main effort with 2 Canadian Corps, but giving Simonds both the space and troop resources of the British 11th Armoured and British 3rd Infantry divisions to take the gap in the rear by executing a southerly turning movement around the Hochwald and Balberger Wald. Crerar instead directed 30 Corps to attack to the northeast with its right flank on the road from Geldern, through Issum and Alpen to Ginderich. On 6 March Montgomery told Crerar to stage a really hard set-piece attack to bust in the bridgehead. This resulted in the 2 Canadian Corps mounting Operation "Blockbuster II" to capture Xanten on 8 March and the towns of Veen and Winnenthal over the next two days, thus securing the heart of the bridgehead now being abandoned by the Germans. By 10 March the Rhineland battles were over.[43]

The battle of the Rhineland represented a real triumph for Canadian arms. In the words of the army COS, Brigadier C.C. Mann, all the fighting strength of the British Empire in northwest Europe with the addition of Poles and other Allied contingents fought under Crerar's command. In Mann's view, the flexibility, cohesion, and unity of the forces of the empire were well and truly demonstrated in the battle and highlighted the advantages that accrued from the policy of uniformity in organization, training, and equipment throughout the empire. Crerar was able to group British formations under Simonds and Canadian formations under British corps commanders with interchangeable ease. The operation of First Canadian Army headquarters further underscored the advantages of a sound staff system with officers, at every level, working from a common script as all had been trained in British staff doctrine and procedures. Notably, army headquarters also functioned under Montgomery's COS system. Unfortunately, as in the case of Normandy, Anglo-Canadian troops again had to face and withstand the greatest concentration of German strength in order to support the development of an American attack. The price paid in Operations "Veritable" and "Blockbuster" together cost 15,634 casualties, of which 5,304 were Canadian, while "Grenade" accounted for a loss of just under 7,300. German losses were much heavier and approximated 90,000 men.[44]

The largest force ever commanded by a Canadian now underwent regrouping as Montgomery turned his attention to crossing the Rhine in Operation "Plunder." On 1 April the British 1 Corps reverted to command of the Second British Army, with Crocker parting good friends with Crerar. This regrouping accorded with the arrival of 1 Canadian Corps from Italy and the final reunification of Canada's overseas army under Crerar from 15 March. The tasks assigned to the First Canadian Army by Montgomery during the final six weeks of the war included opening up a major supply route through Arnhem, clearing northeast Holland and the German coastal belt east to the Elbe, and liberating western Holland. The First Canadian Army experienced further fierce fighting, but never on the scale of "Veritable" and "Blockbuster." During the liberation of Holland, Crerar deliberately attempted to avoid trapping Germans in pockets, which risked committing Canadian troops against savage last-ditch stands, and opted instead to sweep broadly northward, forcing the enemy to conduct a general retreat. The First Canadian Army advance into northern Holland and Germany proceeded rapidly, and by 19 April offensive operations in western Holland had virtually ceased. On 4 May Montgomery received the unconditional surrender of German forces opposing the 21st Army Group and ordered a ceasefire from 0800 the next day.[45]

Crerar was justifiably proud of commanding nearly half a million troops and some eleven divisions in one of the major battles of the Western Front, a feat unlikely to be matched, if ever, by any future Canadian general. That he was allowed this opportunity by Montgomery, who gave him maximum support and his two best corps commanders, could not have failed to register upon him. In purely military respects Crerar remained a Monty man. From the beginning he had earnestly attempted to learn and abide by Montgomery's concepts for waging war. In May 1944 he wrote that he had the utmost confidence in Montgomery's military judgment and noted "his special genius in the matter of military operations." He also expressed faith that Montgomery would never allow Canadian troops to be committed to useless and impossible tasks. In the Battle of the Rhineland Crerar additionally came to appreciate the value of being able to group and regroup British and Canadian elements regardless of nationality to meet the military requirements of the battlefield. At war's end he readily acknowledged Montgomery as a great military commander and professed to having "the greatest, the highest, respect for his former Commander-in-Chief." He did not think that Montgomery as a field commander could be beaten.[46]

On 22 April Crerar returned to Britain for a week of medical check-ups and consultations concerning army policy after the end of hostilities. He left for London again on 21 July leaving Simonds in charge and at the end of the month sailed for Canada. Headquarters First Canadian

Army closed down on 31 July and was replaced by Headquarters Canadian Forces in the Netherlands under the command of Simonds. In Canada, Crerar received a victory parade and government reception, cross-country tour, and several university honorary degrees. Montgomery had tried to get him knighted, but the Canadian government refused, so he was made a Companion of Honour instead. Brooke thought he would have made a fine governor general, but this was not to be. Discharged from service on 27 October 1946, Crerar passed quietly off the Canadian Army stage into relative obscurity. He later reminisced that a major responsibility of senior command in war was to think and plan as far ahead as rationally possible, asserting that there was no such officer in the Allied armies who fulfilled this responsibility more ably than Field Marshal Viscount Montgomery of Alamein.[47]

Chapter Fourteen

Canadian Army Monty Men

Montgomery's military influence over the Canadian Army did not end with the culmination of active operations against the Germans. Much of what he taught continued to characterize the military approach of what was arguably the best little army in the world. Most of the Canadian Army's best commanders were "Monty men" who would hold sway up to the unification of the Canadian Forces. Foremost among these was Simonds who would serve as CGS during the period 1951–55. He also recommended Graham, whose career Montgomery saved in Italy, to be his successor 1955–58. Clark, once Simonds's chief signal officer and no fan of Crerar, followed as CGS during the period 1958–61. Simonds's former corps chief engineer, Walsh, then served as CGS 1961–1964. Simonds, however, did not become CGS in 1945 as his seniority as a commander might have suggested. Although Crerar handed over command of Canadian forces in Holland to Simonds in July 1945, he ensured surreptitiously before his retirement in Canada that Foulkes rather than Simonds would take over as CGS in August. The reasons cited by Crerar were those he broached in Italy, among which that Simonds might not appreciate the nuances of Canadian national command and was unsuited for working with politicians in post-war retrenchment. The latter may have been true, but Crerar attempted to distance himself from his intrigue by telling Montgomery that Simonds had given the impression in Holland that he wanted to remain overseas rather than getting involved in domestic force reduction.[1]

The selection of Foulkes was a blow to Simonds who rightly suspected Crerar's machinations behind the scenes. This was essentially the last act of the latter, however, as his influence over army affairs, especially those related to military operations that were never his strong suit, receded as quickly as he faded away. Foulkes was not chosen for his military ability or expertise, which by most accounts proved unremarkable. Hoffmeister described him as a vain and egotistical man driven only by what was good for himself. To another Canadian division commander, Major General H.W. Foster, he was an incompetent fraud and nasty person. Vokes called him a military nincompoop. Indeed, few soldiers had much good to say about Foulkes. He was most of all a clever and wily careerist survivor who never butted heads with superiors, but regularly offered up the heads of subordinates or fired them. The higher he got in rank, the more he was carried along by competent staff and operationally capable subordinate commanders. Foulkes had a knack for ingratiating himself with superiors, none more than Crerar, and he got the nod to be CGS because he appeared, quite correctly, to be more malleable than Simonds in the drastic downsizing of the army. In fact, he was a master bureaucrat as politically attuned as any civilian politician. He worried, however, about the potentially risky presence of a highly distinguished competitor of equal rank and conspired to keep Simonds out of the country as long as possible. Revealingly, he also retained close to hand the voluminous dossier on Simonds compiled by Crerar in Italy and consigned to a file for future reference.[2]

Montgomery told Ralston in autumn 1944 that he had no confidence in Foulkes replacing Simonds as commander First Canadian Army if the latter became a casualty. After the war he wrote to Simonds stating that he expected him to be a sure bet for the CGS appointment, but added that if Canada had no use for his services the British Army would be glad to have him. In November 1945 Foulkes discussed Simonds's future employment with defence minister Douglas Abbott and after negotiations with Brooke, still CIGS, arranged for Simonds to attend the IDC as a student in 1946. When Montgomery as CIGS suggested that Simonds might be given a corps in Southeast Asia, Foulkes responded that the Canadian government preferred to stay out of imperial conflicts. In this he correctly gauged the government position, but it appeared equally clear that he did not want to allow anything that would enhance Simonds's already lofty reputation. He suggested instead that Canadian policy might be better satisfied by employing Simonds in a training establishment in which Canadian forces personnel were involved. Thus, at the end of the 1946 IDC course Montgomery agreed to Simonds being loaned to the British Army for two years as an instructor at the IDC under Field Marshal W.J. Slim as commandant. Like Montgomery, Slim had been first commissioned into the Warwickshire Regiment. Simonds later revealed that Montgomery had asked him to consider taking on the job of CIGS, a request also repeated later by Slim, possibly because of the retirement of Dempsey in 1947. In both cases Simonds replied that he considered his duty was primarily to the Canadian Army.[3]

In September 1947 Simonds nonetheless sought advice from Montgomery, stating that he would leave the army if Canadians had nothing to offer when his tour ended in 1948. Montgomery replied that he had written to Foulkes to ask the new defence minister, Brooke Claxton, for a firm answer, adding that he was prepared to grant an extension of IDC employment up to 1949. A month later Simonds learned that he was to replace British Major General J.F.M. Whitely as commandant of Canada's new National Defence College opened in Kingston, Ontario, in December 1947. Whitely, on loan from the IDC, advised the Canadian government on the establishment of the NDC and had strongly urged the adoption of the IDC model. Significantly, his view ran counter to that of Foulkes and Air Vice-Marshal W.A. Curtis, Acting Chief of the Air Staff, who both advocated the formation of a Canadian Joint Services Staff College. As envisaged by Foulkes, such a college would "preserve the techniques, mutual understanding, high spirit of joint service cooperation, interdependence of equipment design, and common doctrine, which were major factors in the Allied victory."[4]

In the event, the IDC concept received its greatest support from the civilian sector of the public service. The Secretary to the Cabinet, Mr. A.D.P. Heeney, and the Undersecretary of State for External Affairs, Mr. L.B. Pearson, each sided with Whitely. Pearson, who apparently forgot that the war had not been won by diplomacy, thought that a Joint Services Staff College would be too military and proposed instead an institution wherein military minds could be exposed to civilian modes of analysis. He additionally suggested that if the External Affairs department and other government agencies were to be expected to financially assist and participate, the course of study would have to increase the vocational usefulness of their respective candidates. On 9 July 1947 Heeney and Pearson submitted a paper to this effect to the Canadian COS Committee, calling for the establishment of the NDC by name. Though opposed by both Foulkes and Curtis, the Pearson–Heeney paper received the approval of two civilian members, the Chairman of the Defence Research Board, Dr. O.M. Solandt, and the Deputy Minister of National Defence, Mr. W.G. Mills. The deciding vote in favour of the NDC was cast by the Chief of the Naval Staff, Vice Admiral H.E. Reid, who was less enamoured of a military–civil service college than fearful of an integrated Joint Services Staff College that would adversely affect the interests of the RCN.[5]

Simonds rose to the challenges of the IDC and NDC, comfortably dealing with top-ranking servicemen, politicians, and business leaders of Western alliance nations. As the first Canadian commandant of the NDC from August 1949 he was an outstanding success. There he also headed, through a colonel director in charge, the collocated Canadian Army Staff

College (CASC), the first course of which he had set up and run in war-time Britain before its transfer to Kingston in 1941.[6] Without question such institutional exposure greatly aided Simonds on his assumption of the appointment of CGS in February 1951. Arguably, his CGS tour also benefited from the delay of his appointment, since post-war plans calling for retaining a regular army of 55,788, all ranks, and recruiting a reserve militia of 177,396 men through a universal system of military training were not to be realized. Instead, Defence Minister Abbott announced in October 1945 that the regular army would only comprise between 20,000 and 25,000, all ranks. In fact, Abbott's main task was to initiate a rapid demobilization, which by July 1947 had reduced the regular army to 13,985 troops in two small armoured regiments, three under-strength infantry battalions, and about eight batteries of artillery. The next year witnessed an increase in regular army strength to just over 20,000, while the authorized ceiling of the neglected reserve force militia hovered below 40,000.[7] One doubts that Simonds would have been happy to be CGS in such circumstances.

The delay in being appointed CGS enabled Simonds to benefit on two counts: first, that Abbott was no longer Minister of National Defence and, second, that Canada's forces commenced a rapid peacetime expansion that saw the defence budget tripled. In the year Simonds became CGS almost 7 per cent of GNP was devoted to defence. This reflected the changing international environment set in motion by the Communist coup in Czechoslovakia and the Berlin Blockade of 1948. The Brussels Treaty signed by Britain, France, and the Benelux countries on 17 March 1948 established the Western Union defence pact and eventually led to the formation of the North Atlantic Treaty Organization (NATO) on 4 April 1949. The Korean conflict that broke out in June 1950 added to the urgency and resulted in the dispatch of hastily recruited Canadian troops to support United Nations operations. The vanguard of the Canadian Army Special Force raised to fight in Korea, the 2nd Battalion, PPCLI, first saw action as part of a mixed British-Australian brigade in February 1951. The rest of the 25th Canadian Infantry Brigade arrived in May and from July took its place in the line as part of the 1st Commonwealth Division comprising British, Australian, New Zealand, and Indian troops. The affiliation in this case was considered natural as the brigade used British supply lines and many Canadian troops were Second World War veterans used to British weapons and tactics. The "Uncle" artillery fire system also enabled the divisional artillery to bring all of its fire to bear on a single target in seconds, which American artillery could not do.[8]

The divisional organization further shielded Canadians from militarily unsound orders often emanating from higher American headquarters.

Commonwealth orders tended to be precise and delivered verbally in person at "O" (Orders) Groups by commanders, whereas US Army generals did not personally give orders, but left their planning and issuance to staff after stamping approval. There was thus little opportunity to ask questions, which the Commonwealth system allowed and even encouraged for better understanding and the exercise of initiative by subordinates. The Second World War operation order format of Commonwealth armies also differed in certain respects from that of the American army. Both comprised five paragraphs: in the Commonwealth case, information, intention, method, administration, and intercommunication; and, in the US case, situation, mission, tasks and tactical instructions for subordinate units (including missions), administration and logistics, and command and signal. All paragraphs roughly equated except for mission, which after NATO's adoption of the US format eventually triggered endless "mission analyses" of what a commander's intention might actually be. The Commonwealth format, on the other hand, sowed no such confusion as a commander simply stated his intention up front as intention, not mission. In this respect, it was a far more sensible format that regrettably was not adopted. Under method, Commonwealth commanders assigned tasks to subordinate commanders who then came up with their own intentions as to how to achieve these tasks. They did not assign missions with detailed instructions on how to carry them out.[9]

Notwithstanding the placement of the 25th Canadian Infantry Brigade within the 1st Commonwealth Division, the Korean experience confirmed the army as the most national of Canadian services and largely refuted the charge that Simonds failed to appreciate "the Canadian view." In April 1951 he instructed the brigade commander, Brigadier J.M. Rockingham, to maintain "the principle of the separate entity of the Canadian Force," that Canadian troops were normally to serve together, subject only to the exigencies of combat operations. In stark contrast, the RCAF ended up sending individual fighter pilots to serve with US air (USAF) units, just as they had sent individual aircrew members to the RAF during the Second World War. Canada had purchased 56 F-86 Sabre jets from the US in 1948, but no RCAF fighter squadron was ever sent to Korea. Between November 1950 and July 1953, however, twenty-two RCAF pilots were attached to the US Fifth Air Force to fly F-86 Sabre jets with American formations. The sole RCAF formed unit to serve in the Far East, 426 Transport Squadron, participated only in the airlift of supplies, equipment, and personnel from McChord Air Force Base in Washington state to Tokyo, Japan. The resentment of certain senior RCAF officers toward their supposed colonial relationship with the RAF during the Second World War may partly explain why the RCAF so intimately embraced the USAF in Korea. The irony is that though the RCAF may have thought itself better treated by the Americans, it failed to see that it had again opted for a similar role.[10]

Brooke Claxton, who followed Abbot as defence minister in 1946, had not wanted Canada to get involved in Korea as he feared the conflict would draw Western forces away from the main threat arising in Europe. He also manifested unease about the American conduct of the Korean War and disliked intensely the overly aggressive and bellicose language used by the US military to describe operations. Claxton had served as a battery sergeant major in the Great War and received the Distinguished Conduct Medal and a commission in the artillery. He went on to serve as Minister of National Defence for seven and half years, in which capacity he reshaped defence organization. Although a workaholic with overly sensitive political antennae, Claxton retained the unshakeable conviction that his primary duty was to maintain a viable peacetime defence establishment. In addition to integrating the three service headquarters and creating a single civil service within the Defence Department, he streamlined defence administration, introduced an updated National Defence Act, and established a Defence Research Board. During his tenure, he promoted major land force exercises in the north, set in train the construction of radar warning systems, participated in the formation of NATO, and weathered the conflict in Korea.[11]

Given his military background, Claxton appreciated Simonds's soldierly qualities, and after several visits to the NDC got to know him well, even admitting to liking him a good deal more than he had, and selecting him to be the CGS on the basis of his professional ability. At the same time, Claxton created the post of Chairman of the COS and promoted Foulkes to this position as a full general in 1951. Charged with responsibility for coordinating the operations and training of the Canadian forces, the chairman was the minister's principal military adviser and the senior Canadian military officer. Yet, from the perspective of fostering military professionalism within an expanding army, the choice of Simonds was undoubtedly the more astute move. Foulkes had originally been chosen by Abbott for his diplomatic and political acumen that made him more amenable to compromise. In fact, Foulkes was the consummate bureaucrat who was always prepared to yield to excessive lengths on issues to maintain a cordial relationship with his political masters. By the end of his fifteen-year tour in Ottawa, he reputedly became a man for all seasons and changed direction with the wind. The outspoken Simonds, in contrast, was no diplomat, but he was the better field soldier and possessed of a more imaginative and creative intellect. He also turned out to be the most effective CGS the army ever had, and his legacy of professionalism continued under his successors.[12]

The relationship between Simonds and Foulkes might have proven stormy had the chairman concentrated on adjudicating inter-service squabbles, but as events transpired his primary involvement turned out to be more international in scope. A division of labour thus resulted that kept them out of each other's hair. Foulkes conducted military negotiations with NATO allies, leaving Simonds to run the army. To Claxton, Foulkes was more diplomat than soldier and fought for the Canadian point of view, whereas Simonds hardly knew what the Canadian point of view was. Such judgment cannot be sustained, however, in light of Simonds sophisticated assessment of Canadian interests in the deployment of the 27th Canadian Infantry Brigade to Europe. In January 1951 the Canadian government agreed to send an air division and army brigade group to Europe to augment the NATO integrated force. Recruiting for the brigade subsequently commenced on 7 May 1951, and training on US-pattern equipment and weapons began in July. In exploratory discussions with the US Army COS, General J.L. Collins, Foulkes received assurances that the Americans were prepared to offer quarters and maintenance for Canadian soldiers in the US zone of occupation. As the brigade was to be equipped with US weaponry, it seemed logical to Foulkes to use an American line of communication that provided access to US spare parts and replacement items. Preliminary planning by Supreme Headquarters Allied Powers Europe (SHAPE) likewise indicated that the 27th Brigade would be deployed in the American zone under the operational control of the US Army in Europe. Although no plans had been made for the location of the Canadian air division, due to arrive in 1953, it was assumed that it would be affiliated with the Americans because of RCAF–USAF North American air defence connections dating back to 1946.[13]

At this point the British, who were eager to get more troops for their own zone, expressed an interest in having the Canadian brigade join the British Army of the Rhine. The close relationship of British and Canadian forces during the Second World War plus the fact that the 25th Canadian Infantry Brigade was already serving in the 1st Commonwealth Division in Korea added to the appeal of this possibility. The British further questioned whether logistics should be the determining factor in Canadian deployment as SHAPE planned to place US-equipped Dutch and Belgian forces under British command. Simonds, for his part, could not have agreed more with the British and less with Foulkes. On 16 July 1951 he sent a memorandum to the defence minister recommending that the 27th Canadian Infantry Brigade be placed under

British command to serve in cooperation with British, Dutch, and Belgian troops. In the discussions that followed on this subject the Undersecretary of State for External Affairs, now Arnold Heeney, described Simonds's memorandum as a "powerfully written document" that presented compelling, sophisticated, and persuasive arguments. Heeney, never one to compliment a military mind, found considerable political merit in Simonds's reflections on the balance of power. In stressing that factors other than equipment and logistics should be the ultimate determinants of national force deployments and that purely military concerns should not override political considerations in alliance participation, Simonds displayed a remarkable grasp of international relations and the workings of coalitions.[14]

Correctly assuming that supply would not prove a serious problem, Simonds argued that it would be easier to preserve Canadian identity with the British than with the Americans. The much more powerful Americans were unversed in Commonwealth relations and hence less willing to tolerate constitutional niceties in military affairs. The weaker British accommodated Canadians, the Americans did not, as has been shown in chapter 4. Simonds further asserted that a Canadian army presence in the British zone would bolster Dutch and Belgian efforts. He also stressed that grouping Canadian troops with the British would build upon the mutually beneficial military association that had been so successfully developed during two world wars. And here again, Simonds stood on solid ground, for the precedent of Canadians exercising full command over British soldiers was well entrenched, which was not entirely the case with American field troops. The heart of the case offered by Simonds centred, essentially, on how best to promote Canadian interests within an alliance dominated overwhelmingly by the United States. In order to advance both their national and coalition interests, smaller allies have to be more than just rubber stamps or convenient window dressing for imperial powers. They had to have voices in operational councils, whether to constrain greater powers from the folly of their ways or to assist them in coming up with better courses of action. Such a rationale mandated that Canada cast its lot in with the lesser powers of NATO. In the end, Canada adopted a middle course, sending the 27th Brigade under Brigadier G. Walsh to the British Army of the Rhine and the RCAF air division to the Americans.[15]

Simonds's tenure as CGS ushered in a golden age of military professionalism. Under his able direction the army increased in size in a few short years. He reorganized army headquarters with a properly functioning general staff and decentralized responsibility and power for as many functions as possible to five territorial commands under GOCs. That it was no longer necessary to get approval from the highest authority in order to conduct low-level manoeuvres and training both encouraged and rewarded initiative. The high standard of operational effectiveness reached by the Canadian Army in the period 1951–65 reflected the direct hand of Simonds in establishing the institutional foundations of Canadian military professionalism. As Simonds correctly perceived, with Montgomery's background possibly in mind, staff colleges were the true nurseries of the general staff and had long supplanted cadet academies in the advancement of army field operations. He accordingly assigned the highest priority to the development of the CASC, doubling the size of the student body and improving its facilities and faculty. His appointment of Brigadier George Kitching as commandant in 1951 was also inspired as he was probably the brightest staff officer in the army and had learned from his experiences in war. Brigadier M.P. Bogert, one of the most intellectual officers in the army, succeeded Kitching in 1954 and Brigadier R. Rowley followed as commandant 1958–1962. The CASC constituted the institutional brain of the Canadian Army and aimed not at indoctrinating officers, but at developing military thinkers capable of producing solutions to the problems of modern war.[16]

Standards were high. The first post-war serial of the course commenced in the fall of 1946 under Brigadier J.D.B. Smith and included a guest lecture by Montgomery making his first tour of Canada at the time. Half the students on the first course failed, and of forty-nine candidates who passed entry examinations to attend the ten-month course in 1948, nine, including a colonel and two lieutenant colonels, failed at half-term. The CASC emulated the Staff College at Camberley in using the syndicate system of instruction, which encouraged vigorous criticism of tactical solutions, equally vigorous rebuttal, and general discussion. The object was not to determine whether one solution was better than another (considered a waste of time) but to develop an officer capable of reaching a sound solution to a problem and take appropriate staff action in the minimum time consistent with accuracy. In war, a timely sound solution trumped a late better solution. Several solutions to the same problem could also be sound, yet be very different. The great virtue of the syndicate discussion was that it usually exposed the unsound solution and pointed out overlooked weaknesses in the sound solution. Barring practical experience in the field, the syndicate discussion provided the best possible means of imparting fundamental tactical and administrative knowledge related to command and staff problems. While the unpredictable influences of morale, fatigue, weather, and enemy responses in actual war proved impossible to simulate, the CASC conducted telephone battles and exercises on the ground designed to show that battle situations were frequently not what they seemed to be and that war was not a one-sided affair. Working as teams under stress, students learned to adapt to changing situations and produce alternative solutions to tactical problems that they might encounter in war.[17]

The CASC during the 1950s also tested and developed new concepts for the Canadian Army. Harnessing staff college capabilities in examining future operational structures, however, reflected the hard-earned lessons of the war. A significant *Canadian Army Journal* article of the period summed up an acquired practical fighting doctrine, stressing that the whole essence of tactics was fire, the use of ground, and the handling of reserves. The object of tactical manoeuvre was to destroy the enemy through offensive action taking the form of the "Break-in," the "Dog Fight," and the "Breakout." This was to be initiated by a concentration of force at a time and place of a commander's own choosing, the capture of ground being but ancillary to this object. The infantry division supported by tanks was best suited for the "Break-in" and "Dog Fight," while the armoured division with infantry providing protection against anti-tank fire was best suited for the "Breakout." The armoured division of one armoured and one infantry brigade was also best fought as four-tank regiment/infantry battalion battle groups under either the armoured or infantry brigade headquarters as required by the situation. Maintaining a reserve was mandatory at all levels, and when a reserve was committed, new reserves had to be formed. In either division the best artillery results were always attained when guns were centrally controlled by the CRA.[18] All of this, of course, was pure Montgomery.

In addition to reinforcing the institutional foundations of military professionalism, Simonds emphasized mobilization planning, including the issue of unit mobilization instructions. The Korean mobilization had not gone well largely because of inadequate preparations and a public outcry for action that spurred a hasty intervention by Claxton that resulted in lowering enlistment standards. Having opted to retain the regular army for defence of Canada operations, the government decided to enlist soldiers for eighteen months in a completely new Canadian Army Special Force to fight in Korea. In regard to the NATO commitment, Simonds maintained that the army should be capable of going to war without an extended period of mobilization to call up and train reserves as in 1939. This accorded with the NATO call for a division organized in peacetime not on mobilization. The Canadian commitment was a brigade group forward stationed in Germany and two equivalents in Canada ready to back it up. Preparing for the worst eventuality, however remote, nonetheless called for retaining a professional nucleus to ensure a planned and tidy mobilization. In fielding the NATO brigade from volunteers,

Simonds turned to the reserve force, creating six regionally diverse composite battalions from fifteen regiments, each providing two companies. He reasoned that in the event of war these companies could be expanded into a battalion, thereby providing the basis for a field force of two divisions. Difficulties arising from different terms of service among Korean, NATO, and home brigade soldiers, however, necessitated making them all regular with the same terms of service and unlimited liability to be employed anywhere the government chose.[19]

In another innovative move Simonds created a new four-battalion regiment called the Canadian Guards, which presented a national rather than regional face of the Canadian Army.[20] He now had by the reorganization of 1953 fifteen battalions of infantry, including three battalions of the R22eR and two each of the PPCLI, RCR, Black Watch, and Queen's Own Rifles of Canada. This enabled Simonds to meet his requirements of three battalions for Europe, three for Korea, three for home, and six for rotation. To facilitate the training of this force and to meet the call for a complete division to be at readiness in Germany immediately after NATO mobilization, he reorganized the home army on a divisional basis. This objective in turn identified the need for a large training area near an eastern Canadian all-weather port. It also had to be suitable for all types of training in a temperate climate and be big enough to accommodate the manoeuvres of a 17,000-man division. After an extensive survey in Nova Scotia and New Brunswick, the federal government in the summer of 1952 announced that a permanent military training centre would be built in the Gagetown area of New Brunswick. Roughly 70 miles from the port of St. John by rail and about 55 miles by road, this largest training area in Canada of some 427 square miles measured up well to the requirements established. From November 1953 Simonds set up the 1st Canadian Division with headquarters in Petawawa, Ontario. The first large-scale Gagetown exercise took place in the summer of 1954 when the 3rd Canadian Infantry Brigade moved in for six weeks' training. Between 7 and 12 August 1955 the 1st Canadian Infantry Division under Major General Rockingham conducted Exercise "Rising Star," the first such full-blown divisional level training ever carried out in Canada.[21]

In a further action reminiscent of Montgomery, Simonds also convened a committee to scrutinize the massive amount of paper being generated at army headquarters and sent to commands and schools of instruction and from there, in whole or in part, passed out to subordinate units. Simonds chose the commander of Central Command, Major General Graham, to chair this committee. Graham had been medically evacuated from action in Italy for a duodenal ulcer and returned to Canada in March 1944 to take up the job of Deputy CGS in charge of training. He subsequently served as Deputy Adjutant General and Senior Canadian Army Liaison Officer in London, where he often associated socially with Simonds, frequently playing bridge together, in an amiable and pleasant relationship. In late summer 1948 Graham was promoted and appointed Vice CGS in which capacity he put a stop to the PPCLI having to switch to American small arms to fight in Korea. In January 1951 just before Foulkes's elevation to Chairman of the COS Committee, Graham was moved out to Central Command, where he tackled tasks assigned by Simonds. Exercise "Paper Chase," as termed by Graham, resulted in the elimination of thousands of pounds of paper and countless man hours of writing, producing, and disseminating repetitive and quite unnecessary material. Simonds also tasked Graham with planning and conducting divisional-level exercises, including the one in Gagetown, which highlighted the emphasis the former placed on operations for war. Throughout this period, Graham happily reported, he got on well with Simonds as had been the case in Sicily and Italy after Montgomery's intervention.[22]

One of the great advantages Simonds enjoyed as CGS was his international stature. He knew and was respected by a great many British and American senior military officers, several of whom were close friends. Pearson, a professional diplomat, may even have been a little jealous of the many personal contacts Simonds had made at the IDC. His mentor, Montgomery, with whom he remained in touch, also served as CIGS from June 1946 to 1 November 1948 when he became Chairman of the Commanders-in-Chief Committee of the Western Union. From March 1951 he additionally supported four Supreme Allied Commanders as NATO Deputy Supreme Allied Commander up to the autumn of 1958. Simonds's commandant at the IDC, Slim, replaced Montgomery as CIGS and stayed in that post up to the end of 1952. He was followed by Field Marshal A.J.F. Harding, a Monty man from Alamein, and friend of Simonds. Future Canadian CGS Brigadier S.F. Clark, the Chief Signals Officer of 2 Canadian Corps who had been at the heart of operational planning with Simonds during the war, became the Canadian Military Observer to the Western Union Defence Committee after attending the IDC in 1947. On the creation of NATO in 1949, Clark was promoted to the rank of major general and appointed Canadian Representative on the NATO Military Committee. In 1951 he also became Chairman of the Canadian Joint Staff in London. As can be seen, Simonds remained well connected, never suffering from any lack of high-level contact overseas or paucity of up-to-date information flowing from abroad.[23]

Most significantly, Montgomery became Deputy SACEUR in March 1951 just after Simonds assumed the appointment of CGS in February.

In this capacity Montgomery proved to be a progressive military thinker who recognized that the advent of the atomic weapon had changed the character of the land–air warfare that he had practised so effectively in the Second World War. In May 1947 when CIGS he conducted Exercise "Spearhead" at the army staff college Camberley, which for the first time simulated the tactical use of nuclear weapons in a major training exercise. Developed and organized by Montgomery and set two years in the future, "Spearhead" amounted to a rerun of the 1943 amphibious landing at Salerno in a hypothetical atomic scenario. While cautiously suggesting that atomic bombs would most likely be used against ports, communications centres, maintenance areas, and bridgeheads, he concluded that land forces would have to adjust to operating in more dispersed fashion to avoid presenting large-troop concentration targets for enemy atomic strikes. For an operation like Salerno this meant dispersing widely to achieve a large beachhead in which follow-on forces could deploy in relative safety from atomic bomb attack and push out rapidly to secure larger space in which to operate. This called for improved tactical mobility, greater flexibility, and an increased ability to deceive the enemy. Montgomery acknowledged the experimental nature of "Spearhead," but insisted that as military thought and tactical doctrine must always be well in advance of the time such theoretical inquiry was necessary.[24]

In 1948 Montgomery convened an army doctrine committee under Crocker, his then preferred choice to succeed him as CIGS, which led to the production of the more manoeuvre-oriented publications, "The Conduct of War (1950)," "The Infantry Division in Battle (1950)," and "The Armoured Division in Battle (1952)." Although still reflecting recent war experience, these manuals recognized the need to execute more mobile operations in order to defeat a numerically superior Soviet army. At the end of the year Montgomery assumed the position of Chairman of the Land, Naval, and Air Commanders-in-Chief Committee of the Western Union with its combined headquarters called UNIFORCE in Fontainebleau. From this vantage point he continued to study the matter of how best to defend Central Europe against Soviet invasion. On 2 April 1951 Supreme Headquarters Allied Powers Europe (SHAPE), the direct descendant of UNIFORCE, opened in Paris with Eisenhower designated Supreme Allied Commander (SACEUR) and Montgomery joining him as Deputy SACEUR. Although primarily concerned with strategic planning and higher defence issues, his unique insights into the dilemmas of Western European defence saw him play a leading role in assessing the changing nature of war and how it would affect the actions of NATO ground forces. Through eight annual command post exercises (CPXs) at SHAPE, which he personally designed and directed, he encouraged senior commanders to examine and discuss strategical and tactical concepts aimed at addressing the military problems confronting NATO.[25] Many of these directly affected the development of Canadian army doctrine.

Montgomery retained responsibility for planning CPX scenarios and managing exercise events independent of Eisenhower, who, after CPX 1 held 7–11 April 1952, lauded the exercise as a milestone in SHAPE's accomplishments. More than 200 general officers and top officials from NATO member states, including Canada, attended CPX 1, which studied the stage management and conduct of mobile operations by division and higher commanders in the early phases of a possible war. The strategic setting envisaged the employment of the nuclear-capable fast carriers of the US Sixth Fleet. The following year's exercise, CPX 2, explored in greater detail the effects of nuclear weapons in modern war, including the tactical use of the atomic bomb in land battle. In his closing address Montgomery offered that capitalizing on the tremendous firepower of tactical nuclear weapons could redress the balance of power and be a battle-winning factor of first magnitude. The challenge was to organize and conduct the battle to force the enemy to present targets suitable for atomic attack. In general, this necessitated denying the attacker complete mastery of the air and guarding against being knocked off-balance by the first onslaught. The defence then had to react with swift, sharp blows before the attacker had time to exploit its initial advantage. In order to conduct manoeuvre warfare of this nature, Montgomery called for greater mobility and flexibility in NATO ground forces. Moving more quickly than the Soviets and delivering a hard-hitting punch against them when they were off-balance promised to be the key to victory over Soviet masses.[26]

The inability of NATO to field the necessary ground divisions, air defence, logistics, and command and control systems, however, left Western Europe defence contingent upon the deterrent capability of the US Strategic Air Command. This restricted SACEUR's ability to respond to limited aggressions that might not warrant the massive use of strategic weapons. At Montgomery's insistence, SACEUR therefore authorized the establishment of a New Approach Group to consider equipping NATO conventional forces with tactical nuclear weapons being designed by the Americans. While Montgomery was not completely seduced by the allure of atomic weapons, which he likened to unproven "imponderables" that might not solve the NATO military dilemma, he considered it prudent to assume for planning purposes that the Soviets would use nuclear weapons in any attack and that NATO would be forced to use them in response. In his concept a tough, resilient shield of mobile ground forces would defend Central Europe, with a light screen of covering troops forward of river obstacles manoeuvring to canalize attacking forces so that they presented a profitable target for nuclear strikes. Behind the screening line a highly mobile corps of hard-hitting units would then range swiftly from one end to the other conducting local counter-attacks and breaking up enemy formations. All of this required rethinking land-force doctrine, tactics, and organization that would enable formations to concentrate and disperse with ease. Commanders would at the same time have to be imbued with initiative and imagination in order to operate independently and seize opportunities without precise orders. The integration of atomic weapons with land forces constituted a turning point in NATO strategy and the "New Approach" nuclear posture, of which Montgomery was the chief architect, received North Atlantic Council approval on 22 November 1954.[27]

Like Montgomery, Simonds also gave thought to atomic "imponderables," using the same word, with the military effectiveness of the Canadian Army in mind. In December 1954 he held Exercise "Broadsword," prepared by Brigadier Walsh and conducted at the staff college under Bogert, to provoke discussion on some of the problems the army might encounter in the age of the missile and atom. Whether war would be atomic or non-atomic posed a perplexing problem as operations such as "Totalize" were out of the question in the former case. Citing Montgomery in his closing remarks, Simonds offered that the preponderant conventional strength of the Soviets left NATO no option but to rely on nuclear weapons to dissuade them from attacking. He cautioned, however, that there would come a day of nuclear parity, which raised the question of whether nuclear weapons like chemical usage would be limited because of the threat of retaliation. Whatever the case, the tactics and operations of ground forces had to be tailored to fit both conditions, and "Broadsword" constituted a first step toward examining new concepts related to organizations, supply, and equipment. Simonds noted the political cost appeal of fielding smaller, more flexible formations on the dispersed atomic battlefield, but pointed out that this increased the overhead in commanders and staff without necessarily improving battle effectiveness. Simonds also criticized calls for reducing manpower, pointing out that an infantry section establishment of one NCO and seven men usually resulted in one NCO and two actually fighting owing to casualties, sickness, and other manpower loss. The key was to start with an NCO and seven as the fighting ideal and work back to create a section of one NCO and ten to twelve men, which approach he recommended for each type of arm and service as a means of realistically determining operational requirements.[28]

Simonds also advocated simplifying organization and questioned the value of the armoured division of one armoured and one infantry brigade. In his experience he never found anything that an armoured division could do that the infantry division with an independent armoured brigade attached could not do twice as well, providing that tanks and infantry were properly trained to work together. He recommended instead that independent armoured brigades replace the armoured division, leaving the infantry division as the one major fighting formation. With three infantry brigades giving it more staying power than the armoured division, any combination of tanks and infantry could then be deployed. Armoured and carrier-borne infantry brigades could be grouped together for mass attacks or tank squadrons decentralized to infantry battalions for intimate support of companies in other operations. When Simonds passed on his "Broadsword" remarks to Montgomery, the latter replied that he found them excellent and signalled his agreement on the armoured division. Montgomery went on to say that he had been making the point at SHAPE that the armoured division was now dead, but that the War Office would not come clean and say so because they had three armoured divisions in Germany and several in the Territorial Army. He claimed that they wanted him to say so, however, which he promised to do in his closing address at his CPX Five. Montgomery concluded by saying that he hoped to see Simonds at SHAPE in April for CPX Five.[29]

To Montgomery, land forces had to be prepared for nuclear operations, which called for less manpower and more firepower. He further urged that army formations should be self-contained and capable of maintaining independent combat operations for prolonged periods of time without the need for reinforcement. In his view, the day of the wartime armoured division and infantry division had passed. The armoured division, expensive in overheads, lacked the staying power necessary for sustained battle action. As the infantry division could not fight effectively in most countries without armoured support, tanks had now be an integral part of the formation. Montgomery therefore proposed replacing traditional divisional structures with what he called the standard division, a combined arms formation consisting of small groups of infantry, armour, and artillery. He believed that such standard divisions would be able to fight effectively on a wide front in the mobile battle envisioned by SHAPE planners and would also be well suited to fight static defensive battles if required. He also suggested that the standard division contain a large element of armour since there will come a moment in the tactical battle when a favourable opportunity would arise for launching a flood of tanks against the enemy. In his view, the ultimate governing factor in the organization of armies was that they should be reduced in size as nuclear weapons became available and that they should generally become more streamlined by reducing the administrative tail and the number and size of command headquarters.[30]

To come to grips with the atomic conundrum from a Canadian perspective, Simonds convened structural and conceptual studies under his Deputy CGS, Brigadier R.W. Moncel. Moncel had attended the first war staff course conducted in Britain under Simonds and graduated as top student. From that point onwards Simonds remained Moncel's idol and mentor, "the only one in the whole bunch with talent, brains, and guts."[31] In Normandy on 19 August 1944 Moncel assumed command of the 4th Canadian Armoured Brigade at age twenty-seven and led it with distinction for the rest of the war. In January 1955 Simonds met with Moncel and senior staff officers, including the Vice CGS Major General H.A. Sparling and the QMG, Major General S.F. Clark, and set in train Exercise "Gold Rush": A Study of the Organization and Field Formations to Meet the Conditions of Future Warfare. Headed by Moncel, the "Gold Rush" study team over three years from February 1955 examined the changing characteristics of future warfare and drafted a new tactical and logistical concept for the army that was to be evaluated to the extent possible by divisional level training in Camp Gagetown. While this effort directed at corps level and below initially raised more questions than answers, it eventually produced a reasonable force structure and coherent doctrine designed to enable the Canadian Army to fulfil the mobility and flexibility requirements of the nuclear battlefield as envisioned in NATO tactical concepts fashioned to a large extent by Montgomery.[32] While it is fortunate that a tactical nuclear war was never fought, it would have been folly not to plan for that contingency. An army trained to fight under nuclear conditions could also make the switch to conventional operations, but not the reverse.

Simonds meanwhile, concerned about manning force structures, became increasingly convinced of the need for some form of universal military service in Canada. As far back as May 1951 he had told Claxton that without conscription Canada could not meet its commitments in the event of a major war. In separate speeches in June 1954 and January 1955 that reflected his concern over manning deficiencies, he advocated a period of conscription to establish a stronger reserve force. This brought a rebuke from Ralph Campney, who had taken over as defense minister on 1 July 1954 and resulted in Simonds's resignation, which took effect on 27 August 1955. When Montgomery heard of this he secured the agreement of General Alfred M. Gruenther, NATO supreme commander, to approach the British COS to nominate Simonds for command of Northern Europe at Oslo. John Harding, then CIGS, said no as the British wanted the post to themselves. Montgomery then asked if they would back Simonds for command of the NATO Defence College, but an American general had already been selected for this post. Montgomery then suggested giving Simonds a command in Britain, but Harding again blocked this attempt. British refusal to play, as Montgomery put it, prevented Simonds from getting into the NATO set-up. Admitting to Simonds that he had failed, Montgomery went on to say, "it is ridiculous that the best soldier Canada has ever produced should be retired so young."[33] So ended Simonds's tour as CGS.

The professional approach that Simonds brought to the Canadian Army did not cease with his exit, however, as he was succeeded by Monty men. On 13 June 1954 Graham received a personal handwritten letter from Simonds saying that he thought he had served long enough as CGS and should retire. He then went on to tell Graham of some proposed appointments he intended to make in army headquarters and asked for confidential comments because he had in mind that Graham should succeed him. In a reply letter Graham expressed surprise at the suggestion, stating that he had expected Simonds to stay on as CGS until he reached retirement age at 55. Graham also pointed out that he himself had intended to retire in September 1956 at the age of 58. Here the matter rested until mid-February 1955, when defence minister Campney asked him if he would accept the position of CGS. Graham replied that he would like to take a few days to consider the offer and discuss the matter with Simonds. The same day he had a talk with Simonds, who pretty much repeated what he had said in his personal letter of June 1954. On 21 February 1955 Graham wrote to Campney stating that he had a problem knowing what to do, his main difficulty being that Simonds was probably a better CGS than he would ever be, and that it seemed wrong that he would replace the much younger general officer. He concluded by stating that he hoped Simonds would stay on as CGS. In a second meeting a week later with a somewhat miffed Campney, who said Simonds must go, Graham accepted the CGS appointment to take effect on 1 September 1955.[34]

Graham recorded that on taking over from Simonds he found, as expected, a first-class army designed to carry out the commitments made by the government. He added that he basically continued Simonds's pattern, with most changes related mainly to the development of new weapons and adjustments to comply with NATO plans and policies. Significantly, Simonds's former COS, Major General N.E. Rodger, replaced

Sparling as Graham's VCDS in December 1955. Rodger had filled the appointment of COS in the 2 Canadian Corps from February 1944 to the end of the war and remained a Simonds's loyalist despite describing the latter as "not a man one wanted to go fishing with."[35] Under Graham the "Gold Rush" studies continued as did Gagetown divisional exercises. Between 25 July and 2 August 1956 Rockingham's 1st Canadian Infantry Division participated in Exercise "Morning Star" in Camp Gagetown under simulated tactical nuclear conditions. The next year some 300 Canadian observers attended two American atomic explosion tests in Nevada. Exercise "Eastern Star" followed 27 July–1 August 1957 and experimented with mobile, linear, and area tactical concepts intended to force enemy troop concentrations and allow the exploitation of friendly nuclear strikes. In the meantime, as a result of the 1956 Suez Crisis that spawned Pearson peacekeeping, Graham transferred responsibility for "Gold Rush" assessments of weapons, equipment, organizations, and tactical concepts to the CASC, which had umpired "Eastern Star." The rise of peacekeeping and the attendant cost of Gagetown divisional troop concentrations also led him, despite the massive Soviet crushing of the 1956 Hungarian revolt, to stand down the 1st Canadian Division as a field formation in 1958. "Gold Rush" studies terminated in the same year with the creation of a directorate of combat development within army headquarters.[36]

On 1 September 1958 Graham handed over the duties of CGS to Simonds's former chief signals officer, Lieutenant General Clark, who in addition to peacekeeping took on responsibility for civil defence and national survival operations in accordance with government direction concerning atomic attack on North America. Clark continued to stay the course set by Simonds and oversaw the procurement of the US "Honest John" nuclear surface-to-surface missile for the NATO brigade.[37] Like his predecessors he also supported the idea of having a mobilization plan just in case larger forces proved necessary. The first requirement of such a plan, in his view, was to deal as fully as possible with the very wide spectrum of problems associated with mobilization. Recruiting soldiers was but one facet of the whole, which included among other things a need for infrastructure, personnel administration, stockpiled equipment, and the retention of large training areas in peacetime. He recognized, however, that the probability of writing the perfect mobilization plan was not high, since so many costly preparatory steps had to be approved and implemented a long time in advance. Still, to have no plan was akin to having no insurance at all. For this reason the pamphlet entitled "Unit Mobilization Instructions for the Canadian Army" continued to be issued on a wide scale.[38]

As a result of previous studies, the year 1960 witnessed the full flood of the Canadian Army Manual of Training (CAMT) series, which established an army doctrine based on existing organizations, but in advance of some equipment such as APCs planned to be acquired. CAMT 1–8, "The Infantry Brigade Group in Battle, Part 1 – Tactics," issued under Clark's signature, stated that the infantry brigade group had to be capable of operating directly under a corps headquarters or in combination with other brigade groups under a tactical divisional commander. The manual had been prepared in light of the advent of nuclear weapons and the reality that Canada would never fight without allies. The aim of the manual was to provide broad tactical and logistic doctrine for infantry brigade group defensive, offensive, and withdrawal operations under conditions of nuclear war, with one chapter devoted to non-nuclear war. CAMT 1–11, "The Infantry Brigade Group in Battle, Part 2 – Administration," was largely a reproduction of the War Office publication "Administration in the Field, Volume 1, Administration in the Corps," differing only where Canadian organizations did not match those of the British Army. Details pertaining to individual arms and services included CAMT 3–1, "The Armoured Regiment in Battle"; CAMT 4–1, "Artillery Training – Artillery in Battle, Organization, Command and Employment"; CAMT 5–1, "The Field Squadron in the Infantry Brigade Group"; CAMT 6–15, "The Infantry Brigade Group Signal Squadron"; CAMT 7–84, "The Infantry Battalion in Battle (1960)"; CAMT 8–1, "RCASC in the Field"; CAMT 10–2, "The Canadian Provost Corps in War"; CAMT 11–2, "RCEME in the Field"; and CAMT 12–1, "RCOC in the Field," all dated 1960.[39] CAMT 2–91, "Survival Operations," followed in 1961.

Some manuals in use pre-dated 1960 and included CAMT 2–90, "Road Movement (1958)"; CAMT 2–12, "Nuclear Warheads – Basic Characteristics and Employment (1959)"; CAMT 2–10, Individual Training Nuclear, Biological and Chemical Warfare (1959)"; CAMT 9–1, "Manual of the Canadian Forces Medical Service in the Field (1959)"; WO 9520, "Notes on the Soviet Army (1959)"; WO 9551, "Manual of Military Intelligence, Pamphlet No 1 – A Guide to Military Intelligence (1959)"; WO 9564 "The Corps Tactical Battle in Nuclear War (1958)"; and DAP 39–1, "Nuclear Weapons Employment (1959)." One of the most important manuals appeared in 1950 as CAMT 1–10 "Training for War," a reprint of the War Office original. Another was WO 8457, "Staff Duties in the Field (1949)," republished in 1963 as CAMT 1–36, a reproduction of the British 1962 edition. The publication of the CAMT works represented a prodigious and prescient effort on the part of the Canadian Army general staff and manifested a confidence borne of practical military expertise acquired in the Second World War. The 1963 issue of CAMT 2–38,

"Principles and Methods of Instruction," institutionalized Montgomery's training methods, stressing that "teaching is … no less important than fighting" and that the "ultimate aim of military training and instruction is FITNESS FOR WAR which is essential to the achievement of SUCCESS IN BATTLE."[40] A rigorous system of officer training and promotion through examinations further ensured the dissemination of CAMT doctrine. This was spelled out in CAMT 2–85, "How to Qualify for Promotion and Staff Courses, Officers – Canadian Army (Regular) 1957," and CAMT 1–9, "War Establishments and Staff Data 1956 (For Study Purposes Only)."

Officer promotion examinations required the detailed study of all training manuals and aimed primarily at testing an officer's fitness for war. Meticulously administered and comprising written and practical portions, these examinations accorded with the principle of training two rank levels up. An officer was expected to attempt "lieutenant to captain" examinations by his third year in rank and "captain to major" by not later than three years after promotion to captain. Preparation for writing each qualification examination was the responsibility of the individual officer. The written theoretical portion consisted of five examinations covering such subject areas as military law, military history, current affairs, staff duties and military writing, organization and administration in peace and war, and tactical operations. To ensure fairness by centralized marking boards, candidates were forbidden to identify themselves by either name or regiment. The practical field portion, which could be attempted only upon successful completion of all written examinations, was divided into a mandatory "common to all corps" section for all officers and a "special to corps" section pertaining to an individual's specialty. To pass these promotion examinations with a "distinguished" mark allowed accelerated advancement. Failure to pass, on the other hand, meant no promotion, and failing three times meant that one would never be promoted again. Up until 1959 prospective officers were also required to pass a staff college entrance examination, but thereafter were selected on the basis of high grades attained on "captain to major" examinations. However highly recommended by a superior, an officer could not get into the staff college without meeting these standards.[41]

Such a high standard of officer training produced a field-oriented army in which almost everyone knew and understood the roles and employment of all arms and services. An infantry officer, for example, even knew how to practically site a supply ordnance field park and maintenance field workshop and appreciate the value of their services. In short, doctrine, force structure, and training were in harmony under a blossoming intellectual leadership that melded theory and practical application. The termination of army qualification examinations in 1966, the equivalent of the legal profession dropping bar examinations, unquestionably led to professional regression. Since entrance to staff college no longer depended on achieving high marks in "captain to major" examinations, educational standards had no place to go but down. The discontinuance of formal competitive theoretical and practical examinations also removed the most reliably objective means of determining an officer's fitness for promotion and command. Individual study for examinations had ensured the steady progressive intellectual development of the peacetime officer corps. With the end of examinations, however, officers merely had to please their bosses and jump through prescribed career hoops. Many who could never possibly have gained entry to the staff college in Simonds's era were now permitted to attend. As staff college graduation remained a prerequisite for promotion, however obtained, some of their number even went on to attain senior rank, several rising as high as lieutenant general – Simonds's last rank, though they were hardly in his league.

Lieutenant General Walsh, Simonds's former chief engineer in 2 Canadian Corps, took over from Clark as the last CGS in October 1961. His bad fortune was the arrival in April 1963 of a new defence minister, Paul Hellyer, bent on first integrating then unifying the Canadian armed services. Walsh, like many others, favoured the integration of management as a means of reducing costs through the elimination of triplication. In August 1964 a single integrated Canadian Forces Headquarters (CFHQ) with four staff branches replaced the three headquarters of the separate services. Air Chief Marshal F.R. Miller headed CFHQ in the new post of Chief of the Defence Staff (CDS) with Walsh as his Vice CDS. The separate administrative, supply, and personnel organizations of the RCN, Canadian Army, and RCAF were, in turn, integrated to form single-service branches. Although many informed observers applauded these actions as long overdue cost savings, the ramifications of the actual steps taken to effect service integration and unification were not entirely fathomed. The general staff, uniquely integral to the field operations of the army and only in the broadest sense similar to the more centralized agencies of the RCN and RCAF, went down the drain in an "unbelievable piece of stupidity."[42] In 1965 Walsh handed over the post of Vice CDS to Lieutenant General Moncel, who expected to take over as CDS. Miller, however, protested unification by resigning in 1966, and when Moncel also questioned the wisdom of unifying fighting elements, Hellyer selected another CDS who accepted unification in order to advance his own personal agenda.[43] Arguably, Moncel, who idolized Simonds, was the last high-ranking Monty man.

What vestiges of the Montgomery–Simonds army remained were largely perpetuated by the valiant rearguard efforts of the CASC and its successors. This institution continued to dispense practical war fighting knowledge, especially the importance of such aspects as all arms and air cooperation, planning by commanders thinking two levels down, grouping fighting elements appropriately, using verbal orders, employing Tac HQ, and training for war through exercises and rehearsals. The teaching medium for doing this was for the longest time a Canadian order of battle based on 30 British Corps, which was only buried in a mock funeral at the CASC site on 11 June 1976, not quite three months after Montgomery's death. In 1984 an RMC biography of Simonds, who died on 15 May 1974, proclaimed him "Canada's Montgomery in the last War."[44]

Conclusion

Montgomery's military influence over the Canadian Army ran deep, arguably even deeper than his influence over the more far-flung British Army owing to the competition of the likes of Alexander and most especially Slim, who ironically sprang from the same Warwickshire Regiment. From the moment he took the Canadian Corps under command in South-Eastern Command, Montgomery began shaping the way in which Canadian commanders and soldiers would train and fight. Notwithstanding his ruthless training approach, this was fortunate for Canadian arms as the generalship of McNaughton had not produced a trained army capable of conducting effective operations against the Germans. The troops loved McNaughton, but the inspired leadership he gave them focused on everything but war fighting. He had distinguished himself in the Great War as counter-battery staff officer of the Canadian Corps, then considered one of the best fighting formations on the Western Front, yet in his meteoric rise to CGS during the interwar years he pursued peripheral activities to the neglect of training for war. Montgomery, in contrast, having been badly wounded and almost killed in the Great War, advanced in rank at a more pedestrian pace, but with a single-minded focus on war fighting to the exclusion of all else.

In progressing through company and battalion commands, Montgomery often painfully learned the hard knocks of handling men. At the same time he gained a reputation for being a superlative trainer and master of a military method that stressed achieving objectives with as little loss of life as possible through meticulous planning. Building on the firm base of minor tactics, which he correctly perceived to be the final arbiter to battle, Montgomery formulated his pragmatic approach to preparing larger formations for battle. His six years of employment as a DS at Camberley and Quetta proved critical in enabling him to do this as staff colleges had long replaced cadet schools like Sandhurst and Canada's RMC as primary centres of military learning. Indeed, the importance of these years in Montgomery's development *cannot be over-emphasized,* since staff colleges were the only institutions concerned with fighting large-scale war on land and producing battlefield commanders capable of handling all arms formations in combat. Unlike many of his contemporaries caught up in careerist peacetime bureaucratic activities in static headquarters such as the War Office and NDHQ, Montgomery remained totally field oriented and committed to the serious study of the conduct of military operations in war. He was thus uniquely qualified for high command when war did come, fortunately for both Britain and Canada.

Montgomery's performance in the fighting withdrawal to Dunkirk was of course exemplary and one his finest hours. Here in the face of adversity he proved himself to be a superlative field commander with nerves of steel. He also fought his division as one cohesive force from a forward Tac HQ that included his artillery and engineer commanders, leaving his COS in charge of his main headquarters and empowered to make decisions. He further ensured that his men were well fed and rested before ordering them into action. Constant rehearsal in night movement additionally found the 3rd Division well prepared when Brooke instructed Montgomery to make a clean break with the enemy and conduct a twenty-five-mile night move through three divisional lines behind a fighting front to occupy a critical perimeter defensive position before dawn. In accomplishing this highly challenging manoeuvre Montgomery earned the lasting respect of Brooke, who in the final evacuation of Dunkirk handed over 2 Corps command to him, even though he was the most junior divisional commander.

While his 3rd Division marched out in good order, Montgomery viewed Dunkirk as a humiliating defeat that reflected the inadequacies of the generalship of the BEF commander. At the same time, the withdrawal conducted by the 3rd Division reinforced his confidence in the fighting approach that he had refined at Quetta. Central to his method was the need to get a good start in the execution of a battle plan to avoid drifting aimlessly into battle, which owing to the speed of motorization and air attack risked losing the initiative and having to conform to the enemy plan. A poor plan with faulty dispositions could only be saved, if at all, by troop gallantry and casualties. Even with limited information a commander still had to make a plan and begin early to force his will upon the enemy through forward command and wide reconnaissance. Among the first to recognize and admire German tactical superiority, Montgomery also noted that they conducted operations mainly by day and highly disliked concentrated artillery fire that, unlike Stuka dive bombers, could attack by day and night regardless of weather. His Dunkirk experience further confirmed the worth of tactical exercises and training by rehearsal so that all commanders would know the broad plan of operation and general intention so that they could think for themselves within parameters and act as necessary on their own initiative.

Shortly after his return to England, Montgomery assumed command of the coastal 5 Corps and began to instil his fighting doctrine with a vengeance. Fear of German invasion now lent a real sense of urgency and, as a first step, he set about ruthlessly culling senior officers in corps headquarters, divisions, and garrisons. In May 1941 Montgomery sidestepped to command 12 Corps defending the most likely German landing area on the southeastern coast. Here he repeated the approach he had taken with 5 Corps, sacking three brigadiers plus six COs and raising the standards of field craft and minor tactics. Montgomery conducted seven division and corps headquarters exercises in 5 and 12 Corps that so impressed Brooke, then C-in-C Home Forces, that he was selected to be the Chief Umpire for Exercise "Bumper," a full-scale army manoeuvre. "Bumper" brought Montgomery into contact with the Canadian Corps for the first but not the last time, since he received a promotion on 17 November 1941 to head South-Eastern Command that comprised both 12 Corps and the Canadian Corps.

On 28 November Montgomery issued his first personal memorandum setting out operational policy that covered the individual training of the soldier, field exercises with troops, and handling formations in battle. The Canadian Corps received this memorandum after Major General Pearkes had assumed temporary corps command on 14 November 1941 following the "breakdown" of McNaughton and his departure on extended medical leave. What Pearkes (and probably Montgomery) did not know, however, was that Crerar as CGS had angled for the corps command appointment, which he successfully attained in December 1941. This resulted in a rancorous relationship with the resentful Pearkes, who by measure of command experience considered himself better qualified for the job than Crerar. Faced with what he perceived to be an intolerable situation, Crerar began to contemplate making command changes and in discussing his general concerns with Montgomery readily accepted the latter's offer to visit Canadian formations and give his personal views. Crerar's lack of experience, in short, increased Montgomery's influence on Canadian army training.

In a series of informal visits during February and March 1942 Montgomery inspected all nine Canadian infantry brigades and twenty-seven infantry battalions. In May he also visited the three regiments and headquarters of the 1st Canadian Army Tank Brigade. After each of his brigade visits Montgomery offered a number of comments acquired through interviews in which he listened patiently to key personnel, quietly taking in information that underpinned his conclusions. Since there was a need for urgency at the time, Montgomery did not hold back in offering snap judgments, most of which were spot on. In his personnel assessments Montgomery differentiated between those who were "completely useless" and those who were "teachable" and worth retaining. Out of nine brigadiers observed, he found two unfit for command, but three others divisional command material and another four as more than satisfactory. Of the twenty-eight COs he met, Montgomery considered eight to be unacceptable, but there were more who were keen and able, some even potential brigadiers. In respect of infantry battalion 2ICs, Montgomery categorized nine out of sixteen as unsatisfactory. He assessed many company commanders, on the other hand, as adequate through excellent. He considered all but three of seventeen adjutants encountered to be in the same category. Among NCOs, he recommended the removal of eight RSMs for reasons of age or incompetence. He further noted to his dismay that officer and NCO training was hardly carried out at all. In all of his candid assessments, however, Montgomery evinced an even-handed treatment no different than that handed out in 5 and 12 Corps.

Canadian Captain Trumbull Warren, who became a close confidant of Montgomery, accompanied him as an aide on his visits. In April Montgomery told Warren that he aimed to make the Canadian Corps the finest war machine ever, and that he was not going to fail in this endeavour. He thus set out to rid the corps of what he termed a peacetime atmosphere in which such things as courts of inquiry, traffic accidents, and paper reports and returns left little time or no time for the study of the things that really counted in war. Brigades foundered under paper, making everyone office bound when officers should have been out keeping in touch with their troops and seeing that training was being conducted properly. Montgomery appeared to have a soft spot for Canadian volunteer soldiers and considered them probably the best material in any army of the empire. He warned, however, that they would be killed in large numbers unless commanders learned how to launch them properly into battle. It was no use having battle schools for officers and NCOs if generals did not know their stuff. The key to readying an army for battle was to teach the generals, who could then teach their subordinate commanders, who could then teach their soldiers. The problem was that the Canadian high command did not know how to train troops for action and, but for Montgomery's intervention, would have left them totally unprepared for modern war and prone to incurring unnecessary casualties.

McNaughton's claim that ceaseless training by day and night had thoroughly prepared the Canadian Corps for battle appeared baseless, especially in the view of Hoffmeister, who felt that he had not learned a thing about how to do his job as a company commander. McNaughton's scientific and engineering interests diverted his attention from field operations to the point that he presented no seriously thought-out guidance for training for war. On his return to Britain in March 1942 he was nonetheless elevated to command the First Canadian Army, which gave rise to his title "Father of the Canadian Army." In fact, Crerar as CGS from July 1940 had actually worked to father this formation, arguing that Canada possessed enough manpower to form an army of eight divisions, two of which would remain in Canada, for a war period of six years. He envisaged an overseas field army of two corps sustained by voluntary enlistment. To some extent McNaughton's elevation amounted to kicking him upstairs by leaving him responsible for administering a skeleton headquarters then slated to play a role in a cross-Channel invasion. He was in any case removed from training 1 Canadian Corps, which remained under the operational control of Montgomery, who by military measure became the godfather of Canada's army.

In December 1941 Montgomery promulgated a policy directive listing fourteen points essential to success in battle. The never-ending challenge, however, was to ensure that these points were thoroughly absorbed within the ranks of large numbers of citizen soldiers and their leaders. The only solution was constant training, but the problem, which he also addressed in 5 and 12 Corps, was that officers had never been taught training as distinct from fighting in battle. With little knowledge of training principles and techniques, they employed methods that wasted time and left soldiers bored. Commanders appeared content just to know that training was happening when they should have been out supervising to ensure it was properly organized and conducted along sound lines. That progress made at lower levels was not matched in the training of Canadian brigadiers, CRAs, and unit COs caused Montgomery additional concern. He identified the weak point here as lack of knowledge by commanders of how to stage-manage battle employing all arms in combination. Against an enemy as good as the German it was almost impossible for a formation or unit to recover from errors caused by blundering forward without balanced dispositions. If generals could only learn how to put their divisions into battle properly and how to retain firm control throughout a rough fight, he asserted, the Canadian Corps would be unbeatable.

While stressing the need for all-arms cooperation, Montgomery looked upon artillery as key to dominating forward areas, retaining the initiative, and winning the battle. After Exercise "Bumper" commanders of reserve artillery formations were reintroduced and the positions of CRAs and CCRAs strengthened within a dedicated artillery chain of command that enabled designated artillery officers to order the fire of all guns within range. Artillery commanded at the highest level for deployment and allotment, with control of fire decentralized to the lowest level, was thus able to produce a massive blow in a matter of minutes to smash unexpected resistance or repel a counter-attack. To take advantage of this capability Montgomery stressed that the business of artillery COs was first to train their regiments, and then to train infantry brigadiers to use them properly. He strongly criticized the Canadian practice of assigning a task to a battalion, stating it would be supported by a field regiment, and leaving the battalion CO, who possessed few artillery coordination means, to work out details alone. In all such cases he found no proper fire plan laid on and precious artillery resources wasted as COs had neither the time nor the staff to do so. To Montgomery, it was the duty of the higher headquarters to assist the lower, which meant the fire plan had to be done by brigade headquarters that had an artillery staff. His emphasis on brigade-level coordination of artillery firepower does not appear to have registered to the extent it should have, however, judging from operations in Normandy that have been noted. By October, however, battle groups were largely formed on a brigade basis.

Montgomery closely observed the performances of Canadian formations during field exercises and found several commanders wanting. Doubtless to Crerar's delight, he recommended the relief of Pearkes for his blinkered handling of a divisional attack and leaving out critical timings and coordination details in his order to conduct a withdrawal. Two of his brigade commanders, Potts and Ganong, the last favourably assessed earlier, received similarly adverse assessments. Montgomery also found Price's performance as a divisional commander lamentable and completely ineffective. The notable indecisiveness of his senior brigadier, Haldenby, additionally prompted Montgomery to have second thoughts about his suitability for brigade command. As was his customary practice, Montgomery intentionally came down harder on officers than men. He did not think it possible to produce good divisions unless they had good commanders fully capable of handling a division in battle and competent to train their subordinates. Since men's lives were at stake, Montgomery insisted that plain speaking was necessary. Commanders known to be bad had to be told they were bad, but they also had to be taught so that they would become good. Significantly, Montgomery believed that most Canadian brigadiers and unit commanders were excellent material and needed only to be taught.

In Exercise "Tiger," which tested formation-fighting organization, doctrine, and troop capabilities to the limit, the Canadian Corps performed well. Montgomery visited eight Canadian brigades during "Tiger" and praised Crerar for his handling of the corps, astutely noting that he had an excellent BGS in Simonds. The importance of the staff officer behind the commander was nothing knew, of course, and Montgomery had earlier noted that the sound divisional performance of Roberts reflected the positive influence of Mann, his GSO 1. He predicted that Roberts would always do well if he had a good GSO 1. Significantly, Mann ultimately became Crerar's COS in First Canadian Army. Crerar for his part took Montgomery's schooling seriously, embracing his military concepts related to stage-managing the battle, seizing the initiative, fighting for information, retaining control, and forcing the enemy to dance to your tune. His speaking notes and later directives all essentially dispensed Montgomery's teachings.

Montgomery assumed command of the Eighth Army in August 1942 and fought the battles of Alam Halfa and Alamein using combined arms methods that he had developed and taught to the Canadian Corps. At Alamein he fought a flexible air–land battle on his own terms, adapting quickly to changing situations and never losing the initiative. Alamein turned the tide in North Africa, propelled Montgomery into the limelight, and enhanced his standing among Canadians, especially Crerar, who indicated that he wanted to learn more about the practical side of war. In response, Montgomery invited him to attend a study period at Eighth Army headquarters in February 1943. Here Montgomery confirmed the wisdom of fighting as divisions, the war-winning capability of centrally controlled artillery, the importance of army–air coordination, the need for all-arms cooperation, and the importance of tactical surprise and deception. At this point relations between Montgomery and Crerar were cordial and positive.

With the exception of the disastrous Dieppe raid, which some blamed on Montgomery, though he had cancelled the raid before going to the Western Desert, Canadian troops had not yet seen major action. The push to get them into action increased, however, after the 1942 invasion of North Africa saw American soldiers in action before Canadians. Crerar, who had authorized sending Canadian units to garrison Hong Kong and bore more responsibility than Montgomery for ensuring Canadian participation in the Dieppe raid, worked to make this happen, partly for his personal desire to gain operational experience. In Ottawa, where Stuart the CGS shared Crerar's views, McNaughton's reluctance to divide his First Canadian Army incurred growing opposition, especially from defence minister Ralston, who sought to get Canadian troops into action to satisfy public opinion. Crerar subsequently colluded with Ralston and Stuart to remove McNaughton from command. In this effort he received support from the British, who had observed McNaughton's questionable field performance in Exercise "Spartan." In April 1943 largely owing to pressure exerted by Ralston and the CGS in response to growing public demand to get Canadian soldiers into action, the 1st Canadian Infantry Division and the 1st Canadian Army Tank Brigade replaced equivalent British formations in the order of battle for the invasion of Sicily.

Montgomery's relationship with Canadians got off to a quick start in Sicily, where shortly after landing Simonds fired his 1st Brigade commander, Graham, for not advancing aggressively enough and being too lenient on his battalion commanders. When Simonds informed his British corps commander of his action, the latter replied that while he did not wish to interfere in a Canadian affair, he would be inclined to give Graham another chance. Montgomery, on the other hand, personally intervened when he first heard of the matter. Having given Graham high marks during his Canadian Corps visits, he immediately interviewed Graham and reinstated him in command. In his view, sacking popular brigadiers like Graham risked upsetting the 1st Division, and he asked Simonds to do the big thing and take Graham back. This was an astute move as Simonds, quick to anger, still had much to learn about command. Montgomery went on to say that difficult subordinates had to be led, not driven, and that higher commanders had to keep calm and not be too ruthless. From this point on, Simonds and Graham got along well, much to the satisfaction of Montgomery, who increasingly won the hearts and minds of Canadian troops. Noting that they were fast learners, he praised their field performance and the leadership of Simonds. Simonds, in turn, became a foremost disciple of Montgomery.

Montgomery's involvement in another Canadian incident did not end so happily. In preventing McNaughton from visiting Simonds's division in Sicily he triggered a political tempest. Montgomery always considered visitors a nuisance and had even banned Mackenzie King from observing 3rd Canadian Infantry Division training prior to D-Day, but in this case he overstepped. McNaughton's decision to visit Simonds when he had only commenced operations days before put him at odds with Montgomery, who wanted to shield his protégé from being bothered by extra commitments unrelated to the conduct of battle. Yet, despite his arrival at an inconvenient time, McNaughton had the constitutional right to visit Canadian troops. Brooke recognized this and considered the incident an unnecessary clash brought about by Montgomery's arbitrariness and Alexander's failure to overrule him. McNaughton for his part exacerbated the situation by making a political issue of the incident, which

Brooke attributed to his tendency to always look for some slight to his position as a servant of the Canadian government. One suspects, however, that McNaughton under considerable strain from threats to parcel off his Canadian land forces, also fanned the fire to distract attention from his shortcomings as a field army commander on Exercise "Spartan."

That the British actually bent over backwards to accommodate Canadian demands was nowhere better illustrated than the politically motivated dispatch of Crerar's 1 Canadian Corps and the 5th Armoured Division to Italy. The experience of Dieppe and anticipated heavy casualties in the invasion of France partly drove this deployment as Mackenzie King feared that such losses might lead to conscription. Casualties in Italy, on the other hand, appeared to be relatively lighter and just as likely to satisfy public clamour to get Canadian troops into action. Crerar supported the Italian deployment for reasons related to gaining corps battle experience and personal ambition. The trouble was that there was no need for another armoured division in the rugged terrain of Italy or an inexperienced corps headquarters. Montgomery therefore delayed the activation of 1 Canadian Corps headquarters and suggested that, in the interim, Crerar take command of the 1st Canadian Infantry Division to gain operational experience. Crerar declined to step down to divisional command, however, on the grounds that he had been charged by his government to command 1 Canadian Corps to gain experience at that level. Given this response, Montgomery appears to have begun to lose the confidence he formerly placed in Crerar.

Montgomery's confidence was further eroded by Crerar's disparagement of Simonds, who by this time had won his spurs in command of an infantry division in action. Simonds's success apparently kindled Crerar's jealously and resentment, to the extent that he seized upon the caravan incident to allege that Simonds's nerves were shot and might adversely affect his decision making. Crerar went so far as to inform Montgomery that he had serious doubts about Simonds's suitability for higher command, and that further strain might see him go off the deep end with disastrous results. Montgomery not surprisingly dismissed Crerar's allegations, which he must have found highly bizarre, stating that he held Simonds in the highest esteem and considered him to be a very valuable Canadian officer as there was no one else with his experience. Crerar reacted by compiling a file of all documentation emanating from the caravan incident and passing it on to Stuart at CMHQ for safekeeping and possible use in a future problem with Simonds. He also sought advice from medical and psychiatric authorities as to the mental fitness of Simonds assuming higher responsibilities in the area of Canadian policies and business. That Crerar stooped to such backroom measures clearly revealed a nasty streak in his character, but his efforts to cast aspersions on Simonds only planted further doubts about his own suitability for operational command in Montgomery's mind.

While Crerar worked to undermine Simonds, he also worried about his chances of gaining command of First Canadian Army after the departure of McNaughton on 26 December 1943. His concern was that the loss of 1 Canadian Corps and its replacement by the British 1 Corps had left the First Canadian Army half-British. The former CGS, Stuart, had been named acting commander on 27 December 1943, but only as a secondary appointment to his principal job as COS, CMHQ. His refusal to get involved in operational planning owing to health and security reasons further ensured that the army drifted essentially leaderless, which vacuum Crerar attempted to fill from distant Italy while jockeying for command. This extraordinary situation lasted for almost three months and reflected the inadequate state of Canada's war machinery from the top down. Mackenzie King's policies not only resulted in the loss of a strategic voice for Canada in Allied councils, but also, given his suspicion of things military, affected army command arrangements at intermediate levels. The low esteem in which he held the CCOS, to the point of limiting their attendance at War Committee meetings, resulted in the denigration of the position of CGS. When Stuart left to become COS, CMHQ, the post was not even filled for four months. Arguably, Canada's most senior generals should have occupied that position instead of exercising field command, which pattern both the British and Americans followed.

Crerar nonetheless retained the support of Brooke for his good showing in Exercise "Spartan," and Canadian government pressure to keep a Canadian in command of the First Canadian Army reinforced his status as heir apparent to McNaughton. On 20 March 1944 he took command of First Canadian Army without ever having fulfilled his desire to command a corps in action. Ironically, 1 Canadian Corps would not even fight a corps battle before the Canadian government began to press politically for its return to First Canadian Army. Canadian participation in the Normandy invasion meanwhile had devolved to Keller's 3rd Canadian Infantry Division Group assaulting under the operational control of Crocker's 1 Corps in Second British Army. In Operation "Windsor" Crocker faulted Keller for not giving more divisional guidance when things started to go wrong. Dempsey and Montgomery both agreed and recommended his removal, but left official action to be taken by Canadians. Crerar, however, retained a blind faith in Keller and considered him a candidate for corps command. Although he later admitted that he would not consider Keller for higher appointment, he left him in divisional command. To Montgomery, this showed that Crerar, who had made Price a divisional commander yet questioned Simonds's suitability for higher command, was a poor judge of men.

Canadian operations in Normandy experienced teething problems largely because of the weakness of division commanders. In Operation "Charnwood" where the 3rd Canadian Division struggled in a series of close-quarter battles for defended villages and Caen suburbs, Keller blamed Cunningham, 9th Brigade commander, for his failure to aggressively exploit opportunities and recommended his relief. On investigating Keller's allegations, however, Simonds found that while Cunningham had failed on occasion to show the necessary speed and determination, he generally appeared to have carried out his instructions intelligently and well. Simonds further observed that Cunningham had not always received the direction and guidance from above that he was entitled to expect. Keller at this time also pleaded ill health on being shown the adverse reports rendered by Crocker, Dempsey, and Montgomery on his performance as a divisional commander in Operation "Windsor." Later, in Operation "Atlantic," the similarly slow advance of the 3rd Canadian Infantry Division prompted Montgomery to note that if Crerar had followed his advice and fired Keller the progress of the division would have been better. Keller definitely should have been cashiered.

Later still in Operation "Spring," divisional commanders also performed poorly. Mounted to prevent German deployments against Operation "Cobra" in the west, "Spring" succeeded on a higher plane by leading the German high command to think that "Cobra" was diversionary to the main threat posed by the Anglo-Canadians. Tactically, however, "Spring" turned out to be a disaster largely because many 2nd and 3rd Canadian Division attacks had been delivered only by battalions. Stronger divisional direction that ensured properly launched brigade attacks employing infantry, tanks, and artillery in concert would most certainly have produced better results in a number of instances. Montgomery's emphasis on the critical need for higher headquarters to assist lower ones in the coordination of all three fighting arms does not appear to have registered however. They key here was tactical planning at brigade level as battalions did not have the staff and communication means that brigades possessed to effect the proper coordination of artillery fire support. In "Spring" Simonds considered firing Foulkes, GOC 2nd Division, for incurring unnecessary casualties because he had no idea of what was going on at the front and made little effort to intervene to set things right. Keller's 3rd Division battalion attack on Tilly-la-Campagne also foundered against stiff resistance, but a second attack never occurred as Cunningham and two unit commanding officers refused to reinforce failure. While all three were fired for their refusals, Simonds in later years stated that he should have sacked Keller instead of Cunningham.

Throughout this period Montgomery maintained his faith in Simonds, but on several occasions he told Brooke that he considered Crerar quite unfit to command a field army. Brooke in response emphasized making the best use of the material available, including Crerar, whom he insisted had to be retained as First Canadian Army commander. He added that Montgomery could keep his army small with a less important role, but that he must also teach him. While agreeing to do so, Montgomery nonetheless asserted that Simonds was far and away the best Canadian general, the equal of any British corps commander and much better than Crerar. As if to prove this point, when First Canadian Army became operational on 23 July 1944 taking charge of the British 1 Corps that was holding the eastern sector, Crerar almost immediately got into a spat with his one and only corps commander. At issue was the written order Crerar sent to Crocker giving detailed tactical direction that the latter refused to accept on the grounds that it lay more properly within the purview of a corps commander. Once again Crerar sought the assistance of Montgomery, who instructed Crocker to be a loyal subordinate, but also pointed out to Crerar that it was always better to deal verbally with corps commanders who could then give their views. Montgomery then counselled Crerar that a field army commander should give his corps commanders a task and let them decide how to do it, intervening only when success looks to be fading. Crerar appears to have absorbed this lesson from a command altercation that was largely of his own making.

Crerar's first major undertaking ordered by Montgomery resulted in Operation "Totalize," an attack toward Falaise aimed at cutting off enemy forces that were facing Second British Army as it advanced from the west. The promise of this operation appealed to Crerar, who sought to emulate the achievement of the Canadian Corps at Amiens on 8 August 1918. He later claimed that the "Totalize" plan reflected an earlier directive he had issued, but it was in fact the brainchild of Simonds, who produced a highly innovative plan to launch a night armoured attack in the wake of strikes by strategic bombers, using APCs to transport infantry. Artificial moonlight, wireless directional beams, and a Bofors tracer barrage were also used to keep direction. The plan called for a two-phase corps attack, the first to be executed by two infantry divisions each spearheaded by an armoured brigade and supported by a massive weight of artillery. Although armoured movement by night proved a nerve-racking experience, it worked brilliantly and, within hours, chaos spawned success. While mopping-up operations continued, the first phase of "Totalize" had cracked a hole in the German front line for the relatively light total of 380 casualties. The shock effect on the Germans was enormous, causing the C-in-C West, von Kluge, to remark on 8 August that a breakthrough had occurred near Caen the likes of which had never been seen before.

But it was not a breakthrough. Simonds's plan to pause until 1400 hours before launching the second phase guaranteed the very loss of momentum that Crerar had specifically sought to avoid. The potential danger of such a long pause so worried the commanders of the two armoured divisions slated to attack in phase two that they asked Simonds to call off the bombing. This could have been done up to 1100 hours and, ironically, was quickly done in the event when bombs erringly fell on 2 Corps troops. Simonds refused to cancel the planned bombing, however, as he was under the mistaken perception that the 1st SS Division defended the second German defensive zone. He did not want a repeat of "Atlantic" and "Spring" in which that division delivered stunning counter-attacks. Yet, the best time to have launched a second attack upon the Germans was when the shattered German defence was in turmoil. This opportunity presented itself on the morning of 8 August, but it was a fleeting moment. Every passing minute allowed the Germans time to catch their breath and regroup. Since breakthroughs were rarely easy to discern, an early advance down the route to Falaise should at least have been tested by probing. As Montgomery preached, vague and imprecise information about the enemy should never preclude fighting for information or quick and aggressive action by reserves.

Crerar could have intervened by ordering Simonds to hit the enemy immediately to ascertain his true strength while seeking to shape a more favourable development of the situation. To have overruled Simonds, of course, would have taken a field army commander with the confidence to do so. Crerar was certainly aware of the adverse implications of the loss of momentum in an attack, but with less operational expertise than Simonds, he apparently did not think that he could do much to influence matters. He thus played a passive role in "Totalize," finding refuge in his responsibility for arranging air support, the one planning area that remained the sole prerogative of the First Canadian Army. Simonds did not therefore receive the nudging that might have been forthcoming from a field army commander like Dempsey. Having expended so much effort in arranging strategic bomber support, moreover, Crerar may also have been reluctant to request a cancellation for fear of jeopardizing future support from "Bomber" Harris. His recent dispute with Crocker could also have predisposed him to heed Montgomery's advice not to interfere in corps operations. Yet the essence of Montgomery's counsel was that a higher commander should interfere to prevent things going badly.

When Simonds's armoured divisions finally attacked after largely ineffective bomber strikes they only managed to advance under four kilometres in sector. Simonds had decentralized a more than ample amount of artillery to enable the 4th Canadian Armoured Division to blast its way forward, but this resource was not effectively used to deal with German anti-tank guns. The 4th Armoured Brigade commander spearheaded the division advance with a battle group based on a tank regiment and infantry battalion. The problem was that he did not provide supplemental artillery fire planning assistance to the battle group tank CO, who did not possess the means to generate adequate artillery fire, which was the only way of overcoming enemy anti-tank screens at that time. Simply unleashing battle groups saddled unit commanders with artillery coordination problems that brigade fire planning staff were better equipped to handle. Montgomery in his training of the Canadian Corps had constantly warned against this practice, asserting that leaving unit COs to shoulder responsibility for all arms operations was an abrogation of tactical responsibility. In this case, he was absolutely right, for when the 4th Armoured battle group desperately required artillery support, whether it knew it or not, as well as strong intervention, the brigade commander was two miles away sleeping in his tank.

As an alternative to overriding Simonds on bombing, Crerar could have directed Simonds to use the reserve 3rd Canadian Infantry Division to outflank the Germans from either the east or the west, as eventually done by the 2nd Division via Claire Tizon. In any case, with this reserve available, Montgomery did not need to reinforce Crerar, but instead directed Dempsey to advance his left flank on Falaise and join up with the First Canadian Army. Although Montgomery had agreed to attempt a shorter envelopment of German forces at Falaise and Argentan, he had originally planned to effect a longer envelopment on the River Seine. To insure against Falaise not falling, he resorted to generalship, ordering Crerar to effect the shorter envelopment farther east in the Trun-Chambois sector, leaving the Germans to run a gauntlet of fire. Here Montgomery displayed great flexibility, adjusting to the reality of the situation on the ground while looking days ahead to trapping the Germans on the Seine. By 18 August the withdrawal of German forces through the Falaise Gap reached full flood, and by 25 August Montgomery's four field armies were on the Seine, ten days earlier than forecast in D-Day planning.

Simonds's innovative attacks in the thrust on Falaise greatly impressed Montgomery, but he criticized the ponderous advance of the First

Canadian Army beyond the Seine. To him this reflected poor handling by Crerar, who had grouped his army badly for what was wanted in securing the ports of Le Havre and Dieppe and clearing the coastal belt up to Bruges. On learning of 4th Armoured Division intentions to refit, Montgomery signalled that with the Second Army over one hundred miles ahead this was not the time to stop for maintenance. As armoured divisions were ideally suited to the pursuit of a fleeing enemy, he urged Crerar to push the 1st Polish and 4th Armoured forward with all speed. This rankled Crerar, who replied that there was no lack of push or rational speed on the part of his army. He then added fuel to the fire by missing a conference called by Montgomery to discuss future operations with his four field army commanders. Without even bothering to send his COS in his place, Crerar chose instead to attend a commemoration ceremony at Dieppe where those killed in the disastrous raid of 19 August 1942 lay buried. Arguably, this choice reflected the personal guilt he felt about the Dieppe raid, since he more than anyone else had ensured its resurrection as a Canadian operation after it had been cancelled by Montgomery.

When Crerar arrived at Montgomery's headquarters later on in the day he received a chewing out to which he angrily retorted that he had acted as Canadian national commander and would take the matter up with his government if necessary. Faced with this threat Montgomery asked his Canadian personal assistant what he should do. On being told that he should apologize, Montgomery obliged, accepting full blame. This incident has often been cited to show that Montgomery had to be forced to acknowledge Canadian national command, but this is not completely true as he told Stuart that he agreed a Canadian commander responsible for the general welfare of Canadian troops must have the right of appeal to the Canadian government. Montgomery just disagreed that this role should be exercised by a field army commander, since this was a full-time job in itself. Non-operational administrative involvements were better handled by Stuart as COS, CMHQ, which had been set up to relieve field commanders of such responsibilities. Montgomery accepted that Crerar had the right to refer any matter to his government through CMHQ. Stuart confessed that he did not attempt to argue against this point, because he felt that Montgomery was probably right. Crerar, however, disregarded Stuart's warning against being too "bloody minded" over constitutional issues and went on to assert that he as senior Canadian army officer had primary responsibility for the tactical and administrative problems of Canadian field formations. Here, of course, Canada was out of step with the British and Americans, whose most senior army generals did not assume field command abroad.

Tasks assigned to the First Canadian Army on 9 September included the capture of Boulogne, Dunkirk, and Calais, and then the mouth of the Scheldt. After a message from Brooke urging the early opening of Antwerp and clearance of the Scheldt estuary, however, Montgomery asked Crerar for his views on how he would go about tackling such an operation as a priority. To ensure simplicity, concurrent activity, and speed, Montgomery suggested that Crerar use one of his corps headquarters to control operations from Boulogne to Dunkirk and the other to plan and execute the opening of Antwerp. Crerar replied that he needed his staff to examine what was involved and ultimately declined to have the headquarters of the British 1 Corps, which had captured Le Havre on 12 September, continue with operations from Boulogne to Dunkirk while Simonds's 2 Corps headquarters dealt with opening the Scheldt. His decision to not follow Montgomery's advice eventually resulted in the four divisions of 2 Canadian Corps being stretched between Boulogne and Antwerp. Simonds allegedly protested giving priority to investing Channel ports, suggesting instead that 2 Canadian Corps conduct a pursuit along the coast to Breskens, masking German coastal defences, and then turn east to cut the Fifteenth Army off from the Scheldt. To facilitate movement and ensure adequate supply, he proposed beaching landing craft loaded with ammunition, fuel, and bridging along the route of advance. He also expressed confidence that Montgomery would have approved this operational approach as it promised an earlier opening of the Scheldt.

Crerar clearly experienced difficulty in trying to resolve coastal belt and Scheldt operations. Two Canadian military historians even charged that they were conducted so poorly that had Crerar been a British rather than Canadian general, he would most surely have been sacked. Involvement in non-operational issues likely diverted Crerar's attention as did recuring bouts of dysentery that left him fatigued and irascible. During the planning stages for the Battle of the Scheldt he suffered several severe attacks that resulted in his medical evacuation on 27 September. Before his departure Crerar handed over command to Simonds, whose arrival was described as electrifying and a breath of fresh air. Whereas Crerar often appeared stumped by the problems facing him and thus relied heavily upon his staff for solutions, Simonds personally thought things through for himself. Over strong objections, he also insisted on flooding Walcheren, much of which lay below sea level, by breaching the sea dykes through heavy bomber attacks in order to isolate German forces and leave them open to amphibious attack. Throughout the Scheldt campaign Simonds distinguished himself as a dynamic field army commander, dealing with daunting military challenges that would have confounded many other generals. In his innovative use of amphibious assaults to turn flanks and gain surprise, in his employment of floating smoke screens, and in his detailed coordination of complex bombing and artillery firepower, he demonstrated superior generalship.

That Montgomery would have preferred to see Simonds continue in command of the First Canadian Army is beyond question. Indeed, he revealed this preference when he told Ralston on 8 October that Crerar was neither a ball of fire nor in the same league as Simonds as a field army commander. Ironically, however, he may have unintentionally ensured Crerar's return by increasing Ralston's fears that Canadian command of the First Canadian Army might conceivably be lost owing to its Anglo-Canadian composition and command succession order. If Crerar became a casualty while in command, this would not be a problem as Simonds would succeed him as a Canadian commander. Yet, if Simonds as army commander became a casualty, Montgomery said, he would most likely have to be replaced by an experienced British corps commander as no Canadian, including Foulkes, possessed the requisites. The upshot of all this was that after receiving a clean bill of health, Crerar returned to take command of First Canadian Army on 9 November. He also received promotion to the rank of general seven days later, which prompted Montgomery to request that Brooke not convey the impression that the promotion was in any way linked to distinguished service in the field.

In the meantime, Montgomery had laid plans for a major operation to attack and clear the west bank of the Rhine opposite the Ruhr. Owing to his suspicion of Crerar's abilities, Montgomery would have preferred the Second British Army to conduct the operation, but because of troop dispositions he had no option but to assign the task to First Canadian Army. Resigned to having Crerar, he decided to massively reinforce him with British formations. For what he termed the "great winter offensive effort of the British Empire," Crerar commanded almost half a million troops, including Horrocks's 30 Corps of five divisions. Although Montgomery left the decision to Crerar, the deployment of the 30 Corps on the right of First Canadian Army largely determined that it should spearhead the offensive, now code-named "Veritable." Before the operation could be launched, however, the Germans initiated the Battle of the Bulge, which saw Montgomery assume command of Hodges's First US Army. Unfortunately, Montgomery's superb generalship during the battle was eclipsed by the American resentment he fostered through ill-chosen words spoken at a final press conference. His experience in dealing with the shattered Hodges could only have made him look more favourably upon Crerar nonetheless. The Canadian was certainly a far better field army commander than the American, who deserved to be fired.

Crerar's performance in the Battle of the Rhineland was respectable, but not inspired. Allegedly more of a quartermaster general than field commander, he focused on the highly important administrative and logistical preparations for "Veritable," addressing the enormous requirements for food, fuel, equipment supply, force movement and assembly, ammunition dumping, field engineering tasks, communications, and medical support. This reflected his view that success in war was mainly a matter of the more effective movement of tonnage made up of men, weapons, ammunition, motor transport, fighting vehicles, and essential supplies. The commander who could quickly move the right mixture of such tonnage to the decisive point, in a manner unexpected by the enemy, would have victory in his grasp. Montgomery, however, gained the impression that Crerar was not too good at fighting an army-level battle and that his operations were thus liable to become disjointed. Rather than conduct one army battle as Simonds had done in the Scheldt, Crerar left Horrocks to fight his 30 Corps battle and Simonds to fight his 2 Canadian Corps battle. An army-level battle, in contrast, would have involved regrouping formations and changing inter-corps boundaries as necessary, creating new reserves after existing ones had been committed, and mounting alternate thrusts as the situation demanded. Crerar, for example, had an opportunity to effect an end run around the Hochwald by transferring a British division from Horrocks to Simonds, but chose not to do so.

The Battle of the Rhineland nonetheless represented a real triumph for Canadian arms. By this time, largely owing to Montgomery's tutelage and methods, the Canadian Army had come of age as a superb battle-hardened force. As Crerar's COS put it, all of the fighting strength of the British Empire in northwest Europe with the addition of Poles and other Allied contingents fought under Canadian command. The battle not only demonstrated the flexibility and cohesion of the forces of the empire, but also highlighted the advantages of the imperial policy of uniformity in organization, training, and equipment. Crerar was able to group British formations under Simonds and Canadian formations under British corps commanders with remarkable ease. The operation of First Canadian Army headquarters further underscored the advantages of a sound staff system with officers at every level working from a common script as all had been trained in British staff doctrine and procedures. Crerar was justifiably proud of commanding nearly half a million troops and some eleven divisions in one of the major battles of the Western Front. That he was allowed this opportunity by Montgomery, who gave him maximum support and his two best corps commanders, could not have failed to register upon him. In military respects Crerar remained a Monty man. From the beginning he had earnestly attempted to learn and abide by Montgomery's concepts for waging war. In May 1944 he wrote that he had the utmost confidence in Montgomery's military judgment and noted his special genius in the matter of military operations.

Crerar vanished quickly from the Canadian military scene after the war, but not before one of his last intrigues prevented Simonds, despite his seniority, from becoming the CGS. Montgomery, in contrast, became CIGS and assisted as much as he could in looking after his disciples' fortunes. Simonds eventually did become CGS in February 1951, benefiting from the delay in his appointment, since post-war plans initiated a rapid demobilization that he would have disliked. The beginnings of the Cold War and the Korean conflict that broke out in June 1950, however, enabled Simonds to preside over a rapid peacetime expansion that saw close to 7 per cent of GNP devoted to defence. As CGS, Simonds ushered in a golden age of Canadian military professionalism, vicariously continuing and inculcating Montgomery's methods, including his emphasis on troop morale, verbal orders, thinking two down, correctly grouping tanks and infantry for tasks, forward command from Tac HQs, artillery fire planning, and realistic training based on good teaching and exercise rehearsals. He also assigned the highest priority to staff college education and studies reminiscent of his mentor.

At roughly the same time that Simonds assumed the appointment of CGS, Montgomery became Deputy SACEUR in which capacity he played a leading role in assessing the changing nature of war and how it might affect the actions of NATO ground forces. The inability of NATO to field sufficient ground forces to counterbalance Soviet masses left Western defence dependent upon strategic nuclear deterrence that appeared excessive in the case of limited aggressions. Through the medium of annual CPXs that he personally designed and directed, Montgomery addressed such strategical and tactical problems, including the conduct of mobile operations by division and higher commanders in the early phases of a possible war. From these exercises Montgomery concluded that tactical nuclear weapons could redress the balance of power. At his insistence, SACEUR therefore established a New Approach Group to consider equipping NATO conventional forces with such weapons. While Montgomery considered these weapons unproven "imponderables" that might not solve the NATO military dilemma, he considered it prudent to assume for planning purposes that the Soviets would use nuclear weapons in any attack and that NATO would be forced to use them in response. On 22 November 1954 the North Atlantic Council approved the integration of atomic weapons with land forces in a "New Look" nuclear posture, of which Montgomery was the chief architect.

NATO's "New Look" posture directly affected the development of Canadian Army doctrine. Simonds considered Monty's "imponderables" in his Exercise "Broadsword," which examined some of the problems the Canadian Army might encounter in the age of the missile and atom. Whether war would be atomic or non-atomic posed a perplexing problem as operations such as "Totalize" were out of the question in the former case. In his closing remarks, Simonds cited his mentor and concluded that the overwhelming conventional strength of the Soviets left NATO no option but to rely on nuclear weapons to deter them from attacking. The tactics and operations of ground forces had to be tailored to fit both conditions, however, and "Broadsword" constituted a first step toward examining new concepts to do this. That Simonds passed on his "Broadsword" remarks to Montgomery attested to their continued close relationship.

In January 1955 Simonds launched Exercise "Gold Rush": A Study of the Organization and Field Formations to Meet the Conditions of Future Warfare. Under the direction of his Deputy CGS, Brigadier Moncel, the "Gold Rush" study team explored the changing characteristics of future warfare and produced a new tactical and logistical concept for the army that was to be tested and evaluated in the field by divisional-level training in Camp Gagetown. This effort directed at corps level and below eventually produced a force structure and coherent doctrine designed to enable the Canadian Army to meet the mobility and flexibility requirements of the nuclear battlefield as envisioned in NATO tactical concepts developed largely by Montgomery. Fortunately, a tactical nuclear war was never fought in Europe, but not to have planned for such contingency would have been professionally irresponsible. Reason also suggested that an army trained to fight under nuclear conditions could, with appropriate adjustment, undertake conventional operations.

When Simonds retired as CGS in August 1955 Montgomery vainly attempted to get him commands in Northern Europe, NATO Defence College, and in Britain. In admitting the failure of his efforts, Montgomery commented that it was ridiculous that the best soldier Canada had ever produced should be retired so young. Yet the professional approach that Simonds brought to the Canadian Army continued with successive Monty men. On 1 September 1955 Graham, whom Montgomery had saved in Sicily, replaced Simonds as CGS, basically continuing his policies that included the "Gold Rush" studies and, up to 1958, divisional exercises in Camp Gagetown under simulated tactical nuclear conditions. Notably, Simonds's loyal COS in 2 Canadian Corps, Major General

Rodger, became Graham's VCDS in December 1955. In September 1958 Graham handed the job over to Clark, who stayed the "Gold Rush" course set by Simonds and oversaw the introduction of the US "Honest John" nuclear surface-to-surface missile for the Canadian NATO brigade.

Clark's term also saw the publication of numerous training manuals, which established an army doctrine based on existing organizations, but presciently in advance of some equipment acquisitions such as APCs. CAMT 1–8, "The Infantry Brigade Group in Battle, Part 1 – Tactics," issued under Clark's signature, provided broad tactical and logistic doctrine for infantry brigade group defensive, offensive, and withdrawal operations under conditions of nuclear war, with one chapter devoted to non-nuclear operations. Recognizing that Canada would never fight without allies, the manual further stipulated that the infantry brigade group had to be capable of operating directly under a corps headquarters or in combination with other brigade groups under a tactical divisional commander. Tough officer-promotion examinations also required the detailed study of all training manuals and aimed primarily at testing an officer's fitness for operations in war. However highly recommended by a superior, an officer could not get into the staff college without passing these exams. This high standard of officer training produced an operationally oriented army in which almost everyone knew and understood the roles and employment of all arms and services. Doctrine, force structure, and training were thus at this juncture harmonized under a flourishing, pragmatic military leadership.

Lieutenant General Walsh, Simonds's former chief engineer in 2 Canadian Corps, replaced Clark in October 1961. He was destined to be the last CGS as a new defence minister, Paul Hellyer, arrived in April 1963 determined to integrate, then unify, the Canadian armed services. In August 1964 a single integrated CFHQ came into being under Air Chief Marshal Miller as CDS and Walsh as Vice CDS. In due course the separate administrative, supply, and personnel organizations of the RCN, Canadian Army, and RCAF were integrated to form single-service branches. While Walsh and many others favoured the integration of management as a means of reducing costs through the elimination of triplication, the unintended consequences of service integration and subsequent unification were not entirely foreseen. The general staff, uniquely integral to the field operations of the army ceased to exist along with its professional examinations. In 1965 Walsh handed over the post of Vice CDS to Lieutenant General Moncel, who had expected to take over as CDS after Miller. When Moncel balked at unifying fighting elements, however, Hellyer chose a more opportunistic candidate. Thus passed the last high-ranking Monty man from the Canadian military scene.

The Montgomery Touch

Montgomery was CIGS when he made his first visit to Canada in September 1946 at the invitation of Mackenzie King. Before embarking from Liverpool on 19 August with 1,000 Canadian and American war brides, he had written to Foulkes asking for Trumbull Warren to be attached to him to help run the trip.[1] Montgomery had, of course, maintained a regular correspondence with Warren both during and after the war. As far back as July 1942 he had promised to visit Canada when Warren's mother kindly invited him to stay at Glenlonely, her home in Aurora, Ontario.[2] She also wrote to say that she would be sending a care parcel now and then to Montgomery's son, David.[3] The flow of care parcels and hampers to Montgomery and his son continued throughout the war and included such items as an embroidered hanky, honey, cheese, chocolates, razor blades, and Alphamin-canned Canadian sunshine pills that apparently kept the former very well over winter. During this time Montgomery also exchanged letters with Warren's wife, Mary, to whom he explained that he had to send Trumbull to the staff college even though it meant losing a highly efficient officer. He further promised that on Trumbull's return overseas he would watch over him and do everything within his power to deliver him back safely to her. "And then I shall come and stay with you both at your home in Canada," he added.[4]

While in Canada Montgomery consulted with defence officials and delivered a lecture at the Canadian Army Staff College stressing the need for cooperation and combined action in addressing the Soviet threat. Granted honorary degrees from the universities of Dalhousie, McGill, and Toronto, he also paid tribute to Canada's role in the war during cross-country visits to major cities from Halifax to Victoria, receiving tumultuous welcomes wherever he went.[5] In planning the trip Montgomery asked for four days in Jasper, a day in Toronto, and a visit to Niagara, but he especially insisted on attending the christening of the Warren's newly born daughter, Ann, to whom he became godfather. On his return to Britain, Montgomery continued to correspond with the Warrens, even on one occasion asking for hard-to-obtain sheets and pillow cases for his newly refurbished home in Isington, Hampshire. He also tried to get back to Canada to see them, informing Trumbull that for his planned visit in April/May 1953 he had written Foulkes telling him that the only engagement he wanted included in the program "was a visit to see you and Mary to see my God-daughter." Apart from that, he added, the program could be as Foulkes wished. In September 1953 he further advised Trumbull that he planned his next visit for November 1954.[6]

During and after the war many places, streets, and centres in Canada were named after Montgomery. In 1953 the board of education in Hamilton, Ontario, wrote to him asking his permission to name a new school in the city's east end after him. When Viscount Montgomery Elementary School officially opened on 18 April 1953 it was touted as the most modern school in North America and the largest single-storey school in Hamilton. Montgomery took a personal interest in his "beloved school," which he visited on five separate occasions[7] coinciding with his visits to the Warrens. Montgomery returned for a cross-country visit to Canada in 1956 and spent a week with them in Hamilton.[8] Here he extended an invitation for them to stay with him during their trip to England planned for the next year. He also made arrangements for Mary to meet the Queen as he had promised her long ago. In a letter to Trumbull dated 7 June 1957 Montgomery announced that the Queen had agreed to receive both him and Mary after the Garter Service in Windsor Castle, adding that he looked forward to seeing them at Claridges at 4:30 p.m. on Tuesday 11 June.[9]

Montgomery made another visit to Canada in April 1960, intentionally financing the trip himself so as not to be beholden to anybody.[10] During this time he also made his last visit to Viscount Montgomery School, where he urged "his" students to make the school the best in Hamilton, the best in Ontario, and the best in Canada. According to his brother Brian, Montgomery also visited Canada in October 1961.[11] Montgomery accepted an Empire Club invitation to speak to a Canadian audience on the 25th anniversary of D-Day in 1969 and asked Trumbull in June 1968 if he could stay with him and Mary in their home. A month later, however, he wrote to Trumbull saying that he had to cancel the trip owing to health reasons. As he told Trumbull, at the age of nearly eighty-one, he had to reduce to a lower gear. Announcing that his travelling days were over, he added that he would spend the evening of his life quietly in England. In January 1969 he asked Trumbull and Mary to please come and see him if they visited England in June. He also expressed delight to learn that his god-daughter was expecting a child.[12]

Appendix: Some General Notes on What to Look for When Visiting a Unit

Bernard Law Montgomery

1. The underlying object is obviously to find out what the C.O. is worth, and generally if it is a good or bad unit. The method adopted, and the length of time it will take, will depend entirely on the inspecting officer's own military knowledge, on his own experience in actual command, and generally on whether he can be "bluffed" by the C.O.
2. Most C.O.s will want to lay on a tour of the unit area, looking at the training and so on. This would be quite suitable for *later* visit. But for the first visit, if you really want to find out all about the unit there is only one way to do it. And that is to sit with the C.O. in his orderly room and cross-examine him on certain points which are "key" points, and which will show at once whether or not he knows his job. The Brigadier should be present, but no one else. The C.O. is then put through it. And if he begins to wriggle and to give evasive answers, he is pinned down at once. The C.O. will welcome such an interview and will learn a great deal from it. On no account must he be bullied or rattled. The great point is to show him that you really want to know all about his unit and that you are all out to find out his difficulties and worries and to help him. I have found all C.O.s in the Canadian Corps most friendly, and very willing to tell me how they run their show. It is very important that the C.O. should realise early in the proceedings that you really do know what you are talking about, it is quite easy to show him this by cross-examining him on some point of detail about which he probably thinks you know nothing. Once he sees this, he will be perfectly frank and will welcome any ideas you may give him. Both parties will learn a great deal from the discussion – the visiting officer and the C.O. And so will the Brigadier. And all the time you are summing up the C.O.

and finding out what he knows. It must all be very friendly and natural from the beginning; you then get the C.O.'s confidence; this is most important.

3. An investigation into the following points will show you at once what the unit is worth, and if the C.O. knows his job.

(a) *The system of selection, promotion, and inspection of N.C.O.s.* This is a very important point, and its importance is not always realised by the C.O.s. The N.C.O.'s are the backbone of the battalion; a good solid foundation must be built up on the L/Cpl. level, and the standard of this foundation must be the C.O.'s standard and NOT five different company standards. The C.O. must interest himself directly in everything connected with his N.C.O.s and W.O.s.

(b) *Organization of individual training, i.e., training of the rank and file.* The usual fault here is that men are not graded *before* the training begins, and put into categories in accordance with their knowledge and efficiency. This must always be done, so as to ensure that men get instruction in accordance with their needs. The principle of piece work is also very important.

(c) *Training of the N.C.O.s.* The training of the N.C.O.s in all duties in the field, tactical and administrative, must be carried out by the Coy. Comds. The Adjutant and the R.S.M. must take a very definite hand in keeping the N.C.O.'s up to the mark, in instruction in discipline matters, and generally in ensuring that the non-commissioned ranks are a credit to the battalion, are able to maintain a high standard in all matters, are not afraid of the men, and are trained on for promotion.

(d) *Training of the Officers.* The C.O. must handle this himself, personally. No one else can do it for him. *He must do it himself.* The best results are obtained when the C.O. has an officers day once a week. Officers have got to be taught the stage-management of the various operations of war, the technique of movement, the co-operation of all arms in battle, the technique of reconnaissance and deployment, administration in the field, and so on.

(e) *Organization and conduct of collective training.* Before beginning Coy or Bn. Training the C.O. must issue instructions as to how it is to be done. He should assemble his officers and lay down:
1. The object of the training.
2. The principles on which it is to be based.
3. The standard aimed at.

4. The phases of war to be studied.
5. His views on operations by night.
6. How he wishes the time available to be used. etc.

The great point in collective training is to mix the training. During platoon training the whole company should go out once a week. During company training the whole battalion should go out once every 10 days or so. During Battalion training the whole Bde. should go out once a fortnight. This is far better than having long periods devoted separately to each subject.

The next point is that when you embark on unit training every exercise must include the dusk and the dawn. These are the times when things happen in war.

A small number of exercises lasting 24 hours or more are much better than a large number of short exercises. The exercise lasting from after breakfast till tea-time is of little use. A good exercise is one that tests out the administrative arrangements, and involves the dusk and the dawn.

During collective training the following operations must be taught and practised:

1. The set-piece attack, ie., the Brigade battle.
2. Breaking down the Brigade battle and carrying on the advance by means of resolute fighting in small self-contained groups of all arms.
3. The dusk attack.
4. The night attack.
5. Forcing the crossing of obstacles.
6. Re-organization and holding the ground gained.
7. Disengagement and withdrawal.
8. Defensive tactics.
9. Counter-attacks.

Teaching "Training" as Distinct from Teaching "War"

4. It is the exception to find a commander who teaches his subordinates how train troops. In the F.S.R. we have laid down the principles of war, categorically. In no book do we find laid down the principles of training; officers are supposed to know all about this subject; actually, very few know anything about it and a great deal of time is wasted in consequence.

Training is a great art; there are principles of training just as there are principles of war. Training in war time must be carried out somewhat differently to training in peacetime, as we have to be ready to meet the enemy at any time.

5. In the training of his unit the C.O. has got to consider the following points:

   (a) Training of the rank and file.
   (b) Training of the N.C.O.'s in their duties as leaders.
   (c) Training of the officers.
   (d) Organization and conduct of collective training generally.
   (e) The best way to run sub-unit training, i.e., platoon and company training.
   (f) Battalion training.

If he will think it out on these lines he has got a firm basis from which to start.

6. But he will do no good in his training unless he realises very clearly the importance of the following basic points, and has a good system for carrying them out:

   (a) Interior economy and administration, and life generally within the unit.
   (b) The training of the leaders, i.e., the officers and the N.C.O.'s.

Some C.O.s realise the necessity for training the officers; not a great many, but only some. Very few bother about the N.C.O.s; in fact practically none. But the N.C.O.s are the backbone of the unit; the whole question of their selection, promotion, instruction, and welfare must be on good and sound lines. Sgts. Messes are very important.

The R.S.M.

7. The R.S.M. is one of the most important people in the unit. I always ask to see the R.S.M., treat him like an officer, and shake hands with him. When inspecting the S. Saskatchewan Regt. I called the R.S.M. out in front and shook hands with him in front of the whole Bn; It may seem a small point but in my view it means a great deal.

The R.S.M. is the senior non-commissioned rank in the unit; his authority over the N.C.O.s is supreme, and he must be backed up and given opportunities to pull his weight. He should frequently assemble the W.O.s and N.C.O.s by Coys and address them, getting across to them various points in the daily life of the unit that want attention.

He and the Adjutant should work together as a team; and they should go out together round the battalion area whenever they can, keeping an eye on the general show.

It is very difficult, in fact practically impossible, to have a good cadre of N.C.O.s without a good R.S.M.

Visiting Collective Training

8. When visiting a unit or inter-Bde exercise, or a Divisional exercise, you want to be clear as to what you want to find out. Generally I suggest that this will be as follows:

   (a) What the commander is worth, and whether he is able to handle his ship when in full sail in a rough sea.
   (b) Whether his machinery for exercising command is good, and runs smoothly.
   (c) Broadly, how the formation or unit re-acts. Does it answer to the helm, or is it awkward and unsteady in a rough sea?

As far as the Corps Commander is concerned, or in fact any senior general officer, the above points are the ones that really matter. The points of detail such as the minor tactics, the fieldcraft, and so on, are the province of subordinate commanders. If you want to get a line on this it can be done by getting a staff officer to watch the operation in the front line and to keep an eye on such things as:

   technique of movement;
   deployment;
   battle drill;
   quick manoeuvre;
   outflanking tactics;
   sub-unit tactics generally;
   cooperation with other arms on the sub-unit level.

9. As regards para 8(a) and 8(b). The points here are:
   (a) What orders did the commander receive?
   (b) What did he know about the enemy when he received those orders?
   (c) What orders did he then give?

Once you have got this *from the commander himself*, then you are well on way to what you want to find out.

You then go on as follows:

(d)   What are his present dispositions?

(e)   What is his view as to the general situation, i.e., how does he view the problem?

(f)   What are his plans for future action?

A few questions as to the layout of his H.Q., and a quick tour round his H.Q. follows. I should then leave him.

10. As regards para 8(c). You now visit the next commander below, e.g. if para 9 has been done with a Brigadier you visit one of the forward battalion H.Q. There you go for the same points as outlined in para 9.

11. You have now got the answer to what you want to know. But you want to check up on it, so you must find out from the Director when some important change or event in the battle is to take place. There may be a moment when a very fast ball is going to be bowled at the commander of one side.

You want to be in on this, and study the reactions. In particular it is a good thing if you can be present when the commander is giving out his orders; by listening to this you will find out a good deal.

12. In general the art lies in being at the right place at the right time, and knowing when that time is.

The next point is to get all your information from the commander himself. You want to sum *him* up; therefore you must deal with *him personally*. If he is out, you must chase him till you find him.

The last point is to remember what is the object of your visit; see para 8. You will not have time to also visit sub-units in the front line; if you want a line on how they are working, send some other officer to get that information for you.

6.Mar.42.
B. L. Montgomery
Lieutenant-General.
General Officer Commanding-in-Chief
South Eastern Command.

Notes

Introduction

1 J.L. Granatstein, *The Best Little Army in the World: The Canadians in Northwest Europe, 1944–1945* (Toronto: Harper Collins, 2015), 268.

2 Carlo D'Este, *Decision in Normandy: The Unwritten Story of Montgomery and the Allied Campaign* (London: Collins, 1983), 455, 504, 510, "Monty: World War II's Most Misunderstood General," *Armchair General*, 11 July 2005, and *Bitter Victory: The Battle for Sicily, July-August 1943* (London: Collins, 1988), 614–20; and Williamson Murray and Allan R. Millett, *A War to Be Won: Fighting the Second World War* (Cambridge, MA: Belknap Press, 2000), 270, 417, 470. Even Russell Weigley, one of Montgomery's harshest critics, granted that he was a commander of greater audacity than Americans sometimes like to admit. Russell F. Weigley, *Eisenhower's Lieutenants: The Campaign of France and Germany, 1944–1945* (Bloomington: Indiana University Press, 1981), 175.

3 Imperial War Museum (IWM), Montgomery of Alamein Papers (MAP), BLM 20/4 Brooke to Montgomery, Aug 5/40; and D'Este, *Sicily*, 92, 105.

4 Brian Montgomery, *A Field-Marshal in the Family* (London: Constable, 1973), 144–5, 170, 176–7; Nigel Hamilton, *Monty: The Making of a General 1887–1942* (Sevenoaks: Coronet, 1984), 141–3.

5 Nigel Hamilton, *Monty: The Field-Marshal 1944–1976* (London: Hamish Hamilton, 1986), 225–34; *The Memoirs of Field-Marshal The Viscount Montgomery of Alamein, K.G.* (London: Collins, 1958), 41–4; Hamilton, *Making*, 248–60; and Tom Carver, *Where the Hell Have You Been?* (London: Short Books, 2009), 36–44.

6 IWM, Trumbull Warren Papers (TWP), Montgomery to Warren, 27-6-42.

7 U.S. Army Military History Institute, Carlisle Barracks, Pennsylvania, Oral History: The General James A. Van Fleet Papers, Senior Officers Debriefing Program Conversation with Colonel Bruce H. Williams (1973).

8 Fort Frontenac Library, Kingston, Ontario, bound copy B. Greenhous and W.A. McAndrew, Interview with General B.M. Hoffmeister (1980), 114–6.

9 Hamilton, *Field-Marshal*, 19–20, 34–6.

10 IWM,MAP, Personal Diary, 6, 16, 22, 24, and 30 October and 1 November 1944; and Jeffrey Williams, *The Long Left Flank: The Hard Fought Way to the Reich 1944–1945* (Toronto: Stoddart, 1988), 165–6. Eisenhower made his one and only visit to First Canadian Army on 29 November 1944 at Breda, east of the Scheldt.

1. The Germination of Generalship

1 *The Memoirs of Field-Marshal The Viscount Montgomery of Alamein, K.G.* (London: Collins, 1958), 17–37; Nigel Hamilton, *Monty: The Making of a General 1887–1942* (Sevenoaks: Coronet, 1984), 3–5, 30–131; Gary Sheffield, *Forgotten Victory: The First World War: Myths and Realities* (London: Headline, 2001), 206, 211–2; Brian Montgomery, *A Field-Marshal in the Family* (London: Constable, 1973), 109–77; and Alun Chalfont, *Montgomery of Alamein* (London: Methuen, 1976), 80–6.

2 Montgomery, *Memoirs*, 35; Hamilton, *Making*, 97, 105, 117–20, 131; and Chalfont, *Montgomery of Alamein*, 88–90.

3 Tom Carver, *Where the Hell Have You Been?* (London: Short Books, 2009), 36.

4 Montgomery, *Memoirs*, 36–9; Montgomery, *Field-Marshal in the Family*, 177–81; Hamilton, *Making*, 143–4; and John A English, *The Canadian Army and the Normandy Campaign* (Mechanicsburg: Stackpole, 1991), 63.

5 Hamilton, *Making*, 144–166; and Chalfont, *Montgomery of Alamein*, 96–9, 101–2. Chalfont presents a harsher treatment of Montgomery than Hamilton, which serves to render some balance.

6 Hamilton, *Making*, 159, 171–9; and Chalfont, *Montgomery of Alamein*, 100.

7 Montgomery, *Memoirs*, 40–4; MAP, Montgomery to Tom Reynolds, 6-10-42; Hamilton, *Making*, 180–4; Chalfont, *Montgomery of Alamein*, 103–9; and Alistair Horne with David Montgomery, *Monty: The Lonely Leader, 1944–1945* (London: Macmillan, 1994), 23.

8 Hamilton, *Making*, 199–202; and Chalfont, *Montgomery of Alamein*, 112–13.

9 Hamilton, *Making*, 202–8; and Chalfont, *Montgomery of Alamein*, 115.

10 Hamilton, *Making*, 213–23; and Chalfont, *Montgomery of Alamein*, 116–18.

11 Hamilton, *Making*, 224–7.

12 Ibid., 227–36, 240–5; Montgomery, *Memoirs*, 43; *The First Fifty Years of the Staff College Quetta, 1905–1955* (Quetta: Staff College, 1962), 14–15, 61–2; Chalfont, *Montgomery of Alamein*, 119–22.

2. Canadian Corps Legacy and Loss of Professionalism

1 Hamilton, *Making*, 120–1; Montgomery, *Field-Marshal in the Family*, 144–5, 170; J.L. Granatstein, *Canada's Army: Waging War and Keeping the Peace*

(Toronto: University of Toronto Press, 2002), 123–4; and Gary Sheffield, *Forgotten Victory: The First World War: Myths and Realities* (London: Headline, 2001), 204–16.

2 A.M.J. Hyatt, *General Sir Arthur Currie: A Military Biography* (Toronto: University of Toronto Press, 1987), 73, 78–89; Granatstein, *Canada's Army*, 128–30; Chris Coulthard-Clark, *Where Australians Fought: The Encyclopaedia of Australia's Battles* (St. Leonards: Allen and Unwin, 1998), 132–4; John Swettenham, *McNaughton* (Toronto: Ryerson, 1968), I, 97, 108–11; C.P. Stacey, *Canada and the Age of Conflict: A History of Canadian External Policies*, vol. 1: *1867–1921* (Toronto: Macmillan, 1977), 213–16; and William Stewart, "'Byng Boys': A Profile of Senior Commanders of Canadian Combat Units on the Somme, 1916," *War in History* 23, no. 1 (2016): 55–78.

3 Swettenham, *McNaughton*, 1:68–76, 84–92; Herbert Fairlie Wood, *Vimy* (London: Transworld, 1972), 64–111; Jeffrey Williams, *Byng of Vimy: General and Governor-General* (London: Leo Cooper, 1983), 142–70; Hyatt, *General Currie*, 63–7, 99; and Tim Cook, *No Place to Run: The Canadian Corps and Gas Warfare in the First World War* (Vancouver: UBC Press, 1999), 108–10.

4 Col. C.P. Stacey, "The Staff Officer: A Footnote to Canadian Military History," *Canadian Defence Quarterly* (*CDQ*) 3 (Winter 1973/74): 47–8; English, *Canadian Army*, 4–5; and Swettenham, *McNaughton*, 1:67, 75.

5 Hyatt, *General Currie*, 63–7, 99, 114–15; Shane Schreiber, *Shock Army of the British Empire: The Canadian Corps in the Last 100 Days of the Great War* (Westport: Praeger, 1997), 17–24.

6 Schreiber, *Shock Army*, 33–132; Sheffield, *Forgotten Victory*, 237–51, 256–63.

7 Colonel G.W.L. Nicholson, *Official History of the Canadian Army in the First World War: Canadian Expeditionary Force 1914–1919* (Ottawa: Queen's Printer, 1962), 347–53; Robert Craig Brown and Ramsay Cook, *Canada 1896–1921: A Nation Transformed* (Toronto: McClelland and Stewart, 1974), 310–38; James Eayrs, *In Defence of Canada: Appeasement and Rearmament* (Toronto: University of Toronto Press, 1964), 56; James Eayrs, *In Defence of Canada: From the Great War to the Great Depression* (Toronto: University of Toronto Press, 1964), 224–69, 274–87; English, *Canadian Army*, 22; and Stephen J. Harris, *Canadian Brass: The Making of a Professional Army 1860–1939* (Toronto: University Press, 1988), 152–7, 196–8.

8 Eayrs, *Great War*, 88–93; and English, *Canadian Army*, 13, 32–3.

9 John Nelson Rickard, *The Politics of Command: Lieutenant-General A.G.L. McNaughton and the Canadian Army 1939–1943* (Toronto: University of Toronto Press, 2010), 23–6; Eayrs, *Great War*, 258; English, *Canadian Army*, 23–4; and Swettenham, *McNaughton*, 1:187–93, 229–44, 249.

268 Notes to pages 28–32

10 Swettenham, *McNaughton*, 1:213–24, 251–62, 269–85, 292–7, 304–17;
   Eayrs, *Great War*, 124–36; Rickard, *McNaughton*, 27–33; Reginald H. Roy,
   For Most Conspicuous Bravery: A Biography of Major-General George R. Pearkes,
   V.C., through Two World Wars (Vancouver: UBC Press, 1977), 117–18, 122;
   Richard H. Gimblett, "'Buster' Brown: The Man and his Clash with 'Andy'
   McNaughton" (unpublished BA thesis, Royal Military College, 1979), 64–5;
   and English, *Canadian Army*, 23–4, 26–7.
11 Brig. B.L. Montgomery, "The Problem of the Encounter Battle as Affected
   by Modern British War Establishment," *CDQ* 1 (October 1937): 13–25;
   Lt.-Col. E.L.M. Burns, "A Division That Can Attack," *CDQ* 3 (April 1938),
   282–98 and "Where Do the Tanks Belong?" *CDQ* 1 (October 1938):
   28–31; Capt. G.G. Simonds, "An Army That Can Attack – A Division That
   Can Defend," *CDQ* 4 (July 1938): 413–17, "What Price Assault without
   Support?" *CDQ* 2 (January 1939): 142–7, and "The Attack," *CDQ* 4 (July
   1939): 379–90; Col. T.A. Hunter, "The Necessity of Cultivating Brigade
   Spirit in Peace Time," *CDQ* 1 (October 1927): 22–23; and English,
   Canadian Army, 13, 29–30, 36.
12 *As You Were! Ex-Cadets Remember* (Kingston: The R.M.C. Club of Canada,
   1984), 2:41.

3. Montgomery in Command of British Formations

 1 Brigadier B.L. Montgomery, "The Problem of the Encounter
   Battle as Affected by Modern British War Establishment," *CDQ* 1
   (October 1937): 13–25, republished from the *Royal Engineer's Journal*
   (September 1937); "The Major Tactics of the Encounter Battle," *Army*
   Quarterly 36, no. 2 (July 1938): 268–72; and Hamilton, *Making*, 245,
   249–50, 303–4.
 2 MAP, BLM 11/2, 9th Infantry Brigade Officers Study Week – Dec 1937; and
   Hamilton, *Making*, 249–55, 266–71, 304.
 3 Montgomery, *Memoirs*, 46–9; Hamilton, *Making*, 273–98, 304; Chalfont,
   Montgomery of Alamein, 128–32; and Ronald Lewin, *Montgomery as Military*
   Commander (New York: Stein and Day, 1971), 27–9.
 4 MAP, BLM 17, Div Exercises No. 3 and No. 4, March 1940, BLM 18,
   Exercise No. 5, April 1940, and 3rd Division Exercises carried out in France
   during winter 1939/40; Hamilton, *Making*, 308–16, 320–9, 358; and Julian
   Thompson, *Dunkirk: Retreat into Victory* (London: Sidgwick & Jackson,
   2008), 186–7.
 5 Field Marshal Lord Alanbrooke, *War Diaries 1939–1945*, ed. Alex
   Danchev and Daniel Todman (London: Weidenfeld & Nicolson, 2001),
   71–2 (28 May 1940); Hamilton, *Making*, 329–58; Montgomery, *Memoirs*,
   60–1.

6 Hamilton, *Making*, 343–4, 347, 360–71, 376; Montgomery, *Memoirs*, 61–6; and Thompson, *Dunkirk*, 240–1. Lieutenant General M.G.H. Barker on Montgomery's recommendation was removed from 1 Corps command. Major General Lloyd, GOC 2nd Division, was also sacked.

7 MAP, BLM 19/4, Dill to Montgomery, 5 June 1940 and BLM 19/3 Lt. Gen. Sir Henry Pownall to Montgomery, 5 June 1940; Montgomery, *Memoirs*, 51–8; and Hamilton, *Making*, 301–2, 310–11, 342–3, 372–5.

8 Hamilton, *Making*, 383–94.

9 Ibid., 395–400.

10 Ibid., 400–2.

11 Ibid., 399, 401.

12 Ibid. 403–6, 410–12.

13 MAP, BLM 24/4 Address – Minley Manor – 25 October, 1943; and Hamilton, *Making*, 418, 421–49.

14 Lewin, *Montgomery as Military Commander*, 46–8; and Hamilton, *Making*, 412, 419–20, 442, 446.

15 Library and Archives Canada (LAC), MG30 E157 Crerar Papers (CP), Vol. 23, Corps Commander's Personal Memoranda for Commanders dated 7 May 1941 from B.L. Montgomery, Lieutenant-General, 12 Corps.

16 CP, Vol. 23, Corps Commander's Personal Memoranda for Commanders dated 16 May and 27 Aug 1941 from B.L. Montgomery, Lieutenant-General, 12 Corps.

17 CP, Vol. 23, Corps Commander's Personal Memoranda for Commanders dated 16 May and 29 August 1941 from B.L. Montgomery, Lieutenant-General, 12 Corps.

18 CP, Vol. 23, Corps Commander's Personal Memoranda for Commanders dated 16 May and 30 October 1941 from B.L. Montgomery, Lieutenant-General, 12 Corps.

19 CP, Vol. 23, Corps Commander's Personal Memoranda for Commanders dated 28 May 1941 from B.L. Montgomery, Lieutenant-General, 12 Corps; and Hamilton, *Making*, 454–5, 464.

20 CP, Vol. 23, Corps Commander's Personal Memoranda for Commanders dated 16 May, 1 June, and 9 Aug 41 from B.L. Montgomery, Lieutenant-General, 12 Corps.

21 CP, Vol. 23, Corps Commander's Personal Memoranda for Commanders dated 1 November 1941 from B.L. Montgomery, Lieutenant-General, 12 Corps.

22 CP, Vol. 23, Corps Commander's Personal Memoranda for Commanders dated 16 and 28 May, 20 July, and 1 November 1941 from B.L. Montgomery, Lieutenant-General, 12 Corps; and David Sommerville, *Monty: A Biography of Field Marshal Montgomery* (London: Bison 1992), 46.

23 This included the selection of all senior command and staff appointments down to lieutenant colonel in the field army at home as well as abroad. CP, Vol. 8, Memoranda signed by Lt. Gen. A.G.L. McNaughton, 15 and 24 Jun 42, 3 Apr and 11 Jun 43; and Memorandum by Lt. Col. McNeill, A.A.G. (MS), 13–6-42.

4. Canada's Erratic March to War

1 C.P. Stacey, *Canada and the Age of Conflict: A History of Canadian External Policies*, vol. 2: *1921–1948: The Mackenzie King Era* (Toronto: |University of Toronto Press, 1984), 173, 178, 187, 194–211; C.P. Stacey, *Six Years of War. The Army in Canada, Britain and the Pacific* (Ottawa: Queen's Printer, 1966), 111–12; and J.L. Granatstein, *The Ottawa Men: The Civil Service Mandarins, 1935–1957* (Toronto: Oxford University Press, 1982), 121–2.

2 C.P. Stacey, *Arms, Men and Governments: The War Policies of Canada, 1939–1945* (Ottawa: Information Canada, 1974), 8–9; and Stacey, *Conflict*, 2:10–13, 201, 215, 219, 221–3, 236, 257. Limited liability, most adroitly advanced by British military theorist B.H. Liddell Hart, presumed the superiority of the defence over the offence and proposed committing only minimal British land forces to the direct assistance of European allies at a critical juncture. This concept exerted a powerful appeal for a variety of reasons, among them the still-vivid memories of Great War slaughter, mistrust of the French, inter-service rivalry, army unpreparedness for continental operations, an accepted military need to buy time, and Treasury concern for financial and economic stability. Although the limited liability concept undoubtedly impressed King and his External Affairs advisers, it failed to convince the Canadian military. See, for instance, A.H. Bourne, "Limited Liability War," *CDQ* 3(1939): 282–90.

3 Stacey, *Arms*, 9–10, and *Six Years*, 9, 29–33. The Canadian COS Committee established in January 1939 consisted of the CGS and the chiefs of the air and naval staffs, with the most senior acting as chairman.

4 Stacey, *Conflict*, 2:272–4, 292, *Arms*, 10–13, and *Six Years*, 58–65; and English, *Canadian Army*, 39–40.

5 Stacey, *Arms*, 22, 140–8, 211–12; Stacey, *Conflict*, 2:253–4, 275, 294; Paul Douglas Dickson, *A Thoroughly Canadian General: A Biography of General H.D.G. Crerar* (Toronto: University of Toronto Press, 2007), 163–73; and Granastein, *Canada's Army*, 195–200.

6 Queen's University Archives (QUA), Power Papers, Minutes of the Cabinet War Committee Meeting, 14 June 1940; J.L. Granatstein, et al., *Twentieth Century Canada* (Toronto: McGraw-Hill Ryerson, 1986), 272–3; Stacey, *Conflict*, 2:280–1, 296–9; *Arms*, 11, 31–7, 118; and *Six Years*, 74–80, 86.

7 Stacey, *Arms*, 146–8, 156.

8 Ibid., 117, 145–7, 154–5, 180; and Alan F. Wilt, *War from the Top: German and British Military Decision Making during World War II* (Bloomington: Indiana University Press, 1990), 35–7.

9 Stacey, *Arms*, 69–71, 99–100, 112–22, 126–9, 139; and QUA, Power Papers, Private Secretary of the Minister of National Defence for Air to Chief of the Air Staff, 18 June 1942; and C.P. Stacey, "Canadian Leaders of the Second World War," *Canadian Historical Review* 1 (1985): 69. Lt. Gen. K. Stuart served as CGS from 24 December 1941 to 26 December 1943. He then headed Canadian Military Headquarters in London between 27 December 1943 and 11 November 1944. The post of CGS remained vacant until filled by Lt. Gen. J.C. Murchie on 3 May 1944. Stacey, *Six Years*, 540.

10 Steven T. Ross, ed., *U.S. War Plans 1938–1939* (Boulder: Lynne Rienner, 2002), 67–101; QUA, Power Papers, Minutes of the Cabinet War Committee Meeting, 2 and 29 October 1941; and Stacey, *Arms*, 159–62, 354–7. The full title of ABC-1 was "United States-British Staff Conversations Report" and it stipulated that in the event of American belligerency in a two-ocean war, the priority of both Allies would be to defeat Germany and its allies first.

11 Wilt, 39–41,106; Samuel P. Huntington, *The Soldier and the State: The Theory and Politics of Civil-Military Relations* (Cambridge: Belknap Press, 1979), 317–29, 337. The BJSM comprised the British Admiralty delegation, the RAF delegation, and the British army staff. The JCS consisted of the chiefs of the army, army air, and naval staffs, with Admiral William D. Leahy from July 1942 acting as chairman to provide naval balance. Alex Danchev, *Very Special Relationship: Field Marshal Sir John Dill and the Anglo-American Alliance 1941–44* (London: Brassey's, 1986), 10, 12–16, 19–25, 58; and Stacey, *Arms*, 162–4, 354–7.

12 QUA, Power Papers, Minutes of the Cabinet War Committee Meeting, 14 January, 11 March, and 4 June 1942; and Stacey, *Arms*, 162–7, 180, 354–7.

13 Stacey, *Arms*, 182.

14 QUA, Power Papers, Minutes of the Cabinet War Committee Meeting, 11 August 1943; Stacey, *Arms*, 178–88 and Stacey, *Conflict*, 2:326–30, 334–8.

15 QUA, Power Papers, Minutes of the Cabinet War Committee Meeting, 25 March 1943; Stacey, *Arms*, 153–4, 180–1, 557–9.

16 Stacey, *Arms*, 189–96, and *Six Years*, 212–29.

5. Dagger Pointed at the Heart of Berlin

1 Stacey, *Six Years*, 189–94, 230–4, 257–73.

2 Swettenham, *McNaughton*, 2:15–16, 41; Stacey, *Six Years*, 233; Strome Galloway, *A Regiment at War. The Story of the Royal Canadian Regiment 1939–1945* (London: Regimental Headquarters, 1979), 28–9; and LAC, RG 24, Vol. 13,722, War Diary (WD) 1st Canadian Infantry Division,

Training Progress Report for Week Ending 27 April 1940; RG 24, Vol. 13,722, 1 CD/4-0-2 Vol. 2, 1 Canadian Division Training Instruction No. 3, 27 April 1940; 1 CD/GS 4–0 H.Q. 1 Cdn Div., Imber Trench Warfare Training and Experimental Centre (TWTEC), 2 May 1940; Security G. 300, letter from Commandant of Trench Warfare Training and Experimental Centre to GOC 1st Canadian Division, 30 April 1940; and RG 24, Vol. 13,723, WD 1 CID, Canadian Force Notes for Conference at 4 Corps Headquarters.

3 LAC, Record Group (RG), 24, Vol. 13,723 WD 1 CID, Minutes of Conference at 1100 hours on 20 June 1940, held at Pinewood, Farnborough; Stacey, *Six Years*, 234–6, 273, 286–8; Roy, *Pearkes,*143–5; Col. G.W.L. Nicholson, *The Gunners of Canada: A History of the Royal Regiment of Canadian Artillery*, vol. 2: *1919–1967* (Toronto: McClelland and Stewart, 1972), 72; and RG 24, Vol. 13,723, Cablegram 1 CD/GS 4–8 Canmilitry to Defensor, 8 June 1940.

4 Greenhous and McAndrew, Interview with General B.M. Hoffmeister, 12–13; and Douglas E. Delaney, *The Soldiers' General: Bert Hoffmeister at War* (Vancouver: UBC Press, 2005), 21–3, 27–30.

5 Swettenham, *McNaughton*, 2:150–1, 213; and Stacey, *Six Years*, 74–80, 85–7, 288–9, 420.

6 Nicolson, *Gunners*, 2:57.

7 Swettenham, *McNaughton*, 2:155–6; Stacey, *Arms*, 212–13, and *Six Years*, 43–5, 294–5; and LAC, MG 30, E300, Maj.-Gen. V.W. Odlum Papers, Vol. 26, Memorandum on a meeting held at H.Q. 7 Corps at 1200 hrs, 8 August 1940.

8 Stacey, *Six Years*, 87–93.

9 Swettenham, *McNaughton*, 2:153–4, 167, 193–5; "Commander of the Canadians," *Life*, 18 December 1939, 9; Stacey, *Six Years*, 544–6 and his DHist, CMHQ Historical Report 46, 19 September 1941, The Problem of Equipment; CP, Vol. 1, Crerar to McNaughton, 26 June 1941; Rickard, *The Politics of Command*, 90–3; and Nicholson, *Gunners*, 2:55, 85, 94, 101.

10 Stacey, *Six Years*, 238; Swettenham, *McNaughton*, 2:163–4, 213–33; Roy, *Pearkes*, 161–3; and Rickard, *McNaughton*, 100–1.

11 Rickard, *McNaughton,*, 103–9; Stacey, *Six Years*, 238–9; and *Alanbrooke War Diaries* (3 May and 10 April 1942), 58, 151.

12 Swettenham, *McNaughton*, 2:185, 209; Rickard, *McNaughton*, 52; and "His Dagger was pointed at Berlin," *Time* cover, 10 August 1942.

13 DHist, CMHQ Historical Officer Report No. 49, Conference on Exercise "Bumper," dated 27 October 1941; and LAC, RG 24, Vol. 13,746, WD 2nd Canadian Infantry Division, Exercise "Bumper" Exercise Instructions and Narratives; Stacey, *Six Years*, 239–40, 297–8; and Hamilton, *Making*, 467–70.

14 Stacey, *Six Years*, 93–104, and *Arms*, 44–5; Swettenham, *McNaughton*, 2:188–9; Nicholson, *Gunners*, 111; and LAC, RG 24, Vol. 12,558, McNaughton to Stuart, 21 Dec 42.

15 Stacey, *Six Years*, 108–9. The British in autumn 1942 formed Army Groups Royal Artillery (AGRA), army-level artillery brigades that usually comprised three medium artillery regiments, a field regiment, heavy anti-aircraft regiment, and a rocket and radar battery.

6. Inspecting the Canadian Corps

1 Gen. H.D.G. Crerar Papers (CP), MG 30, E57, Vol. 2, Notes re Enclosed Correspondence with C-in-C., South-Eastern Command; Swettenham, *McNaughton*, 2:187; Roy, *Pearkes*, 136, 152, 166; English, *Canadian Army*, 85–6; and Rickard, *McNaughton*, 115, 297nn5–6.

2 CP, Vol 1, Crerar "Most Confidential," Note to File, 9 May 1942, and letters Crerar to McNaughton, 11 January 1942 and Crerar to Montgomery, 6 January 1942; Vol. 2, Notes re: Enclosed correspondence with C in C South-Eastern Command; Dickson, *Thoroughly Canadian General*, 175,178–80; and Stacey, *Six Years*, 212–15, 540–2. Whereas "the headquarters of the other divisions and formations had invited me to dine with them," complained Crerar, "the 1st Division had done no such thing." On 9 May 1942, he told Pearkes that during "the last months his attitude had, perhaps unknowingly, made my position and our relationships extraordinarily difficult." CP, Vol. 1, Crerar "Most Confidential," Note to File, 9 May 1942. Stacey dated Crerar's assumption of corps command as 23 December, but Dickson provides convincing evidence of 31 December being the official date.

3 CP, Vol 2, File 958C.009 (D182) Some Notes on What to Look For When Visiting a Unit, signed B.L. Montgomery, Lieutenant-General, General Officer Commanding South Eastern Command, 6 Mar 42 (see Annex A); Stacey, *Arms*, 231; and Hamilton, *Making*, 567.

4 English, *Canadian Army*, 87–9; and Rickard, *McNaughton*, 123–4, 244–5.

5 CP, Vol 2, Notes on Inf. Bdes of Canadian Corps – 28 Jan: 6 Inf Bde signed B.L. Montgomery, Lieut-General 3-2-42; and Lt. Col. G.B. Buchanan, *The March of the Prairie Men* (Weyburn: South Saskatchewan Regiment, 1957), 10. Gostling was killed at Dieppe where Southam was captured. Lett commanded the 4th Brigade at Dieppe and in Normandy.

6 CP, Vol 2, Notes on Inf. Bdes of Canadian Corps – 29 Jan: 8 Inf Bde signed B.L. Montgomery, Lieut-General 3-2-42; and Will R. Bird, *North Shore (New Brunswick) Regiment* (Fredericton: Brunswick Press, 1963), 130–49. Spragge went on to command the 7th Canadian Infantry Brigade.

7 CP, Vol 2, Notes on Inf. Bdes of Canadian Corps – 2 Feb: 1 Inf Bde signed B.L. Montgomery, Lieut-General 3-2-42.

8 CP, Vol 2, Crerar to Montgomery, 3 Feb 42. Snow went on to command the 11th Canadian Infantry Brigade in Italy.

9 CP, Vol 2, Notes on Inf. Bdes of Canadian Corps – No. 2, 23 Feb – 7 Inf Bde. Gibson went on to command the 7th Infantry Brigade after Spragge. Brian A. Reid, *Named by the Enemy: A History of the Royal Winnipeg Rifles* (Winnipeg: Robin Brass Studio, 2010), 141, 222.

10 CP, Vol 2, Notes on Inf. Bdes of Canadian Corps – No. 3, 25 Feb 1942–9 Inf Bde under cover letter Montgomery to Crerar, 26-2-42; Lieut-Colonel W. Boss, *The Stormont, Dundas and Glengarry Highlanders 1783–1951* (Ottawa: Runge Press, 1952), 159, 165; and Will R. Bird, *No Retreating Footsteps: The Story of the North Novas* (Hansport: Lancelot Press, 1983), 9–10, 21–5. Both Murdock and Rutherford made brigadier.

11 CP, Vol 2, Notes on Inf. Bdes of Canadian Corps – No. 4, 27 Feb 1942–4 Inf Bde under cover letter Montgomery to Crerar, 26-2-42; Sandy Antal and Kevin R. Shackleton, *Duty Nobly Done: The Official History of the Essex and Kent Scottish Regiment* (Windsor: Walkerville Publishing, 2006), 386–7. Both Jasperson and Labatt were captured at Dieppe.

12 CP, Vol 2, Notes on Inf. Bde of Canadian Corps – No. 5, 28 Feb 1942–2 Inf Bde; Lieut-Colonel G.R. Stevens, *A City Goes to War: History of the Loyal Edmonton Regiment (3PPCLI)* (Brampton: Charters Publishing, 1964), 201, 215.

13 CP, Vol 2, Notes on Inf. Bdes of Canadian Corps – No. 6, 2 March, 1942–3 Inf Bde under cover letter Montgomery to Crerar, 3-3-42. Bernatchez rose to command the 3rd Canadian Infantry Brigade.

14 CP, Vol 2, Notes on Inf. Bdes of Canadian Corps – No. 7, 3 March, 1942–5 Inf Bde; Colonel Paul P Hutchison, *Canada's Black Watch: The First Hundred Years 1862–1962* (Montreal: The Black Watch (R.H.R.) of Canada, 1962), 205–6, 217–18; David Bercuson, *Battalion of Heroes: The Calgary Highlanders in World War II* (Calgary: Calgary Highlanders Regimental Funds Foundation, 1994), 38–42, 80.

15 CP, Vol. 2, File 958.C.009 (D182), Confidential 1 Canadian Army Tank Brigade, 7.5.42 [at the time comprising three tank battalions]. Andrews died at Dieppe.

16 Imperial War Museum (IWM), Trumbull Warren Papers (TWP), Montgomery to Warren, 6-2-42, 11-3-42, 25-4-42, and 1 June.

17 TWP, Montgomery to Warren, 27–6-42 and 10 August. An exemplary officer, Don Mackenzie rose to become CO of the 48th Highlanders and was killed in action on 11 April 1945 during the liberation of Holland.

7. Military Godfather of the Canadian Army

1 Tactical Doctrine Retrieval Cell, Staff College Camberley, Bartholomew Committee Final Report (1940); Ronald Lewin, *Man of Armour: A Study of*

Lieut.-General Vyvyan Pope and the Development of Armoured Warfare (London: Leo Cooper, 1976), 127–8, 143–4; Shelford Bidwell, *Gunners at War: A Tactical Study of the Royal Artillery in the Twentieth Century* (London: Arms and Armour, 1970), 132–6; and Shelford Bidwell and Dominick Graham, *Fire-Power: British Army Weapons and Theories of War, 1904–1945* (London: Allen and Unwin, 1982), 195–201. The Bartholomew Committee included Gen. Sir William H. Bartholomew as chairman, Major Generals C.C. Malden and N.M.S. Irwin, and Brigadiers D.G. Watson and W. C. Holden (three infantrymen and two gunners).

2 DHist CMHQ, Historical Officer Report No. 60, Canadian Corps Study Week 19–23 January 1942, Corps Training Programme, Winter, 1941–42, dated 29 January 1942.

3 CP, Vol. 2, General Notes and Points that Came to Notice added to Notes on Inf Bdes of Canadian Corps, Numbers 1–7, 28 January to 3 March 1942. "The desirability of reducing the large amount of paperwork required of H.Q. was raised by me shortly after I took over command," Crerar commented, "and an analysis has been under way for the last week." CP, Vol. 2, letter Crerar to Montgomery, 3 February 1942.

4 CP, Vol. 2, CP, Vol. 2, General Notes and Points that Came to Notice added to Notes on Inf Bdes of Canadian Corps, Numbers 1–7, 28 January to 3 March 1942.

5 CP, Vol. 2, CP, Vol. 2, General Notes and Points that Came to Notice added to Notes on Inf Bdes of Canadian Corps, Numbers 1–7, 28 January to 3 March 1942; CP, Vol. 2, Crerar to Montgomery, 2 March 1942; RG 24, Vol. 13,685, letter Crerar to All Commanders and Commanding Officers, 1 Canadian Corps, 18 June 1943; and RG 24, Vol. 9764, Report on First Course at G.H.Q. Battle School.

6 CP, Vol. 2, Crerar to Montgomery, 2 Mar 42.

7 CP, Vol. 2, CP, Vol. 2, General Notes and Points that Came to Notice added to Notes on Inf Bdes of Canadian Corps, Numbers 1–7, 28 January to 3 March 1942; and CP, Vol. 1, memorandum Crerar to B.G.S., Cdn Corps, 11 January 1942.

8 CP, Vol. 2, CP, Vol. 2, General Notes and Points that Came to Notice added to Notes on Inf Bdes of Canadian Corps, Numbers 1–7, 28 January to 3 March 1942; RG 24, Vol. 13,684, South Eastern Army Commander's Personal Memorandum No. 2, dated 21 March 1942; RG 24, Vol. 13,746, WDGS 2 CID, 2 DS(G)1-1-23 H.Q. 2 Cdn Div Operation Instruction No. 12 Defence of Sussex, 27 November 1941, and 2 DS(G)1-1-23 H.Q. 2 Cdn Div Plan to Defeat Invasion Amdmts to 2 Cdn Div Operation Instruction, 3 January 1942.

9 CP, Vol. 2, Notes on Beaver IV, 13 May 1942; RG 24, Vol. 13,746, WDGS 2 CID 2 DS(G)1-5 HQ 2 Cdn Div, 9 April 1942, signed by GOC; CP, Vol. 2,

Notes on Exercise "Flip," 14 April 1942; CP, Vol. 2, Exercise "Conqueror,"
16 April 1942; and TWP, Montgomery to Warren, 27 June 1942.

10 MAP, Montgomery to Simbo (Brigadier F.E.W. Simpson), 5-4-43.

11 LAC, RG 24, Vol. 9804, Notes on Address by Army Commander, 22
December 1941, "Some Lessons Learnt during the First Two Years of War
Sep 1939-Sep 1941"; and CP, Vol. 2, Comments Exercise "Conqueror,"
6.4.42.

12 Brigadier B.L. Montgomery, "The Problem of the Encounter Battle as
Affected by Modern British War Establishment," *CDQ* 1 (October 1937):
13–25; "The Major Tactics of the Encounter Battle," *Army Quarterly* 2
(July, 1938): 268–72; and his "Address to the Middle East Staff College,
Haifa, 21 September1942," in Stephen Brooks, ed., *Montgomery and the
Eighth Army* (London: The Bodley Head for the Army Records Society,
1991), 47–61.

13 Notes on Address by Army Commander, 22 December 1941, "Some Lessons
Learnt during the first Two Years of War Sep 39-Sep 41," B.L.M. Nov 1941.

14 CP, Vol. 2, File 958C.009 (D182), Notes on Exercise "Flip" and Remarks
on 2 Cdn Div Exercise "Flip"; Notes on Beaver IV, 13 May 1942; and Some
further notes on Beaver III, 25 April 1942.

15 Bidwell, *Gunners*, 132–136; Hamilton, *Making*, 434–435; and Bidwell and
Graham, *Fire-Power*, 199–201.

16 Brig. A.L. Pemberton, *The Second World War, 1939–1945, Army, The
Development of Artillery Tactics and Equipment* (London: War Office, 1951), 99,
118–19, 149–50, 161–2, 169; and Bidwell, *Gunners*, 132–44.

17 LAC, MG 30 E133 McNaughton Papers (MNP), Vol. 156, Handling of
Divisional and Corps Artillery, 2 Nov 43; The Employment of Army Groups,
Royal Artillery and RG 24, Vol. 9793, GHQ Exercise "Spartan" Comments
by Commander-in-Chief Home Forces March 1943. The CCRA was
responsible for coordinating bombardment as well as counterbattery. He
had no staff for fire planning, details of which were worked out by CRAs
and AGRA commanders (CAGRA). The Brigadier Royal Artillery (BRA)
at army level was responsible for directing the coordination of artillery
throughout the army and for advising the army commander in all artillery
matters.

18 CP, Vol. 2, Exercise "Conqueror," 16.4.42; Some further notes on Beaver
III, 25 April, 1942; and Notes on Beaver IV, 13th May 1942 all signed by
Montgomery.

19 CP, Vol. 2, Some Notes on the Broader Aspects of Beaver III, 23 April 1942;
and Notes on Beaver IV, 13 May 1942.

20 CP, Vol. 2, Some Notes on the Broader Aspects of Beaver III, 23 April, 1942;
Beaver III Notes on Commanders, 25 April 1942; Notes on Beaver IV, 13
May 1942; and Notes on Inf Bdes of Canadian Corps, No. 6, 2 March 1942–3

Inf Bde. On Montgomery's opinion of Pearkes, Price, Potts, and Ganong see also TWP, Montgomery to Warren, 25 April 1942, 1 June 1942, 27 June 1942, 27 July 1942, and 10 August 1942.

21 J.L. Granatstein, *The Weight of Command: Voices of Canada's Second World War Generals and Those Who Knew Them* (Vancouver: UBC Press, 2016), 14, 61, 79; Roy, *Pearkes*, 172–4; Stacey, *Six Years*, 99; and Dickson, *Thoroughly Canadian General*, 185, 191–5.

22 CP, Vol. 2, Notes on Inf Bdes of Canadian Corps, No. 2, 23 February, 7 Inf Bde, 24-2-42; CP, Vol. 2, Montgomery notes on Exercise "Conqueror," 16 April 1942; Notes on Beaver IV, 13th May 42, and Appendix "A" Notes on Commander 3 Div, 13-5-42; and, on Haldenby, CP, Vol.7, Crerar to Montgomery, 8 April, 1943. Price's GSO 1, Charles Foulkes, apparently gave no help to his commander. Haldenby was sent back to command a reinforcement unit. CP, Vol. 7, Crerar to Montgomery, 8 April 1943.

23 CP, Vol. 1, Crerar to McNaughton, 5 March 1941.

24 CP, Vol. 1, Crerar to McNaughton, 10 Aug 1942.

25 CP, Vol. 2, Some Notes on the Broader Aspects of Beaver III, 23 April, 1942; Some further notes on Beaver III, 25 April, 1942; Beaver III Notes on Commanders, 25 April 1942; Notes on Beaver IV, 13 May 1942.

26 Swettenham, *McNaughton*, 2:172; and Rickard, *McNaughton*, 115.

27 RG 24, Vol. 13,760, memorandum Army Commander's Address, 22 December 1941 under Trg 7-1-1 H.Q. Cdn. Corps, Brigadier, General Staff to Distribution, 12 December 1941.

28 Notes on Beaver IV, 13 May 1942; and Exercise "Conqueror," 16-4-42.

29 CP, Vol. 2, Crerar's Notes on Conqueror, undated, following Exercise "Conqueror," 16.4.42 signed by Montgomery; and CP, Vol. 1, GOC/3–6 Comd 1 Cdn Corps to all Commanders and Commanding Officers 1 Canadian Corps, 6 October 1943.

30 CP, Vol. 2, Notes re Enclosed correspondence with C in C South Eastern Command; and Memorandum on Conversation with Lt.-Gen. B.L. Montgomery, Commanding S.E. Army on 4 July 1942 Commencing 1800 hrs.

31 CP, Vol. 2, Montgomery to Crerar, 30 May 1942 and Vol. 19 Crerar to Lt. Col. G.W.L. Nicholson, 5 February 1952.

32 RG 24, Vol. 12,301, S.E. Army, Exercise "Tiger," Final Conference – 4 June, 1942, Remarks of Army Commander, 4-6-42; and Fire Planning Exercise, 3rd Canadian Division – 1st Canadian Army Tank Brigade, Eastern End of Field Firing Area No. 4–6 Jul 42.

33 CP, Vol. 2 Exercise "Tiger" Observations under Montgomery to Crerar, 3-6-42; RG 24, Vol. 12,301, S.E. Army, Exercise "Tiger,' Final Conference – 4 June,1942, Remarks of Army Commander, 4-6-42; and CP, Vol. 2, Montgomery to Crerar, 17 May 42.

34 Strome Galloway, *The General Who Never Was* (Belleville: Mika, 1981), 182.

8. Montgomery and Dieppe

1 Hamilton, *Making*, 516–23; *Alanbrooke War Diaries* (7, 10 March, 13 May, 17–23 July, and 7–8 August 1942), 237–8, 257, 281–4, 295; Stacey, *Six Years*, 328–9, 332; and Brigadier General Denis and Shelagh Whitaker, *Dieppe: Tragedy to Triumph* (Toronto: McGraw-Hill Ryerson, 1992), 90–4, 141–2.

2 Hamilton, *Making*, 520; Terrence Robertson, *The Shame and the Glory: Dieppe* (Toronto: McClelland And Stewart, 1962), 47–53; Mark Zuehlke, *Tragedy at Dieppe: Operation Jubilee, August 19, 1942* (Vancouver: Douglas & McIntyre, 2012), 41–9; and Whitakers, *Dieppe*, 11, 162–4.

3 Theodore L. Gatchel, *At the Water's Edge: Defending against the Modern Amphibious Assault* (Annapolis: Naval Institute Press, 1996), xiii, 1–2, 8, 60, 210, 216.

4 Hamilton, *Making*, 520, 524; *Alanbrooke War Diaries* (1, 10 March 1942), 234, 237–8; Dominick Graham, *The Price of Command: A Biography of General Guy Simonds* (Toronto: Stoddart, 1993), 293; Brian Loring Villa, *Unauthorized Action: Mountbatten and the Dieppe Raid* (Toronto: Oxford University Press, 1990), 223–7, 271, 301; Whitakers, *Dieppe*, 73–5; and Stacey, *Six Years*, 308, 333.

5 Graham, *Price*, 61–2, 293–4; Stacey, *Six Years*, 329–33; Whitakers, *Dieppe*, 11, 75, 94–8, 289; Robertson, *Shame and the Glory*, 55–6, 60–7; Zuehlke, *Dieppe*, 66–8, 70–2; and Villa, *Unauthorized Action*, 90–1, 193, 281n38, 301n25.

6 Villa, *Unauthorized Action*, 12, 90, 151–7, 271n11, 289n62, 294n10; Stacey, *Six Years*, 336–7; Robertson, *Shame and the Glory*, 95–6; Whitakers, *Dieppe*, 13, 160–3; Hamilton, *Making*, 523; and Montgomery, *Memoirs*, 76. Fighter Command committed 800 aircraft, including 600 Spitfires, 24 Hurricane fighter-bombers, 24 medium Blenheim and Boston bombers, 36 Blenheims to lay smoke, and 48 reconnaissance planes.

7 CP, Vol.2, Memorandum on Conversation with Lieut.-General B.L. Montgomery, Commanding S.E. Army on 4 Jul 42 commencing 1800 hrs; Stacey, *Six Years*, 338; and Zuehlke, *Dieppe*, 116–18.

8 Villa, *Unauthorized Action*, 271n6.

9 Ibid., 91, 189–93, 197, 228; Robertson, *Shame and the Glory*, 124–6, 133–5, 139–40; Stacey, *Six Years*, 335, 340–4; Whitakers, *Dieppe*, 12, 162, 172, 182–4; Hamilton, *Making*, 524–5; Zuehlke, *Dieppe*, 134–5; and Rickard, *McNaughton*, 63, 276–7.

10 Robertson, *Shame and the Glory*, 141–4; and Dickson, *Thoroughly Canadian General*, 461.

11 Stacey, *Six Years*, 344–388; Graham, *Price*, 295; Whitakers, *Dieppe*, 290; and Villa, *Unauthorized Action*, 3–4, 17–18; Zuehlke, *Dieppe*, 369–70; CP, Vol. 7, Crerar to Major-General M.A. Pope, 27 October, 1942 and Vol. 21 Crerar to Stacey, 24 February, 1947. On removing Roberts from command in April 1943, Crerar expressed concern that public criticism in Canada about plans

for the Dieppe raid might be interpreted as delayed condemnation of his performance. He therefore prepared a file for record purposes showing examples of Roberts's poor field performances in Exercises "Beaver III," "Maple I and II," and "Spartan." CP, Vol.1, Crerar to McNaughton, 9 Apr 43. One suspects, however, that he just wanted the once highly regarded and now-tainted Roberts out of the way.

12 MAP, Montgomery to Major General F.E.W. Simpson, 5-4-43.

13 Figures vary, but on their respective D-days roughly 170,000 troops landed on Sicily compared with around 133,000 on Normandy. About 1,350 warships supported Sicily and 1,213 Normandy.

14 Hamilton, *Field-Marshal*, 946.

15 D'Este, *Sicily*, 114–26, 144–53, 567, *Normandy*, 299, 482, 504–5, and *Patton; A Genius for War* (New York: HarperCollins, 1995), 494; Richard Lamb, *Montgomery in Europe 1943–1945: Success or Failure?* (New York: Franklin Watts, 1984), 24, 396, 402; and Brooks, *Montgomery and the Eighth Army*, 129. Despite Montgomery's unequalled qualifications, it took the intervention of Brooke to get him appointed as ground force commander for "Overlord." Contrary to popular belief, the greatest amphibious operations of the Second World War were not carried out in the Pacific, but in Europe.

9. Monty's Eighth Army and Canadians

1 Hamilton, *Making*, 527. Brooke later said that Gott, although first class, was much too tired for the job. MAP, BLM 55/3 Brook to Montgomery, Jan 23/48.

2 Liddell Hart Centre for Military Archives (LHCMA), Kings College London, Prime Minister's Personal Minute to CIGS, 8 Feb 43, covering "Situation in August, 1942," submitted by Montgomery; Brooks, *Montgomery and the Eighth Army*, 20–8; Chalfont, *Montgomery of Alamein*, 186; Hamilton, *Making*, 543, 548–9, 586–90. 609, 618–19; and Michael Carver, *El Alamein* (London: B.T. Batsford, 1962), 34–5.

3 David Fraser, *And We Shall Shock Them: The British Army in the Second World War* (London: Hodder and Stoughton, 1983), 235–6; Carver, *El Alamein*, 36–40, 50–74; Brooks, *Montgomery and the Eighth Army*, 26–7, 30–3; Major-General Sir Francis de Guingand, *Operation Victory* (New York: Charles Scribner's Sons, 1947), 136–49; Brigadier Peter Young, *World War 1939–1945* (London: Pan, 1966), 236–9; Hamilton, *Making*, 601–11, 631–56. The Grant sported a 75mm gun, which surprised the Germans.

4 MAP, Speaking notes Tactical Discussions: Tripoli 15 and 16 Feb 1943; Brooks, *Montgomery and the Eighth Army*, 18–84; Montgomery, *Memoirs*, 118–20, 131–7; de Guingand, *Operation Victory*, 195–208; Fraser, *And We Shall*

Shock Them, 238–46; Carver, *El Alamein*, 96–8, 195–205; Young, *World War 1939–1945*, 255–62; and Hamilton, *Making*, 606–7.

5 Montgomery later wrote that at 0200 on 25 October Lumsden lost his nerve, saying all was lost. "I had to take charge of his corps for an hour and gave orders to his division commanders myself." MAP, Montgomery to S of S, 16 October, 1946. Some 980 guns fired roughly 1,000 rounds per gun. LHCMA, Alanbrooke Papers (AP) 14/61 Montgomery to CIGS, 10-11-42; and Col. C.P. Stacey, *Official History of the Canadian Army in the Second World War*, vol. 3: *The Victory Campaign. The Operations in North-West Europe, 1944–1945* (Ottawa: Queen's Printer, 1966), 533.

6 Brooks, *Montgomery and the Eighth Army*, 78–9, 84–5; de Guingand, *Operation Victory*, 208; and Hamilton, *Making*, 770, 797.

7 CP, Vol. 7, Crerar to Montgomery, 5th November 1942, 8 February, 1943, and 8 April, 1943 and Montgomery to Crerar, 10-12-42 and 9-1-43.

8 General B.L. Montgomery, "Some Brief Notes to Senior Officers on the Conduct of Battle," Eighth Army, December 1942.

9 MAP, Tactical Discussions: Tripoli 15 and 16 Feb 1943; Directorate of History, NDHQ, Report on Visit to 8th Army, Lt.-Gen. H.D.G. Crerar, C.B.,D.S.O.; and CP, Vol. 1, GOC/3–6 Comd 1 Cdn Corps to all Commanders and Commanding Officers, 1 Canadian Corps. 6 October 1943.

10 MAP, Report of "Staff Information" in an Army – "J"; Montgomery, *Memoirs*, 111, 137–8; and Brooks, *Montgomery and the Eighth Army*, 308–9, 383nn127, 145. Montgomery credited the invention of "J" service to "a most able officer on my staff called Hugh Mainwaring."

11 Commander Royal Engineers at division level.

12 "Some Brief Notes to Senior Officers on the Conduct of Battle"; and Brooks, *Montgomery and the Eighth Army*, 145.

13 Montgomery, *Memoirs*, 167–8; de Guingand, *Operation Victory*, 191–3; Richard S. Malone, *A Portrait of War* (Don Mills: Totem Press, 1985), 171; Brooks, *Montgomery and the Eighth Army*, 150; and Michael Howard, *The Causes of Wars* (Cambridge: Harvard University Press, 1983), 213. Montgomery apparently had a knack for creating an oasis of serenity around himself. Lewin, *Man of Armour*, 36. For more on the pleasant atmosphere of his Tac HQ see Lamb, *Montgomery in Europe*, 398–9.

14 Montgomery, *Memoirs*, 530–1; Malone, *Portrait*, 171–2; Lewin, *Man of Armour*, 339; and Winston S. Churchill, *Triumph and Tragedy* (Boston: Houghton Mifflin Company, 1953), 414–15. Malone, BM of 2nd Canadian Infantry Brigade until badly wounded in Sicily, served with Montgomery's Tac HQ from the Eighth Army's invasion of Italy. When Malone left for another posting Montgomery asked the GOC 1st Canadian infantry Division for Warren as "he knows me and my ways, and these frequent

changes – with new people – are a great nuisance." RMC, Major General C. Vokes Papers (VP), Montgomery to Vokes, 18-12-43.

15 Stacy, *Six Years*, 248–9; English, *Canadian Army*, 102, 299n20; and Strome Galloway, *The General Who Never Was* (Belleville: Mika, 1981), 89–125.

16 Dickson, *Thoroughly Canadian General*, 211–25; Rickard, *McNaughton*, 43–4, 70–1, 75–7; and C.P. Stacey, *A Date with History* (Ottawa: Deneau, 1982), 124–5.

17 English, *Canadian Army*, 98–100; Tony Foster, *Meeting of Generals* (Toronto: Methuen, 1986), 165; Roy, *Pearkes*, 165–6; Stacey, *Arms*, 231–47; and Rickard, *McNaughton*, 73, 140–9, 156–7.

18 Maj. Gen. Harold E. Pyman, *Call to Arms* (London: Leo Cooper, 1971), 93–4. As a rule of thumb, a CRE had to plan for tomorrow and a CCRE three days ahead. Rickard, *McNaughton*, 155.

19 MNP, Vol. 157, Adv HQ 1 Cdn Corps, GOC 4-0-4-13, Memorandum by GOC, 1 Cdn Corps on Particular Training Requirements as Revealed by Exercise "Spartan," 18 Apr 43; and English, *Canadian Army*, 100–1.

20 *Alanbrooke War Diaries* (7 March 1943), 388; and LHCMA, AP, 12/XII/5 Grigg interview by M.C. Long, November 1954.

21 LHCMA, AP, 12/XI/4/61 Crerar interview by M.C. Long, November 1954; and *Alanbrooke War Diaries* (18 June 1943), 422.

22 Major General M.P. Bogert, letter to author, 1 February 1992.

23 Graham, *Price*, 65–9; and English, *Canadian Army*, 142.

24 Graham, Price, 88–92; General George Kitching, *Memoirs: Mud and Green Fields* (Langley, BC: Battleline Books, 1985), 169–70; Lieutenant-General Howard Graham, *Memoirs: Citizen and Soldier* (Toronto: McClelland and Stewart, 1987), 158–64; Nicholson, *Italy*, 65–72, 78–90; and Daniel G. Dancocks, *The D-Day Dodgers: The Canadians in Italy, 1943–1945* (Toronto: McClelland and Stewart, 1991), 54–5.

25 Montgomery to Lieutenant-General Sir Oliver Leese, 16 July 1943, in Brooks, *Montgomery and the Eighth Army*, 246–7, 374; and Graham, *Price*, 93–4, quoting Montgomery to Simonds, 17 July 1943.

26 MAP, BLM 52/33, Ralston to Montgomery, 27 Nov 43; Stacey, Arms, 224–7, 234–9, 245–7; Dancocks, *D-Day Dodgers*, 49–50; Rickard, *McNaughton*, 171–86; and Swettenham, *McNaughton*, 2:299–302, 318–20.

27 *Alanbrooke War Diaries* (23 April and 21 July 1943), 396, 431–2; and Stacey, *Arms*, 228–9.

28 Montgomery to Brooke, 27 July 1943, in Brooks, *Montgomery and the Eighth Army*, 255; Nicholson, *Italy*, 120–34, 159–163; Dancocks, *D-Day Dodgers*, 60–96; D'Este, *Sicily*, 405–6; English, *Canadian Army*, 308n20; and Graham, *Price*, 94–8.

29 Nicholson, *Italy*, 186–228; Rick Atkinson, *The Day of Battle: The War in Sicily and Italy 1943–1944* (New York: Henry Holt, 2007), 180, 184–5, 209–37;

Brooks, *Montgomery and the Eighth Army*, 289; Young, *World War 1939–1945*, 342–3; and Chalfont, *Montgomery of Alamein*, 251–2.

30 Nicholson, *Italy*, 229–69, 274–339, 386; MAP, Montgomery to Simpson, 10 Nov 43 and 8-11-43; Young, *World War 1939–1945*, 343; Atkinson, *Battle*, 298–306; and Chalfont, *Montgomery of Alamein*, 252–3.

31 Stacey, *Arms*, 42, 229, 237–47; Dancocks, *D-Day Dodgers*, 129–33; Dickson, *Thoroughly Canadian General*, 225; and CP, Vol. 3, Bigot-Timberwolf PA-1-18-1 HQ First Cdn Army, 20 October 1943, Instructions to Lt.-Gen. H.D.G. Crerar and to any other officer who may succeed; and Stacey, *Arms*, 42, 229, 237–47.

32 VP, The Adriatic Front – Winter 1944.

33 VP, The Adriatic Front; and CP, Vol. 1, Crerar to Malone, 27 Feb 44 covering Personal and Confidential letters to formation Commanders dated 18 Feb 44, 21 Feb 44 and Responsibilities of the Comd, The Staff and The Services HQ 1 Canadian Corps, 11 Dec 44. According to Vokes, Crerar was not vigorous like Montgomery or Leese, who called in his division commanders to discuss real and hypothetical tactical problems, but acted like a chairman of the board. Major General Chris Vokes with John P. Maclean, *My Story* (Ottawa: Gallery Books, 1985), 154–5.

34 CP, Vol. 15, WD Comd 1 Cdn Corps, 29–30 Oct 43; Kitching, *Memoirs*, 176–9. Kitching further speculated that the main intent behind Crerar's decision to equip his corps headquarters with vehicles before the 5th Armoured Division was "to make Simonds sit idle for some ten weeks and thus not be able to command the division in operations."

35 Nicholson, *Italy*, 354–8; English, *Canadian Army*, 102–4, 142, 146, 309n24; and Dickson, *Thoroughly Canadian General*, 232. British officer staff representation peaked at 14 per cent.

36 CP, Vol. 7, Crerar to Simonds, 10 Dec 43; and Simonds to Crerar, 15 Dec 43; and English, *Canadian Army*, 144–7, 308nn18–19; and Dickson, *Thoroughly Canadian General*, 223–4.

37 Crerar was not always kind and in fact treated many lower-ranking subordinates very poorly. According to Stacey, who witnessed him publicly tear a strip off his personal pilot much to the embarrassment of many within earshot, there was some element of terror in his manner of command. C.P. Stacey, "Canadian Leaders of the Second World War," *CHR* 1 (March 1985): 68; and Foster, *Meeting of Generals*, 394.

38 CP, Vol. 7, Crerar to Montgomery, 17 Dec 43.

39 Crerar to Simonds, 15 Dec 43; CP, Vol. 7, Simonds to Crerar, 17 Dec 43; and Simonds to Crerar, 2 January 1944.

40 CP, Vol. 7, Montgomery to Crerar 21-12-43. According to de Guingand, Montgomery used this term to describe a British commander whom he held in considerable regard. De Guingand, *Operation Victory*, 180. Vokes, in

fact, learned a great deal from Montgomery and practised much of what he taught.

41 CP, Vol. 7, Crerar to Stuart, 13 Jan 44 covering Memorandum by GOC 1 Cdn Corps on contents of letter dated 15 Dec 43 from Major-General Simonds 5 Cdn Armd Div; and Dancocks, *D-Day Dodgers*, 206.

42 LHCMA, AP 14/24, Montgomery to Brooke, 28–12–43; and Hamilton, *Master of the Battlefield 1942–1944* (London: Hamish Hamilton, 1983), 476. Montgomery recommended that Dempsey be given command of the First Canadian Army and Leese the Second British. Hamilton, *Master*, 465.

43 Montgomery, *Memoirs*, 185; CP, Vol. 15, WD Comd 1 Cdn Corps, 19 Jan 44; VP, The Adriatic Front and Vokes, *My Story*, 152–153; and Malone, *Portrait*, 214–15.

44 Omar N. Bradley, *A Soldier's Story* (New York: Henry Holt, 1951), 209.

45 Galloway, *General*, 180–1; Chalfont, *Montgomery of Alamein*, 244, 254; and D'Este, *Sicily*, Appendix L Montgomery and the Canadians, 614–20.

46 Related by Hoffmeister during Italian Battlefield Tour retracing the path of the 5th Canadian Armoured Division in the Gothic Line battles, 18–23 September 1983.

47 Greenhous and McAndrew, Interview with General B.M. Hoffmeister, 21, 110–11, 114–16; and Delaney, *The Soldiers' General: Bert Hoffmeister at War* (Vancouver: UBC Press, 2005), 34–5, 38–9, 176–7.

48 Dancocks, *D-Day Dodgers*, 221, 238–9, 291–2, 408, 431, 435; Nicholson, *Italy*, 380; and Dickson, *Thoroughly Canadian General*, 233.

49 Crerar "regretted intensely the idea of leaving my present command, before I have successfully fought them [*sic*] in a large scale action." CP, Vol. 8, GOC 11-0-2 Crerar to Stuart, 12 Feb 44.

10. Handling Canadians in Normandy

1 Col. C.P. Stacey, *Official History of the Canadian Army in the Second World War*, vol. 3: *The Victory Campaign. The Operations in North-West Europe, 1944–1945* (Ottawa: Queen's Printer, 1966), 18–21, 28–30; English, *Canadian Army*, 139–40; LAC, MNP, Vol. 161, Memorandum of Conversation Gen. McNaughton-Gen. Paget, 1130 hrs, 17 June 1943; and Hamilton, *Master*, 485–95.

2 IWM, Montgomery of Alamein Papers (MAP), Personal Diary, 10, 15, 27, and 30 June; Bradley, *A Soldier's Story*, 201–4, 213–18, 239–41; Hamilton, *Master*, 497–9, 501–2, 513–19, 549–52, 562–3; Chalfont, *Montgomery of Alamein*, 278–86; Public Record Office (PRO) 70473, CAB 106/1064, Crerar Diary, Notes on Conference given by C-in-C 21 Army Group on 22 June 1944; and CP, Vol. 2, M505 Tac HQ 21 Army Group, 30 June 44. On 15 June Montgomery expressed satisfaction that the main enemy weight had been drawn onto Second British Army, thus easing the pressure on First US Army.

3 Chalfont, *Montgomery of Alamein*, 265–7.

4 Hamilton, *Master*, 301, 325, 601–3; TWP, Simonds to Warren, 27 Jan 72; English, *Canadian Army*, 106, 140–1; D'Este, *Sicily*, 323, 483–6 and *Patton*, 533–5, 549; and Dickson, *Thoroughly Canadian General*, 240–1.

5 Stacey, *Six Years*, 222–8 and *Victory*, 31; Dickson, *Thoroughly Canadian General*, 222, 240–1. Stuart was "not fit and if things get too strenuous he is likely to crack up." CP, Vol. 1, Crerar to McNaughton, 4 March 1941.

6 CP, Vol. 7, Operational Policy – 2 Cdn Corps, 17 Feb 44; MAP, BLM 120, Simonds to Warren, 19 Feb 44, Simonds to Montgomery, 22 Feb 44, and Montgomery to Simonds, 23-2-44.

7 Stacey, *Six Years*, 249–51; English, *Canadian Army*, 98–9, 143; Rickard, McNaughton, 147, 153, 157, 161–4; and J.L. Granatstein, *The Generals: The Canadian Army's Senior Commanders in the Second World War* (Toronto: Stoddart, 1993), 192.

8 Commander Corps Royal Engineers.

9 Granatstein, *Weight of Command*, 61, 79, 125, and *Generals*, 163–4; and Stacey, *Six Years*, 417, and *Victory*, 33.

10 Crerar wanted a replacement for the Leyland caravan he had been issued as corps commander in Italy. A special requisition gave Crerar and his staff the opportunity to design the general layout of the caravan and an office trailer. The firm of Car Cruiser Caravans at Haves, Middlesex, produced the van, a long-wheelbase Diamond T 975 chassis/cab, and Crerar's batman drove up to their works weekly to inspect progress. Although orders in June 1945 stated that no personal military vehicles were to be returned to Canada, Crerar had the Diamond T with trailer shipped from Antwerp to Montreal around September 1945. Colonel D.B. Walton, "Restoration of General Crerar Caravan February 1989," *Quadrant* 6, no. 1 (June 1989): 12–13.

11 CP, Vol. 3, Crerar to Stuart, COS CMHQ, 13 May 44 and Vol. 25, Address by Lt-Gen HDG Crerar, GOC-in-C First Canadian Army to Senior Officers, First Canadian Army on 14 May 1944; MAP, Stuart to Brooke, 18 May 1944; and Dickson, *Thoroughly Canadian General*, 232, 235, 243–4, 253–4, 266.

12 F.W. Perry, *The Commonwealth Armies: Manpower and Organization in Two World Wars* (Manchester: University Press, 1988), 162–4, 180–2, 194–7; David Horner, *Blamey: The Commander in Chief* (St. Leonards: Allen & Unwin, 1998), 136–7, 150–6, 163–8, 181, 208, 210, 215–40, 243–66; Mark Johnston, *At the Front Line: Experiences of Australian Soldiers in World War II* (Cambridge: University Press, 1996), 206–8. Montgomery impressed Australians with his visit to the 9th Australian Division within three days of taking command. A New Zealand divisional officer commented that there had been a remarkable improvement in the Eighth Army after the arrival of Montgomery.

13 MAP, Montgomery to Stuart, 26 May 1944; CP, Vol. 3, Stuart to Crerar, 29
    May 44; Stacey, *Six Years*, 226–8; and Dickson, *Thoroughly Canadian General*,
    245. Stacey suggested that a more logical organization would have placed
    the more senior officer at CMHQ.

14 CP, Vol. 3, Stuart to Crerar, 26 May 44.

15 CP, Vol. 3, Stuart to Crerar, 29 May 44.

16 CP, Vol. 3, Stuart to Crerar, 30 May 44.

17 Dickson, *Thoroughly Canadian General*, 224, 245

18 CP, Vol. 8, Crerar to Stuart, 28 Mar 44; Stuart to Crerar, 1 May 44; and
    Crerar to Stuart, 3 May 44.

19 CP, Vol. 3, First Cdn Army OO Number 1, 23 May 44 and Vol. 1, Keller to
    Crerar, 27 Apr 44.

20 MAP, BLM, 119, Crerar to Montgomery, 14 May 1944 and Montgomery to
    Crerar, 15 May 1944; CP, Vol. 5 Memorandum Keller to Crerar, 13 May 44
    and Vol. 15, WD GOC-in-C First Cdn Army, 14–18 May 44; Stacey, *Victory*,
    37–8; and Dickson, *Thoroughly Canadian General*, 238, 247–53, 263–6.
    Montgomery also brought Churchill to tears when he refused to allow the
    Prime Minister to confer with his staff about Normandy plans. Hamilton,
    Master, 590–3.

21 Griffin had been mentioned by name in the 3rd Division operation order
    and been ordered to "report to the Commander 9 Cdn Inf Bde Gp ... to
    arrange Fire Plan" for the brigade advance. Only upon final reorganization
    were artillery units to revert to command of the CRA. Personal copy 3rd
    Canadian Infantry Division Group Operation Order No. 1, 13 May 44 and
    RG 24, Vol 14,152, 9 Canadian Infantry Brigade Group Operation Order
    No. 1, 18 May.

22 MAP, Personal Diary, 11–15, 18–19 June and 24 June–2 July 1944; English,
    Canadian Army, 155–6; and Stephen Ashley Hart, *"Colossal Cracks": The 21st
    Army Group in Northwest Europe, 1944–45* (Westport: Praeger, 2000), 103, 114,
    141. Since Caen commanded the main routes into Normandy and was the
    linchpin of their defence, the Germans could not afford to let Montgomery
    capture the city as this would have left their forces trapped. The seizure
    of the city in a quick stroke was not an unreasonable objective to set, but
    furious enemy attacks on the 6th British Airborne Division landed east of
    the Orne threatened to jeopardize the entire Normandy landing. Crocker
    quite correctly decided to shore up the airborne bridgehead with the
    massed fire support of the 1 Corps artillery, without which the bridgehead
    would not have survived. Crocker's additional decision to divert the 3rd
    British Division's reserve 9th Brigade from its original task of helping to
    take Caen to, instead, assisting the beleaguered 6th Airborne constrained
    3rd Division operations as only by committing its reserve 9th Brigade was
    there any hope of taking Caen. D'Este, *Normandy*, 112, 120–45, 160; Stacey,

Victory, 98, 115–17, 121–3, 126–33; and John A. English, "I Corps" in *D-Day Encyclopedia*, ed. David G. Chandler and James Lawton Collins, Jr. (New York: Simon & Schuster, 1994), 242–3.

23 MAP, Personal Diary, 25 June–2 July 44, including Summary; PRO 70473, WO 285/9-11, Dempsey Diary (DD), 19–30 Jun and 1 Jul 44; D'Este, *Normandy*, 235–46, 250; Stacey, *Victory*, 147–9; and Hart, *Cracks*, 95.

24 On 25 July 1944, before Cobra, the Germans had an estimated 30,000 fighting men and 150–180 tanks in the area north of Coutances between the Vire River and the ocean. Most of these belonged to the 2nd SS "Das Reich" Panzer Division come from the south. Dwight D. Eisenhower (DDE) Library, Abilene, Kansas, J. Lawton Collins Papers, Box 7, Selected Intelligence Reports, Volume I, June 1944–November 1944, Office of the AC of S, G2, First United States Infantry Division, Germany (6 December 1944), 25.

25 MAP, Personal Diary 3 July 1944–4 August 1944, Montgomery to DCIGS 6 July 1944 covering Memorandum n British Armour, and DCIGS to Montgomery 10 July 1944; English, *Canadian Army*, 157–8, 313n9, 319n11; Bradley, *Story*, 322–3; and Russell A. Hart, *Clash of Arms: How the Allies Won in Normandy* (Boulder: Lynne Rienner, 2001), 307. Montgomery suggested offering one Firefly per tank platoon to the Americans after the British possessed two per tank troop, then building the British up to three per tank troop. The Americans were quick to notice the British advantage in the Sabot round. Marshall Library, Lexington Virginia, George C. Marshall Papers, Eisenhower to Marshall, 5 July 1944.

26 CP, Vol. 3, Crocker to Dempsey, 5 July 1944; Stacey, *Victory*, 153–5; and English, *Canadian Army*, 148, 168–9.

27 Told to the author in 1990 by General (Retired) P.A.S. Todd, who was Keller's CRA at the time.

28 DD, 8 Jun 44.

29 CP, Vol. 3, Crocker to Dempsey, 5 July 1944 and Dempsey to Montgomery, 6 July 1944; and DD, 1–5 Jul 44. The direct and plain-speaking Crocker had also castigated Major General Charles W. Ryder and his 34th US Infantry Division during 9 Corps operations in Tunisia. Although press leakage of the incident upset the Americans, Bradley later admitted that Ryder overlooked the shortcomings of ineffective subordinates and thus penalized his division as well as himself. Bradley, *Story*, 67–8, 100; and Rick Atkinson, *An Army at Dawn* (New York: Henry Holt, 2003), 470–8.

30 Montgomery to Crerar, 8 July 1944; MAP, Personal Diary, 4 and 8 July; and Dickson, *Thoroughly Canadian General*, 274.

31 MAP, BLM 126, M508 Montgomery to Brooke, 7 July 1944. Brooke expressed concern that Keller had been nominated to replace the 1 Canadian Corps commander in Italy who had been found wanting. MAP, BLM 1 /101 Brooke to Montgomery 11 July 1944.

32 MAP, Personal Diary, 15, 31 July and 2 August 44; BLM 119/9,
    Montgomery to CIGS, 15 Jul 44, and Reports on Bucknall, 2 Aug 44, and
    Erskine, 3 Aug 44; D'Este, *Normandy*, 174–97, 272–7, 422–3; and Hamilton,
    Master, 715, 772. Montgomery wrote that Bucknall was almost always 24
    hours too late and admitted that he had made a mistake in selecting him
    for corps command, ruefully adding that "I must now remove him from
    command."

33 CP, Vol. 5, Crerar to McNaughton, 6 June 1942, and Vol. 2, SO CMHCR
    to Crerar, 17 April 1942. Keller and Salmon each took command of their
    respective divisions, the 3rd and 1st, on 8 September 1942, several months
    ahead of Simonds who, after brief service as a brigade commander under
    the latter, became GOC 2nd Division on 13 April 1943.

34 CP, Vol. 1, GOC 6-1-7 Crerar memorandum to file, 3 May 1943 and Crerar
    to Keller, 13th November, 1942.

35 CP, Vol. 8, Crerar to Stuart, 16 May 1944.

36 CP, Vol. 2, Crerar memorandum to COS, CMHQ 24 April 1944.

37 MAP, Personal Diary, 9 July 44; DD, 7–9 Jul 44; English, *Canadian Army*,
    169–173; D'Este, *Normandy*, 305–6, 309–18; and Stacey, *Victory*, 153–64.
    "Charnwood" cost the 3rd Canadian Infantry Division 1,194 casualties, 330
    of them fatal, a heavier loss than on D-Day.

38 CP, Crerar to Simonds, 10 July 1944, Crerar to COS, CMHQ, 10 July 1944,
    and Memo to Army Comd from DA&QMG, First Cdn Army, by Brigadier
    A.E. Walford, 13 July 1944; and English, *Canadian Army*,178–9.

39 CP, Vol. 3, Crerar memorandum to file, 14 July 1944.

40 CP, Vol. 3, Crerar to Stuart, 15 July 1944.

41 PRO 70519, WO 285/16, Main Army Speaking Notes, 27 November 1944;
    LHCMA, LHI/230/22, Dempsey to Liddell Hart, 28 March 1952 covering
    "Operation Goodwood," 18 July 1944, Dempsey's expansion (18.3.52) of
    the notes he wrote down in brief form 21.2.52; Liddell Hart to Dempsey,
    31 March 1952, covering amended notes; and Dempsey to Liddell Hart,
    16 April 1952; DD, 12 Jul 44; Hart, Cracks, 70, 145; and D'Este, *Normandy*,
    354–9; Dempsey's role in selling the Goodwood concept to Montgomery
    certainly refutes Patton's first impression of him as a "yes-man." USMA West
    Point Archives, Original Patton Diary, 1 June 1944.

42 LAC, RG 24, Vol. 10,797, Atlantic – 18 Jul 44; MAP, Personal Diary, 19 July
    44; and English, *Canadian Army*, 173–82.

43 Weigley, *Eisenhower's Lieutenants*, 167; and English, *Canadian Army*, 136–7.

44 LAC, RG 24, Vol. 10,800, Report on "Spring" 25 July 1944 by Lieutenant
    Colonel McLellan, GSO1 (Liaison), 3rd Canadian Infantry Division;
    RG Vol. 13,750, Ops Log Main HQ 2 Cdn Inf Div, 25 Jul 44; RG 24, Vol.
    13,711, 2 Cdn Corps Main, 5–31 Jul 44; English, *Canadian Army*, 187–97;
    Douglas E. Delaney, *Corps Commanders: Five British and Canadian Generals at*

War, 1939–45 (Vancouver: UBC Press, 2011), 267–72; and Personal copy, Memorandum in the Case of Lt. Col. G.H. Christiansen. The RHLI attack never received the credit it deserved in the official history. Personal copy DHist 001. (D5), Brigadier J.M. Rockingham to Col. C.P. Stacey, 27 October 1948.

45 CP, Vol. 3, Simonds to Dempsey on Command Situation in 3 Canadian Division, 27 July 1944.

46 Graham, *Price*, 319.

47 PRO, Crerar Diary, Notes on Conference given by C-in-C 21 Army Group on 22 June 1944; CP, Vol. 2, Montgomery to Crerar, 17-4-44, Notes on Conference C-in-C – GOC-in-C First Cdn Army, 24 Jun 44, and Memorandum of Conference with C-in-C 21 Army Group held at Tac HQ 21 Army Group at 2100 hrs 20 Jul 44; Tac HQ 21 Army Group M512, 21-7-44 and M515, 27-7-44; and Stacey, *Victory*, 208, 265, 368, 642.

48 MAP, Personal Diary, 20 Feb 44 and Montgomery to DGIS, 19 Mar 44; Weigley, *Eisenhower's Lieutenants*, 51; D'Este, *Normandy*, 242–4, 260–3; Stacey, *Victory*, 149, 163, 166; Hart, *Cracks*, 49–61, 64, 145; DD, 10 Jul 44; and Eversley Belfield and H. Essame, *The Battle for Normandy* (London: Pan, 1983), 144–5. Other formations and units disbanded included the 27th Armoured Brigade, the 70th Brigade of the 49th Division (replaced by the independent 56th Infantry Brigade), two tank regiments in the 33rd Armoured Brigade, and a regiment each in the 8th and 34th Armoured Brigades.

49 MAP, Personal Diary, 8 Jul 44.

50 MAP, BLM 126, M508 Montgomery to Brooke 7 July 1944.

51 MAP, BLM 1/101 Brooke to Montgomery 11 July 1944. Brooke had noted earlier that he had full confidence that Crerar would not let him down. *Alanbrooke War Diaries* (29 March 1944), 535–6.

52 MAP, BLM 126, M511 Montgomery to Brooke, 14-7-44; and LHCMA, AP, 14/28 Montgomery to Brooke, 14 July 1944.

53 MAP, BLM, 126/12 Montgomery to Brooke, 14 July 1944.

54 CP, Vol. 2, Main HQ First Cdn Army GOC-in-C 1-0-4 Crerar to GOC 1 Corps, 1930 hrs 22 Jul 44.

55 CP, Vol. 2, Memorandum Crocker to Crerar, 24 Jul 44.

56 CP, Vol. 8, Crerar to Montgomery, 24 Jul 44 and Comments by GOC-in-C First Cdn Army on Memorandum dated 24 Jul 44 submitted by GOC 1 Brit Corps. Awarded a DSO and MC as a Second Lieutenant in the Machine Gun Corps, "Honest John" Crocker was an exemplary general officer who led by example. According to Field Marshal Lord Carver, to serve him was an education in itself. "Thoughts on Command in Battle," *British Army Review* 1 (July 1978): 5. For thorough treatment of this fine officer, see Delaney, *Corps Commanders*, 122–71. For detailed coverage

of the dispute see my *Canadian Army*, 149–52. Following a map study and enemy information from Oberst Helmut Ritgen, I concluded that Crocker had the better case.

57 MAP, Personal Diary, 26 July 44 and Crerar to Montgomery, 26 Jul 44.

58 CP, Vol. 8, Memorandum on Meeting with C-in-C 21 Army Group at Tac HQ 21 Army Group, commencing 1500 hrs 25 July.

59 CP, Vol. 8, Montgomery to Crerar, 26 July 1944.

60 Personal copy, GOC-in-C 3–4 Tactical Directive by Comd, First Cdn Army, Tac HQ First Cdn Army, 22 July with Appx Extracts from Address by Comd, First Cdn Army, given on 14 May 44; and GOC-in-C 3–4 Main HQ First Cdn Army to Crocker, A/Comd 2 Cdn Corps, and A/Comd 4 Cdn Armd Div, 28 Nov 44 covering Part II of First Canadian Army Intelligence Summary 150, "German Views on Allied Combat Efficiency."

61 Crerar later alleged that Crocker had resented competing with him in the development of tactics and techniques for the Normandy assault landing; Delaney, *Corps Commanders*, 167; CP, Vol. 21, Crerar to Stacey, 12 August 1957; and CP, Vol. 8, Crocker to Crerar, 28.3.45.

62 Dickson, *Thoroughly Canadian General*, 266, 289–90.

63 LHCMA, AP, 14/1, Montgomery to Brooke, 26-7-44; and MAP, Personal Diary, 26 July 44.

11. Cracking German Lines

1 LAC, RG 24, Vol. 13,711, Minutes of Conference Held by General Montgomery, HQ 21 Army Group, 0930 hrs 13 Jan 44, under 53-1/SD G 2 Cdn Corps, 14 Jan 44; and CP, Vol. 3, 21 A.Gp/1001/C.in-C., Montgomery to Crerar, 4 May 44.

2 Ibid.

3 RG 24, Vol. 13,711, Minutes of Conference Held by General Montgomery, HQ 21 Army Group, 0930 hrs 13 Jan 44, under 53–1/SD G 2 Cdn Corps, 14 Jan 44; and MAP, Montgomery to Lt. Gen. Sir Ronald M. Weeks, DCIGS, 3 April, 1944; and English, *Canadian Army*, 131–4.

4 "Notes on the Handling of Armour," *Current Reports from Overseas (CFRO)* 7 (17 July 1943): 9–10; and RG 24, Vol. 13,711, Minutes of Conference Held by General Montgomery, HQ 21 Army Group, 0930 hrs 13 Jan 44, under 53-1/SD G 2 Cdn Corps, 14 Jan 44. The Churchill had heavier armour than the Tiger. MAP, DCIGS to Montgomery, 10 July 1944.

5 MAP, 21 A.Gp/1088/C.-in-C., Montgomery to Comd. Second Army, 25 June 1944, 21 A.Gp/1093/C.-in-C., Montgomery to CIGS, 27 June 1944, Montgomery to DCIGS, 6 July covering Memorandum on British Armour and DCIGS to Montgomery, 10 July 1944; and CFRO 52 (26 August 1944). The British developed armour piercing discarding sabot ammunition that

consisted of a light metal "sabot" with the same diameter as the gun calibre and a smaller diameter tungsten armour piercing rod held within the sabot. On being fired the sabot detached around 100 yards from the armoured piercing rod, which then travelled at greater speed onto the target.

6   CP, Vol. 15,WD GOC-in-C First Cdn Army, 27 July 1944; MAP Personal Diary, 27–30 July 44; RG 24, Vol. 13,712, WD Main HQ 2 Cdn Corps, 5 Aug 44; and English, *Canadian Army*, 198–202.

7   Stacey, *Victory*, 206–7; Reginald H. Roy, *1944: The Canadians in Normandy* (Ottawa: Macmillan, 1984), 144–6; Kitching, *Memoirs*, 203–4, 207–8; and W.E.J. Hutchinson, "Test of a Corps Commander: Lieutenant General Guy Granville Simonds, Normandy 1944" (unpublished MA thesis, University of Victoria, 1982), 188.

8   CP, Vol. 2, 21 Army Group M516, 4-8-44 and M517, 6-8-44; personal copy Memorandum Operation Totalizer [*sic*] Re Planning Full Scale Air/Land battle "Totalizer [*sic*]," Crerar to COS, 2 August 1944; CP, Vol. 2, Crerar to Crocker and Simonds, 6 August 1944 and Remarks to Senior Officers, Cdn Army Operation "Totalize" by GOC-in-C First Cdn Army 051100, August 1944.

9   MAP, Montgomery to CIGS, 9-8-44.

10 CP, Vol. 21, Crerar to Colonel C.P. Stacey, 7 June 1952 and 12 August 1957; and CP, Vol. 3, Tactical Directive by Comd, First Cdn Army, 22 July 1944. Simonds staked his claim to the original conception of the APC in CP, Vol. 8, Simonds to GOC-in-C First Cdn Army 10 June 1945. The APC was the Priest 105mm Self-Propelled tracked artillery piece minus the gun – hence the initial name "unfrocked Priest" or "Holy Roller," and, eventually, the "Kangaroo" with an infantry section inside.

11 CP, Vol. 2, Remarks to Senior Officers, Cdn Army Operation "Totalize" by GOC-in-C First Canadian Army 051100, August 1944 and CP, Vol 2, Crerar to Ralston, 1 September 1944 (report upon the initial phase of operations of First Canadian Army during the campaign in France 7–23 August 1944).

12 LHCMA, AP, 14/29 Montgomery to Brooke, 9-8-44.

13 RG 24, Vol. 10,808, Operation Totalize Appreciation by Lieutenant General G.G. Simonds, 1 August 1944; and British Army of the Rhine (BAOR) Battlefield Tour Operation Totalize: 2 Canadian Corps Operations Astride the Road Caen-Falaise 7–8 August 1944, Spectator's Edition (1947), 1–16.

14 RG 24, Vol. 13,712, WD Main HQ 2 Cdn Corps, 7 Aug 44. Brig. Rodger briefing.

15 BAOR Totalize, 6-15, 37.

16 Dickson, *Thoroughly Canadian General*, 306–8; and BAOR Totalize, 12–13. Neither Harris's Bomber Command nor Lieutenant-General Carl A. Spaatz's United States Strategic Air Forces were willing to take orders from Leigh-Mallory however. To resolve this difficulty it was agreed that direction

of all Overlord air command would be vested in the Supreme Allied Commander, to be exercised by his deputy, Air Chief Marshal Sir Arthur Tedder. Initial "Totalize" details were fleshed out on 4 August in a meeting at First Canadian Army headquarters between Crerar, Leigh-Mallory, and 2nd Tactical Air Force commanders. Crerar's COS flew to England the next day with Brigadier C.L Richardson, 21st Army Group (Plans) for a conference at AEAF headquarters chaired by Leigh-Mallory and attended by Tedder, Spaatz, the No. 83 Group commander, and a key staff officer from Bomber Command. On 6 August the COS visited headquarters Bomber Command to personally convince Harris of the feasibility of night bombing in support of ground troops. Stacey, *Victory*, 211–13; and CP, Vol. 15, WD GOC-in-C, 7 Aug 44.

17 MAP, Personal Diary, 7 August 44; RG 24, Vol. 10,800, "Immediate Report" on Operation "Totalize" 7–9 August 1944; CP, Vol. 15, WD GOC-in-C, 7 Aug 44; Stacey, *Victory*, 216–20; and Stephen Hart, *Road to Falaise* (Stroud: Sutton, 2004), 41–7.

18 RG 24, Vol. 13,712, WD Main HQ 2 Cdn Corps, 8 Aug 44; BAOR Totalize, 17–22. Brigadier Wyman commanding the 2nd Armoured Brigade signalled at 0615 hours that the forward area was securely held and that the situation appeared to be entirely suitable for further operations to begin. Jody Perrun, "Best Laid Plans: Guy Simonds and Operation Totalize, 7–10 August 1944," *Journal of Military History* 1 (January 2003): 164–5.

19 RG 24, Vol. 10,797, GOC's Activities, 0700, 8 August 1944; and CP, Vol. 15, WD GOC-in-C First Cdn Army, 8 Aug 44.

20 RG 24, Vol 10,799, Simonds' Draft of Lessons, 1 July 1944; Kitching, *Memoirs*, 210–11; and Brigadier General E.A.C. (Ned) Amy, "Normandy: 1 Squadron Canadian Grenadier Guards, Phase 2 Operation Totalize 7/8 August 1944," unpublished paper dated 21 February 1993. Amy stressed that "The enemy really had little to do with limiting the success of the [4th Armoured] Division on 8 August."

21 DDE Library, J Lawton Collins Papers, Box 5, Operation Cobra, Chapter I: VII Corps Operations (24–31 Jul 44); James Jay Carafano, *After D-Day: Operation Cobra and the Normandy Breakout* (Boulder: Lynne Rienner, 2000), 185–6, 192–203, 221, 262–3; Russell F. Weigley, *Eisenhower's Lieutenants: The Campaign of France and Germany, 1944–1945* (Bloomington: Indiana University Press, 1981), 155–64; D'Este, *Normandy*, 403–4; and John S.D. Eisenhower, *The Bitter Woods: The Battle of the Bulge* (New York, Da Capo, 1995), 45.

22 The bomb line ran from the north edge of Robertmesnil along the north edge of Gaumesnil to the south edge of the quarry west of Gaumesnil.

23 RG 24, Vol. 10,797, COS Notes 8 August and GOC's Activities, 1245, 8 August 1944; RG 24, Vol. 13,712 WD Main HQ 2 Cdn Corps, 8 Aug 44;

Brian A. Reid, *No Holding Back: Operation Totalize, Normandy, August 1944* (Toronto: Robin Brass, 2005), 130; and PRO, Air 25-704, First Canadian Army Operation "Totalize" Request for Air Support, Part III – The Air Plan, 4 Aug 44.

24 RG 24, Vol. 10,800, "Immediate Report" Totalize; and BAOR Totalize, 25–7. For more detailed treatment of German and Canadian moves gleaned from battlefield tours with Canadian and German SS and army veterans, see my *Canadian Army*, 203–23.

25 CP, Vol. 21, Crerar to Stacey, 3 December 1958. Crerar blamed the Poles, charging that the 4th Armoured Division advance had been checked by the "dog fight" that developed between the 1st Polish Armoured Division and German elements in Quesnay Wood. Had the Poles smoked off and contained the enemy there and pushed on with the bulk of their strength, they would have widened the front and increased the depth for a tactically decisive advance. CP, Vol. 21, Crerar to Stacey 23 Jul 47 and 10 January 1958.

26 21 Army Group, *The Armoured Division in Battle* issued by Montgomery December, 1944; and English, *Canadian Army*, 218–20. From October 1944 the "battle group" was usually at brigade level. James Alan Roberts, *The Canadian Summer* (Toronto: University of Toronto Press, 1981), 97; and Stacey, *Victory*, 500–1, 503–5.

27 Stacey, *Victory*, 222–5; Kitching, *Memoirs*, 213; and English, *Canadian Army*, 218–20.

28 CP, Vol. 29, Report on Survey of Reinforcement Situation – Canadian Army Overseas by Lieutenant General E.W. Sansom, 29 March 1945. At 0710 Simonds ordered both armoured divisions to feed forward. RG 24, Vol. 10,797, COS 2 Cdn Corps Handwritten Telephone Notes, 8 August 1944; and Amy, 5.

29 Hubert Meyer, *The History of the 12. SS-Panzerdivision "Hitlerjugend,"* trans. H. Harri Henschler (Winnipeg: J.J. Fedorowicz, 1994), 170–80.

30 RG 24, Vol. 13,789, WD 4 Cdn Armd Div, 7–10 Aug 44; and English, *Canadian Army*, 220–1.

31 CP, Vol. 21, Crerar to Stacey, 10 January 1958.

32 Stacey, Victory, 218; CP, Vol. 6, Harris to Crerar, 13th September 1944; and English, *Canadian Army*, 226, 328n7, 330n28.

33 CP, Vol. 21, Crerar to Stacey, 23 July 1947.

34 USMA West Point Archives, Thomas R. Goethals Papers, Extracts from Telephone Journal Seventh German Army, 8–9 August 1944; Kreigstagebuch,Panzer-Armeeoberkommando 5, 10.6.44-8.8.44. RH 21-5/44 von Kluge to Hausser, evening 8 Aug 44; and Eisenhower, *Bitter Woods*, 55.

35 MAP Personal Diary, 9–12 August 44.

36 CP, Vol. 2, Operation "Tractable," Crerar to Comd 1 Brit Corps and Comd 2 Cdn Corps, 13 Aug 44, Vol. 15, WD GOC-in-C First Canadian Army, 14 Aug 44, and Vol. 21, Crerar to Stacey, 10 January 1958.

37 Operation "Tractable" Bombing Errors in Close Support Operation of 14 August 1944; PRO Air14/860, XC/A/51202, First Cdn Army COS Memo on Use of Coloured Smoke and Flares to GOC-in-C, 22 August 1944 and Minute by A.T. Harris, 31 August; Report on the Bombing of Our Own troops during Operation "Tractable" by Air Chief Marshal A. T. Harris, 25 August 1944; PRO Air 14/860 and PRO Air 14/861, XC/A/51202, RAF Proceedings of a Board of Officers 16–18 August 1944 for the purpose of investigating errors in bombing that occurred on 14 August 1944 in connection with operation "Tractable"; CP, Vol. 5, Memo COS to GOC-in-C Regarding the Report of the AOC in C Bomber Command, 28 August 1944; RG 24, Vol. 797, Notes COS 2 Corps, 14 Aug 44; and Stacey, *Victory*, 243–5.

38 CP, Vol. 2, 21 Army Group, M517, 6–8-44; RG 24, Vol. 10,797, 2 Cdn Corps COS Telephone Notes, 14 Aug 1944 and Crerar, Notes for War Diary, 16 Aug 44; and D'Este, *Normandy*, 426–7.

39 MAP, Personal Diary, 14–17 August 44; CP, Vol. 2, 21 Army Group M518, 11-8-44; and D'Este, *Normandy*, 424–30, 438–48, 456. The 7th Armoured Division could have easily been shifted to Crerar by Dempsey who was progressing on his own front with relative ease at the time. The Canadians also had their 3rd Infantry Division in reserve for "Totalize."

40 D'Este, *Normandy*, 433.

12. First Canadian Army's Greatest Contribution to Allied Victory

1 MAP, 21 Army Group M519, 20–8-44; and CP, Vol. 2, Crerar to Comd 1 Brit Corps and Comd 2 Cdn Corps, 19 Aug 44.

2 Stacey, *Victory*, 264–8, 279–95.

3 MAP, 21 Army Group, Directive M520, 26-8-44.

4 CP, Vol. 15, WD GOC-in-C First Cdn Army, 30 Aug 44; MAP, Personal War Diary, 26–31 Aug 44; Stacey, *Victory*, 296–300, 308; Jeffrey Williams, *The Long Left Flank: The Hard Fought Way to the Reich 1944–1945* (Toronto: Stoddart, 1988), 27–32; and Marshall Library, Lexington, Virginia, General George C. Marshall Papers (GMP), Box 67, Folder 12, Eisenhower to Marshall, 24 August 1944. Eisenhower stressed driving hard to size V Bomb sites in the Pas de Calais area.

5 LHCMA, 1/230/30, Liddell Hart to Dempsey, 4 February 1953; and Pyman, 74.

6 "Some Administrative Problems Encountered during the Advance of Second Army from Falaise to Brussels, 24 Aug to 3 Sep 44," *CRFO* 68 (20

December 1944): 6–8; MAP, Personal Diary, 31 Aug 44; LHCMA, Dempsey Diary (DD), 23–27 Aug 44; RG 24, Vol. 13,789, WD 4 Cdn Armd Div, 31 Aug 44; Lewin, *Man of Armour*, 300; and Weigley, *Eisenhower's Lieutenants*, 254–5.

7 PRO, Crerar Diary, 1–4 September 1944; Royal Military College of Canada Archives (RMC), Crerar Papers, GOC-in-C 1-0-4, Directive Crerar to Comd 1 Brit Corps and Comd 2 Cdn Corps, 1 September 1944; Stacey, Victory, 297–300; Hart, Cracks, 168–9; and Terry Copp and Robert Vogel, "'No Lack of Rational Speed': 1st Canadian Army Operations, September 1944," *Journal of Canadian Studies* 16 (Fall/Winter, 1981): 147, 154.

8 In a congratulatory letter Churchill explained that he did not intend by this promotion to put Montgomery permanently over the head of Alexander as he thought it would be unfair. He stated that Alexander's forthcoming promotion would therefore be backdated to restore the old order of seniority. MAP, Churchill to Montgomery, September 2, 1944.

9 CP, Vol. 15 WD GOC-in-C First Cdn Army 1–4 Sep 44 and Vol. 15, Crerar to McNaughton, MND, 8 Nov 44; MAP, Personal Diary, 3 Sep 44; Stacey, *Victory*, 303–6; Hamilton, *Field-Marshal*, 34–6; Hart, *Cracks*, 165, 168–9; and Dickson, *Thoroughly Canadian General*, 321, 327–38.

10 MAP, September 1944 File, Tac HQ 21 Army Group M524, Montgomery to Brooke, 10-9-44; Copp and Vogel, "No Lack of Rational Speed," 152, 155; Stacey, *Victory*, 300. The port eventually received 7,000 tons per day. Ostend fell on 9 September and its port opened on the 28th. Allied divisions required maintenance supply in the order of 650–700 tons per day.

11 DDE Library, DDE Collection, Pre-Presidential Papers: 1916–1952, Principal File, Eisenhower to Marshall, 14 September 1944; Martin Blumenson, *United States Army in World War II, The European Theatre of Operations: Breakout and Pursuit* (Washington: Office of the Chief of Military History, 1961), 632, 655–6; and Major General J.L. Moulton, *Battle for Antwerp: The Liberation of the City and the Opening of the Scheldt 1944* (New York: Hippocrene, 1978), 74–8, 228. Cherbourg fell on 27 June, but was not mopped up until 1 July; it took another month to open the port to Allied shipping. Brest was not taken until 20 September. Le Havre opened to Allied shipping on 9 October.

12 DDE Library, Supreme Headquarters Allied Expeditionary Force, Office of AC of S, G-3, Minutes of Meeting Held in the War Room at SHAEF FORWARD at 1430 hours, 22 September 1944; and Stacey, *Victory*, 356.

13 Stacey, *Victory*, 359.

14 Hamilton, *Field Marshal*, 42, 49–50, 99; Moulton, *Battle for Antwerp*, 47, 54–6. The first V2 struck Britain on 8 September.

15 *Alanbrook War Diaries* (5 October 1944), 600.

16 DDE Library, Columbia University Oral History Project, Oral History OH-184, Interview James M. Gavin by Ed Edwin, 20 January 1967. Weigley also argued that "Market Garden" was worth the risk and could have succeeded. *Eisenhower's Lieutenants*, 317–18.

17 Major-General J.F.C. Fuller, *The Second World War 1939–1945: A Strategical and Tactical History* (London: Eyre and Spottiswoode, 1948), 339.

18 Gavin, former commander of the 82nd Airborne Division that seized the bridge at Nijmegen, asserted: "I cannot understand how a historian can avoid placing the responsibility [for failing to open Antwerp] on Eisenhower ... [as] he, more than anyone else, had a keen awareness of the critical nature of the logistics situation in his armies." James M. Gavin, *On to Berlin: Battles of an Airborne Commander 1943–1946* (New York: Bantam, 1981), 154.

19 MAP, Personal Diary, 7 Sep 44; Dominick Graham and Shelford Bidwell, *Coalitions, Politicians, and Generals: Some Aspects of Command in Two World Wars* (London: Brassey's, 1993), 238, 256–76; Lamb, *Montgomery in Europe*, 206–17; and Weigley, *Eisenhower's Lieutenants*, 266–7, 270–7, 281–2. Making routes one-way does not maximize road capacity. Scrounging, looting, and hijacking also became commonplace as a black market developed from lost or dishonest drivers selling or peddling their wares to the nearest bidder. Failure to rotate units or maintain trucks properly also left thousands of them derelict. Another indication of managerial incompetence was that of roughly 22 million jerricans shipped to France, half were lost through careless handling by the beginning of September. At least eighty trains were also lost in Paris, another indication of the inefficiency of the U.S. European Theatre of Operations Communications Zone.

20 MAP, Montgomery to Crerar, 13 September 1944; Montgomery Personal Diary, 9–13 Sep 44; CP, Vol. 15, WD GOC-in-C First Cdn Army, 7–13 Sep 44; Directive Crerar to Comd 1 Brit Corps and Comd 1 Cdn Corps, 9 Sep 44; Stacey, *Victory*, 310–12, 329–36, 357–60; Moulton, *Battle for Antwerp*, 50–1; and Hamilton, *Field-Marshal*, 47, 103–6.

21 MAP, Crerar to Montgomery, 13 September 1944; and Stacey, *Victory*, 359.

22 PRO, Crerar Diary, 15 Sep 44, Appendix F, Army Commander's Directive to Corps Commanders, 15 Sep 44; CP, Vol. 15, WD GOC-in-C, First Cdn Army, 14–19 Sep 44; Stacey, *Victory*, 331–6, 357–60; and Copp and Vogel, "No Lack of Rational Speed," 150–1. Le Havre, with a population of 160,000 in 1936, was second only to Marseilles as a ranking French port before the Second World War. Its population at the time of capture was about 50,000. In the 1 Corps attack, code-named Operation "Astonia," heavy strategic bombers and numerous specialized armoured fighting vehicles, including "flail" and "Crocodile," flame-throwing tanks, and "Kangaroo" APCs, were used.

23 Later masked by the 154th Brigade of the 51st (Highland) Division. On 9 October the 1st Czechoslovak Independent Armoured Brigade assumed this task, eventually receiving the German garrison's surrender. Stacey, *Victory*, 368.

24 MAP, Personal Diary, 14 Sep 44; GOC-in-C 1-0-4 Directive Crerar to Comd 1 Brit Corps and Comd 2 Cdn Corps, 15 Sep 44; PRO, Crerar Diary, Appendix G, Directive to 1 Brit and 2 Cdn Corps Commanders, 19 Sep 44; GOC-in-C 1-0-4 Directive Crerar to Comd 1 Brit Corps and Comd 2 Cdn Corps, 19 Sep 44; Stacey, *Victory*, 358–361; and Copp and Vogel, "No Lack of Rational Speed," 153.

25 When the GOC 2 Canadian Corps complained about this on 22 September, the 2nd Canadian Infantry Division was placed under command of the British 1 Corps effective 26 September. Stacey, *Victory*, 367.

26 Stacey, *Victory*, 331–56, 361–4

27 R.W. Thompson, *The Eighty Five Days: The Story of the Battle of the Scheldt* (London: Hutchinson, 1957), 60. Other criticism can be found in H. Essame, *The Battle for Germany* (New York: Bonanza, 1969), 29.

28 W.A.B. Douglas and B. Greenhous, *Out of the Shadows* (Toronto: Oxford University Press, 1977), 200.

29 Over 11,000 Germans garrisoned Le Havre compared with roughly 10,000 at Boulogne.

30 Stacey, *Victory*, 343–56; and Copp and Vogel, "No Lack of Rational Speed," 150–1.

31 CP, Vol. 21 Crerar to Stacey, 3 December 1958; and Copp and Vogel, "No Lack of Rational Speed," 282–3, 145.

32 MAP, Crerar to Montgomery, 13 Sep 44.

33 Moulton, *Battle for Antwerp*, 69; W. Denis and Shelagh Whitaker, *Tug of War: The Canadian Victory that Opened Antwerp* (Toronto: Stoddart, 1984), 69–70; Williams, *The Long Left Flank*, 37–8; Granatstein, *Weight*, 122; and CP, Vol. 15, WD GOC-in-C First Cdn Army, 13 and 15 Sep 44.

34 MAP, M237 cipher of 26 Sep 44 and Personal Diary, 26 Sep 44; CP, Vol. 15, WD GOC-in-C, 19–26 Sep 44; Crerar to McNaughton, Minister of National Defence, 8 Nov 44; and Dickson, *Thoroughly Canadian General*, 257, 289–90, 307–8, 327, 334, 338, 351, 353–4.

35 Hart, *Cracks*, 160, 170; Granatstein, *Canada's Army*, 287; CP, Vol. 15, GOC-in-C War Diary, 19, 21, 24–7 Sep 44; Stacey, *Date*, 237.

36 Chester Wilmot, *The Struggle for Europe* (London: Fontana/Collins, 1974), 470.

37 RG 24, Vol. 10,799, Simonds's comments on the aim of the G Plan appreciation; and personal copy GOC-in-C 1-0-7/7 Notes on Conference on Operation "Infatuate," 22 Sep 44.

38 Hart, *Cracks*, 166.

39 Whitakers, *Tug*, 108–127; and Stacey, *Victory*, 361, 369–78, 409–12.

40 GOC-in-C/1-0, Folio No. 89–92, 27-9-44; MAP, Personal Diary, 27 September (M.527); Stacey, *Victory*, 369–380; Copp and Vogel, "No Lack of Rational Speed," 152; and Delaney, *Corps Commanders*, 239–45.

41 As commander of the 85th German Infantry Division, Chill had made a formidable name for himself and his formation in shoring up the line of the Albert Canal from 2 September. Another outstanding field soldier, Lieutenant-Colonel Friedrich von der Heydte, commanded the 6th Parachute Regiment. Whitakers, *Tug*, 167–8.

42 MAP, BLM 149, Clearing of the Scheldt Estuary, Oct–Nov 1944, 2–3; Stacey, *Victory*, 381–5; Whitakers, *Tug*, 180–98, 212–35; and Williams, *The Long Left Flank*, 109–10.

43 Douglas and Greenhous, *Shadows*, 203.

44 Williams, *The Long Left Flank*, 107–9; Terry Copp, *The Brigade: The Fifth Canadian Infantry Brigade, 1939–1945* (Stoney Creek: Fortress, 1992), 144–50; and Whitakers, *Tug*, 168–77, 247–50. The Wasp was a Canadian-developed flame-thrower fitted on a Universal carrier. RMC, Sawyer Papers (SP), Brigadier J.M. Rockingham to Sawyer, 2 Feb 45 covering "Notes on the Employment of the Wasp Flame Thrower," 1 Feb 45.

45 Lamb, 279–80; and Stacey, *Victory*, 387. Aachen was not be taken until 21 October.

46 For more detail on "Market Garden" see my *Patton's Peers: The Forgotten Allied Field Army Commanders of the Western Front 1944–45* (Mechanicsburg: Stackpole, 2009), 78–84.

47 Stacey, *Victory*, 387, 390; Lamb, *Montgomery in Europe*, 281; Williams, *The Long Left Flank*, 160–1; D'Este, *Sicily*, 271–4, 468–74, 568–9. There is still debate about the relief of Allen.

48 Stacey, *Victory*, 387–91; MAP, Eisenhower to Montgomery, 13 October 1944; Moulton, *Battle for Antwerp*, 118–23; Hamilton, *Field-Marshal*, 105–12; and Lamb, *Montgomery in Europe*, 284–9.

49 The "Water Rats" of the 3rd Division had assaulted on D-day after a year of intense amphibious training. They appear to have earned their nickname, revived in the Scheldt, while practising drills with the navy in Scottish estuaries. Ben Dunkelman, *Dual Allegiance: An Autobiography* (Toronto: Macmillan, 1976), 75, 122. Williams attributes the plan for an amphibious assault to Simonds. Williams, *The Long Left Flank*, 116, 122–4.

50 The "Buffalo" Landing Vehicle Tracked (LVT) was developed by the United States Navy and Marine Corps to assault over coral reefs. Although used at Tarawa and Makin, Buffaloes arrived in Europe too late for the Normandy assault. The LVT Mark II without ramp carried thirty soldiers in fighting order; the LVT Mark IV with stern ramp could carry a 6-pdr gun, jeep, Bren carrier, scout car, or similar loads. They were used by Royal Engineers

and the 79th Armoured British Division, which provided other specialized armoured vehicles and equipment. Moulton, *Battle for Antwerp*, 97–8, 254–5; and "Notes on the Tactical Handling of LVT (Buffaloes)," *CRFO* 77 (21 February, 1945): 4–7. The "Terrapin" was a British built, eight-wheeled load carrying amphibian that appeared in the latter part of 1944. Moulton, *Battle for Antwerp*, 255.

51 Stacey, *Victory*, 392–400; MAP, BLM 149, Scheldt, 4–8,15; Helmut Ritgen, Oberst A.D., unpublished paper, "Fighting for the Scheldt Estuary"; "The Assault across Savojaards Plaat," *CRFO* 72 (17 January, 1945): 1–12; SP, 21AGp/7143/4/G (CWET) Chemical Warfare Liaison Letter No. 5, 14 Dec 44, Smoke Support in the Schelde [*sic*]; Whitakers, *Tug*, 270–318; Moulton, *Battle for Antwerp*, 111–16; and Williams, *The Long Left Flank*, 114–28.

52 Stacey, *Victory*, 389–91, 401–2, 408–12.

53 MAP, BLM 149, Scheldt, 9–14, 16–26; Stacey, *Victory*, 403–6, 412–22; and Moulton, *Battle for Antwerp*, 134–43, 168, 171–4, 179–90, 207–17.

54 Stacey, *Victory*, 422–5.

55 Personal copy Tac Headquarters, 21 Army Group, B.L.A., Montgomery to Simonds, 3 November 1944. Rising commanders included D.C. Spry, GOC 3rd Division, H.W. Foster, GOC 4th Armoured, and R.H. Keefler, Acting GOC 2nd Division (later GOC 3rd Division), J.G. Spragge, 7th Brigade, J.A. Roberts, 8th Brigade, J.M. Rockingham, 9th Brigade, and R.W. Moncel, 4th Armoured Brigade, and J.F Bingham, 2nd Armoured Brigade.

13. Canadian Army Triumph

1   CP, Vol. 15, GOC-in-C First Cdn Army War Diary, 22, 25, and 26 Oct and 7 Nov 44; Hart, *Cracks*, 172; Granatstein, *Generals*, 172; Dickson, *Thoroughly Canadian General*, 358; and Stacey, *Arms*, 224, and *Date*, 236.

2   MAP, BLM 115/64 Montgomery to Brooke, 18 Oct 44 and BLM 119/35 Montgomery to CIGS, 17 Nov 44; Stacey, *Victory*, 426–30, 438; and Dickson, *Thoroughly Canadian General*, 358–9.

3   PRO, Crerar Diary, 8–17 December 1944 and 7 February 1945; CP, Vol. 8, Report Press Conference for General Crerar 2100 hrs 7 August 1945 and Remarks by GOC-in-C to Warcos – 7 Feb 45 as "Off Record" Background to Operation "Veritable"; MAP, Personal Diary, 9–10 December 1944; Hart, *Cracks*, 176–8; John A. Macdonald, "In Search of Veritable: Training the Canadian Army Staff Officer, 1899 to 1945" (Unpublished MA thesis, Royal Military College of Canada, 1992), 174–7; and Stacey, *Victory*, 427, 436–8.

4   PRO, Crerar Diary, GOC-in-C 1-0-7/11 Directive on Operation "Veritable" dated 14 Dec 44 to Comd 1 Brit Corps, 2 Cdn Corps, and 30 Brit Corps and Remarks by GOC-in-C First Canadian Army on Operation "Veritable" to

Staff Officers HQ First Canadian Army/84 Group RAF, 16 Dec 44; Stacey,
Victory, 437; and Macdonald, "In Search of Veritable," 172, 175–7, 218n41.

5   PRO Crerar Diary, Memorandum GOC-in-C 1-0-4/1 Crerar to COS, 19 Dec
44 and Notes on Conference Held at Tac HQ 21 Army Group 1100 hrs by
C-in-C with Comds First Canadian and Second British Armies, 20 Dec 44;
and CP, Vol. 16, WD GOC-in-C First Cdn Army, Notes on Conference Held
between C-in-C 21 Army Group – GOC-in-C First Cdn Army at Tac HQ 21
Army Group 1200–1300 hrs 16 Jan 45.

6   MAP, BLM 79 Notes on the Campaign in NWE, Part VII, The German
Offensive through the Ardennes; DDE Library, Courtney Hicks Hodges
Papers (HP), Box 20, Operational Highlights of the First Army Speech for
General Courtney H. Hodges, 17; David W. Hogan, *A Command Post at War:
First Army Headquarters in Europe, 1939–1945* (Washington: Center of Military
History, United States Army, 2000), 218–19, 225–7; National Archives and
Records Administration, Archives II, College Park, Maryland, Major William
C. Sylvan Diary (SD), 26 December 1944; and Marshall Library, Lexington,
Virginia, George C. Marshall Papers, Box 1, Folder 7, Lieutenant General
W. B. Smith to Lieutenant General Thomas Handy, War Department,
Washington, 28 December 1944; and Eisenhower, *Bitter Woods*, 463–5.

7   DDE Library, DDE Principal File, Box 83, Message M-384 Montgomery
to Eisenhower, 20 December 1944. Montgomery transferred the 51st
(Highland) Division and 6th Guards Tank Brigade to Ninth Army to replace
the 2nd US Armoured Division, which along with the 84th and later 75th
Infantry Divisions concentrated under Collins. DDE Principal File, Box 83,
Message M-385 Montgomery to Eisenhower, 21 December 1944. The 3rd
Armoured Division was also earmarked for Collins. Eisenhower, *Bitter Woods*,
351; and Hogan, *A Command Post at War*, 219–22.

8   "I was placed practically under Monty's command ... he superseded Hodges
so far as my corps was concerned. The moves that were made up there were
good, sound moves" said Collins. HP, "Reflections of General Courtney
Hodges," Interview J. Lawton Collins by Captain G. Patrick Murray, 45; and
MAP, Personal Diary, 20 December 1944.

9   DDE Library, Oral History OH-397, Interview with Brig. Gen. Thomas J.
Betts, by Dr. Maclyn Burg, 16 August 1976; and Hogan, *A Command Post at
War*, 289.

10 DDE Library, DDE Principal File, Box 83, Message S71982, Eisenhower to
Montgomery, 22 December 1944; and Hogan, 220–221. On 22 December
Montgomery signalled Eisenhower that "Hodges was a bit shaken early on
and needed moral support and was very tired. He is doing better now and
I see him and Simpson every day." DDE Principal File, Box 83, Message
M-389 Montgomery to Eisenhower, 22 December 1944. Both Collins
and Ridgway considered Montgomery's liaison officers more intrusive

than informative, but others saw the Phantom and liaison officer system as a tremendously valuable asset. U.S. Army Military History Institute (USAMHI), Carlisle Barracks, Pennsylvania, George I. Forsythe Papers, Oral History Project 74–1, Interview Lieutenant General (Retired) George I. Forsythe by Lieutenant Colonel Frank L. Henry (1974), 191–2.

11 Hogan, *A Command Post at War*, 219–21.

12 MAP, Memo DMO/BM/705, DMO to CIGS, 31 December 1944; and Weigley, *Eisenhower's Lieutenants*, 528–37.

13 Collins stated that Montgomery used to come to VII Corps every other day and that Ridgway would come over and join him. Collins could not remember Hodges visiting. USAMHI, "Reflections on General Courtney Hodges," Oral History Project 73-5, Interview of J. Lawton Collins by Captain G. Patrick Murray, 48, 53.

14 Hogan, *A Command Post at War*, 224, 227–30; Eisenhower, *Bitter Woods*, 412–30, 462; Weigley, *Eisenhower's Lieutenants*, 523; and Gen. James M. Gavin, *On to Berlin: Battles of an Airborne Commander, 1943–1946* (New York: Bantam, 1981), 270–1. Gavin observed that the First Army staff obviously liked Montgomery and respected his professionalism, but that they deeply resented Patton getting all the publicity.

15 Carlo D'Este, "Monty: World War II's Most Misunderstood General," *Armchair General*, 11 July 2005. US Brigadier General Bruce C, Clarke stated that "the greatest generalship" he saw in the Battle of the Bulge was "the generalship of Marshal Montgomery." Thomas E. Ricks, *The Generals: American Military Command from World War II to Today* (New York: Penguin, 2012), 93.

16 MAP, Personal Diary, 18–21 Jan 45; PRO, Crerar Diary, 19 and 25 Jan 44, Appendix 2, Address to Senior Officers First Canadian Army 22 January 1945; Appendix 2a, Notes on Conference held by C-in-C 21 Army Group at Tac, 21 Army Group 1130–1300 hrs, 23 January 45; and 4 February 1945, Appendix 3, Notes on Conference held by C-in-C 21 Army Group at his Tac HQ 1115 hrs, 4 February 1945 and Notes for [Crerar's] Remarks – C-in-C's Conference 4 Feb 1945; Stacey, *Victory*, 455–6, 460–4; and BAOR Battlefield Tour Operation Veritable: 30 Corps Operations between the Rivers Maas and Rhine, 8–10 February 1945, Spectator's Edition, 2–3.

17 MAP, BLM 153, 21 Army Group Report on Operation "Veritable" Clearing the Area between the River Maas and the River Rhine 10 Feb–10 Mar 1945, 3–9, 15–18; Stacey, *Victory*, 464–5; Sir Brian Horrocks with Eversley Belfield and Major General H. Essame, *Corps Commander* (New York: Charles Scribner's Sons, 1977), 173–89; Macdonald, "In Search of Veritable," 159, 201; and BAOR Veritable, 14–15, 37.

18 MAP, BLM 153, "Veritable," 48–56, 71–80, 92–5; PRO, Crerar Diary, 1 February 1945 and Appendix 3, Notes on Conference held by C-in-C

21 Army Group at his Tac HQ 1115 hrs, 4 February 1945 and Notes for [Crerar's] Remarks – C-in-C's Conference 4 Feb 1945 Stacey, *Victory*, 465, 467; Hart, *Cracks*, 157; and BAOR Veritable, 19–22.

19 MAP, BLM 153, "Veritable," 61–4; Stacey, *Victory*, 465–6; and BAOR Veritable, 23–5.

20 A stonk (standard concentration) laid shells in a straight line along an orchard or hedgerow. The twenty-four guns of a field regiment could stonk a target 840 yards long.

21 MAP, BLM 153, "Veritable," 19–23; Stacey, *Victory*, 468–74; and BAOR Veritable, 45–51.

22 MAP, BLM 153, "Veritable," 23–56; Stacey, *Victory*, 457–8, 471, 475–7; BAOR Veritable, 53–55.

23 Essame, *Battle for Germany*, 153–7; Stacey, *Victory*, 476–7; and Horrocks, *Corps Commander*, 186–7.

24 MAP, Personal Diary, 11 and 15 Feb 44. The DUKW (definition code, not acronym) was a six-wheel-drive amphibious modification of the 2½-ton US truck built primarily to ferry ammunition and equipment from offshore supply ships to dumps and fighting units at the beach.

25 MAP, BLM 153, "Veritable," 28–30; Stacey, *Victory*, 476–80; BAOR Veritable, 57–8; and Horrocks, *Corps Commander*, 173–89.

26 Hart, *Cracks*, 174; and Horrocks, *Corps Commander*, 182–3.

27 Roberts, *Canadian Summer*, 106, 108; and Stacey, "Canadian Leaders of the Second World War," 68–9, 71–2, and *Date*, 126.

28 CP, Vol.16, GOC-in-C WD 8–28 Feb 45 and 1–10 Mar 45 and Vol. 15, 3–22 Sep 44; PRO, Crerar Diary, 8 February –10 March 1945; Horrocks, 31, 182–3; Williams, *The Long Left Flank*, 65, 208; and W. Denis and Shelagh Whitaker, *Rhineland: The Battle to End the War* (Toronto: Stoddart, 1989), 111.

29 Lamb, *Montgomery in Europe*, 253.

30 CP, Vol. 1, Address by Crerar on The Responsibility of the Comd, the Staff and the Services, HQ 1 Canadian Corps, 11 Dec 43 repeated in CP, Vol. 15, D265, Address by Crerar to HQ First Canadian Army on the Responsibility of Command, the Staff and the Services, 31 Mar 44.

31 CP, Vol. 4, Crerar to COS, CMHQ, 28 Feb 45 and Immediate Message Canmilitry to Defensor, 021705A Mar 45.

32 MAP, BLM 153, "Veritable," 12–14, 57, and 59–60; PRO, Crerar Diary, 7 February 1945 and Remarks by GOC-in-C to Warcos – 7 Feb 45; Macdonald, "In Search of Veritable," 160, 199, 202; CP, Vol 27, Address by General H.D.G. Crerar on "Principles and Policies of the First Canadian Army"; and Stacey, *Victory*, 480–1.

33 MAP, Personal Diary, 17 Feb 45.

34 Stacey, *Victory*, 482–6, 489–91; and Whitakers, *Rhineland*, 140–50.

35 MAP, Personal Diary, 21–23 February 1945; CP, WD GOC-in-C, 22–24 Feb 45; and CP, Crerar to Brooke, 22 February 1945.

36 MAP, BLM 153, "Veritable," 36; Stacey, *Victory*, 491–3; and Williams, *The Long Left Flank*, 221–2.

37 Stacey, *Victory*, 495–6, 508–9; Williams, *The Long Left Flank*, 221–4, 233, 238; and Whitakers, *Rhineland*, 219, 223.

38 PRO, Crerar Diary, 25 February 1945 and Appendix 4, Directive GOC-in-C 1–0-7/11 dated 25 Feb 45 to Comds 2 Canadian Corps and 30 Corps.

39 Bounded by the general line Marienbaum-Kevelaer-Geldern-Kempen-Krefeld.

40 Whitakers, *Rhineland*, 220–1, 224, 231; Williams, *The Long Left Flank*, 240; Macdonald, "In Search of Veritable," 218; and Stacey, *Victory*, 438–9, 494, 508–9.

41 MAP, BLM 153, "Veritable," 37–38, 41–42; Stacey, *Victory*, 496–514; Whitakers, *Rhineland*, 194–207, 221–43; and Williams, *The Long Left Flank*, 224–32, 237–43. 28 February was the only day on which 2nd TAF was able to provide air support on a large scale. Williams, *The Long Left Flank*, 252.

42 Stacey, *Victory*, 494, 508, 514; and MAP, BLM 153, "Veritable," 35, 39–40.

43 MAP, Personal Diary, 6 Mar 45; CP, WD GOC-in-C, 7 Mar 45; and Stacey, *Victory*, 513–22.

44 Major General C.C. Mann, "The Campaign in North West Europe 6 June 1944–8 May 1945, "Fort Frontenac Library, Kingston, Ontario: 23; CP, Vol.7, Crerar to Foulkes, 29 January 1945; MAP, BLM 153, "Veritable," 45; Macdonald, "In Search of Veritable," 225; and Stacey, *Victory*, 522.

45 CP, Crocker to Crerar, 28.3.45, GOC-in-C 1–0-4/1 Crerar directive to Foulkes and Simonds, 7 Apr 45, and WD GOC-in-C, 4 May 45; Stacey, *Victory*, 522, 529–30, 545, 587.

46 CP, GOC-in-C 5-0-2, Crerar to Stuart, 30 May 44; CP, Vol. 8, Report Press Conference for General Crerar 2100 hrs 7 August 1945; and CP, GOC-in-C Notes on Conference held by C-in-C 21 Army Group at Tac, 21 Army Group 1130–1300 hrs, 23 Jan 45.

47 CP, Vol. 6, Personal Message from Army Commander, 20 July 1945, Vol. 7, Montgomery to Crerar, 6-7-45, and Vol. 27, Address by General H.D.G. Crerar, CH, CB, DSO, CD, ADC, "A Few Reminiscences of 1939–45"; *Alanbrooke War Diaries* (4 July 1945), 702; Stacey, *Victory*, 522, 530–619; Williams, *The Long Left Flank*, 257–91; Granatstein, *Generals*, 114–15, and *Canada's Army*, 303–6; and Dickson, *Thoroughly Canadian General*, 441–65.

14. Canadian Army Monty Men

1 Dickson, *Thoroughly Canadian General*, 433–44, 441, 448; and S.F. Clark interview, *Weight of Command*, 153.

2 Dickson, *Thoroughly Canadian General*, 455, 457; Delaney, *Corps Commanders*, 255–95; Vokes, *Story*, 200; Granatstein, *Generals*, 173–8. Clark, who retained copies of correspondence related to the Italian caravan incident in his personal papers, considered Crerar's letters "the worst things he'd ever seen." Clark interview, *Weight of Command*, 154.

3 Stacey, *Date*, 236; Graham, *Price*, 221–2, 230; Delaney, *Corps Commanders*, 294–5; Hamilton, *Field-Marshal*, 678; and TWP, Simonds to Warren, 19 Jan 69. Slim retired in 1948 after two years at IDC, but was brought back to be CIGS by Prime Minister Clement Attlee.

4 Graham, *Price*, 232–3; James Eayrs, *In Defence of Canada: Peacemaking and Deterrence* (Toronto: University of Toronto Press, 1972), 70–1; and S. Mathwin Davis, "A Comparative Study of Defence Colleges" (unpublished MA thesis, Royal Military College of Canada, 1974), 11–12. Whitely had served with Simonds as an IDC instructor.

5 Eayrs, *Peacemaking*, 70–1.

6 "The Canadian Army Staff College," *Canadian Army Journal (CAJ)* 4 (Summer 1950): 49–52; Canadian Army Staff College (CASC), *Snowy Owl Annual Review* (Christmas, 1952), x–xi; Courses at the College, *R.M.C. Review* 22 (December 1941): 17–23; and RG 24, Vol. 9874, File 2/Staff 4, Report on the First Canadian Junior War Staff Course by G.C. Simonds, Lieut. Colonel, Commandant.

7 Eayrs, *Peacemaking*, 19, 64, 79, 85–6, 96, 106; Granatstein, *Canada's Army*, 316, 320. In December 1944 the Cabinet War Committee had approved an army occupation force of about 25,000, but only 18,000 men of the 3rd Canadian Infantry Division actually served under the British 30 Corps in that capacity. In the spring of 1946 this Canadian Army Occupation Force, afflicted by sit-down strikes, was withdrawn as part of a general demobilization.

8 Granatstein, *Canada's Army*, 321–9; David Jay Bercuson, *True Patriot: The Life of Brooke Claxton* (Toronto: University of Toronto Press, 1993), 227; William Johnston, *A War of Patrols: Canadian Army Operations in Korea* (Vancouver: UBC Press, 200), 252–3; and Brent Byron Watson, *Far Eastern Tour: The Canadian Infantry in Korea, 1950–1953* (Montreal and Kingston: McGill-Queen's University Press, 2002), 8–14, 32–4, 79. Canadians used British small arms but some US support weapons. They retained the iconic Vickers medium machine gun and the matchless 25-pounder gun-howitzer.

9 Johnston, *A War of Patrols*, 139–43, 372; Herbert Fairlie Wood, *Strange Battleground: The Operations in Korea and Their Effects on the Defence Policy of Canada* (Ottawa: Queen's Printer, 1966), 134–5, 139; Allan R. Millett, *Allies of a Kind: Canadian Army–US Army Relations and the Korean War, 1950–1953* (Fort Leavenworth: Combat Studies Institute Press, 2015), 25–37, 44–6; FM 7-40 Infantry Regiment, Department of the Army, January 1950, 366–7 and FM 7-10 Rifle Company Infantry Regiment, October 1949; and Australian

War Memorial 373, WO 281/49, 1 Comwel Div OO No. 3 Op Cudgel, 27 Sep 51.

10 Wood, *Strange Battleground,* 293–4; Bercuson, *Claxton,* 225; John Melady, *Korea: Canada's Forgotten War* (Toronto: Macmillan, 1983), 113–15; Eayrs, *Peacemaking,* 104–5; and Stacey, *Date,* 258, and *Conflict,* 2:296.

11 Eayrs, *Peacemaking,* 19–28; and Bercuson, *Claxton,* 111–19, 210, 224–6, 231–7. Brooke could see a political implication where nobody else could perceive anything of the kind. Stacey, *Date,* 218.

12 Eayrs, *Peacemaking,* 63–4, 115–16; Graham, *Price,* 241, 248–9; Bercuson, *Claxton,* 223–4; Granatstein, *Canada's Army,* 319; Graham, *Citizen,* 215; and Kitching, *Memoirs,* 302–3.

13 Eayrs, *Peacemaking,* 64–5; David J. Bercuson, "The Return of the Canadians to Europe: Britannia Rules the Rhine," in *Canada and Nato: Uneasy Past, Uncertain Future,* ed. Margaret O. MacMillan and David S. Sorenson (Waterloo, ON: University of Waterloo Press, 1990), 15–19.

14 James Eayrs, *In Defence of Canada: Growing Up Allied* (Toronto: University of Toronto Press, 1980), 210–15; and Bercuson, "Return," 18–21.

15 Bercuson, "Return," 21–6; Eayrs, *Allied,* 213–15. Some argue that this robbed the brigade of RCAF close air support. In fact, air forces like artillery are most efficiently used when centralized, and it made no sense to have the RCAF dedicated to support a mere brigade. Besides, air forces at this time were more interested in maintaining air superiority and delivering deep strikes on the enemy

16 Granatstein, *Canada's Army,* 341–2; Kitching, *Memoirs,* 284–8, 292–3. Kitching claimed that from 1951 to 1965 the Canadian Army, both regular and reserve, reached the highest levels of organizational and operational efficiency and that it became the object of study and analysis by some NATO partners. Primary credit for this belonged to Simonds.

17 Galloway, *General,* 270–2; Brigadier M.P. Bogert, "The Staff Officer and The Staff College," *Snowy Owl* (Christmas 1954), 19–20; and MGen (Retd) J.W.B. Barr, *From Barnyard to Battlefield and Beyond: The Story of a Military Medical Officer* (Ottawa: Borealis Press, 2005), 160–5.

18 Major J. Harris and Captain J.G.W. Haynes, "The Course of '54," *Snowy Owl* (Christmas 1954): 24–35; Major-General Christopher Vokes, "Tactical Manoeuvre – Infantry and Armour," *Canadian Army Journal (CAJ)* 1 (April 1947): 13–15, 32; and Colonel H.G. Coombs and R. Wakelam, "The Rowley Report and the Canadian Army Staff College," *CAJ* 13, no. 2 (Summer 2010), 20–1.

19 Graham, *Price,* 252–4, 259; Kitching, *Memoirs,* 283; Granatstein, *Canada's Army,* 322, 331, 335–9; and Bercuson, *Claxton,* 216–18.

20 The Regiment of Canadian Guards comprised four battalions, one of them French Canadian. The idea was that, since the Queen had recently been designated Queen of Canada, with Canada no longer listed as one

of "her Dominions beyond the Seas," she should have her own regiment of Canadian Guards, just as she had Scots Guards, Irish Guards and Welsh Guards in the United Kingdom. The Guards turned out to be among the finest of regiments.

21 Granatstein *Canada's Army*, 340–1; Graham, *Citizen*, 230, 235; Lt. Col. F.T. Waugh, "Camp Gagetown," *Snowy Owl* (Christmas 1954): 39–42; and Lt. Col. J.A. English, "The Canadian Combat Training Centre," *Jane's Military Review* 4 (1983–8), ed. Ian V. Hogg (London: Jane's Publishing, 1983), 34–51.

22 Graham, *Citizen*, 192–6, 205–10, 214–15, 221–4; and Kitching, *Memoirs*, 296. Interestingly, Graham and Foulkes also had a disagreement rooted in the latter's indication to the minister that the number of men required for a NATO brigade would be 5,000. Whether from ignorance, which Graham doubted, or to encourage the government to make a commitment to provide a brigade, Foulkes had omitted to include the number for a reinforcement pool, which, of course, was absolutely essential. Foulkes was away from Ottawa, and Graham was in his chair when the prime minister wanted to make the relevant announcement. After consulting with and getting the agreement of the adjutant general, Graham gave the prime minister the actual number of men who would need to be enlisted. When Foulkes returned, he was livid with anger and seemed to think Graham had double-crossed him. He gave Graham a terrific blast for giving the prime minister the figures he had. Graham did not argue, but later told Foulkes that he resented his comments and would be happy to retire. Foulkes replied, "Forget it, Howard. I was tired last night." And that, Graham recorded, was the end of the fracas. Graham, *Citizen*, 220.

23 Montgomery, *Memoirs*, 487–513, 515–16; Graham, *Price*, 248; University of Victoria, Donor Biography, Lieutenant-General S.F. Clark, CBE CD Scholarship, by Reginald Roy; and Kitching, *Memoirs*, 283.

24 Simon J. Moody, "Was There a 'Monty Method' after the Second World War? Field Marshal Bernard L. Montgomery and the Changing Character of Land Warfare, 1945–1948," *War in History* 23, no. 2, (2016): 212, 214–15.

25 Ibid., 216–19; and Delaney, *Corps Commanders*, 169–70.

26 Moody, "Was There a Monty Method?," 219–29; and Hamilton, *Field-Marshal*, 811–12, 842–3. While SACEUR, Eisenhower personally painted a highly attractive oil portrait of Montgomery that now hangs in the British Embassy, Washington, DC.

27 Moody, "Was There a Monty Method?," 221–4. In April 1954 at CPX 4 attended by military and civilian officials from all NATO nations, save Iceland, General Alfred Gruenther, then SACEUR, and Montgomery explained and sold the new NATO concept later embodied in Military Committee Report MC 48.

28 Transcript of address given by Lt-Gen GG Simonds, Chief of the General Staff, at closing of Exercise "Broadsword," 8 Dec 54 under cover circular

letter 28 Jan 55 by Lieutenant-Colonel JME Clarkson, Military Assistant to
CGS. Canadian army wrestling with the tactical nuclear conundrum also
approximated on a lesser scale the "pentomic division" experiments of the
US forces that indicated while fewer troops were needed to defend, many
more were needed to replace mass casualties.

29 Ibid.; and Simonds Papers, Montgomery to Simonds, 10-2-55. Between 1952
and 1958 Montgomery conducted eight CPXs designed to rehearse NATO
high command and communications in peacetime. In CPX 4 he sought
to peer into the future with a battlefield dominated by missiles. Hamilton,
Field-Marshal, 835, 842, 850–1.

30 Moody, "Was There a Monty Method?," 226–7.

31 Moncel interview, *Weight of Command*, 78.

32 Andrew B. Godefroy, *In Peace Prepared: Innovation and Adaptation in Canada's
Cold War Army* (Vancouver: UBC Press, 2014), 116–50; and Peter Kasurak,
"Canadian Army Tactical Nuclear Warfare Doctrine in the 1950s: Force
Development in the Pre-Professional Era," *Canadian Military Journal* 11, no.
1 (Winter 2010): 38–44.

33 Graham, *Price*, 252–3, 257–60; Eayrs, *Peacemaking*, 65–6; Granatstein,
Canada's Army, 332 and *Generals*, 177; and Simonds Papers, Montgomery to
Simonds, 5 August 1955.

34 Graham, *Citizen*, 225–7; Kitching, *Memoirs*, 296–7.

35 N.E. Rodger interview, *Weight of Command*, 143.

36 Graham, *Citizen*, 242; Godefroy, *In Peace Prepared*, 131, 136–9, 144–8; and
Kasurak, "Canadian Army Tactical Nuclear Warfare Doctrine," 41–2.

37 Roy, *Pearkes*, 297–302, 306, 332; and Graham, *Citizen*, 243–5. After his
retirement as CGS, Graham accepted a government request to review and
make recommendations regarding civil defence measures. In his report of
31 December 1958 he recommended that the Defence Department assume
responsibility for civil defence, which since 1951 had been the responsibility
of the Health and Welfare Department. In March 1959 the prime
minister announced that the army should undertake primary and direct
responsibility for public warning, locating nuclear explosions and fallout
patterns, damage and casualty assessment, and re-entry rescue operations
into nuclear damaged cities. Roy, *Pearkes*, 297–302, 306; Graham, *Citizen*,
243–5; and CAMT 2-91, "Survival Operations (1961)," 3.

38 The Military Communications and Electronics Museum, Lieutenant
General S.F. Clark Papers, "A Collection of Memories"; and "Unit
Mobilization Instructions for the Canadian Army," June 1960.

39 RCASC, RCEME, and RCOC abbreviated the Royal Canadian Army Service
Corps, Royal Canadian Electrical and Mechanical Engineer Corps, and
Royal Canadian Ordnance Corps, respectively.

40 CAMT 2-38 "Principles and Methods of Instruction (1963)," Introduction:
Success in Battle Depends on *You* – The Instructor!

41 CAMT 2–85, "How to Qualify for Promotion and Staff Courses, Officers –
     Canadian Army (Regular) 1957 revised 1965."
42 Stacey, *Date*, 256. See also Douglas Bland, *The Administration of Defence Policy
     in Canada 1947 to 1985* (Kingston: Ronald P. Frye, 1987), 35–52.
43 Granatstein, *Canada's Army*, 353–5 and *Weight of Command*, 78; and Stacey,
     "The Staff Officer: A Footnote to Canadian Military History," *CDQ* 1, special
     no. 2 (August 1990): 21–8.
44 *As You Were! Ex-Cadets Remember*, 2:12.

Epilogue: The Montgomery Touch

 1 TWP, Montgomery to Trumbull Warren, 12-4-46.
 2 TWP, Montgomery to Trumbull, 27-7-42.
 3 TWP, Montgomery to Trumbull, 10-10-42.
 4 TWP, Montgomery to Mary, 14-5-42, 2 June 42 and 27-6-42, Montgomery to
     Trumbull, 10-6-42, 5-10-45, and Montgomery to Mary, 14-5-42, 27-6-42.
 5 Montgomery *Memoirs*, 438–40; Hamilton, *Field-Marshal*, 648–9, 656–7.
     Vokes claimed that Montgomery was also rude to many people, telling the
     occasional poor fellow, "You are too fat," but that crowds yelled themselves
     hoarse shouting, "Monty, Monty, Monty!" Vokes, *Story*, 212–15.
 6 TWP, Montgomery to Trumbull, 3-8-46, 10-3-48, 2 Sep 52, and 10 Sep 53;
     and Montgomery to Mary, 2-6-48.
 7 http://www.hwdsb.on.ca/viscountmontgomery/about.
 8 TWP, Montgomery to Mary, 27 May 56.
 9 TWP, Montgomery to Trumbull, 7 June 1957.
10 TWP, Montgomery to Trumbull, 12-3-59.
11 Montgomery, *Field-Marshal in the Family*, 340.
12 TWP, Montgomery to Trumbull, 9 June 1968, 26 Aug 68, 1 Jan 69, 20 Nov
     70, and Montgomery to Mary, 15 Dec 70.

Bibliography

Primary Sources

Government Records, Personal Papers, and Manuscript Collections

Current Reports from Overseas

The Armoured Division in Battle, 21 Army Group, December, 1944

Dwight D. Eisenhower (DDE) Library, Abilene, Kansas: DDE Collection, Pre-Presidential Papers: 1916–1952, Principal File, Courtney Hicks Hodges Papers, J. Lawton Collins Papers, Oral History and Columbia University Oral History Interviews

Imperial War Museum (IWM), London: Montgomery of Alamein Papers and Trumbull Warren Papers (TP)

Library and National Archives of Canada (LAC): Record Group 24, National Defence 1870–1981, A.G.L. McNaughton Papers (MNP), H.D.G. Crerar Papers (CP), and V.W. Odlum Papers

Liddell Hart Centre for Military Archives (LHCMA) King's College, London: Sir Basil Liddell Hart Papers, Alanbrooke Papers, Sir Miles Dempsey Papers, Sir Harold Pyman Papers

Marshall Library, Lexington, Virginia: George C. Marshall Papers, Thomas T. Handy Papers, James A. Van Fleet Papers

The Military Communications and Electronics Museum, Kingston, Ontario, Lieutenant General S.F. Clark Papers, "A Collection of Memories"

National Archives and Records Administration (NARA), Archives II, College Park, Maryland: William C. Sylvan Diary

National Defence Headquarters (NDHQ), Directorate of History and Heritage: Miscellaneous Documents

Public Record Office (PRO), London: Cabinet Office Historical Section files (CAB Series), War and Foreign Office (FO) records, 21st Army Group Papers (WO205), Dempsey Papers (WO285), and Crerar Diary (CAB 106)

Queen's University Archives (QUA), Kingston, Ontario: C.G. Powers Papers
Royal Military College of Canada (RMC), Kingston, Ontario: Crerar Papers, Major General C. Vokes Papers (VP), and W.R. Sawyer Papers (SP)
Tactical Doctrine Retrieval Cell, Staff College Camberley, Bartholomew Committee Final Report (1940)
United States Army Military History Institute (USAMHI), Carlisle Barracks, Pennsylvania: George I. Forsythe Papers and Oral History Interviews
United States Military Academy, West Point, New York: Thomas R. Goethals Papers, George S. Patton, Jr. Papers

Memoirs, Journals, and Accounts

Alanbrooke, Field Marshal Lord. *War Diaries, 1939–1945.* Edited by Alex Danchev and Daniel Todman. London: Weidenfeld & Nicolson, 2001.
Bradley, Omar N. *A Soldier's Story.* New York: Henry Holt, 1951.
Churchill, Winston S. *The Second World War: Triumph and Tragedy.* Boston: Houghton Mifflin, 1953.
De Guingand, Major General Sir Francis. *Operation Victory.* New York: Charles Scribner's Sons, 1947.
Dunkelman, Ben. *Dual Allegiance: An Autobiography.* Toronto: Macmillan, 1976.
Gavin, Gen. James M. *On to Berlin: Battles of an Airbome Commander, 1943–1946.* New York: Bantam, 1981.
Graham, Lieutenant General Howard. *Memoirs: Citizen and Soldier.* Toronto: McClelland and Stewart, 1987.
Horrocks, Sir Brian, with Eversley Belfield and Maj. Gen. H. Essame. *Corps Commander.* New York: Charles Scribner's Sons, 1977.
Kitching, Major General George. *Mud and Green Fields: Memoirs.* Langley, BC: Battleline, 1986.
Mann, Major General C.C. "The Campaign in North West Europe 6 June 1944–8 March 1945." Army Historical Section, Fort Frontenac Library, Kingston, Ontario.
Meyer, Hubert. *The History of the 12. SS-Panzerdivision "Hitlerjugend."* Translated by H. Harri Henschler. Winnipeg: J.J. Fedorowicz, 1994.
Montgomery of Alamein, Field Marshal The Viscount. *Normandy to the Baltic.* London: Hutchinson, 1946.
– *Memoirs.* London: Collins, 1958.
Pyman, Gen. Sir Harold E. *Call to Arms.* London: Leo Cooper, 1971.
Ritgen, Helmut. *The Western Front 1944: Memoirs of a Panzer Lehr Officer.* Winnipeg: J.J. Fedorowicz, 1995.
Roberts, James Alan. *The Canadian Summer: Memoirs.* Toronto: University of Toronto Press, 1981.
Snowy Owl, Canadian Army Staff College.

Stacey, C.P. *A Date with History: Memoirs of a Canadian Historian.* Ottawa: Deneau, 1982.

Official Histories

Blumenson, Martin. *United States Army in World War II, The European Theater of Operations: Break Out and Pursuit.* Washington: Office of the Chief of Military History, 1961.

Clarke, Jeffrey J., and Robert Ross Smith. *United States Army in World War II, The European Theater of Operations: Riviera to the Rhine.* Washington: Center of Military History, 1993.

Hogan, David W. *A Command Post at War: First Army Headquarters in Europe, 1943–1945.* Washington: Center of Military History, United States Army, 2000.

Nicholson, G.W.L. *Official History of the Canadian Army in the Second World War,* vol. 2: *The Canadians in Italy, 1943–1945.* Ottawa: Queen's Printer, 1956.

– *Official History of the Canadian Army in the First World War: Canadian Expeditionary Force 1914–1919.* Ottawa: Queen's Printer, 1962.

– *The Gunners of Canada: A History of the Royal Regiment of Canadian Artillery,* vol. 2: *1919–1967.* Toronto: McClelland and Stewart, 1972.

Pemberton, Brig. A. L. *The Second World War, 1939–1945, Army, The Development of Artillery Tactics and Equipment.* London: War Office, 1951.

Stacey, C. P. *Official History of the Canadian Army in the Second World War. Vol. I, Six Years of War. The Army in Canada, Britain and the Pacific.* Ottawa: Queen's Printer, 1966.

– *Official History of the Canadian Army in the Second World War. Vol. III, The Victory Campaign: The Operations in North West Europe, 1944–1945.* Ottawa: Queen's Printer, 1966.

– *Arms, Men, and Governments: The War Policies of Canada, 1939–1945.* Ottawa: Information Canada, 1974.

Secondary Sources

Books

Antal, Sandy, and Kevin R. Shackleton. *Duty Nobly Done: The Official History of the Essex and Kent Scottish Regiment.* Windsor: Walkerville Publishing, 2006.

As You Were! Ex-Cadets Remember. Vol. 2. Kingston: The R.M.C. Club of Canada.

Atkinson, Rick. *An Army at Dawn: The War in North Africa, 1942–1943.* New York: Henry Holt, 2003.

– *The Day of Battle: The War in Sicily and Italy 1943–1944.* New York: Henry Holt and Company, 2007.

Barr, MGen (Retd) J.W.B. *From Barnyard to Battlefield and Beyond: The Story of a Military Medical Officer.* Ottawa: Borealis Press, 2005.

Belfield, Eversley, and H. Essame. *The Battle for Normandy.* London: Pan, 1983.

Bercuson, David. *True Patriot: The Life of Brooke Claxton.* Toronto: University of Toronto Press, 1993.

– *Battalion of Heroes: The Calgary Highlanders in World War II.* Calgary: The Calgary Highlanders Regimental Funds Foundation, 1994.

Bidwell, Shelford. *Gunners at War: A Tactical Study of the Royal Artillery in the Twentieth Century.* London: Arms and Armour, 1970.

Bidwell, Shelford, and Dominick Graham. *Fire-Power: British Army Weapons and Theories of War, 1904–1945.* London: Allen and Unwin, 1982.

Bird, Will R. *North Shore (New Brunswick) Regiment* (Fredericton: Brunswick Press, 1963.

– *No Retreating Footsteps: The Story of the North Nova Scotia Highlanders.* Hantsport: Lancelot Press, 1983.

Bland, Douglas. *The Administration of Defence Policy in Canada 1947 to 1985.* Kingston: Ronald P. Frye, 1987.

Boss, Lieut-Colonel W. *The Stormont, Dundas and Glengarry Highlanders 1783– 1951.* Ottawa: Runge Press, 1952.

Brooks, Stephen, ed. *Montgomery and Eighth Army.* The Bodley Head: Army Records Society, 1991.

Brown, Robert Craig, and Ramsay Cook. *Canada 1896–1921: A Nation Transformed.* Toronto: McClelland and Stewart, 1974.

Buchanan, Lt. Col. G.B. *The March of the Prairie Men.* Weyburn: South Saskatchewan Regiment, 1957.

Buckley, John. *Monty's Men: The British Army and the Liberation of Europe.* New Haven: Yale University Press, 2013.

Caddick-Adams, Peter. *Monty and Rommel: Parallel Lives.* London: Preface, 2011.

Callahan, Raymond. *Churchill and His Generals.* Lawrence: University Press of Kansas, 2007.

Carafano, James Jay. *After D-Day: Operation Cobra and the Normandy Breakout.* Boulder: Lynne Rienner, 2000.

Carver, Tom. *Where the Hell Have You Been?* London: Short Books, 2009.

Chalfont, Alun. *Montgomery of Alamein.* London: Methuen, 1976.

Chandler, David G., and James Lawton Collins, Jr, eds. *The D-Day Encyclopedia.* New York: Simon and Shuster, 1994.

Cook, Tim. *No Place to Run: The Canadian Corps and Gas Warfare in the First World War.* Vancouver: UBC Press, 1999.

Copp, Terry. *The Brigade: The Fifth Canadian Infantry Brigade, 1939–1945.* Stoney Creek: Fortress, 1992.

– *Fields of Fire: The Canadians in Normandy.* Toronto: University of Toronto Press, 2003.

– *Cinderella Army: The Canadians in Northwest Europe 1944–1945.* Toronto: University of Toronto Press, 2006.

– *Guy Simonds and the Art of Command.* Kingston: Canadian Defence Academy, Press, 2007.

Coulthard-Clark, Chris. *Where Australians Fought: The Encyclopaedia of Australia's Battles.* St. Leonards: Allen and Unwin, 1998.

Danchev, Alex. *Very Special Relationship: Field Marshal Sir John Dill and the Anglo-American Alliance 1941–44.* London: Brassey's, 1986.

Dancocks, Daniel G. *The D-Day Dodgers: The Canadians in Italy, 1943–1945.* Toronto: McClelland and Stewart, 1991.

Delaney, Douglas E. *The Soldiers' General: Bert Hoffmeister at War.* Vancouver: UBC Press, 2005.

– *Corps Commanders: Five British and Canadian Generals at War, 1939–1945.* Vancouver: UBC Press, 2011.

D'Este, Carlo. *Decision in Normandy: The Unwritten Story of Montgomery and the Allied Campaign.* London: Collins, 1983.

– *Bitter Victory: The Battle for Sicily, 1943.* London: Collins, 1988.

– *Patton: A Genius for War.* New York: HarperCollins, 1995.

– "Monty: World War II's Most Misunderstood General," *Armchair General,* 11 July 2005.

Dickson, Paul. *A Thoroughly Canadian General: A Biography of General H.D.G. Crerar* Toronto: University of Toronto Press, 2007.

Douglas, W.A.B., and B. Greenhous. *Out of the Shadows.* Toronto: Oxford University Press, 1977.

Eayrs, James. *In Defence of Canada: Appeasement and Rearmament.* Toronto: University of Toronto Press, 1964.

– *In Defence of Canada: From the Great War to the Great Depression.* Toronto: University of Toronto Press, 1964.

– *In Defence of Canada: Peacemaking and Deterrence.* Toronto: University of Toronto Press, 1972.

– *In Defence of Canada: Growing Up Allied.* Toronto: University of Toronto Press, 1980.

Eisenhower, John S.D. *The Bitter Woods: The Battle of the Bulge.* New York: Da Capo, 1995.

English, John A. *The Canadian Army and the Normandy Campaign.* Mechanicsburg: Stackpole, 2009.

– *Patton's Peers: The Forgotten Allied Field Army Commanders of the Western Front 1944–1945.* Mechanicsburg: Stackpole, 2009.

Essame, H. *The Battle for Germany.* New York: Bonanza, 1969.

The First Fifty Years of the Staff College Quetta, 1905–1955. Quetta: Staff College, 1962.

Foster, Tony. *Meeting of Generals.* Toronto: Methuen, 1986.

Fraser, David. *And We Shall Shock Them: The British Army in the Second World War.* London: Hodder and Stoughton, 1983.

French, David. *Raising Churchill's Army: The British Army and the War against Germany 1919–1945.* Oxford: Oxford University Press, 2001.

Fuller, Major-General J.F.C. *The Second World War 1939–1945: A Strategical and Tactical History.* London: Eyre and Spottiswoode, 1948.

Galloway, Strome. *A Regiment at War. The Story of the Royal Canadian Regiment 1939–1945.* London: Regimental Headquarters, 1979.

– *The General Who Never Was.* Belleville: Mika, 1981.

Gatchel, Theodore L. *At the Water's Edge: Defending against the Modern Amphibious Assault.* Annapolis: Naval Institute Press, 1996.

Godefroy, Andrew B. *In Peace Prepared: Innovation and Adaptation in Canada's Cold War Army.* Vancouver: UBC Press, 2014.

Graham, Dominick. *The Price of Command: A Biography of General Guy Simonds.* Toronto: Stoddart, 1993.

Graham, Dominick, and Shelford Bidwell. *Tug of War: The Battle for Italy: 1943–45.* London: Hodder & Stoughton, 1986.

– *Coalitions, Politicians and Generals: Some Aspects of Command in Two World Wars.* London: Brassey's, 1993.

Granatstein, J.L. *The Ottawa Men: The Civil Service Mandarins, 1935–1957.* Toronto: Oxford University Press, 1982.

– *The Generals: The Canadian Army's Senior Commanders in the Second World War.* Toronto: Stoddart, 1993.

– *Canada's Army: Waging War and Keeping the Peace.* Toronto: University of Toronto Press, 2002.

– *The Weight of Command: Voices of Canada's Second World War Generals and Those Who Knew Them.* Vancouver: UBC Press, 2016.

Greenhous, B., and W.A. McAndrew. Interview with General B.M. Hoffmeister, 1980.

Hamilton, Nigel. *Monty: The Making of a General 1887–1942.* Sevenoaks: Coronet, 1984.

– *Monty: Master of the Battlefield 1942–1944.* London: Hamish Hamilton, 1983.

– *Monty: The Field Marshal 1944–1976.* London: Hamish Hamilton, 1986.

Harris, Stephen J. *Canadian Brass: The Making of a Professional Army 1860–1939.* Toronto: University of Toronto Press, 1988.

Hart, Russell A. *Clash of Arms: How the Allies Won in Normandy.* Boulder: Lynne Rienner, 2001.

Hart, Stephen Ashley. *Montgomery and "Colossal Cracks": The 21st Army Group in Northwest Europe, 1944–45.* Westport: Praeger, 2000.

– *Road to Falaise.* Stroud: Sutton, 2004.

Hastings, Max. *Overlord: D-Day and the Battle for Normandy.* London: Pan, 1984.

Horn, Bernd, and Stephen Harris, eds. *Warrior Chiefs.* Toronto: Dundurn, 2000.

Horne, Alistair, with David Montgomery. *Monty: The Lonely Leader, 1944–1945*. New York: HarperCollins, 1994.

Horner, David. *Blamey: The Commander in Chief*. St. Leonards: Allen & Unwin, 1998.

Howard, Michael. *The Causes of Wars*. Cambridge: Harvard University Press, 1983.

Huntington, Samuel P. *The Soldier and the State: The Theory and Politics of Civil-Military Relations*. Cambridge: Belknap Press, 1979.

Hutchison, Colonel Paul P. *Canada's Black Watch: The First Hundred Years 1862–1962*. Montreal: Black Watch (R.H.R.) of Canada, 1962.

Hyatt, A.M.J. *General Sir Arthur Currie: A Military Biography*. Toronto: University of Toronto Press, 1987.

Jarymowycz, Roman Johann. *Tank Tactics: From Normandy to Lorraine*. Boulder: Lynne Rienner, 2001.

Johnston, Mark. *At the Front Line: Experiences of Australian Soldiers in World War II*. Cambridge: University Press, 1996.

Johnston, William. *A War of Patrols: Canadian Army Operations in Korea*. Vancouver: UBC Press, 2000.

Keegan, John, ed. *Churchill's Generals*. London: Weidenfeld and Nicloson, 1991.

Lamb, Richard. *Montgomery in Europe 1943–45: Success or Failure?* New York: Franklin Watts, 1984.

Lewin, Ronald. *Montgomery as Military Commander*. New York: Stein and Day, 1971.

– *Man of Armour: A Study of Lieut.-General Vyvyan Pope and the Development of Armoured Warfare*. London: Leo Cooper, 1976.

Malone, Richard S. *A Portrait of War*. Don Mills: Totem Press, 1985.

Melady, John. *Korea: Canada's Forgotten War*. Toronto: Macmillan, 1983.

Millett, Allan R. *Allies of a Kind: Canadian Army–US Army Relations and the Korean War, 1950–1953*. Fort Leavenworth: Combat Studies Institute Press, 2015.

Milner, Marc. *Stopping the Panzers: The Untold Story of D-Day*. Lawrence: University Press of Kansas, 2014.

Montgomery, Brian. *A Field-Marshal in the Family*. London: Constable, 1973.

Moulton, Major General J.L. *Battle for Antwerp: The Liberation of the City and the Opening of the Scheldt 1944*. New York: Hippocrene, 1978.

Murray, Williamson, and Allan R. Millett. *A War to Be Won: Fighting the Second World War*. Cambridge: Belknap Press of Harvard University Press, 2000.

Perry, F.W. *The Commonwealth Armies: Manpower and Organization in Two World Wars*. Manchester: University Press, 1988.

Reid, Brian A. *No Holding Back: Operation Totalize, Normandy, August 1944*. Toronto: Robin Brass, 2005.

– *Named by the Enemy: A History of the Royal Winnipeg Rifles*. Winnipeg: Robin Brass Studio, 2010.

Rickard, John Nelson. *The Politics of Command: Lieutenant-General A.G.L. McNaughton and the Canadian Army 1939–1943*. Toronto: University of Toronto Press, 2010.

Ricks, Thomas E. *The Generals: American Military Command from World War II to Today*. New York: Penguin, 2012.

Robertson, Terrence. *The Shame and the Glory: Dieppe*. Toronto: McClelland and Stewart, 1962.

Ropp, Theodore. *War in the Modern World*. New York: Collier, 1962.

Ross, Steven T., ed. *U.S. War Plans 1938–1939*. Boulder: Lynne Rienner, 2002.

Roy, Reginald H. *For Most Conspicuous Bravery: A Biography of Major-General George R. Pearkes, V.C., through Two World Wars*. Vancouver: University of British Columbia Press, 1977.

– *1944: The Canadians in Normandy*. Ottawa: Macmillan, 1984.

– University of Victoria, Donor Biography, Lieutenant-General S.F. Clark, CBE CD Scholarship.

Schreiber, Shane. *Shock Army of the British Empire: The Canadian Corps in the Last 100 Days of the Great War*. Westport: Praeger, 1997.

Sheffield, Gary. *Forgotten Victory: The First World War: Myths and Realities*. London: Headline, 2001.

Sommerville, David. *Monty: A Biography of Field Marshal Montgomery*. London: Bison 1992.

Stacey, C.P. *Canada and the Age of Conflict: A History of Canadian External Policies*, vol. 1: *1867–1921*. Toronto: Macmillan, 1977.

– *Canada and the Age of Conflict: A History of Canadian External Policies*, vol. 2: *1921–1948: The Mackenzie King Era*. Toronto: |University of Toronto Press, 1984.

Stevens, Lieut-Colonel G.R. *A City Goes to War: History of the Loyal Edmonton Regiment (3PPCLI)*. Brampton: Charters Publishing, 1964.

Swettenham, John. *McNaughton*. 3 vols. Toronto: Ryerson Press, 1968–9.

Thompson, Julian. *Dunkirk: Retreat into Victory*. London: Sidgwick & Jackson, 2008.

Thompson, R.W. *The Eighty Five Days: The Story of the Battle of the Scheldt*. London: Hutchinson, 1957.

Villa, Brian Loring. *Unauthorized Action: Mountbatten and the Dieppe Raid*. Toronto: Oxford University Press, 1990.

Vokes, Major General Chris, with John P. Maclean. *My Story*. Ottawa: Gallery Books, 1985.

Watson, Brent Byron. *Far Eastern Tour: The Canadian Infantry in Korea, 1950–1953*. Montreal and Kingston: McGill-Queen's University Press, 2002.

Weigley, Russell F. *Eisenhower's Lieutenants: The Campaign of France and Germany, 1944–1945*. Bloomington: Indiana University Press, 1981.

Weinberg, Gerhard L. *A World at Arms: A Global History of World War II.* Cambridge: Cambridge University Press, 1994.

Whitaker, W. Denis and Shelagh. *Tug of War: The Canadian Victory That Opened Antwerp.* Toronto: Stoddart, 1984.

– *Rhineland: The Battle to End the War.* Toronto: Stoddart, 1989.

– *Dieppe: Tragedy to Triumph.* Toronto: McGraw-Hill Ryerson, 1992.

Williams, Jeffery. *Byng of Vimy: General and Governor-General.* London: Leo Cooper, 1983.

– *The Long Left Flank: The Hard Fought Way to the Reich, 1944–1945.* Toronto: Stoddart, 1988.

Wilmot, Chester. *The Struggle for Europe.* London: Fontana/Collins, 1974.

Wilt, Alan F. *War from the Top: German and British Military Decision Making during World War II.* Bloomington: Indiana University Press, 1990.

Wood, Herbert Fairlie. *Strange Battleground: The Operations in Korea and Their Effects on the Defence Policy of Canada.* Ottawa: Queen's Printer, 1966.

– *Vimy.* London: Transworld, 1972.

Young, Brigadier Peter. *World War 1939–1945.* London: Pan, 1966.

Zuehlke, Mark. *Tragedy at Dieppe: Operation Jubilee, August 19, 1942.* Vancouver: Douglas & McIntyre, 2012.

Battlefield Studies

British Army of the Rhine (BAOR) Battlefield Tour, Operation Bluecoat: 8 Corps Operations South of Caumont 30–1 July 1944, Spectator's Edition (1947).

BAOR Battlefield Tour, Operation Totalize: 2 Canadian Corps Operations Astride the Road Caen-Falaise 7–8 August 1944, Spectator's Edition (1947).

BAOR Battlefield Tour, Operation Veritable: 30 Corps Operations between the Rivers Maas and Rhine, 8–10 February 1945, Spectator's Edition.

Theses

Davis, S. Mathwin. "A Comparative Study of Defence Colleges." Unpublished MA thesis, Royal Military College of Canada, 1974.

Gimblett, Richard H. "'Buster' Brown: The Man and His Clash with 'Andy' McNaughton." Unpublished BA thesis, Royal Military College, 1979.

Hutchinson, W.E.J. "Test of a Corps Commander: Lieutenant General Guy Granville Simonds, Normandy 1944." Unpublished MA thesis, University of Victoria, 1982.

Macdonald, John A. "In Search of Veritable: Training the Canadian Army Staff Officer, 1899 to 1945." Unpublished MA Thesis, Royal Military College of Canada, 1992.

Articles

Amy, Brigadier General E.A.C. (Ned). "Normandy: 1 Squadron Canadian Grenadier Guards, Phase 2 Operation Totalize 7/8 August 1944," unpublished paper dated 21 February 1993.

Bercuson, David J. "The Return of the Canadians to Europe: Britannia Rules the Rhine." In *Canada and Nato: Uneasy Past, Uncertain Future*, ed. Margaret O. MacMillan and David S. Sorenson, 15–19. Waterloo, ON: University of Waterloo Press, 1990.

"Biography of General The Honourable Henry Duncan Graham Crerar, P.C., C.H., C.B., D.S.O." *Quadrant* 1 (June 1989): 11, 13.

Bogert, Brigadier M.P. "The Staff Officer and the Staff College." *Snowy Owl* (Christmas, 1954): 19–20.

Bourne, A.H. "Limited Liability War." *Canadian Defence Quarterly (CDQ)* 3 (1939): 282–90.

Burns, Lt.-Col. E.L.M. "A Division That Can Attack." *CDQ* 3 (April 1938): 282–98, and "Where Do the Tanks Belong?" *CDQ* 1 (October 1938): 28–31.

Coombs, Colonel H.G., and R. Wakelam. "The Rowley Report and the Canadian Army Staff College." *Canadian Army Journal (CAJ)* 13, no. 2 (Summer 2010): 20–1.

Copp, Terry, and Robert Vogel, "'No Lack of Rational Speed': 1st Canadian Army Operations, September 1944." *Journal of Canadian Studies* 16 (Fall/Winter 1981): 145–55.

Dickson, Paul D. "The Politics of Army Expansion: General H.D.G. Crerar and the Creation of First Canadian Army, 1940–41." *Journal of Military History* 60 (April 1996): 271–98.

– "The Hand That Wields the Dagger: Harry Crerar, First Canadian Army Command and National Autonomy." *War and Society* 2 (October 1995):113–41.

– "Crerar and the Decision to Garrison Hong Kong" *Canadian Military History*, 3 (Spring, 1994): 97–110.

English, Lt. Col. J.A. "The Canadian Combat Training Centre." *Jane's Military Review 1983–84*, ed. Ian V. Hogg. London: Jane's, 1983: 34–51.

– "I Corps" in *D-Day Encyclopedia*. Ed. David G. Chandler and James Lawton Collins, Jr., 242–3 New York: Simon & Schuster, 1994.

Forrester, Charles. "Field Marshal Montgomery's Role in the Creation of 21st Army Group's Combined Arms Doctrine for the Final Assault on Germany." *Journal of Military History* 4 (October 2014): 1295–1320.

"His Dagger Was Pointed at Berlin." *Time*, 10 August 1942.

Hunter, Col. T.A. "The Necessity of Cultivating Brigade Spirit in Peace Time." *CDQ* 1 (October 1927): 22–3.

Kasurak, Peter. "Canadian Army Tactical Nuclear Warfare Doctrine in the 1950s: Force Development in the Pre-Professional Era." *Canadian Military Journal* 11, no. 1 (Winter 2010): 38–44.

Moody, Simon J. "Was There a 'Monty Method' after the Second World War? Field Marshal Bernard L. Montgomery and the Changing Character of Land Warfare, 1945–1948." *War in History* 23, no. 2, (2016): 210–29.

Montgomery, Brig. B.L. "The Problem of the Encounter Battle as Affected by Modern British War Establishment." *CDQ* 1 (October 1937): 13–25.

– "The Major Tactics of the Encounter Battle." *Army Quarterly* 2 (July 1938): 268–72.

Perrun, Jody. "Best Laid Plans: Guy Simonds and Operation Totalize, 7–10 August 1944." *Journal of Military History* 1 (January 2003): 137–73.

Ritgen, Helmut, Oberst A.D. "Fighting for the Scheldt Estuary." Unpublished paper,

Simonds, Capt. G.G. "An Army That Can Attack – A Division That Can Defend.'" *CDQ* 4 (July 1938): 413–17; "What Price Assault without Support?" *CDQ* 2 (January 1939): 142–7; and "The Attack." *CDQ* 4 (July 1939): 379–90.

Stacey, C.P. "The Staff Officer: A Footnote to Canadian Military History." *CDQ* 3 (Winter 1973/74): 47–8.

– "Canadian Leaders of the Second World War." *Canadian Historical Review* 1 (1985): 64–72.

"The Canadian Army Staff College." *CAJ* 4 (Summer, 1950): 49–52.

"Thoughts on Command in Battle." *British Army Review* 69 (December, 1981): 5.

Stewart, William. "'Byng Boys': A Profile of Senior Commanders of Canadian Combat Units on the Somme, 1916." *War in History* 23, no. 1 (2016): 55–78.

Vokes, Major-General Christopher. "Tactical Manoeuvre – Infantry and Armour." *CAJ* 1 (April 1947): 13–15, 32.

Walton, Colonel D.B. "Restoration of General Crerar Caravan February 1989." *Quadrant* 6, no. 1 (June 1989): 12–13.

Index

of battle, 79 ; Great War lessons,
16–17; Great War service and
wounds, 15–17; grouping fighting
elements for battle, 87, 96, 100,
172, 205; importance of army–air
cooperation, 100–2; impressed by
Simonds, 10, 86, 109–10; impresses
US troops, 122; interwar years,
17–22, 30–1; introduces COS
system, 16, 95; Italy invasion, 111;
"J" service, 101; lack of information
no excuse for not planning, 30,
79; Middle East service, 20–1, 31;
need for broad plan of battle to be
communicated down to soldiers,
100; need to fight field army as an
army battle, not as individual corps
battles, 205; need to reconnoitre
widely and fight for information,
79, 83; need to teach training as
distinct from fighting, 76; never
allow staff to force a plan upon
a commander, 93–4; never call
frontline commanders back for
orders, 101; no bad soldiers, only
bad officers, 8, 41–2; Operation
"Market Garden," 176–7, 184–5;
orchestrates Normandy invasion,
94, 121–2; principles of war, 151;
promoted field marshal, 174; puts
leash on British armour at Alam
Haifa, 96; rapport with soldiers,
119–20; recognizes German
superiority and weaknesses, 34,
236–7; recognizes winning power
of artillery, 9, 35, 81, 98, 240;
service in India, 15, 21–2; Sicily
invasion, 94; staff college duty
Camberley and Quetta, 17, 19,
21–2; stage management to avoid
blundering into battle, 6, 78–9,
82 *passim*; stamps his methods

on Canadian Corps, 80; stresses
physical fitness, 37–9, 74, 87;
superlative generalship in the
Battle of the Bulge, 194; Tac HQ,
102; touts achievable objectives,
101, 151; training generals key to
readying an army for battle, 78,
100; use of liaison officers (LOs),
102–3; on training for war, stressing
field craft, minor tactics, exercises,
and rehearsals, 6–7, 30–4, 37–42,
76–9, 101; vicarious influence on
post-war Canadian army, 13, 213;
vital importance of retaining the
initiative and making enemy dance
to your tune, 82–3, 98, 100, 122,
131, 167, 239–40; vows never to
smoke or drink again, 6, 31
morale, big factor in war, 5, 16, 93,
102, 104, 144, 151, 253
Moreshead, Major General L.J., 98
Morgan, Lieutenant General F.E., 121
Mortain, 160, 166
Morton, Brigadier R.O.G., 116–17
Mountbatten, Lord Louis, 88, 90–1
Moyland Wood, 203–4
Murdock, Lieutenant Colonel W.S., 68
Murray, Williamson, 4

National Defence Act, 217
National Defence College, 214
National Research Council, 28
National Resources Mobilization
Act, 47
New Zealand Army: 2nd New Zealand
Division, 96,
Normandy, D-Day and battle of, xii,
51 *passim*
North Atlantic Council, 226
North Atlantic Treaty Organization
(NATO), 13, 215–16, 221–2 *passim*;
"new approach," 225–8